Blockchain and Smart Contracts

Design Thinking and Programming for FinTech

Singapore University of Social Sciences - World Scientific Future Economy Series

ISSN: 2661-3905

Singapore University of Social Sciences - World Scientific Future Economy Series introduces the new technology trends and challenges that businesses today face, financial management in the digital economy, blockchain technology, smart contract and cryptography. The authors describe current issues that the business leaders and finance professionals are facing, as well as developments in digitalisation. The series covers several increasingly important new areas such as the fourth industrial revolution, Internet of Things (IoT), blockchain technology, artificial intelligence (AI) and many other forces of disruption and breakthroughs that shape today's realities of the economy. A better understanding of the changing environment in the future economy can enable business professionals and leaders to recognise realities, embrace changes, and create new opportunities — locally and globally — in this inevitable digital age.

*Published**

Vol. 4 *Blockchain and Smart Contracts: Design Thinking and Programming for FinTech*
by Lo Swee Won, Wang Yu and David Lee Kuo Chuen

Vol. 3 *Artificial Intelligence, Data and Blockchain in a Digital Economy, First Edition*
edited by David Lee Kuo Chuen, supported by Singapore University of Social Sciences and World Scientific, in support of Singapore Digital (SG:D) and in collaboration with Infocomm Media Development Authority

Vol. 2 *The Emerging Business Models*
by Guan Chong, Jiang Zhiying and Ding Ding

Vol. 1 *AI & Quantum Computing for Finance & Insurance: Fortunes and Challenges for China and America*
by Paul Schulte and David Lee Kuo Chuen

*More information on this series can also be found at
https://www.worldscientific.com/series/susswsfes

(Continued at end of book)

Singapore University of Social Sciences - World Scientific
Future Economy Series 4

Blockchain and Smart Contracts

Design Thinking and Programming for FinTech

LO Swee Won
WANG Yu
David LEE Kuo Chuen
Singapore University of Social Sciences, Singapore

SUSS
SINGAPORE UNIVERSITY OF SOCIAL SCIENCES

World Scientific

Published by

World Scientific Publishing Co. Pte. Ltd.
5 Toh Tuck Link, Singapore 596224
USA office: 27 Warren Street, Suite 401-402, Hackensack, NJ 07601
UK office: 57 Shelton Street, Covent Garden, London WC2H 9HE

Library of Congress Cataloging-in-Publication Data
Names: Lo, Swee Won, author. | Wang, Yu (Fintech research fellow), author. |
Lee, David (David Kuo Chuen)
Title: Blockchain and smart contracts : design thinking and programming for fintech / Lo Swee Won,
Wang Yu, David Lee Kuo Chuen, Singapore University of Social Sciences, Singapore.
Description: New Jersey : World Scientific, 2021. | Series: Singapore University of
Social Sciences--World Scientific future economy series, 2661-3905 ; vol. 4 |
Includes bibliographical references and index.
Identifiers: LCCN 2020041556 (print) | LCCN 2020041557 (ebook) |
ISBN 9789811223686 (hardcover) | ISBN 9789811224867 (paperback) |
ISBN 9789811223693 (ebook) | ISBN 9789811223709 (ebook other)
Subjects: LCSH: Financial engineering. | Blockchains (Databases) |
Cryptocurrencies. | Computer security.
Classification: LCC HG176.7 .L62 2021 (print) | LCC HG176.7 (ebook) | DDC 332.4--dc23
LC record available at https://lccn.loc.gov/2020041556
LC ebook record available at https://lccn.loc.gov/2020041557

British Library Cataloguing-in-Publication Data
A catalogue record for this book is available from the British Library.

For any available supplementary material, please visit
https://www.worldscientific.com/worldscibooks/10.1142/11919#t=suppl

Desk Editors: Balasubramanian Shanmugam/Yulin Jiang

Typeset by Stallion Press
Email: enquiries@stallionpress.com

This book is dedicated to
Prof. Cheong Hee Kiat, President of SUSS,
and
Prof. Tsui Kai Chong, Provost of SUSS.

Preface

Digital economy, cryptocurrency and blockchain have been popular keywords in the news, social media, research articles, investment and strategies for companies and nations over the past few years. Technology is more than just a future trend — it is happening now, developing fast and has a huge impact on every aspect of the society, including the governments, corporations, educational institutes and individuals.

The finance industry has witnessed dramatic changes in the products and services provided in the markets, owing to the rapid developments of new technologies and innovations. At SUSS, we are devoted to becoming the bridge between industry and students. We have organised dozens of meet-ups, seminars, workshops, conferences and summits and invited experts from industry, government agencies and academia to share their thoughts. We are also one of the earliest institutes that provide training and courses on blockchain and cryptocurrencies.

Through these events and other collaborative research projects with industry partners and government agencies, we have learned a lot about the latest development and trends, and such knowledge can then be incorporated in our teaching materials and curriculum design.

To ensure that our curriculum is relevant to the industry developments, the Finance Programme at SUSS has gone through several rounds of curriculum revamp. With a strong industry connection, we were able to invite industry veterans to become our SUSS Fellows to advise on our curriculum updates and give students exposure to the fast-changing finance world. By July 2020, we have appointed more than 100 experts in FinTech and blockchain areas from all over the world to be our SUSS Fellows.

In addition, the Finance Programme at SUSS has developed a series of new courses in the curriculum to equip students with relevant knowledge and skills to meet the needs of the new roles that have been evolving in the finance industry for the past few years. These courses cover areas in business analytics, programming, blockchain technology and the latest developments in financial technology as well as business innovation. The objective is to give students rigorous training in the areas of programming and analytical skills, which are greatly needed in the new economy. Various levels of options are available at SUSS. For example, we offer FinTech minor for the undergraduate, the Master of Finance (MFIN) programme, the Graduate Diploma in FinTech (GDFT) programme, the Graduate Certificate in FinTech (GCFT) programme for professionals who wish to acquire professional advancement and deepen their knowledge of finance, financial technologies and financial innovations, and the Doctor of Business Administration programme for people who further seek sophisticated problem-solving skills required to tackle complex business problems and drive innovations.

Therefore, in this new book, as the 4th Volume of the SUSS-WS Future Economy Series, we discuss both the design thinking ideas and technical details in blockchain and smart contracts to provide in-depth analysis of the conceptual framework of the Bitcoin and Ethereum blockchains and help the readers understand more about the token economics. The content is developed based on several courses at SUSS, to name a few, Financial Cryptography, Financial Technologies and Innovations, Blockchain Security and Privacy, and Hands-On Lab with MultiChain.

Our goal is to equip the students with the following three skill sets in the workplace after they graduate. The first skill is technology analysis. We hope to train more people to know what technologies are about and what the underlying technical details are so that they can truly understand and appreciate the technologies and familiarise themselves with the application and useful scenarios.

The second skill is business strategy. Knowing what tech can and cannot do is important, but what is more important is to choose the most suitable technology for your business. So, the second important

Mr. Vitalik Buterin, Co-Founder of Ethereum, delivering the keynote at the Inclusive Blockchain Conference in 2017.

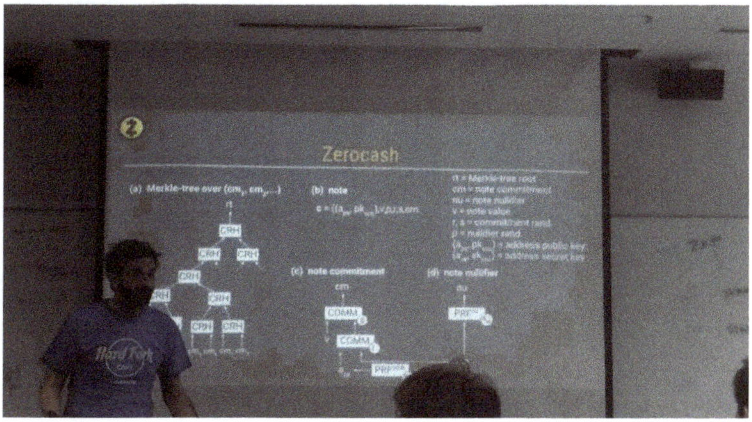

Mr. Zooko Wilcox-O'Hearn, CEO and Founder of Zcash, conducting the Blockchain Privacy Workshop in 2018.

Dr. Xiao Feng, Chairman and CEO of Wanxiang Blockchain, giving a keynote address at the Global Inclusive Blockchain Conference in 2018.

Ms. Hester Peirce, Commissioner of the U.S. Securities and Exchange Commission, delivering a keynote address at the SUSS Convergence Forum in 2019.

Mr. Sopnendu Mohanty, Chief Fintech Officer, Monetary Authority of Singapore (MAS), giving a keynote speech in our very first online summit, China–Singapore Blockchain Leaders Summit 2020.

skill related to technologies is to understand the business strategy — what is the case for your company, what your business can or cannot do and how technologies can help achieve your objectives. Knowledge about the technologies alone is not enough, one must be aware of the companies' strategies such as the KYC, business philosophy, market environment, regulation and compliance, and the firms' competitive edges to make sure the business is sustainable in the long run.

The third skill is project management. Effectiveness of planning and vision depends largely on the execution, so project management also plays an important role. It is the step to bring ideas to the market. Regardless of the decisions on which technologies to use or the level of reliance on technologies, students shall be able to contribute to the company as employees and make the projects work.

Therefore, we consolidate some of the course materials and incorporate them into this book, hoping to provide readers with some insights about the design thinking and technical details behind the blockchain technologies, and to employ the knowledge or the mindset in your future study or work. Like the spirit of decentralised and distributed blockchain, we are happy to make our course materials open-sourced to encourage peer-to-peer learning and we look forward to seeing more people recognising realities, embracing changes and creating new opportunities in this inevitable digital age.

Feel free to visit the SUSS-WS Future Economy Book Series page (https://www.worldscientific.com/series/susswsfes) for our existing books on other relevant topics such as AI, data and quantum computing and more upcoming books, or our website (www.sussblockchain.com) for the latest news on workshops and publications available at SUSS FinTech & Blockchain Group. Enjoy the journey to learn!

Last but not least, we would like to thank the President, Provost and Dean of SUSS for supporting us on this project. Also, without the contribution by the SUSS Fellows to the workshop series and conferences, we would not have accelerated the preparation of these materials. Many students have contributed in one way or another in the preparation of this book by providing feedback and our fellow academics have been very forthcoming in their criticism to enhance our presentation. We will not name everyone but thank all of you for helping us.

About the Authors

Professor David LEE Kuo Chuen is the founder of several companies including California-based Left Coast, Singapore's Ferrell Group and BlockAsset. He is a non-executive director of two listed companies. He is the founding investor in Zcash, Qtum and a few other blockchain companies. He is an advisor to Financial Inclusion Institute, and was the director of the Sim Kee Boon Institute for Financial Economics at the Singapore Management University. He graduated with B.Sc., M.Sc. and Ph.D. from the London School of Economics and Political Science. He was the Group Managing Director of OUE and Auric Pacific. He founded and managed one of the most successful hedge funds in 1998 for property investment in Asia with several commercial buildings and more than 100 units of residential units. He founded Premium Land and was the property developer for Ferrell Residences, a high-end 24-storey residential building, in 2006. His operation and managing experience includes F&B, manufacturing, hospitality, hedge funds, stockbroking, property management, property development, REITs, medical plastic components, listing and de-listing of companies, startups and multinationals. He is the editor and an author of the American Library Association Outstanding Award Reference

Book titled *Digital Currency* by Elsevier and the LASIC model for scalable technology companies. He has been nominated by the Internal Consulting Group as a Global Thought Leader for Fintech and Blockchain.

Dr LO Swee Won is a lecturer at the School of Business, Singapore University of Social Sciences. She graduated with a Ph.D. in Information Security & Trust from Singapore Management University, where her dissertation focused on the security of online distribution of multimedia codestreams. She teaches financial cryptography, FinTech, and blockchain security and privacy courses to postgraduates and undergraduates. She is a content provider and validator for the IBF Future-Enabled Skills series and a member of the Blockchain and Distributed Ledger Technologies Technical Committee (BDLTTC) at ITSC. Her primary research interests include data/user security and privacy, and risks and complexities in blockchain. Her publications include book chapters and papers in top conferences such as WISA, ICME and ESORICS. She serves as a referee for *The Singapore Economic Review* and *IEEE Transactions on Intelligent Transportation Systems*, and is a member of the Editorial Board of *Cybersecurity and Privacy* (specialty section of Frontiers in Big Data) as a Review Editor.

Ms WANG Yu (Cheryl) is a fintech research fellow at the School of Business, Singapore University of Social Sciences. Her main research interests are FinTech, ICO, Financial data analysis and Asset pricing. Prior to SUSS, she worked at the National University of Singapore Business School as a research associate on corporate governance and sustainability. She graduated with an M.Sc. in Applied Economies from Nanyang Technological University and a B.Sc. in Financial Engineering from Huazhong University of Sciences of Technologies. She has written multiple journal papers, including an empirical study on sustainability reporting and firm value published in the SSCI journal, *Sustainability*, and one investigating cryptocurrency as a new alternative investment published in the *Journal of Alternative Investments* that has been cited over 150 times and recommended by *CFA Institute Journal Review*. She also serves as a referee for various journals such as *Singapore Economic Review*, *Quarterly Review of Economics and Finance* and *Journal of Alternative Investments*.

Acknowledgements

We would like to thank our researchers Davina Tham, Sherman Low Wei Dong and Yiheng Liu, as well as Balasubramanian Shanmugam and Jiang Yulin for their tremendous help in the completion of this book.

We are also especially thankful to the Dean of the School of Business, Associate Professor Allan Chia Beng Hock, and the former Dean of the School of Business, Professor Lee Pui Mun, for their support. Thanks are also due to our colleagues Professor Leslie Chew and Dr. Daniel Seah from the School of Law, Associate Professor Ding Ding, Dr. Caroline Lim, Dr. Hung Yuchen, Associate Professor Joseph Lim, Associate Professor Linda Low, Associate Professor Phoon Kok Fai, Dr. Ren Jing, Sherry Li Ying Ying, Dr. Tan Chong Hui, Associate Professor Tan Yan Weng, Dr. Wang Yue, Dr. Xu Weibiao and Dr. Yu Yinghui from the School of Business.

Special thanks also to our close partners and collaborators Professor Zhao Xiaoju, Professor Hou Wenxuan, Professor Liu Liya, Professor Chen Yun, Associate Professor Cindy Deng Xin and Assistant Professor Min Min of Shanghai University of Finance and Economics (SUFE), Professor Pei Sai Fan of Libai Academy, Dr. Yan Li of Nanyang Technological University, Associate Professor Zhang Junwei of Xidian University, Sopnendu Mohanty, Tay Su Hui and team from MAS, Thomas Ho of NRF, Veronica Tan, Koh Wee Siong and team from IMDA, Law Chung Ming, Teh Kai Feng, Low Yue Wen and team from ESG, Juanita Woodward of CTD, Anson Zeall of IDAXA/ACCESS Singapore, Chia Hock Lai of Singapore FinTech Association/Global FinTech Institute, Tan Bin Ru, Yeo Guat Kwang, Tome Oh and others from Blockchain Association Singapore, Dr. Naseem Naqvi from British Blockchain Association, Daphne Ng, Dr. Ernie Teo, Edwan Chiam and team from Dedoco, Paul Neo of SAL, Peter Douglas and team from CAIA Association, and Addy Crezee and team from Blockshow. We are indebted to Emma Cui and her team from LongHash, Wang Lei and his team from 8BTC, Dr Xiao Feng, Du Yu and team from Wanxiang Blockchain Labs, Selina Lin and her team from DRC and Niu Zhiyan and her team from Shanjun Culture Media.

We would also like to thank our SUSS Fellows, workshop instructors and invited speakers for sharing their insights with us. There are so many to thank and their names are all on www.susssblockchain.com but especially to Dr. Aleksandra Bal, Dr. Alex Baranovskyi, Andras Kristof, Anish Srivastava, Anju Patwardhan, Professor Anne-Laure Mention, Anthony Lim, Armen Harutyunyan, Ben Cessa, Ben Chan, Benjamin Soh, Bobby Ong, Dr. Boyd Cohen, Dr. Chan Onn, Charlie Lee, Chua Tju Liang, Clay Lin, Danny Lim, Dave Appleton, Dr. David Hardoon, Debbie Watkins, Diego Gutierrez, Dmitriy Budorin, Edward Tan, Gary Loh, Gongpil Choi, Harry Smorenberg, Henry Wang, Commissioner Hester Peirce, Ian Myles, Jack Lee, James Gong, Jason Lim, Jeff Garzik, Jehan Chu, Jerome Eger, Joseph Thompson, Justin Newton, Dr. Justo Ortiz, Karen Teoh, Prof Kung Chen, Lesly Goh, Lisette Cipriano, Liz Steininger, Joseph Lubin, Dr. Loi Luu, Matthew Tan, Mike Lloyd, Dr. Miguel Soriano, Niall Dennehy, Nicola Paoli, Nizam Ismail, Patrick Dai, Paul Schulte, Dr. Peter Yan, Ramon Vicente, Remington Ong, Renqi Shen, Robert Greene, Roberto Capodieci, Robin Lee, Roland Schwinn, Roland Sun, Roy Lai, Roy Teo, Shaun Djie, Shen Bo Siew Kai Choy, Professor Silvio Micali, Stanley Yong, Sunny Lu, TM Lee, Tomicah Tillemann, Tony Lai, Tony Yeoh, Val Yap, Vitalik Buterin, Associate Professor Wan Zhiguo, Dr. Wang Xinxi, Wijitleka Marome, Dr. Yan Qiang, Yusho Liu, Yvonne Zhang, Professor Zhang Bohui, Zhang Yifeng, and Zooko Wilcox.

Lastly, Cheryl Wang Yu and Lo Swee Won would like to express their thanks to Guo Li and Li Feng.

the CIA triad is no longer considered sufficient to ensure protection against attacks on the data and user. Security practitioners are now also expected to address two additional security objectives: *authentication* and *accountability*. It is important to keep in mind these five objectives, as they guide the design and use of cryptographic techniques. Let us look more closely at what each objective entails.

1.2.1 *Confidentiality*

Confidentiality extends to both data confidentiality and user confidentiality (also understood as user privacy):

- *Data Confidentiality*: There are two primary aims of data confidentiality. The first is to shield data from all unauthorised parties. This is similar to the original objective of classical cryptography, and is achieved through data encryption. The second is to shield data from unauthorised parties who are differentiated on the basis of access rights. For example, a patient's hospital records will contain different types of data, such as identifying information, test results, diagnoses, treatments, prescriptions and medical insurance coverage. To protect the patient's privacy, hospital employees should only have access to the records on a need-to-know basis. Doctors, nurses, pharmacists, hospital administrators and medical social workers should all have different access rights depending on the information they need to carry out their respective roles. The records management system will therefore need an authorisation protocol that gives users different levels of access based on their identity.
- *User Privacy*: There are two primary aims of user privacy, in situations where there is reason to expect that a user remains unidentifiable. The first is to ensure untraceability. We should be able to conceal the routes of goods, money, data and other operations, so that an observer cannot follow the trail to deduce identifying information about a user. The second is to ensure unlinkability. We should be able to conceal the connection between multiple pieces of data from the same user, so that they appear unrelated to an observer. For example, given multiple pseudonymous transactions

on the Bitcoin blockchain, it should not be possible to deduce the real identity of the user who performed the transactions, nor to deduce that they were performed by the same user.

High-profile cases of compromised data confidentiality have made news headlines in recent years, from the unauthorised harvesting of Facebook users' personal data by Cambridge Analytica to the data breach of Sing Health medical records in 2018. In contrast, there are almost no publicly disclosed cases of compromised user privacy, which largely remains an area of theoretical concern in academia but is also gaining more attention as big data, Internet-of-Things (IoT) and the usage of blockchain become more pervasive.

1.2.2 *Integrity*

We cannot trust a message unless we know that its content has been secured from the point that it leaves its origin to the point that it reaches its destination. Data integrity is concerned with ensuring that data are not tampered. Though often conflated with confidentiality, integrity is a distinct objective. It is sometimes assumed that encryption is sufficient to ensure data integrity, in the sense that since encryption conceals the real content of a message, the content cannot be modified in any meaningful way. This is a false assumption as it is possible to manipulate a piece of encrypted data in ways that simply invalidate its content. In this case, the recipient has no idea if the encrypted data are received with errors or were maliciously modified. We therefore need tools specific to integrity protection to secure data from unauthorised modifications.

Integrity is achieved through the use of hash function, message authentication codes and/or digital signature. Integrity is closely associated with authentication and accountability — two security objectives that have evolved above and beyond the traditional "CIA triad". It is important to be able to distinguish the subtle differences among all three.

1.2.3 *Availability*

Data and online services are of no use if they are not available when authorised users need them. Availability as a security objective is closely associated with a malicious activity known as a Denial-of-Service (DoS) attack. As its name suggests, a DoS attack is when an attacker attempts to overwhelm a server with a flood of bogus requests that render the server so busy that it is unable to process normal traffic, and becomes unavailable to other users.

In this era of the IoT, a DoS attack has evolved to a Distributed DoS (DDoS) attack, which uses a network of distributed devices connected to the Internet to carry out the attack. In a DDoS attack, an attacker first injects malicious software (or malware) into any vulnerable devices connected to the Internet. These devices could be mobile phones, routers, personal computers, network printers and Internet Protocol (IP) cameras. Once infected with malware, these devices become bots that can be remotely controlled to send bogus requests to the target server, even down to a stipulated date and time. Availability is usually addressed through good system design, such as intrusion detection or intrusion prevention systems. It is also important to note that provision of availability is closely related to how susceptible a system is to single point of failure, i.e. how decentralised the system is.

1.2.4 *Authentication*

Authentication extends to both data authentication and user authentication:

- *Data Authentication*: The aim is to verify that the origin of a piece of data is what it claims to be. One of the most common ways of ensuring data authenticity is through message authentication codes and digital signatures.
- *User Authentication*: The aim is to verify that a user is who they claim to be. It can be achieved by providing authentication factors to a login system, based on what you know (e.g., username and password), what you have (e.g., access card) or who you are (e.g., biometric information). Similarly, the cryptographic techniques involved are message authentication codes and digital signature, where users are required to demonstrate something they know (i.e., the secret/private key).

1.2.5 *Accountability*

Accountability aims to thwart a user from falsely denying that they have sent or received a particular communication. It is analogous with the concept of non-repudiation. Imagine that we have ensured data integrity and authentication; that is, we have secured a piece of data from tampering while in transit, and we have verified the origin of the data. Accountability goes a step further by creating a digital artefact that makes it impossible for the sender to deny having sent the data. It draws an undeniable link between the data and the users who have processed it, ensuring accountability for actions performed on the data. This is achieved through the use of a digital signature. With the rise of "deepfakes" and disinformation, and eroding public trust in news media, ensuring accountability is increasingly becoming a matter of social and political stability.

1.2.6 *Attacks*

Know thyself, know thy enemy, and in every battle you will be victorious.

— *Sun Tzu,* The Art of War

To respond effectively to a threat to information security, we must know what we are up against. Understanding possible attack strategies enables us to put in place the appropriate safeguards to ensure the security of a system and its cryptographic techniques. We will briefly look at two types of attacks here:

- *Active Attack*: The attacker performs aggressive and often blatant actions with the aim of affecting or altering a system's operations. Examples include e-mail phishing, modifying data in transit between users, mounting a DDoS attack and mounting a brute-force attack (trial and error) to guess a username and password combination. An active attack is easy to detect but difficult to defend, involving a thorough analysis to close all loopholes in a system or cryptographic technique. By the time an attack is detected, the damage may already have been done or underway.

- *Passive Attack*: The attacker uses covert methods to tap into a network and eavesdrop on or record communications. The objective of a passive attack is usually to gain access to a system or steal information surreptitiously. Examples include surveillance, man-in-the-middle attacks and keystroke logging. Designed to avoid detection, passive attacks are difficult to detect but easy to prevent. One of the most straightforward methods is to encrypt communication between users.

1.3 Cryptography

Earlier, we briefly discussed the idea of what is considered secure in cryptography. We stated that cryptography is a suite of algorithms based on the intractability of difficult problems that cannot be solved in a reasonable amount of time. In this section, we will examine the concept of security in cryptography in greater detail, and identify the key properties of a secure cryptographic scheme.

Key Terms: Bit, Scheme, Algorithm, Function

A bit (short for binary digit) is the smallest unit of computer data. Each bit has one of two binary values, either 0 or 1. 4 bits of data therefore have 2^4 or 16 possible combinations:

0000	0100	1000	1100
0001	0101	1001	1101
0010	0110	1010	1110
0011	0111	1011	1111

In the following sections, we use certain terms to talk about parts of a security system. A cryptographic *scheme* is an overall description of how a security system works. Schemes consist of one or more *algorithms*, which are sets of instructions defining a sequence of operations to be carried out by a computer. For example, an encryption scheme may consist of a secret key generation algorithm, an encryption algorithm and a decryption algorithm.

A *function* is a process or relation between values that takes some input and produces some output. For example, the secret key generation algorithm has a KeyGen() function that takes as input the security parameter n, and produces a secret key k of n bits. The encryption algorithm has an Enc() function that takes as input a secret key k and a plaintext m, and produces a ciphertext c. The decryption algorithm has a Dec() function that takes as input a ciphertext c and a secret key k, and produces a plaintext m.

Cryptographic techniques cannot be proven unconditionally secure, as that would require breakthroughs in the analysis of computational complexity that are not yet within our reach. In fact, almost all cryptographic techniques can be broken given enough time and computing power. We still consider them secure because what is "enough" is generally not achievable in our lifetime or several lifetimes. Instead of unconditional security, we aim for cryptographic techniques to be *computationally secure*.

Refining our earlier statement, we say that *a cryptographic scheme is computationally secure if no efficient attacker is able to break it in a reasonable amount of time*. An "efficient attacker" can be understood as an attacker with a reasonable amount of computing power, while "a reasonable amount of time" can be understood as a time frame during which the ability to solve a problem has ceased to be useful or interesting. Cryptographic techniques that meet these conditions have a negligible probability of being broken.

For example, to break a secret key of 4 bits, an attacker needs to try only 2^4 combinations, with the probability of guessing the right key being $1/2^4$. This is easily done through a brute-force attack. A 4-bit secret key is therefore not computationally secure. In contrast, if the key is of 256 bits, mounting a brute-force attack to try 2^{256} combinations would take an attacker several lifetimes, even with a supercomputer. That makes a 256-bit key computationally secure.

Intuitively, it seems that we could make cryptography schemes more secure by setting the highest requirements, such as assuming an attacker with unlimited, rather than reasonable, computing power. Indeed, the study of information-theoretic security (or perfect security) produces security systems that even an attacker with unlimited computing power would not be able to break, as the encrypted message provides no information about the original message. The one-time pad, or Vernam cipher, which we will discuss in Section 1.9, is an example of an information-theoretic secure scheme.

We can think of computational security as a practical balance between security and *efficiency*. All computationally secure cryptographic schemes rely on the provision of *pseudorandomness*. This refers to the fact that the distribution of a string should satisfy statistical tests of randomness, even though it is in fact not truly random. Ciphertexts (encrypted texts) are not truly random; in certain conditions, when enough information is known, a user can know what ciphertext an algorithm will produce. However, to all other users who do not have enough information, the ciphertext is just a pseudorandom string.

Pseudorandomness is important because it prevents a ciphertext from inadvertently disclosing information about the statistical distributions of the secret key or the original message. It does this by ensuring that an attacker cannot distinguish one ciphertext from another. Using the example of an encryption scheme, where an encryption algorithm is denoted as Enc(), m is a message in plaintext, c is the encrypted ciphertext and k is the encryption key,

$$c \leftarrow \mathrm{Enc}_k(m)$$

A computationally secure encryption scheme requires that given two ciphertexts c_1 and c_2, or

$$c_1 \leftarrow \mathrm{Enc}_k(m_1)$$
$$c_2 \leftarrow \mathrm{Enc}_k(m_2)$$

Both c_1 and c_2 are indistinguishable to an efficient attacker. In other words, both c_1 and c_2 have pseudorandom distributions, and do not reveal any information about the statistical distributions of k, m_1 or m_2.

1.4 Blockchain

The concept of a blockchain first appeared in 2008 in a white paper by Bitcoin inventor Satoshi Nakamoto. In the paper, Nakamoto proposes Bitcoin as a peer-to-peer payment system, and "a chain of blocks" as the structure for recording Bitcoin transactions in an immutable and transparent manner.

The idea of using digital currencies for decentralised peer-to-peer payment is not new. However, before Bitcoin, it had never been realised because without a trusted central authority (such as a bank) to oversee transactions, there was no practical way to thwart three possible acts by malicious users: spending without authorisation (i.e., without ownership of the account), spending without having enough balance and double-spending (i.e., sending the same amount of digital currencies to more than one receiver without deduction in the account balance).

Consider the banking system that we are familiar with. To initiate a fund transfer, users first have to log in to their Internet banking account. The act of logging in proves a user's ownership of the account. When the user requests a fund transfer, this involves the bank checking, among others, if the user has enough balance to perform the transaction. If so, the request will be approved. Immediately after, the amount transferred will be deducted from the balance, so double spending will not be possible. If a user were to copy and resend the transaction confirmation, this would not result in multiple duplicate fund transfers to the same receiver, because the bank would prohibit fraudulent transactions.

At its introduction, Bitcoin blockchain was the first sound design of an open and secure *Distributed Ledger Technology* (*DLT*) that thwarts these three malicious acts without the need for a central authority. DLT is a method of record-keeping whereby every person involved in the record-keeping possesses a copy of the ledger. Whenever a new record is created, it is updated in each and every user's ledger. DLT is straightforward to implement in a trusted setting, which assumes either a trusted central authority with no self-interest, or that all users will behave honestly by

- not sending bogus or meaningless transactions that will consume unnecessary computation and storage resources;
- updating the ledger in an honest and timely manner whenever a new transaction comes in;
- not making unauthorised deletions, insertions or modifications to transaction details on the ledger; and
- including only valid transactions on the ledger and rejecting all invalid transactions.

A trusted setting without a central authority is unrealistic in most real-life settings, however, given the self-interested behaviour of individuals. Blockchain, specifically public blockchain like Bitcoin, does not assume trust. Its significance is that it enables a decentralised peer-to-peer payment system where the ledger recording the transactions is maintained and updated by a group of users who do not necessarily trust each other. It is able to bring the community of users together to agree on a single version of the truth through "crypto-economy", which combines cryptography and economic incentives. Cryptography records data on the transactions in a secure manner and ensures that it is costly for a user to cheat or perform unauthorised actions, while economic incentives reward honest and trustworthy users who help to maintain the integrity of the ledger.

"The Tragedy of the Commons" (Ostrom, 2015)

Blockchain can be considered as a modern solution to an age-old economic problem known as the "tragedy of the commons". This term describes the scenario where, given a pool of a common resource that is scarce, rivalrous (i.e. one person's consumption reduces the amount available to another) and non-excludable (i.e., it is not possible to block access to the resource by people who have not paid), individuals acting independently based on their own self-interest will behave contrary to the common good of all, and deplete or spoil the common resource through their collective action. Land, water and other natural resources are prominent examples of such common resources, and the "tragedy of the commons" often emerges in discussions about environmental rights. Solutions to a "tragedy of the commons" situation may be governmental (e.g., regulation, privatisation) or non-governmental (e.g., collective social action) in nature.

In 2009, American scholar Elinor Ostrom became the first woman to win the Nobel Memorial Prize in Economic Sciences for her analysis of economic governance, particularly of common resources. Her work identifies eight design principles for self-organised governance of common resources, which turn out to be very similar to those of blockchain:

1. Clearly define the group of common goods and the group of entitled users.
2. Adapt the rules governing the use of common goods to local conditions.
3. Allow users affected by the rules to participate in the decision-making process.
4. Implement a monitoring system with monitors from within the group.
5. Use graduated sanctions for users who violate rules.
6. Provide accessible and low-cost means for dispute resolution.
7. Ensure that the group's rule-making rights are recognised by any higher authorities.
8. In the case of larger pools of common goods, organise governance through multiple, nested tiers of management.

1.5 Cryptographic Hash Function

We start with a simple definition of a hash function, namely that it is a method of mapping input of arbitrary length onto an output of fixed length. We call this output a hash value, also known as a "hash" or "message digest". A hash function, denoted as Hash(), takes as input a message m of arbitrary length and produces a hash value h of fixed length l:

$$h = \text{Hash}(m)$$

We can also write this process as

$$\text{Hash}()\colon \{0,1\}^* \rightarrow \{0,1\}^l$$

Hash functions have many uses, one of the most common being the generation of hash tables for indexing data to enable efficient data storage and retrieval. However, cryptographic hash functions are different as they possess rigorous security definitions. Cryptographic hash functions can be used for file integrity protection, generation of one-time passwords and digital signature computation, to name a few. We are concerned only with the family of cryptographic hash functions, and will use "cryptographic hash function" and "hash function" interchangeably in the remainder of this chapter. Some examples of hash functions are shown in Figure 1.1.

You might have heard of a blockchain being described as an immutable ledger. This immutability is a result of the use of distributed ledger technology coupled with hash functions, which do not allow any modification to a block and its transactions to go undetected. Informally, a hash function possesses the properties shown in Figure 1.2.

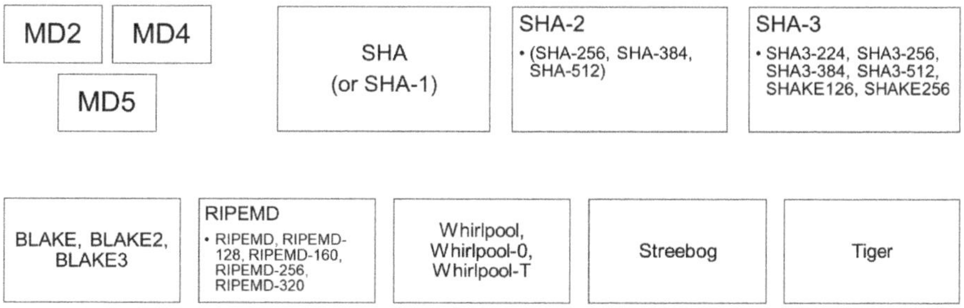

Figure 1.1: Examples of hash functions.

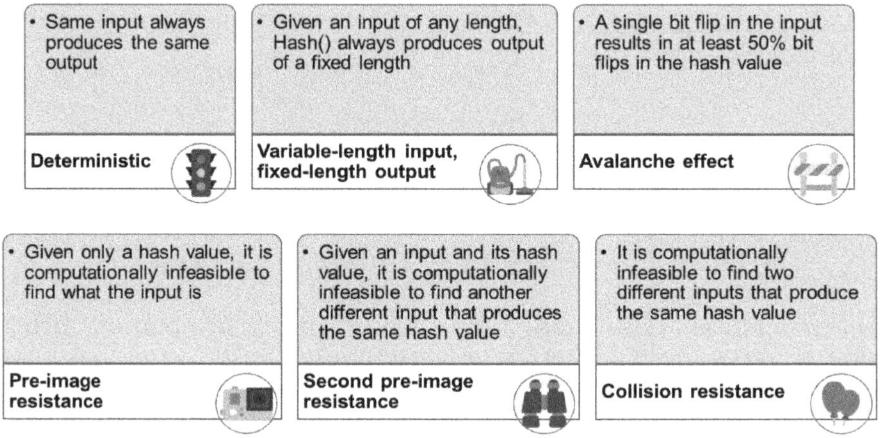

Figure 1.2: Properties of hash function.

Formally, the properties of pre-image resistance, second pre-image resistance and collision resistance can be written as follows:

- Pre-image resistance (or one-wayness): Given h where $h = \text{Hash}(m_1)$, it is infeasible to find out the value of m_1 without trying on average $2^l - 1$ times, where l is the length of the hash value in bits.
- Second pre-image resistance: Given $h_1 = \text{Hash}(m_1)$, it is computationally infeasible to find another message m_2, where $m_2 \neq m_1$ but $\text{Hash}(m_2) = \text{Hash}(m_1)$.
- Collision resistance: It is computationally infeasible for an attacker to find two distinct inputs m_3 and m_4, such that $\text{Hash}(m_3) = \text{Hash}(m_4)$.

Many attacks against hash functions exploit the mathematical underpinnings of collision resistance based on the "birthday problem". In the original birthday problem, we are tasked to find two people who have the same birthday out of a roomful of people. Assuming that all 365 days in a year are equally probable for a birthday (and ignoring leap years), we need at most only 23 people in the room to have a 50% probability of finding two people who share a birthday. It may seem counter-intuitive that a relatively small set

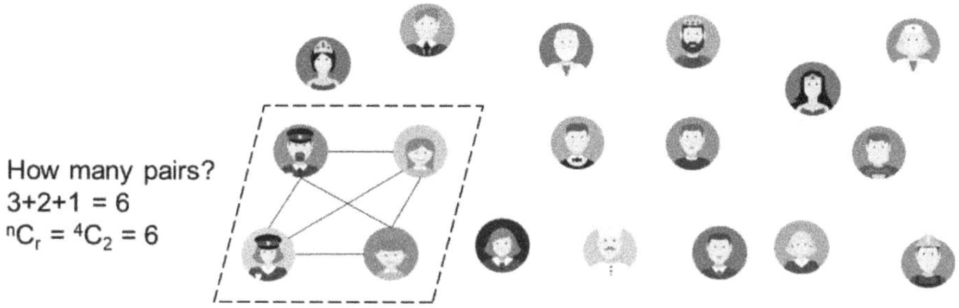

Figure 1.3: Number of pairs that can be formed out of four persons.

produces such a high probability of collision. However, consider the following problem: How many pairs can we form out of four persons? The answer is six, given by the formula for ${}^{n}C_{r} = \frac{n!}{r!(n-r)!}$. Thus, ${}^{4}C_{2} = 6$. See Figure 1.3.

As such, given 23 people in one room, the number of possible pairs is given by ${}^{23}C_{2} = 253$. This number is well over half of the 365 possible birthdays in a year.

An approximation can be devised in that given a function $f()$ that has x number of possible outputs, the number of tries after which we expect to get two different inputs y_1 and y_2 where $f(y_1) = f(y_2)$ is given by $1.25 \times \sqrt{x}$. With respect to hash functions, the birthday problem states that *if the hash function produces a hash value of length l bits, then a collision for that hash value can on average be found in $2^{l/2}$ tries*. This probabilistic model is the basis for so-called "birthday attacks".

Aside from the sound design of a hash function, therefore, the birthday problem reminds us that the length of the hash value is also closely related to security. However, sound design is arguably the more fundamental for security. The cryptographic community witnessed this in 2017 when Google announced that it had achieved the first concrete collision attack on SHA-1, having developed a technique to generate a collision[1]. SHA-1 produces a 160-bit hash value, meaning that on average it takes 2^{80} tries to find a collision

[1]https://shattered.io/.

Figure 1.4: Example of software integrity verification for ghostscript.
Source: https://github.com/ArtifexSoftware/ghostpdl-downloads/releases/download/gs952/SHA512SUMS.

through a brute-force attack, which is still computationally infeasible given today's computing power. However, Google was able to expose a practical attack that exploited flaws in the design of SHA-1 that paved the way for it to be phased out of use.

Hash functions form the basis of a myriad of cryptographic techniques, including message authentication codes, digital signatures, one-time passwords and checksums. For example, when downloading software from the Internet, users should check their download against the checksum, or hash value provided on the software's official website to ensure they have an uncorrupted version of the programme (see Figure 1.4). Note that this act of checking software integrity is based on the assumption that the official website is not compromised. As we will see later, hash function is also used to protect integrity of transactions and blocks; this is built upon the distributed ledger technology. For the rest of this section, we will look more closely at the application of hash functions in blockchain.

1.5.1 *Merkle Hash Tree*

Fundamentally, the Merkle Hash Tree is a binary tree; each parent node has two children nodes. It is created using a bottom-up

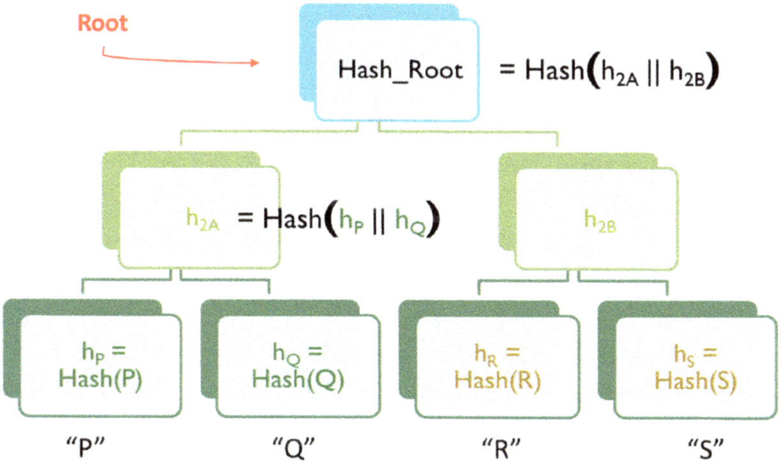

Figure 1.5: An example of Merkle Hash Tree with data "P", "Q", "R" and "S".

construction, where nodes at the bottom are called leaf nodes. Each leaf node contains cryptographic hash of a piece of data and every non-leaf node contains cryptographic hash of its children nodes. An example is illustrated in Figure 1.5. Here, the data of each leaf node are "P", "Q", "R" and "S", respectively. Each leaf node thus contains cryptographic hash of "P", "Q", "R" and "S", i.e., h_P, h_Q, h_R and h_S, respectively. The parent node (i.e., a non-leaf node) of "P" and "Q" records the hash of h_P and h_Q, i.e., $h_{2A} = \text{Hash}(h_P \| h_Q)$, where "$\|$" denotes concatenation. Similarly, the parent node of "R" and "S" records the hash of h_R and h_S, i.e., $h_{2B} = \text{Hash}(h_R \| h_S)$. At this juncture, we are left with only two nodes containing h_{2A} and h_{2B}; the parent of these nodes is called the Merkle Root and it records $\text{Hash}(h_{2A} \| h_{2B})$.

To take a closer look at how Merkle Hash Tree protects data integrity, we notice how h_{2A} is computed based on h_P and h_Q, how h_{2B} is computed based on h_R and h_S, and finally, how the *Hash_Root* is computed based on h_{2A} and h_{2B}. Consequently, any changes in the data "P", "Q", "R" or "S" would always be reflected in the *Hash_Root*.

The construction of a Merkle Hash Tree allows efficient and secure verification of data. If the Merkle Root, *Hash_Root*, is published and immutable to changes (therefore, trusted to be the true representation of data in the tree), then one can verify whether the data "P" is included in the Merkle Hash Tree by asking the Prover to supply proofs consisting of $\{h_Q,\ h_{2B}\}$. The tuple $\{h_Q, h_{2B}\}$ is called the Merkle Path for data "P".

The Merkle Path for data "P" together with the hash of "P" is then sufficient for the Verifier to reconstruct its own Merkle Hash Tree and compare the resulting Merkle Root with the immutable *Hash_Root*; if the hash values match, then the Verifier can be ascertained that the data "P" is included in the Merkle Hash Tree.

If "P" is not, in fact, included in the Merkle Hash Tree but the Prover lies that it is, the Prover needs to find a collision in the Merkle Root hash. For simplicity, suppose the Verifier checks if data "N" is included in the Merkle Hash Tree shown in Figure 1.5. To lie that "N" is in the Merkle Hash Tree (instead of "P"), the Prover must supply proofs that are in one of the following forms:

- $\{h_1,\ h_{2B}\}$, where h_1 is a hash value that will result in the same h_{2A} when computed with h_N, i.e., $\text{Hash}(h_N \| h_1)$ is the same as $\text{Hash}(h_P \| h_Q)$.
- $\{h_Q, h_2\}$, where h_2 is a hash value that will result in the same *Hash_Root* when computed with the $\text{Hash}(h_N \| h_Q)$, i.e., $\text{Hash}(\text{Hash}(h_N \| h_Q) \| h_2)$ is the same as $\text{Hash}(h_{2A} \| h_{2B})$.
- $\{h_3,\ h_4\}$, where h_3 and h_4 are both hash values that when combined with h_N will result in the same *Hash_Root* that has been published and immutable.

To supply either one of the proofs above, the Prover will have to find a collision in the Merkle Root (*Hash_Root*), an act which is computationally infeasible due to the security properties of a hash function. This has an important implication when one wishes to verify if a transaction is included in a Bitcoin block.

1.5.2 *Hash Function in the Bitcoin Blockchain*

A blockchain is essentially a chain of blocks. It is a digital ledger, and the "digital chain" is enabled by the use of hash function. Figure 1.6 shows the structure of a Bitcoin block. In the ith block, denoted as

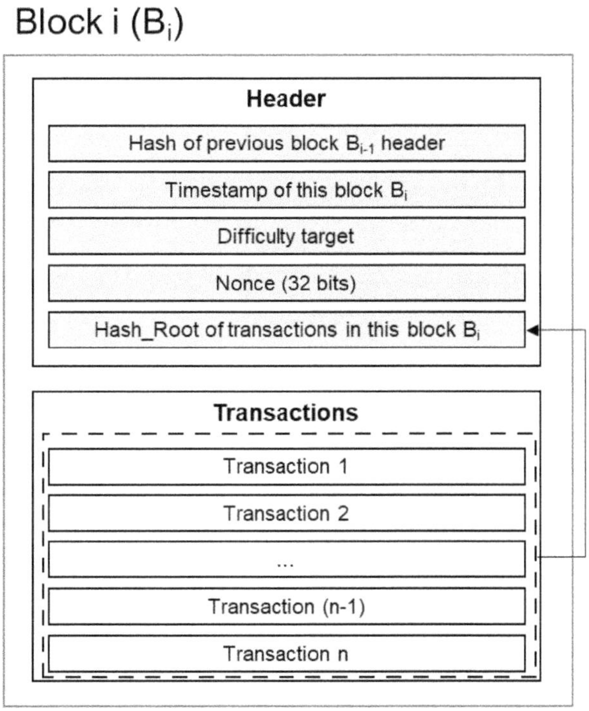

Figure 1.6: Bitcoin block header structure.

B_i, there is a list of transactions. These transactions are integrity-protected using a Merkle Hash Tree, and the Merkle Root is part of block B_i's header as shown in Figure 1.6.

To integrity-protect the block header, Bitcoin does not employ a straightforward calculation of the block header's hash. Instead, the proof-of-work (PoW) consensus algorithm in Bitcoin requires miners to vary the 32-bit nonce and iteratively calculate the block header hash until the resulting hash satisfies the difficulty target (see Figure 1.7). Without loss of generality, we refer to the block header hash that satisfies the difficulty target as the "valid block header hash".

As a secure hash function outputs a hash value that is pseudo-random and it is infeasible to predict which nonce would result in a valid block header hash, the PoW consensus algorithm is essentially

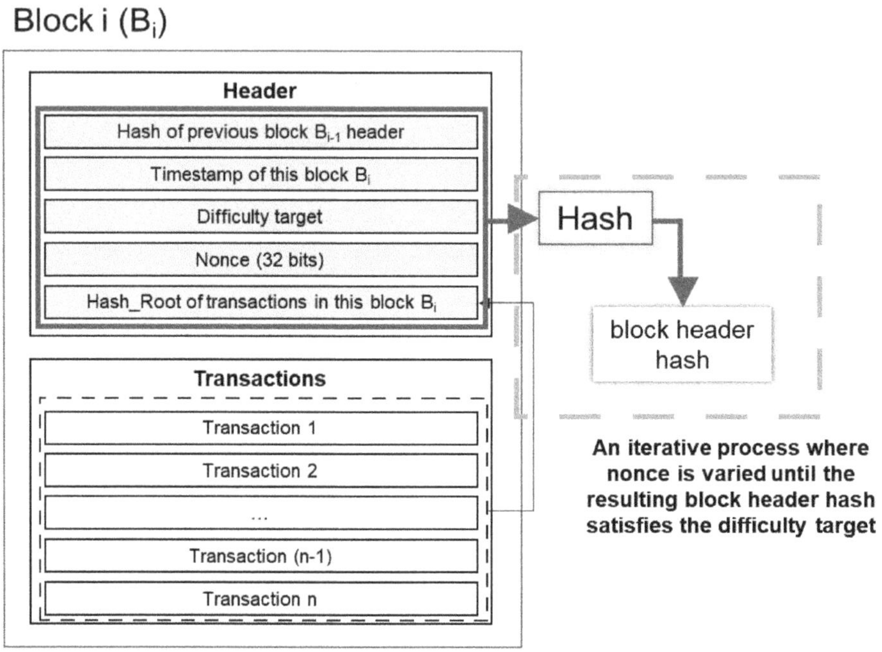

Figure 1.7: Bitcoin calculation of block header hash (Proof-of-Work).

a lottery system among miners. Each miner can only vary the nonce, recompute the block header hash and check if the block header hash is valid. This effort constitutes proof of work. Each miner has equal probability in finding a nonce that gives a valid block header hash. When a valid block header hash is found, the miner will broadcast the block in its entirety (referred to as "the solution") to the network. Other miners in the network will accept this block as valid by checking that after hashing the solution, the resulting block header hash satisfies the difficulty target. The value of a difficulty target is part of the consensus rule globally accepted by miners in the network.

To this end, we note that what constitutes a valid block header hash is a hash value that satisfies the difficulty target. If the difficulty target states that "A valid block header hash is one that starts with at least four zeros in hexadecimal", then, for a block B_i, any one of the following hash values can be regarded as a valid block header hash:

- 00004a89fd89403a36e19c5d67ffcc9bba626cf8dc9a2109bcdbb2471 b952683
- 0000ed4bf83abd0f4b4ce53ed89fe59285f1016ccf85d738d0f6aa9924 e368d4
- 000002eb9ddb8b6d986196f3bf4a3958b2605e917e734c0d9e24d800 dc3cbb6b
- ... and the list goes on.

This presents an opportunity for an attacker who attempts to revert a transaction.

For instance, Eve agrees to pay Bob 1 btc (bitcoin) in exchange for a software license activation code. Eve creates a bitcoin transaction that pays Bob the agreed-upon amount and this transaction is recorded in block 500, B_{500}, with a block header hash value of 00006120ab0fbd24a1b61dbdca856c3795314945f405b4e90d9a1d3452b 85127. Upon seeing the transaction in B_{500}, Bob immediately sends the activation code to Eve. At the same time, Eve creates another block 500 *without* her transaction to Bob (denote this block as B_{500}') and performs the proof-of-work to get a valid block header hash for B_{500}'. Suppose this block has a block header hash value of 000035a474b760c0d13ff431a806553a3364c302117ceff8e08ef5fe37b123 53. Eve broadcasts B'_{500} to the network.

At this point in time, the network would observe two blocks at height 500, namely B_{500} with a header hash value of 00006120ab0fbd24a1b61dbdca856c3795314945f405b4e90d9a1d3452b 85127 and B_{500}' with a header hash value of 000035a474b760c0d13ff 431a806553a3364c302117ceff8e08ef5fe37b12353. To other users in the network, both blocks are considered valid. Bob's fate would then depend on which block is accepted by at least 51% of the users; the block which is accepted by majority users and therefore belongs in the longer chain will be considered as the final state of the ledger. The discarded block is commonly called a stale block.

If block B_{500}' is included in the longer chain and block B_{500} is discarded (because both share the same parent, B_{499}, thus only one would remain), Eve's transaction of 1 btc to Bob would not be part of the final state of the ledger. Therefore, in Bitcoin, transaction finality is characterised by a concept called the six-block confirmation. The idea is that a transaction will become computationally difficult to reverse when it is buried at least six blocks deep in the blockchain.

The Bitcoin PoW's difficulty target is set such that a valid block header hash can only be found in, on average, ten minutes. In the earlier scenario where Eve attempts to reverse her transaction to Bob, the one-block confirmation of Eve's transaction makes it possible for Eve to create another valid block and possibly get the newly created block accepted by majority of the users. However, if Bob sends the activation code to Eve only after B_{500} is appended with six additional blocks, it will make it practically impossible for Eve's attempt to reverse her transaction (for her to do so, she needs to create B_{500}', B_{501}', B_{502}', B_{503}', B_{504}', B_{505}', B_{506}' *and* convince the network to adopt her chain of blocks). Due to the security properties of hash function, there is no faster way for Eve to create the chain of B' blocks other than to run the proof-of-work algorithm honestly and compute block header hashes iteratively. As long as Eve does not possess majority hash power of the network, the six-block confirmation ensures that Eve can never catch up with the rest of the honest miners in her quest of creating the chain of B' blocks.

1.6 Digital Signature

Digital signature achieves user accountability, data authentication and integrity protection. In cryptography, a digital signature is a pseudorandom string that is created via arithmetic computation and secured based on a computationally hard problem. A high-level (but inaccurate) illustration of how a digital signature works is shown in Figure 1.8.

In Figure 1.8, Alice attempts to send Bob a message "hi". This message is converted into its decimal equivalent (from ASCII codes 104 for "h" and 105 for "i" to the binary representation 0110100001101001 to the decimal representation 26,729). A digital signature scheme takes Alice's private key, that is the decimal number 3, and raises 26,729 to the power of 3. The result of the exponentiation is Alice's digital

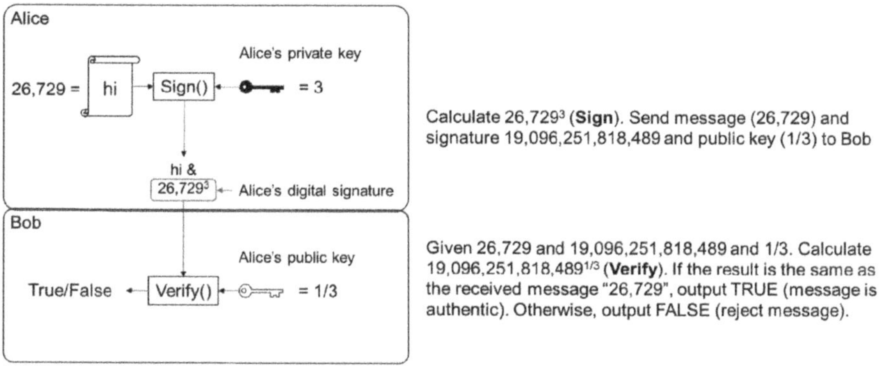

Figure 1.8: A high-level but inaccurate illustration of the working mechanism of a digital signature.

signature. Subsequently, Alice sends her message and the corresponding signature to Bob. Bob will verify Alice's signature using her public key, in this case, it is the number $1/3$, by raising the digital signature to the power of Alice's public key. If the result of the exponentiation is equal to Alice's message, then Bob concludes that the message is authentic and it indeed comes from Alice.

The above example is a high-level example to illustrate how digital signature works, where essentially, signing requires the signer's message and private key and verifying requires the verifier to perform arithmetic comparison using the signer's public key, message, and digital signature. Actual implementation of digital signature addresses the following practical considerations:

1. Our input messages to sign are usually much longer than a statement such as "hi".
2. Our public and private keys are long (around 1024 bits, i.e., a number that is around 309 digits, or 2048 bits) and their relationship is not a simple a and $1/a$. Instead, the relationship between private and public keys is such that given a user's public key, it is computationally infeasible (due to computationally hard problem) to find out or compute the user's private key.
3. Modular arithmetic is used and we leverage many important characteristics of modular arithmetic. This includes the ability

to work only with integers, the provision of groups, rings and fields, and the assumptions of computationally hard problems when modular arithmetic is applied.

1.6.1 *Modular Arithmetic — A Brief Introduction*

Before delving into the more specific RSA digital signature scheme, we first need to lay out some fundamental concepts in modular arithmetic.

A *prime number* is an integer that is only divisible by 1 and itself. By convention, 1 itself is not considered a prime number. All integers greater than 1 can be uniquely expressed as the product of prime numbers. The *greatest common divisor* is defined as the largest number that divides two numbers a and b. This is expressed as $\gcd(a, b)$. If a is a prime number, then $\gcd(a, b)$ will be either 1 or a. If $\gcd(a, b) = 1$, we say that a and b are relatively prime. For example,

$$\gcd(3, 9) = 3$$
$$\gcd(290, 333) = 1$$
$$\gcd(684, 1748) = 76$$

Modular arithmetic revolves around a number called a modulus, denoted as N. Given integers a and N, we define the expression (a mod N) (short for "a modulo N") as the remainder after a is divided by N. Thus,we can also write

$$r = (a \bmod N)$$

The integer a can be expressed as $a = qN + r$, where q is an integer, r is an integer and $0 \leq r < N$.

For example,

$$\text{Let } N = 17$$
$$(6 \bmod 17) = 6$$
$$(17 \bmod 17) = 0$$
$$(425 \bmod 17) = 15$$

The concept of modular arithmetic is commonly used in the 12-hour clock, in which the hour number restarts every time it reaches the modulus of 12. So, when it is 15 hours past midnight, we compute $(15 \bmod 12) = 3$, giving us the clock time of 3.

Given two integers a and b, we say that "a and b are congruent modulo N" if $a \equiv b \pmod{N}$. In this expression, the brackets around "mod N" imply that the modulus is applied to both a and b instead of just b. When we say that $a \equiv b \pmod{N}$, it also means that $(a \bmod N) = (b \bmod N)$.

As an example, $36 \equiv 21 \pmod{15}$ because $(36 \bmod 15) = (21 \bmod 15) = 6$. When $a \equiv b$ (mod N), then it is also true that $a = b + kN$ for any integer k. By taking modulus on both sides,

$$\begin{aligned} a \bmod N &= (b + kN) \bmod N \\ &= b \bmod N + kN \bmod N \\ &= b \bmod N + k(N \bmod N) \\ &= b \bmod N + k(0) \\ &= b \bmod N \end{aligned}$$

With this in mind, a *group* is a set of elements with a defined binary operation, denoted as $^\circ$. In mathematics, a group has the following defined properties:

- *Closure*: For any elements a and $b \in$ G, the result of $a \circ b$ is also in the group, i.e., $a \circ b \in$ G.
- *Identity*: There exists an "identity" element $e \in$ G, where for any element $a \in$ G, $a \circ e = e \circ a = a$.
- *Inverse*: For each element $a \in$ G, there exists an element $b \in$ G such that $\mathrm{a} \circ b = b \circ \mathrm{a} = e$.
- *Associativity*: For any elements a, b and $c \in$ G, $(a \circ b) \circ c = a \circ (b \circ c)$.
- *Commutative*: For any elements a and $b \in$ G, $a \circ b = b \circ a$.

A set of elements with the first four properties is a group. A group that also fulfils the fifth property is called an Abelian group. The *order* of a group, denoted as $\phi()$, is the number of elements in that group. To decide the number of elements in a group requires certain checks.

We are concerned with multiplicative group denoted as Z_N^*, where the binary operation is multiplication mod N. We can see that Z_N^* fulfils all the properties of a group:

- *Closure*: For any two elements a and b in Z_N^*, $(a \times b) \bmod N$ will produce an element of Z_N^*.
- *Identity*: Z_N^* has an identity element $e \in Z_N^*$, such that $(a \times e) \bmod N =$ a. For the group Z_N^*, $e = 1$.
- *Associative*: For any three elements a, b and c in Z_N^*, $(a \times b) \times c \bmod N = a \times (b \times c) \bmod N$.
- *Commutative*: For any two elements a and b in Z_N^*, $(a \times b) \bmod N = (b \times a) \bmod N$.
- *Inverse*: To ensure that each element in Z_N^* has an inverse that returns the identity element $e = 1$, we define the group as $Z_N^* = \{a \in \{1, 2, \ldots, N-1\} | \gcd(a, N) = 1\}$.

In other words, for each element in Z_N^* to have an inverse, the element $a \in Z_N^*$ must satisfy $\gcd(a, N) = 1$. In fact, it turns out that for a group Z_p^*, where p is a prime number, the set of group elements is always $\{1, 2, \ldots, p-1\}$.

As an example, suppose $N = 12$. Recall that any number modulo N will always result in a number between 0 (inclusive) and N, so we start with $Z_{12}^* = \{0, 1, 2, 3, 4, 5, 6, 7, 8, 9, 10, 11\}$. Let us check each possible element in the group for its inverse:

Element a	**Inverse of a**	**gcd(a,N)**	**Comment**
0	Does not exist	Invalid	0 is not in Z_{12}^*
1	Identity element	Identity element	1 is in Z_{12}^*
2	Does not exist	$\gcd(2, 12) = 2$	2 is not in Z_{12}^*
3	Does not exist	$\gcd(3, 12) = 3$	3 is not in Z_{12}^*
4	Does not exist	$\gcd(4, 12) = 4$	4 is not in Z_{12}^*
5	5 $(5 \times 5) \bmod 12 = 1$	$\gcd(5, 12) = 1$	5 is in Z_{12}^*
6	Does not exist	$\gcd(6, 12) = 6$	6 is not in Z_{12}^*

Element a	**Inverse of a**	**gcd(a,N)**	**Comment**
7	7 $(7 \times 7) \bmod 12 = 1$	$\gcd(7, 12) = 1$	7 is in Z_{12}^*
8	Does not exist	$\gcd(8, 12) = 4$	8 is not in Z_{12}^*
9	Does not exist	$\gcd(9, 12) = 3$	9 is not in Z_{12}^*
10	Does not exist	$\gcd(10, 12) = 2$	10 is not in Z_{12}^*
11	11 $(11 \times 11) \bmod 12 = 1$	$\gcd(11, 12) = 1$	11 is in Z_{12}^*

Therefore, $Z_{12}^* = \{1, 5, 7, 11\}$ and $\phi(12) = 4$.

As mentioned previously, where N is a prime number p, the set of group elements for Z_p^* is always $\{1, 2, \ldots, p-1\}$ and the order of Z_p^* is $\phi(p) = p - 1$. This is because for a prime number p, $\gcd(a, p)$ is always 1. Suppose $N = 7$:

Element a	**Inverse of a**	**gcd(a,N)**	**Comment**
0	Does not exist	Invalid	0 is not in Z_7^*
1	Identity element	Identity element	1 is in Z_7^*
2	4 $(2 \times 4) \bmod 7 = 1$	$\gcd(2, 7) = 1$	2 is in Z_7^*
3	5 $(3 \times 5) \bmod 7 = 1$	$\gcd(3, 7) = 1$	3 is in Z_7^*
4	2 $(4 \times 2) \bmod 7 = 1$	$\gcd(4, 7) = 1$	4 is in Z_7^*
5	3 $(5 \times 3) \bmod 7 = 1$	$\gcd(5, 7) = 1$	5 is in Z_7^*
6	6 $(6 \times 6) \bmod 7 = 1$	$\gcd(6, 7) = 1$	6 is in Z_7^*

Therefore, $Z_7^* = \{1, 2, 3, 4, 5, 6\}$ and $\phi(7) = 6$.

Notice that by using modular arithmetic, all numbers that are inverse of each other exist in integer form instead of fractional form. This has important implications in public key cryptography. Furthermore, certain mathematical problems are known to be hard in modular arithmetic, and this lays the basis of security for some cryptographic schemes.

1.6.2 *Scheme*

A digital signature scheme comprises three algorithms:

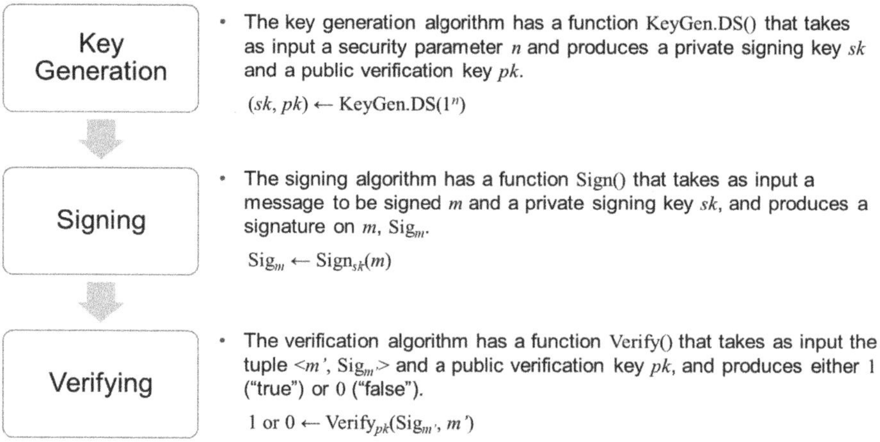

The correctness requirement of a digital signature is as follows:

Given a key pair (sk, pk) and the signature $\text{Sig}_m \leftarrow \text{Sign}_{sk}(m)$, the verification algorithm $\text{Verify}_{pk}(\text{Sig}_m, m)$ will always output 1. In other words, a digital signature produced using the private key sk corresponding to the public key pk will always be successfully verified using the public key pk. Figure 1.9 depicts how a digital signature algorithm works in Alice's communication with Bob.

1.6.3 *RSA Digital Signature (Textbook)*

In more detail:

- *Key Generation*: On input of a security parameter n, the $\text{KeyGen.RSA}(1^n)$ function outputs a prime p and a prime q of n bits; computes $N = pq$; an integer e that satisfies the relation $\gcd(e, \phi(N)) = 1$; and an integer d that satisfies the relation $ed = 1 \bmod \phi(N)$.

$$(sk = d, pk = \langle N, e \rangle) \leftarrow \text{KeyGen.RSA}(1^n)$$

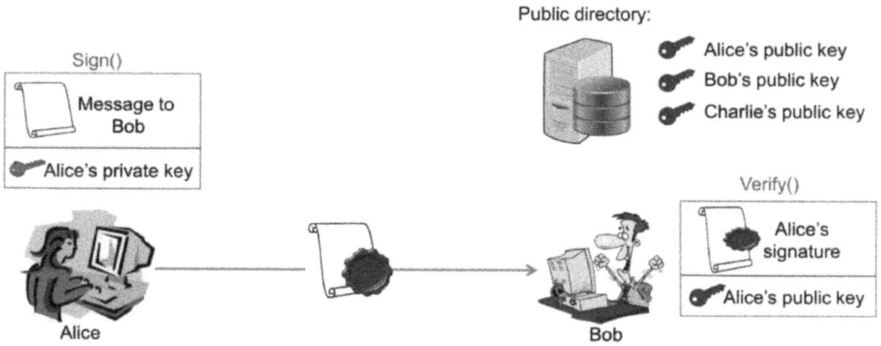

Figure 1.9: A graphical illustration of a digital signature scheme.

- *Signing*: Sign.RSA() takes as input the integer d (the private signing key sk) and a message to be signed m.

$$\text{Sig}_m \leftarrow m^d \bmod N$$

  Here, it is important that the message m is less than the value of N for the verification to succeed.
- *Verification*: Verify.RSA() takes as input the tuple $\langle \text{Sig}_{m'}, m' \rangle$ and the integer e (the public verifying key pk), and produces 1 ("true") if and only if

$$\text{Sig}_{m'}^e \bmod N = m'$$

The correctness requirement of the RSA digital signature scheme is

$$\begin{aligned} \text{Sig}_m^e \bmod N &= (m^d)^e \bmod N = m^{1+\text{k}\phi(\text{N})} \bmod N \\ &= m^1 m^{\text{k}\phi(\text{N})} \bmod N = m^1 = m \end{aligned}$$

The security of the RSA digital signature is based on the RSA factorisation problem. By referring to the Key Generation algorithm, the RSA factorisation problem states that given a very large number $N = pq$, where p and q are both large prime numbers, there is no known efficient method to find out its two prime factors p and q.

The reason that this RSA digital signature scheme in this section is called a "textbook" scheme is because it is insecure for several reasons. Initially, in one form of attack known as a no-message attack, an attacker can arbitrarily choose a public key e of a legitimate user, generate a pseudorandom value as the signature Sig, compute $m = \text{Sig}^e \bmod N$ and produce the tuple $\langle \text{Sig}, m \rangle$ as a supposedly valid signature of the user on the message m. By definition of how the verification algorithm works, this tuple will also be verifiable using public key e of the victim. In this case, the attacker does not need to know the private key, and the message could just as well be gibberish.

One solution to the vulnerability is to hash the message before signing it. The signature would therefore be generated on the hash value rather than directly on the message. In this case, the security of the solution now relies on the security of the underlying hash function:

$$\text{Sig}_m = \text{Hash}(m)^d \bmod N$$

Furthermore, due to property of the hash function, signing on hash value of a message is as good as signing on the message itself, as any changes to the message will result in a completely different hash value. Also, hash value is a compact representation of the message, thus allowing more efficient signature generation compared to operating directly on a potentially large message. Yet, we notice that signing in the above manner produces a deterministic signature. Actual implementation of the RSA digital signature is the RSA Probabilistic Signature Scheme (PSS), which introduces a certain amount of pseudorandomness to the message before signing it, so that a different signature will be generated each time. A simplified breakdown of signing and verification steps under the RSA-PSS is as follows (Stallings, 2017):

Signing in RSA-PSS

S1. Given a message M, the signer performs a message encoding process that takes as input M, $padding_1$, $padding_2$ and $salt$:

a. Let $M' = padding_1 | \text{Hash}(M) | salt$
b. Let $H = \text{Hash}(M')$
c. Let $DB = padding_2 | salt$
d. Using the mask generation function, transform H so that $|H| = |DB|$

e. Let $maskedDB = DB \oplus H_{MGF}$, where H_{MGF} is the transformed H

f. Let $EM = maskedDB|H|bc$

S2. Using the private key d, compute a signature $\text{Sig}_{EM} = EM^d \bmod N$

Verification in RSA-PSS

V1. Given the possibly tampered message $M^\wedge$, $EM^\wedge$ and $\text{Sig}^\wedge_{EM}$, the receiver verifies that $EM^\wedge = \text{Sig}^{\wedge e}_{EM} \bmod N$. If yes, the receiver proceeds to the next step. If not, the receiver aborts.

V2. The receiver performs a message-decoding process that takes as input $M^\wedge$, $EM^\wedge$, $padding_1$ and $padding_2$:

a. Parse the string $EM^\wedge$ and let $maskedDB^\wedge|H^\wedge|bc^\wedge$, keeping $H^\wedge$ for verification

b. Let $DB^\wedge = maskedDB^\wedge \oplus H^\wedge_{MGF}$

c. Parse the string $DB^\wedge$ and let $DB^\wedge = padding_2|salt^\wedge$

d. Let $M^\wedge{}' = padding_1|\text{Hash}(M^\wedge)|salt^\wedge$

e. Let $H^\wedge{}' = \text{Hash}(M^\wedge{}')$

V3. If $H^\wedge{}' = H^\wedge$, accept the message as authentic.

RSA-PSS works on the principle that since the message $EM^\wedge$ is signed, if it has been tampered with, $\text{Sig}^\wedge_{EM}$ would be invalidated and step V1 would not succeed. In addition, the parsing at step V2(a) would result in an incorrect $H^\wedge$, and at steps V2(d) would result in an incorrect $salt^\wedge$. Therefore, verification would fail.

In Python, this can be implemented using the RSA library in Cryptodome. To generate public and private keys, we import the RSA library as shown in Figure 1.10.

```
from Cryptodome.PublicKey import RSA

key = RSA.generate(2048)
private_key = key.export_key()
public_key = key.publickey().export_key()
print(private_key)
print(public_key)
```

Figure 1.10: Python code for RSA keys generation.

```
-----BEGIN RSA PRIVATE KEY-----
MIIEpAIBAAKCAQEAtjUxIehwXZp7lzd5uYFTKKcwMLHPC04G+HSIKBU4waM7V/4D
Otu7jCJo/9DM51ylRzSrA+A/TqyrTkfOiv16UUwk7SZp6pzOHY84l9PcNro6Z32W
ZZQOrugmy1Zgg3el0rH4lVM+Z4sZnzF/8+2Djvst9KXLaI62ZmLiH2l590njEUbC
jVmxrL+BZFJQXpKas9N8HcSfR4p5UlTnvmFEwKoI+sNcuutQoP1GjQO3i8s2ZI50
RqzxhxJNc+X3EwnD9645aSWrXUQ5WIsxhCoQmSxwARAIbpnts+KWD1y7Eo7cgzbc
6KzGFZi9XjTCs2xDtce0piWzv9IH8uZuym7jEwIDAQABAoIBAAOtRh0LjjztUaIn
De9G41E2MnxBEk8Fl5Fq9JZuezM5IojviMwmw/2bcif7ZC8lCPbLYsoUu+JQDLLr
MwlN/Spn0XTxqgCAgo5JJhi2P0Lhdi1BdQf+uV8hMys2RoNQpkl+qugEgoVfYrh6
LL1U5Ss8+Vvu/pBRFPAy/aIppDrvu2yK54Eor+oSLlP3p5yplwfMi9V/lLxLmtHL
Ob9miaH0mEpPT7530DZ6365cqLtWMpJrxGbuQLsZaWaWKpjgU6YFVaCkHMeSH1Yu
WXrgLltLh1OU1G/ihR02TS4kfDzlqmxnN+vZYbJqAm/v63NJ9IfUkgn3JK0pGaLK
/fvaclkCgYEAtnY1OlTq0QEHA3ytCrwFSbybXZol60gqha+cbu3fphzMNiGe6Zxp
x9ls1ereRVLbYPkDpSlubtms6nDNJrm1TMklOLlb/0BAhqG9H48R9kqWXqHhJqtL
pi1MrKryjVL+APr8P2P3RvyYuef2rdAoN7g71K4FH6MyWaPCcRpPuIsCgYEA/6TH
xZId8zQryLEof74AEU0/WjkDmyW7rtcSw/47Jxw5h5EdFWA2fWYVZK7bMWBXtAF+
138QswCa0Bc3K1HkYdJNEC1evRy+OTA8YB4A7QP8cb/wc3tOFgXgQ7Rs0KmdLyRq
K+DKfX3ohfC0eR46HN9tH0K23EFyIkepywB3yJkCgYA9Jx8t3roYtJxyKb4hY+Tt
0r3LwFdHJRfDWJk4gJc9qFc1KU2GhHrblV6pz58RYvTN6oezOlCd7GzM4mOPwBwo
kR3dhhp0UUePF/Q3+I6Pmm4NZ3n7qNug5XvWPzEt9ovVLkmOwWVmMFDLthfyJ1rj
WecLoAttkBfW/VC08ZmYgwKBgQD69Xhnq5lbNswEqGVpgcvvMDYRDAdONyyX5uq1
HM5VBpAzVXGHmnvjfmNiA4WKY1m1jAJI6qQqFV3lCeVO0YWxwhGE4AUxARZ8ba3X
bZzbEB6yTApwU4vEcuBFlsl7zgZQUR8pE/O0XfX2BuYkQFgsH+mv1n5MmrLAlDlK
35q3gQKBgQCbOzJW84bF7ElMXTrXR+AeMtMFi0F7tJoV3QfJbyVD9JtE4NGdCyNR
PXPZRbV1qyZkSpTp5BtYj/1CvVvgppBK7ycM6ZBkWKibOwibgF/PO/ivtq8PkuvI
It9+DZisvXLFPp9emHJ8V8Ggf7fhmc6oiDhcSgrU4dp8qf+vij7pJQ==
-----END RSA PRIVATE KEY-----
```


Figure 1.11: Example of RSA private key.


```
-----BEGIN PUBLIC KEY-----
MIIBIjANBgkqhkiG9w0BAQEFAAOCAQ8AMIIBCgKCAQEAtjUxIehwXZp7lzd5uYFT
KKcwMLHPC04G+HSIKBU4waM7V/4DOtu7jCJo/9DM51ylRzSrA+A/TqyrTkfOiv16
UUwk7SZp6pzOHY84l9PcNro6Z32WZZQOrugmy1Zgg3el0rH4lVM+Z4sZnzF/8+2D
jvst9KXLaI62ZmLiH2l590njEUbCjVmxrL+BZFJQXpKas9N8HcSfR4p5UlTnvmFE
wKoI+sNcuutQoP1GjQO3i8s2ZI50RqzxhxJNc+X3EwnD9645aSWrXUQ5WIsxhCoQ
mSxwARAIbpnts+KWD1y7Eo7cgzbc6KzGFZi9XjTCs2xDtce0piWzv9IH8uZuym7j
EwIDAQAB
-----END PUBLIC KEY-----
```


Figure 1.12: Example RSA public key.

The resulting private and public keys are shown in Figures 1.11 and 1.12, respectively.

Figure 1.13 shows how we can sign using the RSA digital signature scheme in Python. Here, the message is sent as input to the signing algorithm in bytecode and the user's private (signing) key is assumed

```
from Cryptodome.Signature import pkcs1_15
from Cryptodome.Hash import SHA256
from Cryptodome.PublicKey import RSA

message = b"Hello world!"
key = RSA.import_key(open("user_privatekey.pem").read())
h = SHA256.new(message)
signature = pkcs1_15.new(key).sign(h)

print(signature)
```

Figure 1.13: Python code for RSA digital signature signing algorithm.

Figure 1.14: The resulting RSA digital signature in bytecode (upper part) and UTF-8 encoding (lower part).

to be stored in a file named as "user_privatekey.pem". The resulted signature (shown in bytecodes) is shown in Figure 1.14. If we convert the bytecodes into UTF-8 representative, we will see that the signature is essentially a pseudorandom string.

Recall that the verification of a digital signature requires the use of the signer's public key, message and the corresponding digital signature. A successful verification indicates that the signer has indeed created the message because no one else has access to the private key to create the digital signature for that message. Figure 1.15 shows the code that performs an RSA digital signature verification. In this piece of code, we assume that user's message and signature are stored in separate txt files, and the user's public key is stored in a PEM file. Upon successful verification, a message "The signature and the message are valid" will be displayed. In the event that the message or signature has been modified, or if we used a

```python
from Cryptodome.Signature import pkcs1_15
from Cryptodome.Hash import SHA256
from Cryptodome.PublicKey import RSA

message = open("user_message.txt", "rb").read()
key = RSA.import_key(open("user_publickey.pem").read())
signature = open("user_signature.txt", "rb").read()
h = SHA256.new(message)

try:
    pkcs1_15.new(key).verify(h, signature)
    print("The signature and the message are valid.")
except (ValueError, TypeError):
    print("Message modified - Reject.")
```

Figure 1.15: Python code for RSA signature verification.

different public key from the actual signer's, the signature verification will fail.

1.6.4 *Elliptic Curve Cryptography*

Elliptic Curve Digital Signature Algorithm (ECDSA) is adopted in Bitcoin and widely used in the blockchain system. It is the elliptic curve analogue of the Digital Signature Algorithm (DSA), based on the form of cryptography that is called the Elliptic Curve Cryptography (ECC). ECDSA can be considered as an alternative, with enhanced security, of the first-generation public key cryptography methods such as RSA.

ECC uses third-degree and second-degree equation (resulting in an elliptic curve, and thus the name). The general form is $y^2 = x^3 + ax + b$. In ECC, the private key is a random integer d selected from $\{1, 2, \ldots, n-1\}$ where n is the order of the subgroup, and the public key is the point $H = dG$ where G is the base point of the subgroup (Corbellini, 2015).

Bitcoin uses Secp256k1 for parameters of the elliptic curves in its public key cryptography. It is a recommended 256-bit elliptic curve domain parameter over $\mathrm{F_p}$ associated with a Koblitz curve. According to the Standards for Efficient Cryptography Group (SEC)[2], the

[2]http://www.secg.org/sec2-v2.pdf.

parameters are specified by the sextuple $T = (p,\ a,\ b,\ G,\ n,\ h)$ and the finite field F_p is defined as follows:

1. The prime modulo $p = 2^{256} - 2^{32} - 2^9 - 2^8 - 2^7 - 2^6 - 2^4 - 1$ = FFFFFFFF FFFFFFFF FFFFFFFF FFFFFFFF FFFFFFFF FFFFFFFF FFFFFFFE FFFFFC2F

   The below is in hexadecimal form and basically it is an extremely large number.
2. The elliptic curve E: $y^2 = x^3 + ax + b$ where $a = 0$ and $b = 7$.
3. The base point G in compressed form is

   G = 02 79BE667E F9DCBBAC 55A06295 CE870B07 029BFCDB 2DCE28D9 59F2815B 16F81798,

   and in uncompressed form is:

   G = 04 79BE667E F9DCBBAC 55A06295 CE870B07 029BFCDB 2DCE28D9 59F2815B 16F81798 483ADA77 26A3C465 5DA4FBFC 0E1108A8 FD17B448 A6855419 9C47D08F FB10D4B8.

   Both are in hexadecimal forms.
4. The order n of G in hexadecimal form is the following number and cofactor h is 1.

   n = FFFFFFFF FFFFFFFF FFFFFFFF FFFFFFFE BAAEDCE6 AF48A03B BFD25E8C D0364141

Public Key and Private Key

Therefore, for Bitcoin, the private key is a random number between 1 and the order n specified above. The public key is then calculated through point multiplication based on the random number or the private key as

$$\text{public key } P = \text{random number } k * \text{base point } G$$

The equation will generate a new point on the elliptic curve, or the public key, using the base point G. This process can be done in Python with the *ecdsa* module as follows.

We first import the packages or modules necessary for our calculations. The *os* module provides a series of actions that relates to the operating system functionality. We use *os.urandom()* function to generate a string of bytes with random size, which is commonly used in cryptography. The number in the parenthesis refers to the size parameter — *os.urandom(32)* will generate a random 32-digit bytes string. The *ecdsa* module is for us to conveniently use the ECDSA algorithm in Python without the need to write all the equations ourselves. The module will yield results using ECDSA. The *binascii* module is used to convert binary and various ASCII-encoded binary representations — hexadecimal, in our case. So, we use it to convert binary numbers to hexadecimal representation or from hexadecimal to binary for the purpose of function input.

```
import os
import ecdsa
import binascii

private_key = os.urandom(32)
sk = ecdsa.SigningKey.from_string(private_key, curve=ecdsa.SECP256k1)
public_key = ('\04' + str(binascii.hexlify(sk.verifying_key.to_string())))
print(binascii.hexlify(private_key))
print(public_key)
```

Once we generate a random number to use as private key in Python, we can use the SigningKey utility *ecdsa.SigningKey* under ECDSA to get the SigningKey *sk* and then get our public key from it. The *from_string* before *private_key* is needed as the output *of os.urandom()* function is in string type. We specify the secp256k1 parameters by including the *curve=ecdsa.SECP256K1* command in the function. The public key is then derived from the *verifying-key.to_string()* function from the signing key *sk*. The prefix 04 is added to represent uncompressed public keys, while a prefix of 02 or 03 is used for compressed public keys. The results are shown below. *private_key* is a string so we change it to hexadecimal representation using the *binascii.hexlify()* function.

```
b'797bca06b4967e586c3b1fe225aac90da29844ddea91125d74061bbbe0f18e60'
b'6e10afeab03b78bdc2d81fcb6e6da4d36dc9dfc17734b8089dc37a72486ccd8cc57eee0da8cb10f8aceaf65fd4
41b8cef2cb2f23de02546e57292d76e82397e8'
```

Do note that in cryptography the generation of a public key based on a private key is one way only, meaning it is very easy to calculate the public key of a given private key, but extremely difficult the other way around — it is computationally infeasible to generate the private key of a given public key. This feature forms the basis for security in the digital signature or proof of ownership in Bitcoin, so owners of the private key (secret) can easily generate the public key and share it (public key) to the entire network for others to verify his or her ownership of the secret without worrying about the leak of private key (secret) information.

Sign and Signature

A signature will be generated after a signing operation takes place and it is a mathematical process involving the message (what to be signed) and the private key. Since it is a number, the signature is also referred to as digital signature, as opposed to the actual handwritten signature. ECDSA is a variant of the DSA that applied to elliptic curves.

A digital signature allows others, such as the recipient of a message, to verify the authenticity of the message (and other information such as whether the message has been tampered with or proof of ownership in Bitcoin's transactions) using the sender's public key. Once we have the private key and public key, the signature can be generated as follows:

1. To calculate the number $r = x_P \bmod n$ where x_P is the x coordinate of public key P.
2. If $r = 0$, a new random number k needs to be generated and r needs to be calculated again (because r must be different from 0 to be valid).
3. Then, s is computed using scalar operations with message digest m, the private key K and the random number k as inputs:

   $s = k^{-1} * (m + K * r) \bmod n$ where k^{-1} is the multiplicative inverse of k mod n.

4. If $s = 0$, a new random number k needs to be generated and both s and r need to be calculated again (because s must be different from 0 to be valid).

It facilitates a secure bitcoin transaction in the following way: the sender can sign the hashed message m using the private key K and a random number k. The receiver can verify that the message has been correctly signed using the corresponding public key P without the need of knowing the sender's private key.

In Python, this signing procedure can be achieved by the following lines. For a given private key (we use the output from the previous Python section), we convert the string type to hexadecimal format. Then, similar to the private and public keys section, we generate the *sk* variable first using our private key and sign the message using the *sign* function embedded in the Python *ecdsa* module. Again, *binascii.hexlify* is applied to present the output in hexadecimal format.

```
private_key =
bytes.fromhex('797bca06b4967e586c3b1fe225aac90da29844ddea91125d74061bbbe0f18e60')
sk = ecdsa.SigningKey.from_string(private_key, curve=ecdsa.SECP256k1)
message = 'hello'
signature = binascii.hexlify(sk.sign(str.encode(message)))

print(signature, message)
```

The signature and original message are shown below. The hexadecimal string is the digital signature after signing the message "hello" with the private key.

```
b'bbcf497a8cbead93c8a7ba8757cdcea5dd40406dc12553a5525b76750d836e90d751f698f2cf856eca4cb6d90b
a94a0f694b4b25acdd7a5c32764a485cca7c9e' hello
```

Verification

The counterpart of signature generation or computation is signature verification. The receiver can easily verify the authenticity of the message using the sender's public key. Necessary inputs are the hash value of the message, m, the public key P (corresponding to the private key that is used to sign the message) and the signature s. The verification process consists of the following steps[3]:

1. To calculate the integer $w = s^{-1} \bmod n$.
2. To calculate the integer $u_1 = (m * w) \bmod n$.
3. To calculate the integer $u_2 = (r * w) \bmod n$.
4. To calculate point $H = (u_1 * G + u_2 * P) \bmod n$.

If the x-coordinate of point H equals r, the verification is successful and the signature is in fact signed or computed using the private key, meaning the message is authentic or valid. In a bitcoin transaction, this means the sender is indeed the owner of the bitcoin amount.

The mathematic logic behind the verification ensures its validity in the following way (Corbellini, 2015):

1. To replace the public key P with private key k from the previous equation,

$$H = u_1G + u_2P = \mathrm{u}_1G + u_2kG = (u_1 + u_2k)G \bmod n$$

2. According to the definitions of u_1 and u_2, we can further rewrite the equation to

$$H = (u_1 + u_2k)G = (s^{-1}m + s^{-1}rk)G = s^{-1}(m + rk)G \bmod n$$

3. Since we define s as $s = k^{-1}(m + kr) \bmod n$, to multiply each side by k and divide by s, we have $k = s^{-1}(m + kr) \bmod n$, and substitute s in the equation above will yield

$$H = s^{-1}(m + rk)G \bmod n = kG$$

The "mod n" is omitted for brevity, since the cyclic subgroup generated by G has order n, thus making "mod n" unnecessary. Therefore, it proves that this is the public key paired with or generated from the private key (or random number k).

The verification process in Python is shown as follows. We use the public key and signature generated in the previous section. Since they

[3]https://www.maximintegrated.com/en/design/technical-documents/tutorials/5/5767.html.

are in hexadecimal string format, we need to apply *bytes.fromhex()* function convert to bytes before using them as inputs in the *ecdsa* module.

```
public_key =
bytes.fromhex('6e10afeab03b78bdc2d81fcb6e6da4d36dc9dfc17734b8089dc37a72486ccd8cc57eee0da8cb1
0f8aceaf65fd441b8cef2cb2f23de02546e57292d76e82397e8')

message = 'hello'
signature =
bytes.fromhex('bbcf497a8cbead93c8a7ba8757cdcea5dd40406dc12553a5525b76750d836e90d751f698f2cf8
56eca4cb6d90ba94a0f694b4b25acdd7a5c32764a485cca7c9e')

vk = ecdsa.VerifyingKey.from_string(public_key, curve=ecdsa.SECP256k1)
print(vk.verify(signature, str.encode(message)))
```

The results will be *true*.

```
True
```

If we make changes to the public key or signature, even the slightest, the resulting outcome will not be successful and the Python module will raise an Error message — "ecdsa.keys.BadSignatureError: Signature verification failed" — to indicate the failure of signature verification.

1.6.5 *ECDSA vs. RSA*

As we mentioned earlier, ECDSA serves as a next-generation public key algorithm compared to the earlier one such as the RSA. The main reason is that ECC is more secure than the RSA, that is to say, the probability of the ECC algorithm being solved or the risks of ECC being broken are much lower than that of the RSA. The security of any public key algorithm relies on the size and algorithm, so that having a public key, one cannot find the private key; otherwise, it is not safe. The reverse direction is not impossible, just computationally infeasible, because the possibility is very slim given the extremely large number. Breaking an RSA key requires one to factor a large number, but breaking an ECDSA key requires one to solve the Elliptic Curve Discrete Logarithm Problem (ECDLP) and the mathematical community has not made any major progress in improving algorithms to solve this problem (Sullivan, 2014). Therefore, using ECDSA will provide the same level of security as RSA but with smaller keys (160-bit key length in ECC compared with 1024-bit key length in RSA), which has the benefits of faster signature generation, less data for the network and less computing power needed. More comparison is summarised in the table below.

Aspect	ECC	RSA
Time	ECC takes full exponential time	RSA takes sub-exponential time
Security and key size	Same level of security with smaller key sizes	Same level of security with larger key sizes
Data size	Smaller	Larger
Encrypted message	Function of key size and data size; encrypted message is smaller in ECC	Function of key size and data size; encrypted message is larger in RSA
Computational power	Smaller	Larger

Source: Khalique *et al.* (2010).

1.7 Pay to Public Key Hash (P2PKH)

To illustrate how hash and digital signature are used in Bitcoin, we look at the process of a method called Pay to Public Key Hash, or P2PKH. Figure 1.16 shows the Bitcoin transaction fields and their corresponding descriptions. Each transaction may contain more than one input (e.g., 1 btc and 2 btc as inputs to make up for a 3-btc spend) or more than one output (e.g., 1 btc as input and 0.4 btc, 0.6 btc to more than one recipients), or multiple inputs and multiple outputs. Each transaction will also have a unique transaction hash value based on its content; the hash value is recorded in the block Merkle Hash Tree as detailed in Section 1.5.1.

We will use a fiat transaction example to illustrate how the equivalent bitcoin transaction looks. Suppose there are four users,

The equivalent bitcoin transactions' flow can be modelled as follows. In Round 1 (R1), the transaction of 5btc from Alice to Bob will be formatted as shown in Figure 1.17 (we omit other fields and the provision of transaction fees for simplicity). Suppose this (Alice-to-Bob) transaction has a unique hash value of 7b844fe6a2ce9b1c7ea2f02bfb802a095ad3352a092ac83aef0562ee5952b1d7.

Field		Description
ver		Version number
vin_sz		Number of inputs
vout_sz		Number of outputs
lock_time		The time to wait before the coins can be spent
size		Size of the transaction in bytes
in	prev_out	The ID of the transaction containing the input
	scriptSig	The sender's public key and digital signature on this transaction
out	value	The amount to be transferred to the receiver
	scriptPubKey	The receiver's public key hash

This transaction has a unique transaction hash value

Figure 1.16: Structure of a Bitcoin transaction.

Field		Description
vin_sz		1
vout_sz		1
in	prev_out	<A specific transaction hash>
	scriptSig	Alice's public key and digital signature
out	value	5 btc
	scriptPubKey	Bob's public key hash

Transaction hash: 7b844fe6a2ce9b1c7ea2f02bfb802a095ad3352a092ac83aef0562ee5952b1d7

Figure 1.17: Structure of the Alice-to-Bob transaction.

Alice, Bob, Charlie and Eve, and the flow of their fiat transactions with each other is shown below.

	Alice	*Bob*	*Charlie*	*Eve*
Starting balance	$5	-	$1	$1
End-of-R1 balance	-	→ $5	$1	$1
End-of-R2 balance	-	-	→ $5 + $1	$1
End-of-R3 balance	$5 + $1 ←	-	-	$1
End-of-R4 balance	$1	-	-	→ $5 + $1
End-of-R5 balance	$1 + $1 ←			$5

Field		Description
vin_sz		1
vout_sz		1
in	prev_out	7b844fe6a2ce9b1c7ea2f02bfb802a095ad3 352a092ac83aef0562ee5952b1d7
	scriptSig	Bob's public key and digital signature
out	value	5 btc
	scriptPubKey	Charlie's public key hash

Transaction hash: 317b9591b0a9d7 4afacd5735812d 236681e5111982 d2d57be21a598a d1cba628

Figure 1.18: Structure of the Bob-to-Charlie transaction.

Field		Description
vin_sz		2
vout_sz		1
in0	prev_out0	317b9591b0a9d74afacd5735812d236681e 5111982d2d57be21a598ad1cba628
	scriptSig0	Charlie's public key and digital signature
in1	prev_out1	<A specific transaction hash>
	scriptSig1	Charlie's public key and digital signature
out	value	6 btc
	scriptPubKey	Alice's public key hash

Transaction hash: d7a7e3cd01e473 1dacd10bd20c21 8acebdcd2ea3d2 71c1f5a46b886c 2698cd92

Figure 1.19: Structure of the Charlie-to-Alice transaction.

In R2, as Bob sends the 5 btc he has received from Alice to Charlie, he would formulate his transaction as shown in Figure 1.18. As Bob intends to spend the 5 btc he has gotten from Alice, he must specify that the input to this (Bob-to-Charlie) transaction comes from a previous (i.e., Alice-to-Bob) transaction with the hash value 7b844fe6a2ce9b1c7ea2f02bfb802a095ad3352a092ac83aef0562ee5952 b1d7.

In R3, Charlie's transaction to Alice contains two inputs (5 btc and 1 btc), of which the 5-btc input comes from the previous Bob-to-Charlie transaction. Thus, Charlie's transaction is formulated as shown in Figure 1.19.

In R4, Alice intends to pay Eve 4 btc. However, in contrast to fiat currency transactions, Alice has in her wallet 6 btc instead of 5 btc +1 btc due to aggregation. Thus, in her transaction, Alice has

Field		Description
vin_sz		1
vout_sz		2
in	prev_out	d7a7e3cd01e4731dacd10bd20c218acebdcd2 ea3d271c1f5a46b886c2698cd92
	scriptSig	Alice's public key and digital signature
out0	value0	4 btc
	scriptPubKey0	Eve's public key and digital signature
out1	value1	2 btc
	scriptPubKey1	Alice's public key hash

Transaction hash:
be3c7b2c461219
050cc716717778
c552c3e57841b2
26b89912a33ee4
b897fe4b

Figure 1.20: Structure of the Alice-to-Eve transaction.

to specify that she intends to pay Eve 4 btc, and pay herself 2 btc; this is the concept of "change" in bitcoin (see Figure 1.20).

Notice a few things in the example above. First, a bitcoin transaction can contain one or more inputs and one or more outputs. Second, once a previous transaction (e.g., Alice-to-Bob) has been recorded on the blockchain, it effectively transfers the ownership of the 5 btc from Alice to Bob. Third, when Bob intends to spend the 5 btc he has gotten from Alice, he must specify the source of the 5 btc in the "prev_out" field and provide his proof of ownership of the 5 btc by stating his public key and digital signature on this transaction. In order for miners to validate whether Bob has ownership of the 5 btc, they will do the following checks:

1. Extract Bob's public key from the "scriptSig" field in the Bob-to-Charlie transaction.
2. Calculate the hash of Bob's public key obtained in Step 1.
3. Find the transaction specified in the "prev_out" field in the Bob-to-Charlie transaction, i.e., the Alice-to-Bob transaction.
4. Verify that the hash calculated in Step 2 is equal to the recipient's public key hash specified in the "scriptPubKey" field of the Alice-to-Bob transaction.
5. If they are equal, use the public key obtained in Step 1 to verify Bob's digital signature in the "scriptSig" field for the Bob-to-Charlie transaction.
6. If verification succeeds, conclude that Bob has ownership of the 5 btc and thus can spend the 5 btc.

7. Add the Bob-to-Charlie transaction to a block, and run the PoW algorithm.

The fourth point to note in this process is that Bob's public key is not disclosed until he creates the Bob-to-Charlie transaction and announces his intention to spend the 5 btc in his wallet. The usage of public key hash to specify the receiver utilises properties of the hash function — an attacker could not pretend to be Bob because the public key hash reveals nothing about the pre-image. Consequently, only Bob can provide the correct public key that hashes to the public key hash specified by Alice.

Finally, once the miners verified that the hash of Bob's public key is equal to the public key hash specified by Alice, the miners will use Bob's public key to verify his digital signature on the Bob-to-Charlie transaction. When the verification succeeds, miners conclude that Bob has ownership of the 5 btc in the wallet.

To this end, note the relationship between a user's private key, public key and wallet address. For security purposes, private keys are truly random strings. From the private key, a user's public key is calculated using a one-way (irreversible) and predetermined manner. The public key is then hashed and encoded to form the user's bitcoin wallet address. As such, the conclusion that "Bob has ownership of the wallet containing the 5 btc if his digital signature on the transaction can be verified using his public key" is based on the fact that Bob can only provide the (correct) public key if and only if he has the private key to create the digital signature. Consequently, only Bob can give Alice the (correct) public key hash. The act of specifying the receiver's public key hash in a bitcoin transaction is a mechanism called "Pay to Public Key Hash (P2PKH)".

1.8 Public Key Infrastructure

In a digital signature, the signature and message are verified using the sender's (i.e., signer) public key to prove that the message originates from the signer. As the name indicates, a public key is widely disseminated. However, the public key is a pseudorandom number

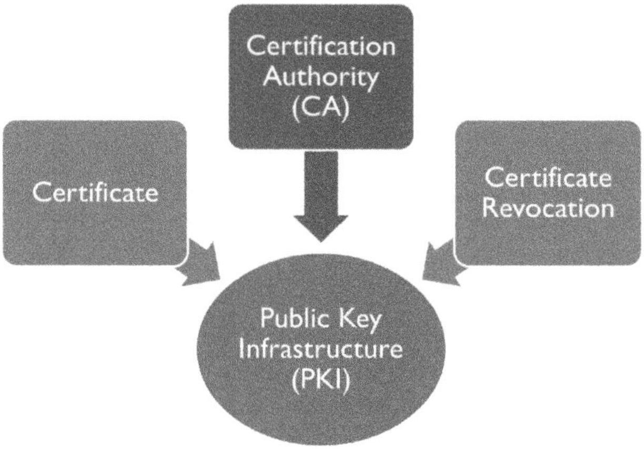

Figure 1.21: Components of a public key infrastructure.

that by itself does not contain any identifiable information about its owner.

This leaves a potential security loophole — how can a verifier be sure that the public key belongs to the right signer? Without a method of verification, an attacker could exploit this loophole by intercepting the public key and replacing it with his own, thereby compromising the objective of data authentication and accountability in the digital signature. Therefore, there is a need for us to ensure that a public key belongs to a specific user. Public key infrastructure (PKI) solves this problem by providing a method for associating a public key with a specific user in a secure manner. As shown in Figure 1.21, the PKI framework comprises certificates, certification authorities and certificate revocation.

A *certificate* is a digital document that serves as proof that a particular public key belongs to a specific user (the subject). A certificate contains the following information: version number, serial number, type of digital signature scheme used, issuer's name, validity period, subject's name, subject's public key and issuer's signature. Aside from users, certificates can also state a website's information. A screenshot of Facebook's certificate is shown in Figure 1.22.

Figure 1.22: Example of certification path for facebook.com.

To obtain a digital certificate, we must approach a third-party *certification authority* (CA, also known as the issuer). Certification takes the form of the CA's digital signature appended at the end of the certificate. CAs are usually organised according to geographical distribution. For example, Netrust is a CA that covers the Southeast Asia region, and is the only accredited CA in Singapore. We know which CAs to trust as one CA can vouch for another. This takes the form of a hierarchical relationship, with a root CA at the top vouching for intermediate CAs that issue certificates to end users (see Figure 1.23). A list of such root CAs is hard-coded into our browsers. Whenever we install a browser and visit a website, our browsers trace the website's certification path back to the root CA. Examples of root CAs include Comodo, Symantec, GoDaddy, GlobalSign, DigiCert and Verizon.

Certificates are revoked when they expire, if the user's credentials change or if the user's private key is lost or compromised. To avoid inadvertently sending confidential messages to a compromised user,

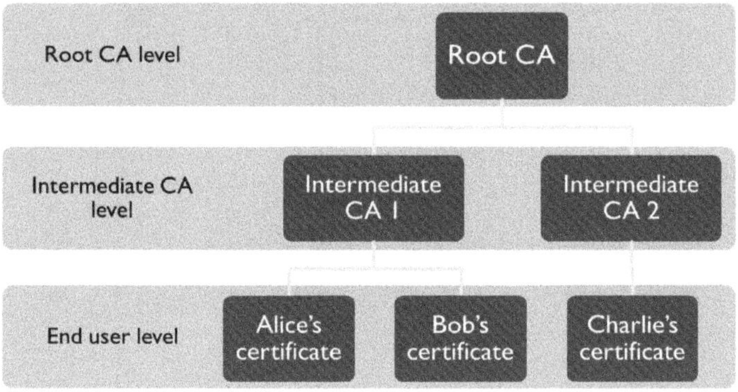

Figure 1.23: The certification path for facebook.com.

we maintain repositories of revoked certificates to perform checks on the status of a certificate. One way to do this is for root CAs to maintain a certificate revocation list (CRL) that users can check against. However, over time, the CRL may grow to such a magnitude that it becomes either difficult to maintain or inefficient to perform a search. Alternatively, the online certificate status protocol (OCSP) uses IP to obtain the status of a certificate. This is a much more efficient method that is supported in most browsers used today.

The PKI is a setting in which we can ensure user authentication and build trusted, secure communication networks. Its usage can be found in our daily applications as well as private blockchain settings such as in Project Ubin.[4] In public blockchain, however, a public key is not associated with an identity in the conventional sense. Here, we should note that public blockchain is typically pseudonymous, meaning that it provides some, but not full, anonymity. In the Bitcoin blockchain, all transactions are linked to public key hashes, which on their own do not provide any identifying information pertaining to the wallet's owner. That said, it can be possible to prove a user's ownership of a wallet given certain information, such as her possession of a private key corresponding to the public wallet address.

[4]https://www.mas.gov.sg/schemes-and-initiatives/project-ubin.

In the Bitcoin blockchain, the usage of public and private keys to ensure bitcoin ownership in a decentralised manner is executed through methods such as Pay-to-Public-Key-Hash (P2PKH), which relies on the security of hash function and digital signature, as detailed in Sections 1.5 and 1.6, respectively. Double spending is prevented with a global view of the transaction hashes on the distributed ledger.

1.9 Encryption

Encryption was an early component of classical cryptography and continues to be an important part of modern cryptography, where it is the means of achieving confidentiality. In this section, we will first look at the concepts of perfect secrecy and computational secrecy, and then discuss the distinctions between symmetric and asymmetric encryption schemes.

1.9.1 *Perfect Secrecy*

A perfectly secret encryption scheme is one with a ciphertext that does not leak any information about the secret key or the plaintext. It therefore cannot be broken by any attacker, even with unlimited computing power. The one-time pad (or Vernam cipher) is the most prominent example of such a scheme. The Vernam cipher uses an Exclusive-OR logical operation, denoted as $\oplus$, that only produces an output of "true" (i.e., Boolean value of 1) when the inputs differ. It is a bijective function, meaning that each bit in the plaintext has exactly one corresponding bit in the ciphertext, and vice versa. There are no unpaired bits. Given a plaintext m and a secret key k of equal length, the truth table of the cipher is as follows:

Input		**Output**
m	k	c
0	0	0
0	1	1
1	0	1
1	1	0

To encrypt the plaintext m to a ciphertext c, we compute this as

$$c = m \oplus k$$

Let the plaintext $m = 1010111010$, and the key $k = 1100101100$. A sender will use k to compute ciphertext c as

m	1	0	1	0	1	1	1	0	1	0
k	1	1	0	0	1	0	1	1	0	0
c	**0**	**1**	**1**	**0**	**0**	**1**	**0**	**1**	**1**	**0**

To decrypt c, we compute this as

$$m = c \oplus k$$

The receiver will use the same key k to compute the plaintext m as

c	0	1	1	0	0	1	0	1	1	0
k	1	1	0	0	1	0	1	1	0	0
m	**1**	**0**	**1**	**0**	**1**	**1**	**1**	**0**	**1**	**0**

The Vernam cipher is a relatively simple scheme in that it is based solely on the Exclusive-OR operation. However, it can provide perfect secrecy because without knowledge of the key, which is chosen uniformly at random, there are countless possibilities for the plaintext. Specifically, if c has the length of l bits, then there are 2^l possible plaintexts, and each plaintext is equally probable.

As an example, suppose the secret key is given by k = A1 B1 C1 D1 E1 F1 AA BB CC DD EE FF 10 34. An illustration on encryption of the message "I have 100 btc" using k, and decryption of the resulting ciphertext using the same k, is shown in Figure 1.24.

Suppose an attacker is observing the network and intercepted the ciphertext c. In the attempt to decrypt, the attacker will try all possible keys to see if the decrypted text resulted in a coherent content (this is known as a brute-force attack). In this process, suppose the secret key tried by the attacker is k' = AC F0 C7 90

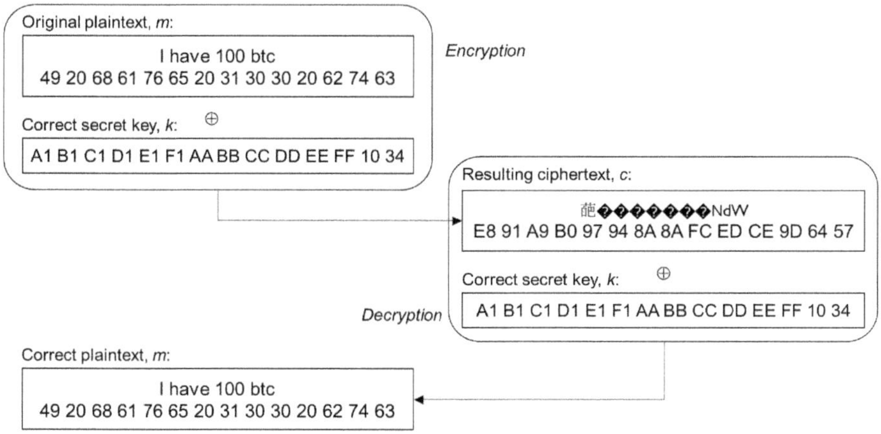

Figure 1.24: Vernam cipher decryption using the same secret key k used for encryption.

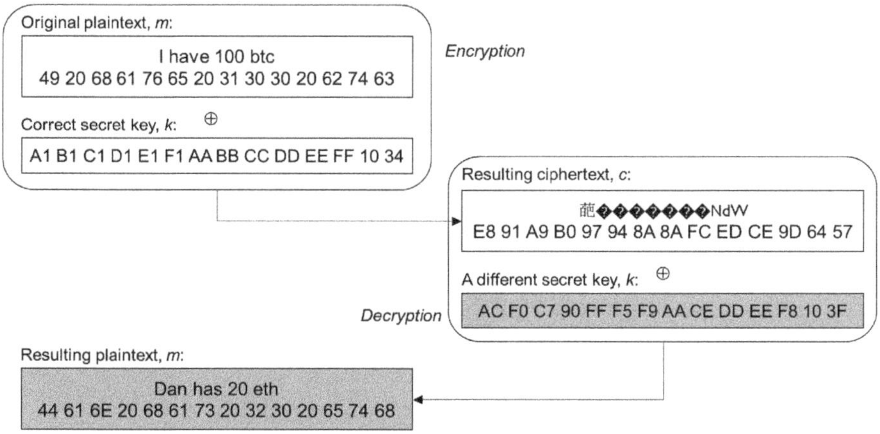

Figure 1.25: Vernam cipher decryption using a different secret key k'.

FF F5 F9 AA CE DD EE F8 10 3F, the resulting plaintext becomes "Dan has 20 eth" (see Figure 1.25). In another instance, if $k'' =$ A9 E5 DD D1 F4 FF AA EB 88 CD AA FC 13 39, the resulting plaintext is "Attack at dawn" (see Figure 1.26).

The Vernam cipher is perfectly secret without knowledge of the secret key because the ciphertext leaks no information about

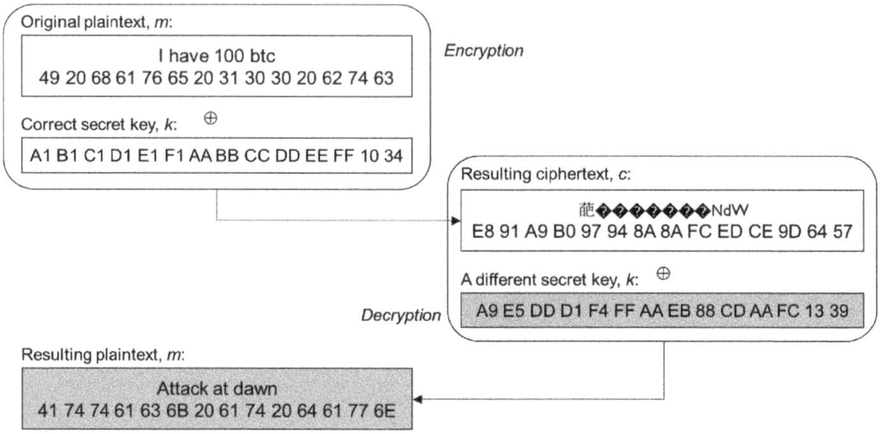

Figure 1.26: Vernam cipher decryption using a different secret key k".

the plaintext given the countless number of possible plaintexts. If the Vernam cipher is so secure, why do we not use it all the time? There are two major drawbacks to the Vernam cipher. First, each key can be used to encrypt only one plaintext. Suppose the same key is used to encrypt plaintext m_1 producing ciphertext c_1, and plaintext m_2 producing ciphertext c_2. If an attacker has both ciphertexts, they can compute the following:

$$\begin{aligned} & c_1 \oplus c_2 \\ & = m_1 \oplus k \oplus m_2 \oplus k \\ & = m_1 \oplus m_2 \oplus k \oplus k \\ & = m_1 \oplus m_2 \text{ since } k \oplus k \text{ results in } 0 \end{aligned}$$

This will leak information about the plaintexts.

Second, each key in a Vernam cipher must be truly random and equal in length to the plaintext. Otherwise, it is vulnerable to a frequency analysis attack and will leak information about the plaintext as well. Certain alphabet or combinations of alphabet are known to recur frequently in human communications. For example, in the English language, "e" is the alphabet that appears most frequently and "th" is the most common combination of two alphabets. If a key is shorter than the plaintext, it will need to be repeated across the length of the plaintext to encrypt the whole string. If the key happens to coincide with the most common alphabet or words multiple times, the attacker can then deduce information about the plaintext.

The requirements of no repeated keys and a unique and truly random key that is equal to the length of each plaintext to be encrypted make the Vernam cipher an inefficient scheme with a high cost of construction. In any case, for most practical purposes, it is not necessary to construct a perfectly secret encryption scheme as a computationally secure scheme will suffice. In the rest of this section, we will look at computationally secure encryption.

1.9.2 *Symmetric Encryption*

Modern encryption schemes belong to one of two categories: symmetric or asymmetric. A symmetric encryption scheme (Figure 1.27) performs both encryption and decryption with the same secret key. It is structured around three algorithms:

- *Key Generation*: The key generation algorithm has a function KeyGen.SE() that takes as input a security parameter n and produces a secret key k of n bits.

$$k \leftarrow \text{KeyGen.SE}(1^n)$$

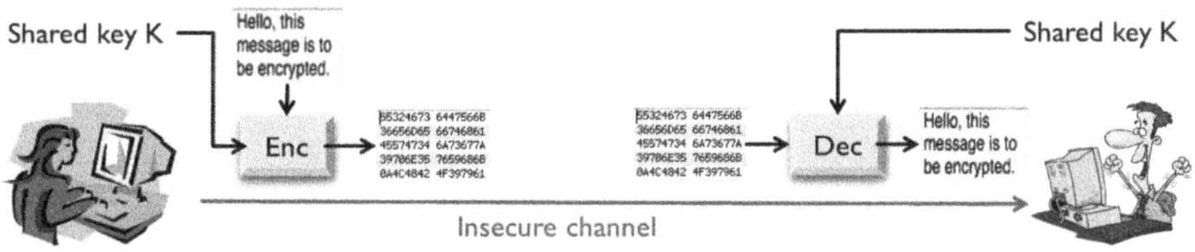

Figure 1.27: A graphical illustration of a symmetric encryption scheme.

- *Encryption*: The encryption algorithm has a function Enc.SE() that takes as input a secret key k and a plaintext m, and produces a ciphertext c.

$$c \leftarrow \text{Enc.SE}_k(m)$$

- *Decryption*: The decryption algorithm has a function Dec.SE() that takes as input a secret key k and a ciphertext c, and produces a plaintext m.

$$m = \text{Dec.SE}_k(c)$$

The correctness requirement of a symmetric encryption scheme is

$$m = \text{Dec.SE}_k(\text{Enc.SE}_k(m))$$

In other words, for any m and k, $\text{Dec.SE}_k(c) = m$ if and only if $c \leftarrow \text{Enc.SE}_k(m)$.

The Vernam cipher is a form of symmetric encryption as encryption and decryption use the same secret key. The most well-known ones in use now are the Data Encryption Standard (DES) and Advanced Encryption Standard (AES). DES and AES are block ciphers, meaning that to encrypt a plaintext, both will partition the plaintext into blocks of equal length and encrypt one block at a time with the same key. The DES block cipher partitions data into blocks of 64 bits, while the AES block cipher partitions into blocks of 128 bits. DES was published in 1975 and standardised by NIST in 1977, while AES was published in 1998 and standardised in 2001. AES is still widely used today, and underlies most applications that require the provision of data confidentiality.

Earlier, we said that the key of the Vernam cipher is chosen uniformly at random. We can regard the Vernam cipher as a truly random permutation, whereas DES and AES are pseudorandom permutations. In a simplified expression, whereas the Vernam cipher encryption is given as

$$c = m \oplus k$$

DES and AES encryption are given as

$$c = m \oplus f_k(x)$$

where $f_k()$ is a pseudorandom function producing an output with a pseudorandom distribution. We will now look more closely at the design principles underlying DES and AES.

1.9.3 *DES and the Feistel Network*

DES is one of many block ciphers based on a structure called the Feistel network. The Feistel network is a multi-round cipher that divides a plaintext m into blocks of 64 bits each, and further divides each block into a 32-bit left half L_0 and a 32-bit right half R_0:

$$m = \mathrm{L}_0|\mathrm{R}_0$$

In each round of encryption, the DES round function swaps the right and left sides, and applies a function $f_i()$, also called a mangler function, to one side. The mangler function uses a 48-bit subkey, also called a round key, generated from a 56-bit master secret key. The mangler function carries out four operations: expansion of the 32-bit half-block to 48 bits; Exclusive-OR operation with the round key; substitution using substitution boxes (S-boxes); and permutation. Mathematically, we write this as

$$\begin{aligned} \mathrm{L}_i &= \mathrm{R}_{i-1} \\ \mathrm{R}_i &= \mathrm{L}_{i-1} \oplus f_i(R_{i-1}) \end{aligned}$$

This process is repeated for the stipulated number of rounds (16 rounds for DES). The ciphertext is the combination of both half-blocks in the final round of encryption.

To decrypt the ciphertext, we use the same structure but apply the round function in reverse. The plaintext is the combination of both half-blocks in the final round of decryption. We invert the algorithm by computing the following:

$$\begin{aligned} \mathrm{R}_{i-1} &= \mathrm{L}_i \\ \mathrm{L}_{i-1} &= \mathrm{R}_i \oplus f_i(R_{i-1}) \end{aligned}$$

This method of decrypting the left half-block works because of the nature of the Exclusive-OR operation, which has the property that

$A \oplus A = 0$, since the inputs are identical. Similar to the decryption of a Vernam cipher, we can see that

$$\text{Given } A = B \oplus C$$
$$A \oplus C = B \oplus C \oplus C = B \oplus 0 = B$$
$$B = A \oplus C$$

We can therefore effectively "cancel out" the round function from the left half of the ciphertext:

$$\text{Given } \mathrm{R}_i = \mathrm{L}_{i-1} \oplus f_i(\mathrm{R}_{i-1})$$
$$\mathrm{R}_i \oplus f_i(\mathrm{R}_{i-1}) = \mathrm{L}_{i-1} \oplus f_i(\mathrm{R}_{i-1}) \oplus f_i(\mathrm{R}_{i-1}) = \mathrm{L}_{i-1} \oplus 0 = \mathrm{L}_{i-1}$$
$$\mathrm{L}_{i-1} = \mathrm{R}_i \oplus f_i(\mathrm{R}_{i-1})$$

The table below illustrates how we compute a four-round encryption and decryption, with arrows indicating the order of computation:

Encryption Input: $m = L_0 \mid R_0$ Output: $c = L_4 \mid R_4$		**Decryption** Input: $c = L_4 \mid R_4$ Output: $m = L_0 \mid R_0$	
L_0	R_0	$L_0 = R_1 \oplus f_1(R_0)$	$R_0 = L_1$
$L_1 = R_0$	$R_1 = L_0 \oplus f_1(R_0)$	$L_1 = R_2 \oplus f_2(R_1)$	$R_1 = L_2$
$L_2 = R_1$	$R_2 = L_1 \oplus f_2(R_1)$	$L_2 = R_3 \oplus f_3(R_2)$	$R_2 = L_3$
$L_3 = R_2$	$R_3 = L_2 \oplus f_3(R_2)$	$L_3 = R_4 \oplus f_4(R_3)$	$R_3 = L_4$
$L_4 = R_3$	$R_4 = L_3 \oplus f_4(R_3)$	L_4	R_4

A notable feature of the Feistel network is that the entire operation is invertible even though the mangler function $f_i()$ itself is not invertible. The Feistel network therefore allows us to construct an invertible algorithm from non-invertible functions. This is an important security feature, as requiring a function to be invertible necessarily introduces more structure, but more unstructured behaviour will allow a cipher to appear more random, and hence be more secure.

In DES, the mangler function $f_{k\_i}()$ is designed to have an additional input of a subkey k_i. DES requires a subkey because the scheme's 56-bit secret key is insufficient for the 16 rounds in its Feistel network. In 1999, DES famously fell victim to a brute-force attack that found the secret key in 22 hours and 15 minutes, using a machine that cost US$250,000 to build. After this attack, the use of DES with three subkeys, called triple-DES (3DES), was proposed. In 3DES, three different subkeys, k_1, k_2 and k_3, are generated from the 56-bit master secret key. The plaintext is encrypted with k_1, decrypted with k_2 and then encrypted with k_3. As long as the master key k is kept secret, then the output of $f_{k\_i}()$ should be indistinguishable from a truly random permutation. 3DES is still widely used today, but AES is now considered a better choice for symmetric encryption using a single secret key.

1.9.4 *AES and the Substitution–Permutation Network*

The current design of AES was selected by the NIST in 2000 after a call for submissions in 1997. Also known as the Rijndael cipher, AES is a block cipher based on a substitution–permutation network. As we saw earlier, the Feistel network in DES also runs on substitution and permutation operations applied to two halves of the plaintext. The difference between a substitution–permutation network and a Feistel network is that the former has to be invertible, while the latter does not.

In AES, the plaintext is split into 128-bit blocks. The cipher uses a secret key, the length of which affects the key schedule to generate subkeys as well as the number of rounds — 10 rounds for a 128-bit key, 12 rounds for a 192-bit key and 14 rounds for a 256-bit key. The design of AES is very complex, as its round function needs to be invertible. For our purposes, it suffices for us to have a general idea of its operation. Similar to DES, the master secret key first goes through a key expansion to produce a round key for each round. Each round of AES comprises the following: Exclusive-OR with the round key; substitution using S-boxes; permutation; and further substitution using a matrix.

AES is the structure underlying the encryption schemes of many applications we use today, such as file encryption on our hard disks (as well as ransomware attacks) and Secure Sockets Layer (SSL) protocol for secure communication. As forms of symmetric encryption, DES and AES can be used to encrypt large plaintexts efficiently and possess shorter key lengths than asymmetric encryption. However, the main drawback of symmetric encryption is that the sender and receiver will need to share the secret key prior to any encryption. To communicate with n number of peers, a user will also need n number of secret keys. These inefficiencies can be addressed through asymmetric encryption.

1.9.5 *Asymmetric Encryption*

An asymmetric encryption scheme (Figure 1.28) is also structured around three algorithms, but uses a public key for encryption and a private key for decryption:

- *Key Generation*: The key generation algorithm has a function KeyGen.AE() that takes as input a security parameter n and produces a private key sk and a public key pk.

$$(sk, pk) \leftarrow \text{KeyGen.AE}(1^n)$$

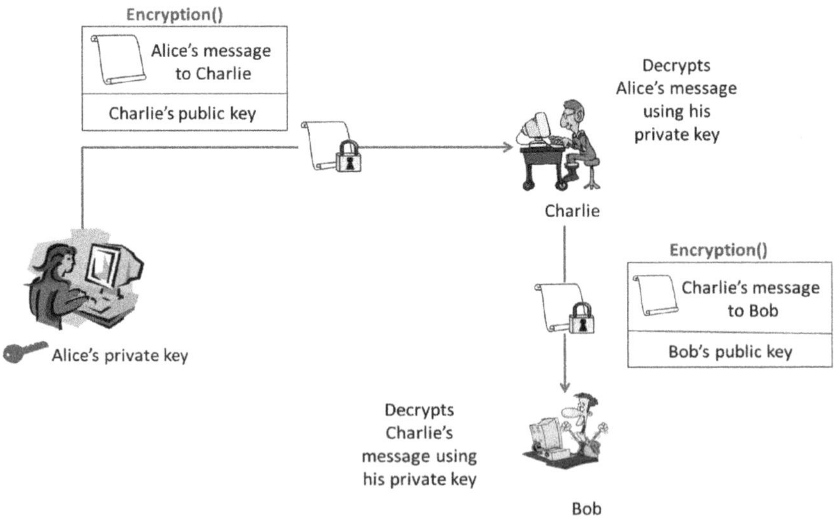

Figure 1.28: A graphical illustration of an asymmetric encryption scheme.

- *Encryption*: The encryption algorithm has a function Enc.AE() that takes as input a public key *pk* and a plaintext m, and produces a ciphertext c.

$$c \leftarrow \text{Enc.AE}_{pk}(m)$$

- *Decryption*: The decryption algorithm has a function Dec.AE() that takes as input a private key *sk* and a ciphertext c, and produces a plaintext m.

$$m = \text{Dec.AE}_{sk}(c)$$

The correctness requirement of an asymmetric encryption scheme is

$$m = \text{Dec.AE}_{sk}(\text{Enc.AE}_{pk}(m))$$

In other words, for any pair of $\langle sk, pk\rangle$ and m, $\text{Dec.AE}_{sk}(c) = m$ if and only if $c \leftarrow \text{Enc.AE}_{pk}(m)$. In asymmetric encryption, users first choose a private key *sk*, which is used to compute the public key *pk*. The computation of the public key is one-way only — given *pk*, it must be computationally infeasible to compute *sk*. The resulting $\langle sk, pk\rangle$ are always a pair that belongs to a single user. The sender always encrypts the plaintext with the receiver's public key, so that the receiver can decrypt it with her own private key. Note that the public key by itself does not contain any identifiable information about its owner. In Section 1.8, we showed how certificates are used to legally bind a user's identity to a public key to prevent impersonation by an attacker.

We use the textbook RSA encryption as an illustration of public key encryption as follows:

- *Key Generation*: KeyGen.RSA() takes as input a security parameter n and produces a modulus $N = pq$ where p and q are uniform n-bit prime numbers; an integer e that satisfies the relation $\gcd(e, \Phi(N)) = 1$; and an integer d satisfying the relation $ed = 1 \bmod \Phi(N)$.

$$(sk = d, pk = \langle N, e\rangle) \leftarrow \text{KeyGen.RSA}(1^n)$$

- *Encryption*: Enc.RSA() takes as input N, the integer e (the public key pk) and a plaintext m, and produces a ciphertext c.

$$c \leftarrow m^e \bmod N$$

- *Decryption*: Dec.RSA() takes as input N, the integer d (the private key sk) and a ciphertext c, and produces a plaintext m.

$$m = c^d \bmod N$$

The correctness requirement of the RSA encryption scheme is

$$c^d \bmod N = (m^e)^d \bmod N = m^{ed\, mod\phi(N)} = m^1 = m$$

Similar to the RSA digital signature, RSA encryption is backed by the difficulty of solving the integer factorisation problem for N. That is, it is computationally infeasible for an attacker to find the two unique prime numbers p and q given only N. In asymmetric encryption, only the public key tuple $\langle N, e\rangle$ is sent over an open, insecure network, while p and q are kept secret. If the factorisation of N were known, then $(p-1)(q-1) = \phi(N)$ would be known, and it would be easy for the attacker to break the algorithm and find the private key d.

In RSA, the size of N is 4096 bits, which is around 1234 digits. That said, the RSA encryption scheme described above is not secure because it is deterministic — given the same plaintext, the resulting ciphertext is always the same if the key pair (sk, pk) is the same. An attacker could intercept the ciphertext and replay it at a later time. This is therefore a "textbook" RSA encryption scheme that should not be implemented as is, as it is vulnerable to a number of attacks. One solution to these attacks is the RSA Optimal Asymmetric Encryption Padding (OAEP) scheme, which adds a pseudorandom number to the plaintext in every instance of encryption, generating a different ciphertext each time.

1.9.6 *Hybrid Encryption*

Apart from RSA encryption, other notable encryption schemes include ElGamal encryption, based on the difficulty of the discrete logarithm problem, and encryption schemes based on elliptic curves.

Although asymmetric encryption addresses the drawbacks of symmetric encryption, it is much slower than the latter as it relies on the algorithmic computation of large numbers. Asymmetric encryption schemes like RSA are therefore rarely used to encrypt messages themselves. Instead, the hybrid encryption scheme is used in practical implementation (see Figure 1.29 for a graphical illustration of hybrid encryption).

Suppose Alice wants to send a confidential message to Bob:

1. Alice generates her pair of private and public keys $\langle sk\_\text{Alice}, pk\_\text{Alice}\rangle$ and Bob generates his pair of private and public keys $\langle sk\_\text{Bob}, pk\_\text{Bob}\rangle$.
2. Alice encrypts the secret key k using asymmetric encryption with Bob's public key pk_Bob.

$$c_k \leftarrow \text{Enc.AE}_{pk\_\text{Bob}}(k)$$

3. Alice encrypts her message m using symmetric encryption with the secret key k.

$$c_m \leftarrow \text{Enc.SE}_k(m)$$

4. Alice sends $\langle c_k, c_m\rangle$ to Bob.
5. Bob decrypts c_k using his private key sk_Bob to obtain the secret key k.

$$k = \text{Dec.AE}_{sk\_\text{Bob}}(c_k)$$

6. Bob decrypts c_m using the secret key k to obtain the message from Alice.

$$m = \text{Dec.SE}_k(c_m)$$

Because the secret key k for symmetric encryption is short — in particular, it is likely to be shorter than Alice's message to Bob — it is more efficient to use asymmetric encryption to encrypt the secret key. This also addresses the performance issue of having to pre-share a secret key over an open, insecure network without a pre-shared key prior to that.

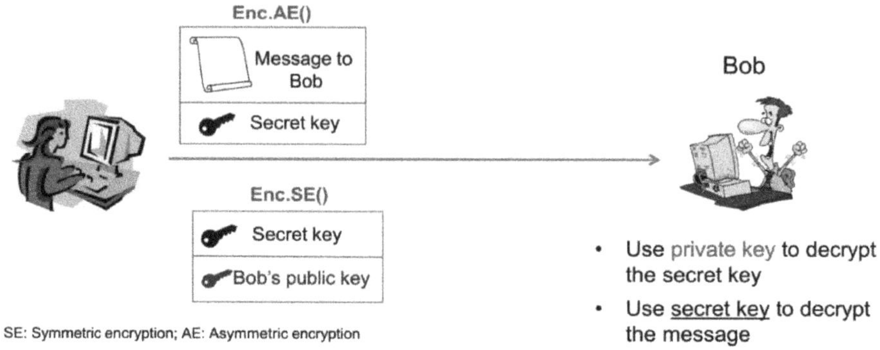

Figure 1.29: A graphical illustration of the hybrid encryption scheme.

```
# RSA Encryption (Hybrid, encrypt-then-authenticate)

from Cryptodome.PublicKey import RSA
from Cryptodome.Random import get_random_bytes
from Cryptodome.Cipher import AES, PKCS1_OAEP

data = b"This is my answer to your question. The merkle hash tree summarises the hashes of transaction into a
merkle root hash." #Key in your text here.
file_out = open("for_receiver.txt", "wb")

recipient_key = RSA.import_key(open("receiver_publickey.pem").read()) # recipient's public key
session_key = get_random_bytes(16) # Generate a secret key for symmetric encryption

# Encrypt the session key with the public RSA key
cipher_rsa = PKCS1_OAEP.new(recipient_key)
enc_session_key = cipher_rsa.encrypt(session_key) # Encrypt the secret key using recipient's public key

# Encrypt the data with the AES session key
cipher_aes = AES.new(session_key, AES.MODE_EAX)
ciphertext, tag = cipher_aes.encrypt_and_digest(data) # Encrypt the data using the secret key
[ file_out.write(x) for x in (enc_session_key, cipher_aes.nonce, tag, ciphertext) ] # Send the encrypted secret
key and the encrypted data & other necessary info
file_out.close()

print(ciphertext)
```

Figure 1.30: Python code for hybrid encryption using RSA and AES.

Hybrid encryption using RSA and AES can be implemented in Python using the RSA, AES and PKCS1_OAEP libraries in Cryptodome. In the Python code shown in Figure 1.30, we assume that the user has generated a pair of public and private keys and the public key is stored in the file "receiver_publickey.pem". The result of the encryption is shown in Figure 1.31.

To decrypt, we extract the ciphertexts of the secret key and the message, use the recipient's private key to obtain the secret (session) key and then use the secret key to decrypt the message as shown in Figure 1.32.

Figure 1.31: The resulting ciphertexts from hybrid encryption using RSA and AES.

```python
from Cryptodome.PublicKey import RSA
from Cryptodome.Cipher import AES, PKCS1_OAEP

file_in = open("for_receiver.txt", "rb") # the ciphertexts

private_key = RSA.import_key(open("receiver_privatekey.pem").read()) # Receiver's private key

enc_session_key, nonce, tag, ciphertext = \
   [ file_in.read(x) for x in (private_key.size_in_bytes(), 16, 16, -1) ]

# Decrypt the session key with the private RSA key
cipher_rsa = PKCS1_OAEP.new(private_key)
session_key = cipher_rsa.decrypt(enc_session_key) # decrypt using private key to get the secret key

# Decrypt the data with the AES session key
cipher_aes = AES.new(session_key, AES.MODE_EAX, nonce)
data = cipher_aes.decrypt_and_verify(ciphertext, tag) # decrypt the data using the secret key
print(data.decode())
```

Figure 1.32: Python code for hybrid decryption using RSA and AES.

1.10 Privacy

User privacy in a blockchain rests on the untraceability and unlinkability of transactions. To recap, untraceability means we should be able to conceal the details of a transaction so that an observer cannot follow the trail. Unlinkability, in general, means that two events occurring under observation of an attacker should appear unrelated to the observer. Earlier, we said that blockchain technology is pseudonymous, as opposed to anonymous. By simply observing the blockchain, there is no identifying information linked to the wallet addresses or transactions. However, we are able to trace the source of every transaction, and therefore, able to obtain a graphical visualisation of transaction paths.Through prior knowledge or social engineering, it is possible to link an identity to a wallet address. We therefore need security schemes in place to protect user privacy.

Furthermore, suppose an attacker observes the following transaction traces (Figure 1.33) at time t.

At time t+1, a new transaction as shown in Figure 1.34 takes place.

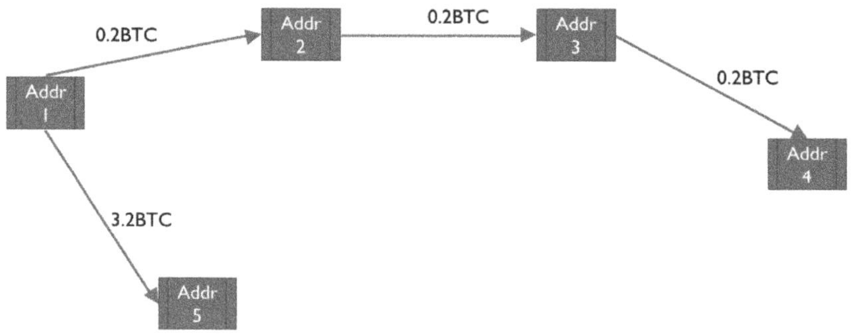

Figure 1.33: Trace of transactions that can be obtained from a public blockchain.

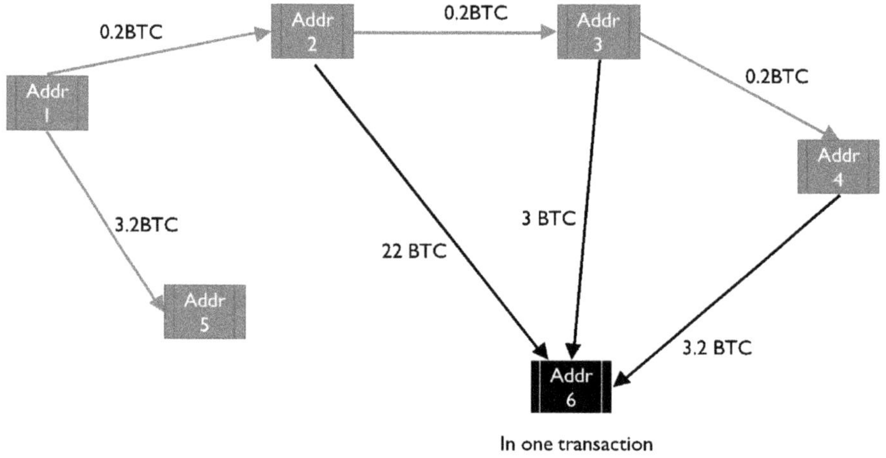

Figure 1.34: A new transaction that takes user inputs from three different addresses may reveal user private information.

An observer can deduce, with certain probability, that addresses 2, 3 and 4 belong to the same user. In fact, such an attack is similar to a dusting attack, where an attacker sends users tiny amounts of cryptocurrencies to their wallets. After that, the attacker performs analysis of these wallet addresses in an attempt to identify which ones belong to the same user.

Understanding user privacy as a form of confidentiality might lead us to consider encryption as a solution. The two main types of data in a Bitcoin transaction are the transaction amount and the addresses of the sender and receiver. Immediately, some problems are evident with encrypting this information. Encryption alone does not allow blockchain to function properly or securely as a decentralised P2P payment system, and encryption alone does not ensure untraceability and unlinkability. For example, encrypting transaction data or wallet addresses does not provide untraceability if the same wallet is reused. Furthermore, encrypting transaction data and wallet addresses without providing additional information will impede miners in the effort of validating transactions (e.g., check for double-spending and proof of ownership).

Blockchain developers have managed to develop algorithms that ensure user privacy while addressing these concerns. In this section, we will briefly discuss five methods: CoinJoin, stealth addresses, ring signature and Ring Confidential Transaction (RingCT) in Monero and zero-knowledge proofs.

1.10.1 *CoinJoin*

CoinJoin is a trustless method that allows multiple bitcoin spenders to come together and mix their input and output, so that observers cannot easily trace how they are spending their bitcoin. Suppose Alice has received 2 btc from Bob, which she now wants to spend. But, Bob can easily track the 2 btc to see which addresses Alice pays the amount to. For privacy, Alice decides to spend her 2 btc in a CoinJoin transaction.

Alice finds at least one other user who agrees to spend the common denomination of 2 btc. Among them, they identify a user who will facilitate the transaction. They then provide their respective input of 2 btc to the facilitator, as well as their respective public key hashes specifying where their output should go. All the users then sign the transaction and broadcast it to the network. This single transaction spends the agreed common denomination of bitcoin from each user at one go. Purely by observing the CoinJoin transaction, other users, including Bob, will not be able to identify which particular public key hash belongs to Alice. From that point onwards, Bob will lose trace of Alice's spending behaviour. In effect, CoinJoin employs a mixing technique that gives users plausible deniability regarding how they spend their bitcoin.

The more users are involved in the CoinJoin transaction, the more difficult it will be to trace the transactions of any one user. This method depends on a mixture and obfuscation of data, but does not involve additional cryptographic techniques. It therefore retains certain vulnerabilities. CoinJoin does not preclude any of the users involved in the transaction from announcing to the network which public key hash belongs to them, thereby making it easier for observers to deduce the public key hashes of other users in the transaction. Furthermore, the users involved in the CoinJoin transaction will know which public key hashes belong to the other users. The solution to this is CoinShuffle,[5] a method for encrypting public key hashes.

1.10.2 *Stealth Addresses*

The concept of stealth address is used in many privacy coins. An example is the Monero blockchain. The idea of stealth address is used to hide the real recipient of a transaction. Instead of specifying the public key hash of the recipient in a transaction, the sender creates a random number r, and "randomises" the public key hash to create a "one-time stealth address". The manner of randomising and creation of stealth address is designed in such a way that only the real, intended recipient, can de-randomise the stealth address and discover his/her own wallet address.[6] We use Monero to illustrate the usage of stealth addresses.

In Monero, every user holds four keys: a pair of private and public view keys $\langle pv, PV\rangle$, respectively, and a pair of private and public spend keys $\langle ps, PS\rangle$, respectively. The public keys are generated from the respective private keys through elliptic curve multiplication:

$$PV = pv \times G$$

$$PS = ps \times G$$

Each user's wallet address is made up of their public PV and PS. Every time a user wants to carry out a transaction, a one-time stealth

---

[5]https://bitcoinmagazine.com/articles/shuffling-coins-to-protect-privacy-and-fungibility-a-new-take-on-traditional-mixing-1465934826.

[6]We use public key hash and wallet address interchangeably.

address for the receiver is generated. Suppose Alice wants to send XMR (the Monero coin) to Bob. She obtains Bob's PV_{Bob} and PS_{Bob}. These two keys constitute Bob's permanent wallet address. Alice then chooses a random number r. She computes Bob's one-time stealth address X_{Bob} that will be used for this particular transaction only:

$$X_{\text{Bob}} = \text{Hash}(r \times PV_{\text{Bob}}) \times G + PS_{\text{Bob}}$$

Alice also computes a random one-time transaction number R:

$$R = r \times G$$

Alice includes both values X_{Bob} and R in her transaction to Bob.

Alice's transaction:

$R = r \times G$

$X_{\text{Bob}} = \text{Hash}(r \times PV_{\text{Bob}}) \times G + PS_{\text{Bob}}$

...

Other info

Since every transaction hides the receiver's address, users do not know whether they are the intended receiver of a transaction. This means that every user will need to check every single transaction to see if he/she is an intended receiver.

From the example above, given a transaction with X' and R', Bob will use his private view key pv and public spend key PS to verify whether a transaction is meant for him. He would check if the following equation is true:

$$\text{Hash}(pv \times R') \times G + PS = X'$$

If Bob comes across Alice's transaction, the calculation on the left-hand side will be equal to

$$\begin{aligned} &\text{Hash}(pv_{\text{Bob}} \times R) \times G + PS_{\text{Bob}} \\ &\quad = \text{Hash}(pv_{\text{Bob}} \times r \times G) \times G + \text{PS}_{\text{Bob}} \\ &\quad = \text{Hash}(r \times \text{PV}_{\text{Bob}}) \times G + \text{PS}_{\text{Bob}} \\ &\quad = X_{\text{Bob}} \end{aligned}$$

Thus, each time a user wants to send a new transaction, she will choose a different r value, generating a unique stealth address. To an observer, it will be computationally infeasible to work out which addresses are meant for the same receiver, granting the receiver untraceability.

However, suppose another user, Charlie, is also sending XMR to Bob. On the blockchain, Alice's and Charlie's transactions to Bob will not reveal that they are sending XMR to the same receiver. But, if Alice and Charlie were to meet in real life and compare their transaction details, it would be possible to deduce that both had made transactions with Bob. To provide untraceability even in such a scenario, Monero uses subaddresses. Bob can send different subaddresses to Alice and Charlie, which are not identifiable as belonging to the same user. For more information about subaddresses, the reader may refer to (SerHack and the Monero Community, 2018).

1.10.3 *Ring Signature*

To provide privacy to the sender, Monero employs a ring signature scheme that is structured around a pool of unspent coins of the same denomination belonging to multiple users. Recall that the scheme of a digital signature comprises three algorithms: key generation, signing using a private key sk and verification using a public key pk. Given a group of n users, each user holds a pair of private and public keys $(\langle sk_1, pk_1\rangle, \langle sk_2, pk_2\rangle, \ldots, \langle sk_n, pk_n\rangle)$. In the signing stage, a user holding the key pair $\langle sk_i, pk_i\rangle$ uses her own secret key sk_i and the public keys pk of all n users to generate a ring signature Sig_m on a message m. In the verification stage, the message and signature pair $\langle \mathrm{Sig}_{m'}, m'\rangle$ can be verified using the pk of all n users.

A ring signature can be used to sign any transaction created by a member of the group. This scheme allows the blockchain to specify a set of possible signers without revealing which individual user actually signed on a particular transaction. Ring signature inherits all the security properties of a normal digital signature scheme, with the additional property that it is computationally infeasible to determine which user in the group has signed a particular message. This anonymity cannot be revoked.

1.10.4 *Ring Confidential Transaction*

The RingCT method in Monero uses two ways to hide transaction amount. First, it encrypts the transaction amount using the receiver's public key. Then, it uses cryptographic commitment and range proof to prove that the transaction amount is valid. The proof is computed to verify that the sum of all inputs is greater than or equal to the sum of all outputs using commitments (thus, the sender is not creating cryptocurrencies in a transaction), and the input values are non-negative using range proof. For a deeper dive into Monero, readers may refer to (SerHack and the Monero Community, 2018).

1.10.5 *Zero-Knowledge Proofs*

Zcash is the first public blockchain to implement a full privacy protection scheme on transactions. It encrypts all transaction data, and uses a zero-knowledge succinct non-interactive arguments of knowledge (zk-SNARKs) algorithm to provide user anonymity and transaction untraceability and unlinkability in a more efficient manner than the traditional zero-knowledge proof.

A good illustration of zero-knowledge proofs can be found (Quisquater *et al.*, 1989). Traditional design of a zero-knowledge proof is interactive and requires multiple iterations to be convincing. The non-interactive zk-SNARKs algorithm used in Zcash is more succinct in terms of proof size and efficient in terms of verification time.

Typically, when we want to convince someone that we possess knowledge of a secret statement, such as a password, we do so by exchanging the statement with a verifying authority or user who also possesses knowledge of it. But, what if the user who is verifying the information does not — and should not, for privacy — possess knowledge of the secret statement itself? Zero-knowledge proofs allow us to prove to a verifier that a secret statement we hold is true, without actually revealing any information about that statement to the verifier. Such proofs have three properties:

- *Completeness.* If the prover is honest, the prover will eventually convince the verifier.

- *Soundness.* The prover can only convince the verifier if the statement is true.
- *Zero-knowledge.* The verifier learns nothing about the statement aside from the fact that it is true.

We proceed with a high-level overview of Zcash based on the Zcash protocol specifications (Hopwood *et al.*, 2019). In a Zcash transaction, the value of the transaction can be either transparent or shielded. Transparent transfers are essentially the same as Bitcoin and shielded transfer is the key differentiating factor for Zcash. There are two types of addresses in Zcash, namely private (z-address) or transparent (t-address). Transactions can be between two t-addresses, two z-addresses, or between a z-address and a t-address.

Transactions between two t-addresses are essentially the same as Bitcoin transactions where the sender, receiver and transaction amount are public information.

Transactions between two z-addresses are private, where the sender, receiver and transaction amount are encrypted.

A transaction from a t-address to a z-address is a shielding transaction, whereas a transaction from a z-address to a t-address is a deshielding transaction.

In Zcash, each user possesses the keys as depicted in Figure 1.35.

In Zcash, the concept of JoinSplit Description is discussed. A JoinSplit Description contains, among others, one or more encrypted Notes for shielded transfers and values for transparent transfers (Figure 1.36). It also contains nullifiers and commitments for shielded

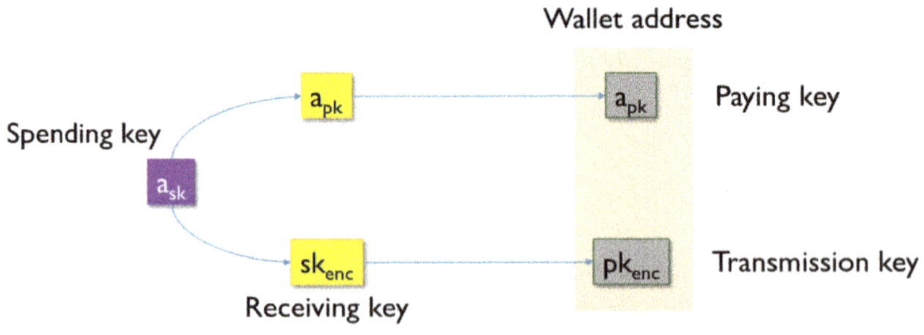

Figure 1.35: Keys in Zcash.

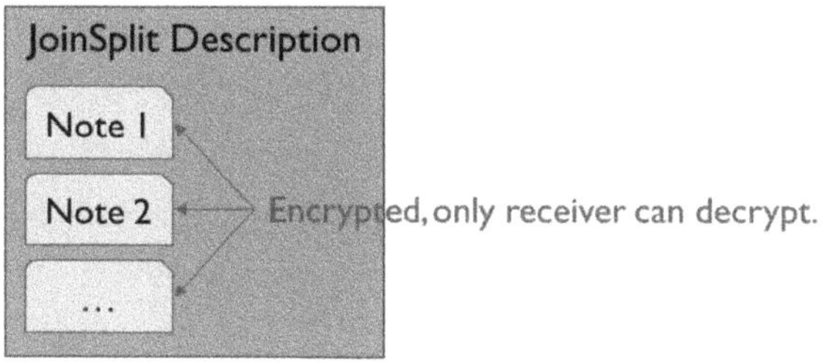

Figure 1.36: Illustration of a JoinSplit Description containing encrypted Notes.

transfers, an ephemeral public key to derive encryption key used to decrypt the Notes, and zero-knowledge proofs for all necessary components. We will discuss these components next.

Shielded transfers are carried in encrypted Notes. Each Note contains the recipient's paying key a_{pk}, the value of transfer v, a ρ to be used by the recipient to compute the nullifier when spending the Note and a commitment trapdoor rcm.

When a sender, e.g., Alice, creates a transaction to Bob, the output of this transaction must be accompanied by a commitment. Commitment is calculated as $\text{Hash}(10110000||\text{a}_{\text{pk}}||v||\rho||rcm)$, where a_{pk} belongs to Bob and $||$ denotes concatenation.This commitment is also recorded on a Merkle Hash Tree.

As Bob intends to spend the output given to him by Alice, at which the output is now the input to Bob's transaction, Bob would need to prove that the commitment of the input exists in the Merkle Hash Tree without revealing which commitment it is. He would also need to calculate a nullifier for the input. The nullifier is calculated as $\text{Hash}(1110||\text{a}_{sk}||\rho)$. This nullifier is added to the nullifier set and used by the miners to verify if there is a double-spending. An input where the nullifier exists in the nullifier set is a double-spending. To this end, notice that because the Note is encrypted such that only the intended recipient can decrypt, only the recipient will be able to obtain ρ to calculate the nullifier.

Encryption of Notes is performed using an ephemeral secret key that only the receiver can derive. Zcash uses a key agreement protocol that allows only the sender and the intended receiver to agree on a common secret without pre-sharing a secret key.

With the above operations in mind, zk-SNARK is used in Zcash for a sender of a transaction to prove that, among others,

- For the input — a Note commitment exists and the Merkle Path is valid; the nullifier is computed in a correct manner so that double-spending can be accurately detected.
- For the output — the Note commitment is computed correctly, and the nullifier is unique.

The proof using zk-SNARKs is beyond the scope of this chapter. It involves a multitude of techniques including homomorphic encryption, arithmetic circuit constructions to model cryptographic functions and secure creation of common reference string. Interested readers may refer to a step-by-step introduction by the Zcash team (Electronic Coin Company, 2020) and advanced readers may refer to the Zcash protocol specifications (Hopwood *et al.*, 2019) for more details.

References

Corbellini, A. (2015). Elliptic Curve Cryptography: ECDH and ECDSA. Retrieved from https://andrea.corbellini.name/2015/05/30/elliptic-curve-cryptography-ecdh-and-ecdsa/.

Electronic Coin Company. (2020). *How it works* | Zcash. Retrieved from Privacy Protecting Digital Currencies | Zcash: https://z.cash/technology/.

Hopwood, D., Bowe, S., Hornby, T. and Wilcox, N. (2019). *zips/protocol.pdf at master. zcash/zips.* Retrieved from GitHub: https://github.com/zcash/zips/blob/master/protocol/protocol.pdf.

Khalique, A., Singh, K. and Sood, S. (2010). Implementation of Elliptic Curve Digital Signature Algorithm, *International Journal of Computer Applications*, 2(2), 21–27.

Ostrom, E. (2015). *Governing the Commons: The Evolution of Institutions for Collective Actions* (*Canto Classics*). Cambridge University Press.

Quisquater, J.-J., Quisquater, M., Quisquater, M., Quisquater, M., Guillou, L., Guillou, M.,... Guillou, S. (1989). How to Explain Zero-Knowledge Protocols to Your Children. *Advances in Cryptology — CRYPTO' 89.*

SerHack and the Monero Community (2018). *Mastering Monero — The Future of Private Transactions.* LernoLibro LLC.

Stallings, W. (2017). *Cryptography and Network Security: Principles and Practice*, (7th Global Edition). Pearson Education.

Sullivan, N. (2014). ECDSA: The Digital Signature Algorithm of a Better Internet. Retrieved from https://blog.cloudflare.com/ecdsa-the-digital-signature-algorithm-of-a-better-internet/.

Chapter 2

Bitcoin Mining and Python Programming Demonstration

2.1 Getting Started

Decentralised as the bitcoin network is, the bitcoin mining process may be difficult to understand for many. Basically, the underlying blockchain technology is a distributed public ledger where bitcoin transaction data are recorded. Each block in the bitcoin blockchain contains transaction data and blocks of data are chained together using cryptography (see Figure 2.1).

Transactions are grouped into a block that will be added to the end of the current blockchain. The process is called mining and the node that does it is known as the miner. As a reward, miners get certain amount of bitcoins (currently 12.5 BTC) for every block successfully mined and they can also collect the transaction fees of the transactions included in the block. How to determine when a block is successfully mined, or the consensus rule, in the bitcoin network is the Proof of Work (PoW) algorithm. The bitcoin blockchain architecture is summarised in Figure 2.2.

This chapter aims to provide a demonstration of mining in Python and a better understanding of the mining process of bitcoins. Do note that this is a simplified version and may differ from the real-life bitcoin mining as we hope to provide you with some interactive and programming experiences. When explaining the code line by line, we will go through the bitcoin mining process step by step and illustrate the meaning of each step as well.

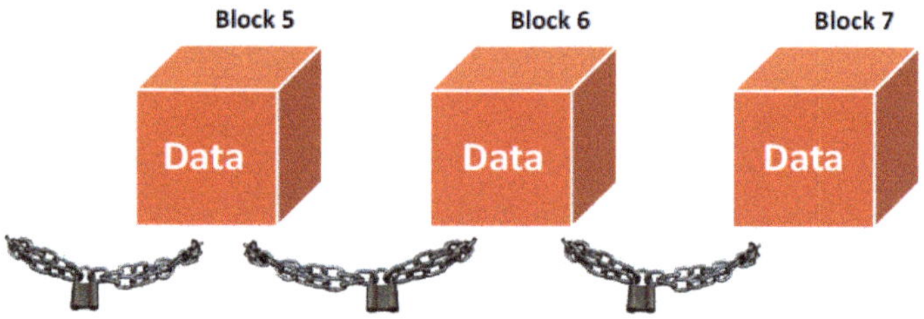

Figure 2.1: Blockchain structure.

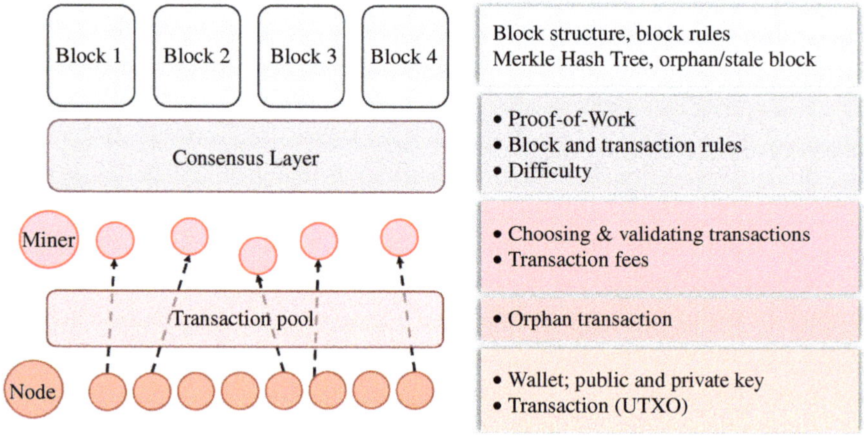

Figure 2.2: Summary of blockchain architecture.

2.2 Introduction of Python Programming

There are two ways to insert comments in Python: (1) to start with "#" and whatever follows the hashtag in that line will become comments or notes; (2) to start a line with `"""` and end it with `"""` so that whatever is in between will become comments for notes (see Figure 2.3). The former is usually used for shorter comments such as one line or a few words at the end of a line, while the latter is usually used for longer comments such as several lines. These comments or notes will not be run as codes.

In Python, there are many functions, codes or libraries readily available for users to use, instead of writing one from scratch. Such codes or scripts can be saved in a file named module. In order

```
"""
Python code for bitcoin mining demonstration
"""

import pandas as pd
```

Figure 2.3: Importing modules in Python.

to use an existing module or a set of libraries or modules (also referred to as packages) in your Python IDE (Integrated Development Environment) like PyCharm, you need to import the library first. Importing a library means loading it into the memory and then it is there for us to work with. "pandas" is an important module in Python, especially for dealing with financial data. It stands for "Python Data Analysis Library", which is derived from the term "panel data". It allows us to see the data as a table format or "series"/"data frame" type in Python. The code "import pandas as pd" in Figure 2.3 means we can call the module using two letters "pd" instead of the full six letters "pandas" for brevity. "pd" is widely used as abbreviation for "pandas".

2.3 Data Import

For the demonstration, we can use a simplified version of transaction data and transaction ID, but the idea is the same: miners need to import the transaction data first and select the transaction IDs before they can proceed to the mining.

Assume that the transactions available, or the transaction pool in bitcoin, are stored in a local file named "transactions.txt". We can use the "with open" command to import the text file into Python (see Figure 2.4). We can include the full directory of the file (e.g., "C:/$\cdots$/transaction.txt") or we can include the file in the same Python project folder and use only the file name "transaction.txt". The "with open" command is also applicable if the data are stored in other formats such as csv. We can also use other methods such as the csv or pandas module to import a csv file.

```
# From local file
with open('transactions.txt', 'r', encoding='utf-8') as f:
    tx = f.readlines()
# To create an empty list
tx_list = []
# To change the tx data from txt file to a list
for t in tx:
    t = t.replace('\n', '')
    tx_list.append(t.split(', '))

# To change it to the data frame type using the "pandas" library for better
display
tx_data = pd.DataFrame(tx_list, columns=['id', 'content', 'tx_fee'])
```

Figure 2.4: Importing transaction data.

The data in the text file are then stored as a list in *tx*, with each line as an element of the list (see Figure 2.4). To clean the transaction data, we would like to store each row in different columns (similar to Excel) and remove the line breaker "\n" at the end of each line. So, we create a new list named *tx_list* and leave it empty ("[]" refers to a list). For each element t in *tx*, we delete the line breaker "\n" by replacing it with an empty string. *t.split* will convert each line (t) in transaction data (*tx*) into different columns using the separator — comma. Then, we store the separated line data in the list *tx_list* with each line as a list.

In the last line of Figure 2.4, we convert the list to dataframe type by calling the pandas module, with the column names as "id", "content" and "tx_fee" (here we use simplified transaction data; the column names can be specified according to the data using the following format). The transaction data are now well organised with transaction id, transaction content and transaction fee data in separate columns.

Next, with reference to Figure 2.5, we choose the transaction IDs from the transaction data. The input() function allows users to use the keyboard to key in data, which will be stored as strings. The sentence in the parenthesis is what shows on the screen preceding the cursor. The "\n" at the end of the line allows the user to key in data in a new line. We can split the string input by space and get a

```
tx_in = input("Please key in the transaction IDs (separated by spacing):\n")

tx_in_list = tx_in.split(' ')
tx_in_list = [t.replace('\\s+', '') for t in tx_in_list]  # To remove one or
more space
tx_in_list = [int(t) for t in tx_in_list]

instr_list = []
for t in tx_in_list:
    print(t)
    if t not in list(tx_data['id']):
        print('The ID of %s is not a valid input and has been excluded. ' % t)
        continue
    instr_list.append(t)

print('='*30)
print('The list of valid transaction IDs selected is: ', instr_list)

in_data = pd.DataFrame()
for id in instr_list:
    in_data = in_data.append(tx_data[tx_data['id']==id])

print(in_data)
```

Figure 2.5: Selecting transaction IDs.

list of transaction IDs selected. There may be extra spacing in *tx_in* and thus *instr_list*, so we delete the spacing from *instr_list*. This will generate a list of transaction IDs without extra spaces, but they are still string type resulting from the input() function. So, we convert the IDs to integer type using the int() function.

Transaction IDs that are not included in the transaction data *tx_data* should be removed from the list (see Figure 2.5). So, in the *for* loop, for every element *t* or every transaction ID in the *tx_in_list*, we use the *if* statement to skip the step of appending the transaction ID to the ID output list *instr_list* using "continue" (which means to skip the following lines in the loop and continue to the next loop) if that transaction ID is not in the ID column of the transaction data (*tx_data*['id']). If all the transaction IDs selected are valid, all the IDs will be included in the final ID output *instr_list*.

Then, we create an empty data frame using *pandas* to store the full transaction records for the transaction IDs selected using the "*for* loop" (see Figure 2.5). The *for* loop and *tx_data[tx_data['id']==id]* return only the rows in *tx_data* where the ID in *tx_data['id']* appears in the *instr_list* (the list that stores the transaction IDs selected). The print output will be the list of valid transaction IDs selected and the corresponding transaction data. Printing 30 equation symbols is just to make the layout nicer.

Then, we can have the transaction data imported and nicely presented in Python. This is a demonstration of data files import and data clean in Python. In the following sections, we will use a simple four-transaction example to further elaborate the mining process.

2.4 Transaction

Before we proceed to deal with the transaction data in Python, let us run through the information contained in a Bitcoin transaction and how it works. As mentioned earlier, transaction data will be recorded in the bitcoin blockchain. Like any other conventional transaction, a bitcoin transaction needs information on the receiver, sender and the amount of money. First, a sender needs to have a certain amount of bitcoins to spend, and he can initiate a transaction by specifying a bitcoin amount and a sender. This transaction will then go to a transaction pool for miners to validate and be included in a block with other transactions. The Bitcoin blockchain ensures that transaction data included in a block cannot be altered. How can it achieve that? The answer is the bitcoin blockchain structure and information included in the transaction. Whether the transaction data included in a specific block have been tampered with can be easily verified using the Merkle Hash Tree method in the cryptography. Understanding transaction, transaction data and Merkle Hash Tree is important to understand bitcoin mining and blockchain.

2.5 Bitcoin Transaction

Similar to the bank account in a conventional online banking transaction, each bitcoin transaction has a sender and receiver (Nakamoto, 2019). But, a bitcoin transaction contains more information and it can have several transactions. So, the term input and output are used

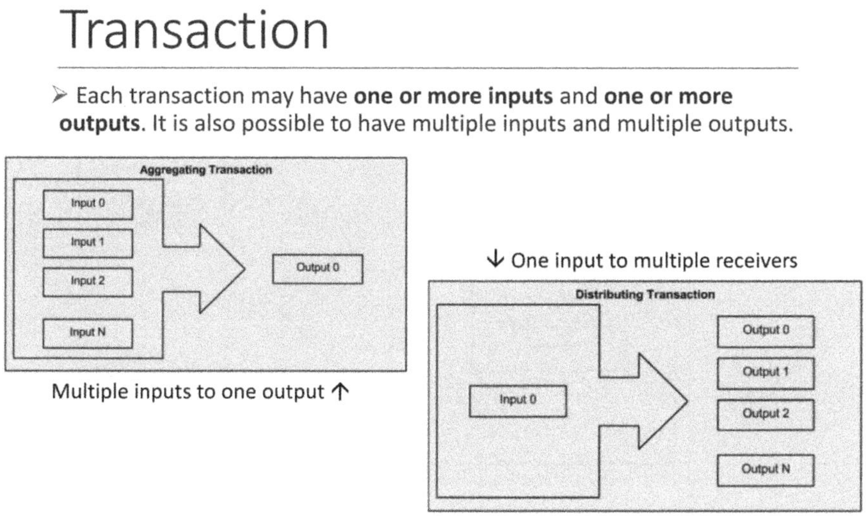

Figure 2.6: Inputs and outputs in a transaction.

in Bitcoin and a bitcoin transaction may have one or more inputs and one or more outputs (see Figure 2.6). Consider it as a one-way flow of bitcoins. Input shows where the bitcoins came from (could be multiple sources) and output points to where they are going (could be multiple receivers). The number of inputs in a transaction is called "Input Counter" and the number of outputs "Output Counter", both of which will be included in the bitcoin transaction data.

As we all know, a key aspect of blockchain is that once the information is recorded, it is there forever and cannot be changed. This spirit of blockchain can be viewed in a single transaction as well. Although the bitcoins are non-fungible (meaning we do not distinguish between different bitcoins), the sender needs to specify the source of the transacted amount of bitcoins as part of the input information in a transaction, and the concept of remaining account balance is not applicable in bitcoin. Unlike a bank account, we can see the balance left in a lump sum and we can spend it all together without linking to previous transactions; the balance of bitcoins goes by transactions. In each transaction, the input information will point to previous transactions, to which a specific amount of bitcoins is

➢ The concept of a change in bitcoin.

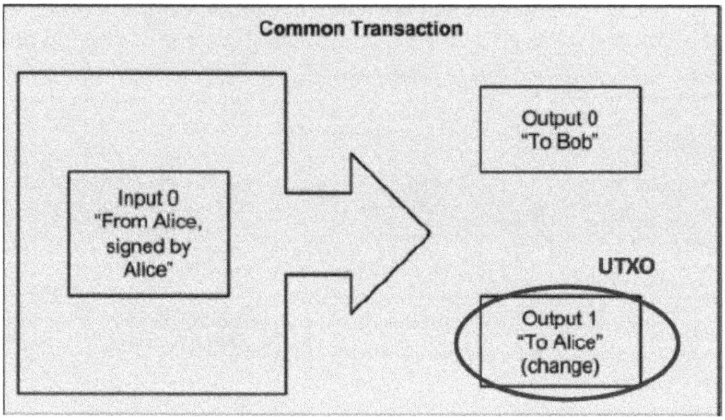

Figure 2.7: UTXO and the concept of change.

linked. In this way, it would be very effective and easy for miners to verify whether the sender owns the bitcoins.

Furthermore, the receiver information, or the transaction output in bitcoin, is different from conventional online transactions. In a bank transfer, we can simply transfer the money to another account with the rest remaining unchanged as long as the amount we are trying to send is no more than the total amount available, while in bitcoin, we need to include the bitcoins left as part of the transaction output. For each transaction, if there are unspent bitcoins left, this amount will be sent to the sender's address again as an unspent transaction output (UTXO), which refers to bitcoins from a previous transaction that has not yet been spent (or unspent) and can be the input of another transaction in the future (Figure 2.7). All transaction inputs in bitcoin are UTXOs and can be linked to previous transactions that indicate the source of unspent bitcoins.

In summary, a typical bitcoin transaction contains the following information as shown in Figure 2.8:

- Version that indicates the consensus rules to follow.
- Input counter that shows the total number of inputs.

Version		Rules (consensus) to follow	
Input Counter		Number of inputs	
Inputs	Prev output hash	Previous UTXO identifier	
	Prev output index	Previous UTXO index	
	scriptSig size	Size of sender's signature	**Proof of**
	scriptSig	Sender's signature	**Ownership**
	Sequence number	Currently disabled; set "FF FF FF FF"	
Output Counter		Number of outputs	
Outputs	Amount	Bitcoin amount to send	
	scriptPubKey size	Size of receiver's scriptPubKey	
	scriptPubKey	Condition to spend the output (Receiver's public key)	
Locktime		Time before the tx can be added to blockchain	

Figure 2.8: Information contained in a Bitcoin transaction.

- Input information such as previous output hash (previous UTXO identifier), previous output index (previous UTXO index), scriptSig size (size of the sender's signature), scriptSig (sender's signature) and sequence number (currently disabled).
- Output counter that shows the total number of outputs.
- Output information such as amount (bitcoin amount to send), scriptPubKey size (size of receiver's public key) and scriptPubKey (condition to spend the output which is the receiver's public key).
- Locktime that suggests the time before the transaction can be included in a block and added to the blockchain.

Among them, the inputs and outputs in a transaction provide the information about the sender and receiver, including the sender's source of wealth, proof of ownership (see Figure 2.8) or proof that the sender owns the bitcoin by a digital signature signed using the sender's private key, receiver's address or public key, and the amount to receive. The input counter shows the number of sources or previous transactions linked (where the bitcoins come from) in this transaction and the output counter shows the number of outflows (where the bitcoins go) with unspent amount transferred to the sender's own address.

2.6 Hash

Since there is a lot of information included in a transaction, bitcoin adopts a more efficient way to incorporate the transaction data in the mining while ensuring the integrity of the data at the same time. Namely, the transaction information will then be taken into a hash function and the generated hash value of the information will be used as transaction ID that is used to identify the transaction. The hash value of any input has the same length and any slight changes in the input will cause the resulted hash value to be completely different with no pattern. Such features of hash ensure that as long as we have the same transaction ID, the data and information in a transaction have not been tampered with.

What is hash and why is used in bitcoin transactions? Hash, or hashing, refers to a function that takes data input of any length and returns a value of fixed length (Sobti & Geetha, 2012). The value returned by a hash function is also known as hashes, hash values, hash codes or digests. We can create hashes of all kinds of digital content of any length and form (e.g., numbers, letters, and symbols; documents, images and music) and the output will be a value of fixed length, which makes the calculation process neater and easier. The use of a hash function can also easily suggest whether the transaction information remains unchanged or not. This is because hashing the same input will always generate the same hash values and any changes, even the slightest, in the input will result in a totally different hash value.

The hash function used in bitcoin is SHA-256, which returns a fixed length of 256 bits (32 bytes). So, the transaction ID in bitcoin would look like this:

B94d27b9934d3e08a52e52d7da7dabfac484efe37a5380
ee9088f7ace2efcde9

Now, that we use the hash values to represent a transaction (at transaction level), is there an efficient way to aggregate multiple transactions or hash values (at block level) as many transactions may be included in a single block? In fact, for each block, the transactions selected by the miner are aggregated by Merkle Hash Tree and reflected as a single number, the Merkle Root.

The Merkle Hash Tree is a binary tree that would calculate the hash value of every two transactions until the Merkle Root is reached. The Merkle Root summarises all the transactions gathered within this block and is used as an efficient way to determine if a particular transaction is included within a block and to verify if all transactions have not been tampered with (Merkle, 1980). A simplified version of Merkle Hash Tree is shown in Figure 2.9. If the information within a transaction is changed, the hash value of the transaction will change (also known as the leaf) and the second layer (or the branch) will change, leading to a different Merkle Root because any changes in the input of a hash function will generate a completely different output or hash values. We will demonstrate this process in Python using an example of four transactions.

What does this imply? This means that if an attacker tries to modify a transaction (say Alice to Bob: 1 btc), he is effectively trying to find another transaction with the same hash value as Alice to Bob: 1 btc in order to be not detected. This is not possible because it is computationally not feasible as to find two different inputs

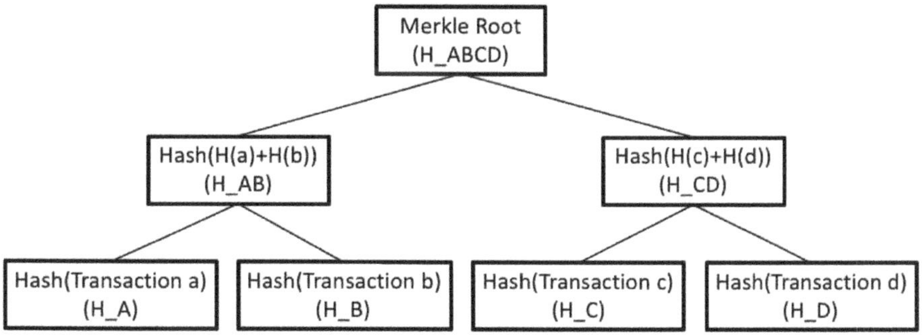

Figure 2.9: Structure of a Merkle Root.

(or transaction data) with the same hash output (or hash values) is extremely difficult with current computing power.

Same as earlier, we need to import the packages needed. Since Bitcoin uses SHA-256 cryptographic hash function, we can import it from the Python library available named "hashlib" (see Figure 2.10). Note that if we use "import hashlib" instead of "from hashlib import sha256" at the beginning, the code would be "hashlib.sha256()" instead of "sha256()", and if we would like to call the function as Python, it would only recognise "hashlib" not "sha256" as a valid function.

Next, looking at the functions in Figure 2.11, we define two functions: dsha() and rev(). Bitcoin uses double hashing, meaning for the input, we need to use the sha256() function twice. In Python, "sha256(tx).digest()" returns the hash value, or digest, of the input "tx". So, for bitcoin, the code would be "sha256(sha256(tx).digest()).digest()". Instead of writing so many strings every time, we can define a function named "dsha()" to return the double hash results. Similarly, we can define a function named "rev()" to reverse the elements in the input "buf", which will be used later in the calculation. "buf[::−1]" means to cover all elements (by default as there are no numbers specified before each colon), from the last to the first and one at each time (determined by the "−1" after the second colon).

```
from hashlib import sha256  # The hash algorithm used in Bitcoin
```

Figure 2.10: Importing *sha256*.

```
def dsha(tx):  # Double hashing the transaction data 'tx' in Bitcoin
    return sha256(sha256(tx).digest()).digest()

def rev(buf):  # Reverse the elements in 'buf'
    return buf[::-1]
```

Figure 2.11: Defining functions *dsha* and *rev*.

Let us start with the following four transactions, A, B, C and D (see Figures 2.12 and 2.13). The strings in the parenthesis are the corresponding transaction IDs. The "bytes.fromhex()" function converts hexadecimal, or hex, strings to binary strings.

The hash values of the four transactions can be calculated using the following commands (see Figure 2.14). Note that output from the "dsha()" function is binary, but it is easier for us to see the hash

```
tx_A =
bytes.fromhex('0000000003ce000000000000000000000000000000000000000000000000000
00000000000ffffffff08044c86041b020602ffffffff0100f2052a010000004341041b0e8c256
7c12536aa13357b79a073dc4444acb83c4ec7a0e2f99dd7457516c5817242da796924ca4e99947
d087fedf9ce467cb9f7c6287078f801df276fdf84ac00000000')

tx_B =
bytes.fromhex('000000001032e38e9c0a84c6046d687d10556dcacc41d275ec55fc00779ac8
8fdf357a187000000008c493046022100c352d3dd993a981beba4a63ad15c209275ca9470abfcd
57da93b58e4eb5dce82022100840792bc1f456062819f15d33ee7055cf7b5ee1af1ebcc6028d9c
db1c3af7748014104f46db5e9d61a9dc27b8d64ad23e7383a4e6ca164593c2527c038c0857eb67
ee8e825dca65046b82c9331586c82e0fd1f633f25f87c161bc6f8a630121df2b3d3ffffffff020
0e32321000000001976a914c398efa9c392ba6013c5e04ee729755ef7f58b3288ac000fe208010
000001976a914948c765a6914d43f2a7ac177da2c2f6b52de3d7c88ac00000000')
```

Figure 2.12: Transaction A and B.

```
tx_C =
bytes.fromhex('0f00000001c33ebff2a709f13d9f9a7569ab16a32786af7d7e2de09265e41c6
1d078294ecf010000008a4730440220032d30df5ee6f57fa46cddb5eb8d0d9fe8de6b342d27942
ae90a3231e0ba333e02203deee8060fdc70230a7f5b4ad7d7bc3e628cbe219a886b84269eaeb81
e26b4fe014104ae31c31bf91278d99b8377a35bbce5b27d9fff15456839e919453fc7b3f721f0b
a403ff96c9deeb680e5fd341c0fc3a7b90da4631ee39560639db462e9cb850ffffffff0240420
f00000000001976a914b0dcbf97eabf4404e31d952477ce822dadbe7e1088acc060d2110000000
01976a9146b1281eec25ab4e1e0793ff4e08ab1abb3409cd988ac00000000')

tx_D =
bytes.fromhex('0c400000670b6072b386d4a773235237f64c1126ac3b240c84b917a3909ba1c
43ded5f51f4000000008c493046022100bb1ad26df930a51cce110cf44f7a48c3c561fd977500b
1ae5d6b6fd13d0b3f4a022100c5b42951acedff14abba2736fd574bdb465f3e6f8da12e2c53039
54aca7f78f3014104a7135bfe824c97ecc01ec7d7e336185c81e2aa2c41ab175407c09484ce969
4b44953fcb751206564a9c24dd094d42fdbfdd5aad3e063ce6af4cfaaea4ea14fbbffffffff014
0420f00000000001976a91439aa3d569e06a1d7926dc4be1193c99bf2eb9ee088ac00000000')
```

Figure 2.13: Transaction C and D.

```
ha = dsha(tx_A)
hb = dsha(tx_B)
hc = dsha(tx_C)
hd = dsha(tx_D)

# To print the hash values in hex string of the four transactions
print("H_A:", ha.hex())
print("H_B:", hb.hex())
print("H_C:", hc.hex())
print("H_D:", hd.hex())
```

Figure 2.14: Calculating hash values of transactions.

```
H_A: 607fd0327a3b7773690219764d9df3188b3df63dc927a62e088295838c5c52d2
H_B: f5a205e1aa269d59c0e4f17b6d3f934d5c3e32826949b777710cf61276512ef9
H_C: 59e0e7fbd76c65b24371899472ffa5f39514a8eca2de48e800c65dd53ea85940
H_D: bc2a504bcbf5e3e4c938394cd7b53f39f34acc73870dc23dac34b1540de1ddee
```

Figure 2.15: Output of the four transactions.

```
hab = dsha(ha+hb)
hcd = dsha(hc+hd)

print("H_AB:", hab.hex())
print("H_CD:", hcd.hex())

habcd = dsha(hab+hcd)

print("H_ABCD:", habcd.hex())
print("Merkle root:", rev(habcd).hex())
```

Figure 2.16: Calculating the Merkle Root.

values in hex strings, so we present the result in hex strings using ".hex()" function.

The output is displayed as follows in Figure 2.15.

Following the Merkle Hash Tree, the Merkle Root can then be calculated as the hash of the sum of *hab* and *hcd* (see Figure 2.16).

The output is shown in Figure 2.17.

```
H_AB: 33878862fd223395836ecb79b090370f571a579cea8330cc34eb0515c6038e28
H_CD: 24770cb6ff08789585d492d7e4fd4b2f19f78bce57fb17b8259fdefb37d470ac
H_ABCD: e947ad0314c5d58e0165282159584c04f0eb58200743a4f2c4fa3adf6a10f4c1
Merkle root: c1f4106adf3afac4f2a443072058ebf0044c5859212865018ed5c51403ad47e9
```

Figure 2.17: Output of the Merkle Root.

Therefore, the Merkle Root of our four transactions is

"c1f4106adf3afac4f2a443072058ebf0044c5859212865018 ed5c51403ad47e9"

This will then be used to mine a block and stored in the block header.

Why do we need the reverse function for the Merkle Root? Basically, this has something to do with how data is stored in the computer and how we prefer it to appear. When considered as input of the hash, or double hash, in the case of Bitcoin function, transaction IDs need to be in binary strings and little endian machines, which refer to an order that stores the low-order byte of the number ("little-end", or the least significant value in the sequence) first (at the lowest address) and high-order byte ("big-end", or the most significant value in the sequence) last (at the highest address). But, the blockchain explorers display the data in hexadecimal and big endian machines, which store the "big-end" first and "little-end" last. Therefore, we need to reverse the characters in the hexadecimal Merkle root strings to convert it back to big endian machines, thus the usage of reverse function defined earlier on.

2.7 Block Structure

Each block consists of a block header and transaction data (see Figure 2.18). Full transaction data are included in a block, but only the Merkle Root is included in the block header as an aggregation and presentation of the transactions in that block. Some nodes can keep and sync merely the block header information, instead of the full transaction data, to save space. The block header is crucial in blockchain and mining as each block is cryptographically chained

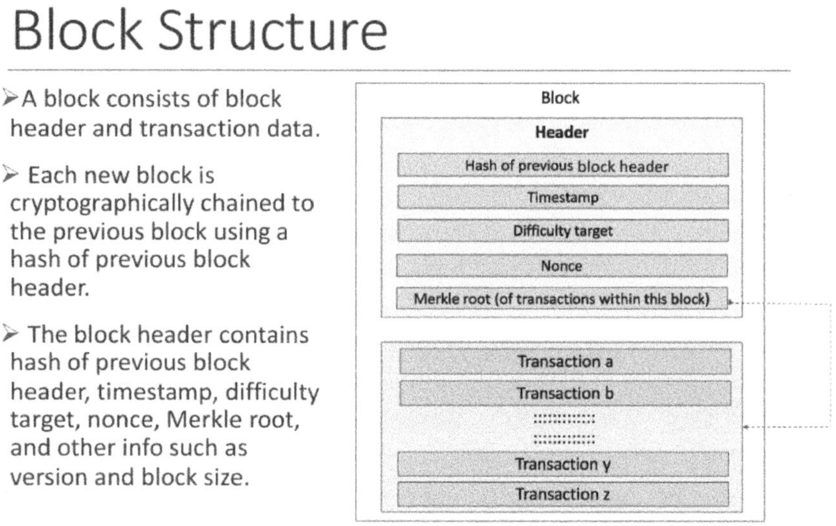

Figure 2.18: Overview of block structure.
Source: https://luxsci.com/blog/understanding-blockchains-and-bitcoin-technology.html.

to the previous block using a hash of the previous block header. It contains the hash of the previous block header, timestamp, difficulty target, nonce, Merkle Root and other information such as version and block size.

The blockchain is designed in such a way that is constantly appending new blocks of validated transactions to the end of its chain. The chain can only grow and blocks cannot be removed or amended once confirmed and appended. Since every block contains a unique hash value of the previous block, if an attacker tries to change content of the previous block, its hash value will change. Thus, the attack will be detected because all subsequent hash values will not match. Just as the hash of a transaction reflects the information within the transaction and the Merkle Root reflects the transactions included in a block, the hash value of the block header reflects all the information in the block.

Here, looking at the codes in Figure 2.19, we include the version, the hash value of previous block and time information, to be included

```
ver = 2
prev_block =
"00000000000000117c80378b8da0e33559b5997f2ad55e2f7d18ec1975b9717"
time_ = 0x5D21A868  # 2019-07-07 08:08:08
```

Figure 2.19: Given information to be included.

in the block header later. The above number for *time_* is the Unix epoch (or Unix time or POSIX time or Unix timestamp), which is the number of seconds that have elapsed since January 1, 1970 (midnight UTC/GMT), not counting leap seconds (in ISO 8601: 1970-01-01T00:00:00Z). It is equivalent to 2019-07-07 08:08:08.

2.8 Mining

Mining refers to the process of finding a valid block to add to the current blockchain and it follows certain rules or consensus rule, which is Proof of Work (PoW) in bitcoin. Miners are the nodes that do mining. Since there are no centralised parties like banks or governments to control the issuance or validate the account balance and transactions, the consensus rule, or PoW, is what the bitcoin network relies on. The nodes in the bitcoin network reach the consensus that a block is genuine through the block header's hash value — whether it satisfies a given condition or meets a given target (Nguyen and Kim, 2018). Just like solving a math problem, this condition is explicit and stated in the bitcoin protocol so that everyone in the community must comply, which ensures trust among the bitcoin community.

In Bitcoin's Proof-of-Work mechanism, the blockchain that was created with the greatest cumulative effort expended is the one considered to be the latest and to which new blocks are attached. That is to say, the longest blockchain in the system is the accepted state of the bitcoin ledger as it requires the greatest effort to create. Since the rest of the information included in the block header hash value computation is more or less given, the most variable factor is the nonce, so miners will keep trying different nonce values to generate different hash values of the block header. That said, without changing any other data in the block header (definitely not the transactions), the Proof-of-Work process is a competition among miners to find "the Golden Nonce" that will result in a block fingerprint (i.e., the hash value of the block header) that satisfies a given condition or meets a given target.

2.9 Target and Mining Difficulty

In the bitcoin blockchain, the target is a 256-bit number that all bitcoin nodes share. It is sometimes referred to as the difficulty target as it measures how difficult it is to mine or generate a new block. The SHA-256 hash of a block's header must be lower than or equal to the current target for the block to be accepted by the network. It is usually expressed in hexadecimal. An example of target is as follows:

0x0000000000FFFFFFFFFFFFFFFFFFFFFFFFFFFFFFFFFFFFFFFFFFFFFFFFFFFFFFFFFFFF.

The more the leading zeros, the lower the target (meaning in decimal the number is lower), and thus the more difficult it is to find a block fingerprint that satisfies the condition or meets the target. What is hexadecimal? The hexadecimal numeral system, often shortened to "hex", is a numeral system made up of 16 symbols (base 16). The standard numeral system is called decimal (base 10) and uses ten symbols: 0,1,2,3,4,5,6,7,8,9. Hexadecimal uses the decimal numbers and six extra symbols (see Figure 2.20). We often see the block hash represented as hexadecimal numbers (64 digits) which result from SHA-256 hashing. Each hexadecimal number is four bits, so the output of SHA-256 is a 256-bit number (64 hexadecimal digits $\times$ 4 = 256 bits), and thus the name.

Sometimes, a target is given in "bits" or a "compact" format of the target such as "1903a30c" or 0x1903a30c. The exponent is 0x19 and the coefficient is 0x03a30c. The target can be calculated using the following formula:

$$Target = Coefficient * 2^{8*(Exponent-3)}$$

So, for a difficulty bits value of 0x1903a30c, we have

$$Target = \text{0x03}a\text{30c} * 2^{\text{0x08}*(\text{0x19}-\text{0x03})}$$

Hexadecimal	Binary	Decimal
0	0000	0
1	0001	1
2	0010	2
3	0011	3
4	0100	4
5	0101	5
6	0110	6
7	0111	7
8	1000	8
9	1001	9
A	1010	10
B	1011	11
C	1100	12
D	1101	13
E	1110	14
F	1111	15

Figure 2.20: Hexadecimals, binary and decimal.

The target is then 0x0000000000000003A30C0000000000000 0000000000000000000000000000000.

What does "0x" mean? It simply means that what follows is in hexadecimal, to avoid confusion with other data types such as decimal or strings.

Since it is difficult to compare two targets using the hex strings or decimal values as they are very large integers, difficulty can be viewed as another representation of the target that makes the comparison easier.

Difficulty is expressed as follows:

$$difficulty = \frac{difficulty\_1\_target}{current\_target}$$

Difficulty_1_targets is defined as the easiest allowed target value, 0x1d00ffff, which gives us a hex target of

$$0x00ffff * 2 * * (8 * (0x1d - 3))$$
$$= 0x00000000FFFF000000000000000000000000000000000 0000000000000000000$$

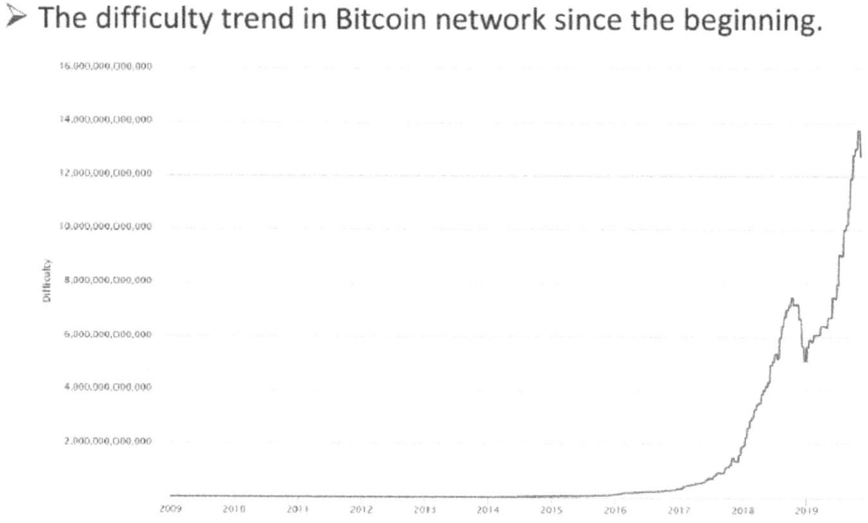

Figure 2.21: Increase in difficulty of mining Bitcoins.
Source: https://www.blockchain.com/charts/difficuly?timespan=all.

Difficulty is a network-wide setting that controls how much computation is required to produce a proof of work. It is a relative measure of how difficult it is to find a hash below a given target or to find a new block. The bitcoin network has a global block difficulty, which is adjusted periodically as a function of how much hashing power has been deployed by the network of miners to ensure that it takes 10 minutes on average to add a new block to the bitcoin blockchain (O'Dwyer and Malone, 2014).

How often does the network difficulty change? It changes roughly every two weeks, depending on the network block generation speed or the overall computing power (see Figure 2.21).

The formula for a new difficulty level is as follows:

$$\text{New difficulty} = \text{Old difficulty} * \left(\frac{\text{actual time taken for last 2016 blocks}}{\text{20160 minutes}}\right)$$

Let us assume a simpler target to demonstrate how the target is calculated using bits value in Python (see Figure 2.22). Exponent

```
bits = '0x1e03a30c'   # 5 zeros difficulty target
exponent = bits[2:4]
coefficient = bits[4:]
exponent2 = int("8", 16) * (int(exponent, 16) - int("3", 16))

target = int(coefficient, 16) * (int("2", 16)) ** exponent2
print("The target is: ", target)

target1 = format(target, 'x')  # To convert the string back to hex
print("The target (in hex) is: ", str(target1).zfill(64))
```

Figure 2.22: Calculating the difficulty target.

```
The target is
25100974094617268335075366062347480202344008198530079569242512873750528
The target (in hex) is:
000003a30c000000000000000000000000000000000000000000000000000000
```

Figure 2.23: Output of the target.

is the third and fourth digit in bits, so it is the second and third element in the *bits* string since the number starts with 0 in a list and *bits[2:4]* means the second and third in *bits*, which is 0x1e. *bits[4:]* gets the 5th digit to the last digit in the bits value, which is 0x03a30c. Then, we can calculate the target using the abovementioned formula. While *int(var)* gives the integer of *var* in decimal, *int(var, 16)* tells the program that this integer *var* is in hexadecimal.

The output will be as follows (see Figure 2.23). We can see that the target in decimal is an extremely large number. It is much more neatly expressed in hex strings, which is why hex strings are widely used in the bitcoin blockchain. Without the zfill(64), the target would be 000003a30c and the function fills the rest of the places so that the final number is 64 digits.

2.10 Finding the Golden Nonce

If we recall the whole mining process again, once the miner selected the transactions, the Merkle Root will be calculated and remain the same as long as the transactions selected do not change. In previous sections, we calculated the difficulty target. The next step is to put

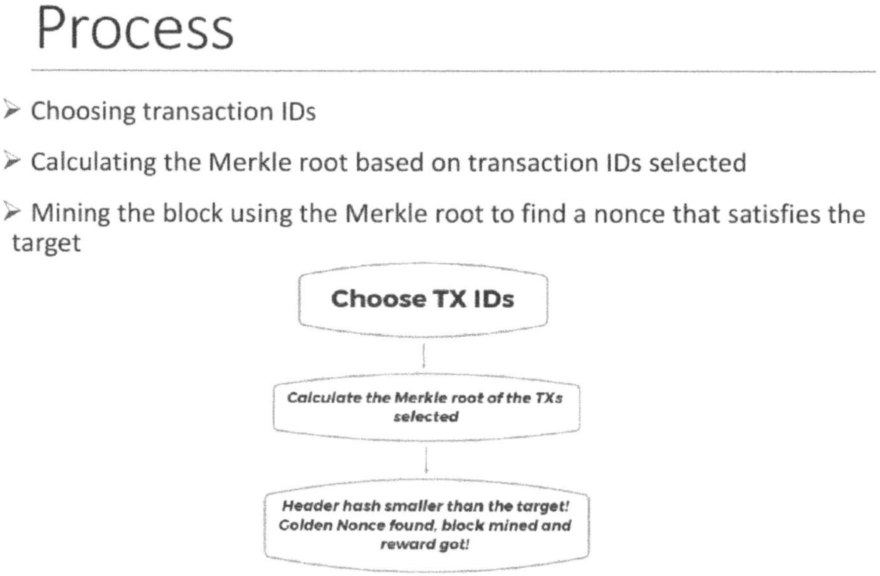

Figure 2.24: Process of Bitcoin consensus.

the rest of the information into the header and start finding the Golden Nonce in the mining process (see Figure 2.24).

The target value in bytes is stored in *target_byte* for block mining later (see Figure 2.25). We can also prepare the *partial_header* using the information we have now, including version, hash of previous block header, Merkle Root that aggregates the transactions included in this block and timestamp. *struct.pack(“< L”, x)* returns the input x as little-endian ordered unsigned long value. As mentioned in the transaction section, the endianness is a convention that determines in which direction a sequence of bits is interpreted as a number: from (Big-endian) left to right, or from (Little-endian) right to left. This is to follow the rules in bitcoin network.

From the *partial_header* (see Figure 2.25), we can see that among the information included in a block header, all the rest of the data are given and can be easily obtained except for the nonce. So, to successfully mine a new block is equivalent to finding a correct nonce that makes the hash value of the block header equal to or smaller than the target. Any change to the block header input (such as the

```
target_byte = bytes.fromhex(str(target1).zfill(64))
partial_header = struct.pack("<L", ver) \
               + bytes.fromhex(prev_block)[::-1] \
               + bytes.fromhex(mrkl_root)[::-1] \
               + struct.pack("<LL", time_, int(bits, 16))
```

Figure 2.25: Partial header and block header information.

nonce) will make the block hash completely different. Since it is believed infeasible to predict which combination of bits will result in the right hash, many different nonce values will be tried and the hash recomputed for each nonce value until a hash less than or equal to the current target of the network is found. As this iterative calculation requires time and resources, the presentation of the block with the correct nonce value (known as the golden nonce) constitutes PoW in Bitcoin (MacKenzie, 2019). The mining process can also be referred to as the process of finding the golden nonce.

What is a nonce? In cryptography, a nonce is an arbitrary number that can be used just once in a cryptographic communication (Gordon and Jeffrey, 2004). It is similar in spirit to a nonce word, hence the name. The "nonce" in a bitcoin block is a 32-bit (4-byte) field whose value is adjusted by miners so that the hash of the block will be less than or equal to the current target of the network. The rest of the fields may not be changed, as they have a defined meaning. It is important to realise that block generation is not a long, set problem (like doing a million hashes), but more like a lottery. Each hash basically generates a random number between 0 and the maximum value of a 256-bit number (which is huge). If the corresponding hash is below the target, the miner wins. If not, the miner needs to increment the nonce (completely changing the hash) and try again. Therefore, the process requires a huge amount of computing power.

The next step is to find the golden nonce, or to examine whether the block hash meets the target using different nonce values. In Python, we can start with a nonce that we choose by the *input()* function. The *while True* loop ensures that the user can keep keying in values if there are any wrong entries (see Figure 2.26).

```
print('='*30)

# To specify a nonce
while True:
    user_input = input('Please key in an non-negative integer: \n')
    try:
        nonce = int(user_input)
        if nonce < 0:
            print('It is a negative integer. Please key in again. ')
            continue
        else:
            break
    except ValueError:
        print('That is not an integer. Please key in again. ')
        continue
```

Figure 2.26: To input a nonce.

The *nonce* = *int(user_input)* statement is necessary to convert the user input to integer. Otherwise, what the user keyed in will be a string type. It is possible that the user keyed in strings or other symbols that cannot be used for the *int()* function, which will raise a value error message. So, the "*except ValueError:*" statement is meant for such cases and allows the user to key in again without the program being ended by the error message.

Once we have keyed in a nonce value, we can start the trial with this nonce value and keep trying to use a *while* loop. 0x100000000 in hex is 4294967296, so this is the max number of loops run if the golden nonce is not found. With the nonce, we can have the hash of block header (used to determine if the target is met). Do note that in this example, we use a relatively easy target. In reality, to mine a block in bitcoin is very difficult and the number of loops or the time it takes to find the golden nonce is much larger and longer than our example.

Generating a *mining_start_time* variable that shows the start time is for us to see how long it takes to find a golden nonce or mine a block with the target set compared to the time when we find the golden nonce (see Figure 2.27). Current time minus start time is the

```
mining_start_time = time.time()
while nonce < 0x100000000:  # The number is 4294967296
    header = partial_header + struct.pack("<L", nonce)
    hash = dsha(header)

    if nonce in range(50000, 20000000, 50000):
        mining_time = time.time() - mining_start_time
        hash_rate = nonce / mining_time
        print(nonce, hash[::-1].hex(), hash_rate, " per second")

    if hash[::-1] < target_byte:
        print('Success!', nonce, binascii.hexlify(hash[::-1]))  # in hexstring
        break

    nonce += 1
```

Figure 2.27: Finding the golden nonce.

time taken. We will show the nonce, hash of the block header and the hash rate per second every 50,000 times the loop runs.

For every loop, we try a larger nonce value until the golden nonce is found or nonce value reaches 4294967296 (can set to larger value with smaller target). If the block header hash is smaller than the target, the loop will be broken with a "Success!" message. The nonce that satisfies the condition is the golden nonce.

This is an example of trying different nonce values to see if we get a hash value that is smaller than the target given. Here, we start with a small nonce and try a bigger nonce every time the loop runs. Of course, it can be other methods to try out different nonce values, such as to randomly select a nonce number in a range or to start with a large number and try a smaller value in every round.

Once the target is met, miners can broadcast the new block they find to the network. If recognised, more miners will use this block as the latest block and calculate the hash value of the next block to mine another new block. Successful miners can collect the reward generated with the new block and the transaction fees via the transactions included in and confirmed with the block. This is the economic incentive for miners to keep the bitcoin network running.

References

Gordon, A. D. and Jeffrey, A. (2004). Types and effects for asymmetric cryptographic protocols. *Journal of Computer Security*, 12(3–4), 435–483.

MacKenzie, D. (2019). Pick a nonce and try a hash. *London Review of Books*, 41(8), 35–38.

Merkle, R. C. (1980). Protocols for public key cryptosystems. *In Proc. 1980 Symposium on Security and Privacy, IEEE Computer Society*, (pp. 122–133).

Nakamoto, S. (2019). Bitcoin: A peer-to-peer electronic cash system. *Manubot.*

Nguyen, G. T. and Kim, K. (2018). A survey about consensus algorithms used in blockchain. *Journal of Information Processing Systems*, 14(1), 101–128.

O'Dwyer, K. J. and Malone, D. (2014). Bitcoin mining and its energy footprint. Conference working paper.

Sobti, R. and Geetha, G. (2012). Cryptographic hash functions: A review. *International Journal of Computer Science Issues* (IJCSI), 9(2), 461.

Chapter 3

Consensus for Blockchain and Distributed Ledger Technologies

Ernie Teo*

3.1 Introduction

When a group arrive together at a decision and agree to support it, the group would have achieved consensus among its members. The decision is what is considered an acceptable resolution, a decision that the group can support even if it is not the preferred option of individuals in the group. A government election is one example of a group coming together to make such a decision.

Consensus is an important concept for blockchain networks and distributed ledgers as there is no central authority to provide the source of truth. The network members have to arrive at a conclusion about the state of the network by following some rules. These rules are the consensus algorithms programmed into the blockchain protocol. In Bitcoin, the consensus algorithm used is Proof of Work or Bitcoin mining. Nodes on the Bitcoin blockchain can choose which transactions to include into a block they are mining or validating. They can also choose to ignore transactions that are broadcasted to the network. When a block is mined, a majority of nodes on the

*Adjunct Senior Lecturer, National University of Singapore; Co Vice-Chairman, Blockchain Association Singapore, Singapore.

network agree on the state if they choose to mine on top of the previous block. Consensus is thus achieved when a block is accepted into the blockchain.

A good consensus protocol needs to maintain a consistent ledger. It should keep the network up to date, fix errors and ignore malicious nodes. In a blockchain network, it also needs to ensure that the transactions put on the ledger are valid. For consensus algorithms to achieve the objective to maintain a valid blockchain ledger, it needs to be able to do the following:

- If bad actors try to broadcast invalid transactions, they should be ignored by the good nodes and not included in the ledger.
- When bad nodes try to mine a block with invalid or fraudulent transactions, the majority of the network should agree not mine on top of it.

In Figure 3.1, suppose there are four nodes on the network and the correct action is to "Proceed". Node B has the wrong information "Wait" and Node D is maliciously trying to get the nodes to "Cancel". A good consensus algorithm needs to update Node B such that it chooses "Proceed" and successfully ignores Node D.

To achieve this, the blockchain nodes need to do the following:

- be able to keep track of historical transactions;
- authenticate and validate current broadcasted transactions;

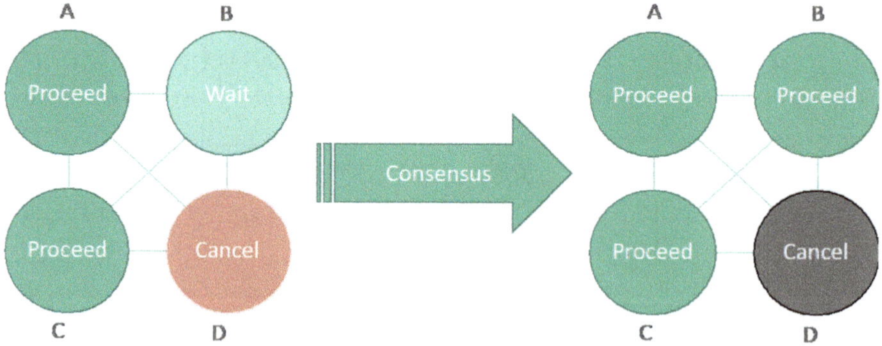

Figure 3.1: Example of a good consensus algorithm.

- reach an agreement on what goes in the ledger with the other nodes;
- receive appropriate incentives to "do the right thing".

Incentive is a key element for blockchain consensus for a public network. Since anyone can join the blockchain, the right type of reward needs to be in place such that the members would do what is required to get rewarded. The rewards need to be aligned with actions we want the members to take such that a goal of a consistent and correct network is achieved. This is also known as the network economics or mechanism design of the network.

Proof of Work (PoW) is not the only method to achieve consensus in a blockchain network. Since the inception of Bitcoin more than 10 years ago in 2008, several shortcomings were found in PoW. Bitcoin PoW incentivises miners to pool resources and compete in hardware, which causes centralisation on the network where there are only a few large miners controlling the network. PoW also consumes large amounts of electricity as a result and is not very environmentally friendly. These short comings were recognised early and there were many attempts to replace PoW as the industry evolved and matured. In this chapter, we will go through a survey of the types of consensus methods being used. First, we start with the concept of network fault tolerance in the next section.

3.2 Fault Tolerance

Fault tolerance is the ability of a system to operate in the event of failure of one or some of its components. There are two types of failures that can occur on a distributed network: network and node failures. A network fails when it loses connectivity fully or partially. In the event of partial loss in connectivity, segregated parts of the network should be able to continue operating and sync up again when the network is reconnected. The linear nature of blockchain networks does not allow this to happen and hard forks will result. Structures like Directed Acyclic Graph (DAG) address this and will be discussed in Section 3.3.3.

The other type of failure is node failure. A node can experience faults such as crashes, power outages, hardware problems or running out of memory. These are generally known as crash faults. In the event of a crash fault, the node should be able to rejoin the network and sync up after it recovers. There is another type of fault when a node acts maliciously to send conflicting messages to other nodes. This is known as a Byzantine failure. When a Byzantine failure has occurred, the system may respond in any unpredictable way, unless it is designed to have Byzantine fault tolerance. Byzantine faults include the following:

- omission failures (e.g., crash failures, failing to receive a request, or failing to send a response);
- commission failures (e.g., processing a request incorrectly, corrupting local state, and/or sending an incorrect or inconsistent response to a request).

Most blockchain consensus is designed to deal with Byzantine faults or at least crash faults. The term Byzantine fault comes from the Byzantine Generals Problem. It describes a situation where a network of actors needs to agree on a strategy where some of these actors are malicious. Several armies, each led by a general, are closing in on an enemy fortress from different directions. They have made camp and can observe the enemy from their point of view. The generals must decide whether to attack or retreat. The armies must all attack at the same time in order to succeed. The only way to communicate is to send messengers between the army camps. Some of the army generals are unreliable and could be traitors. Traitors can prevent a decision from being made by influencing decisions like attacking when most generals do not wish to attack or confusing some generals to the point that they are unable to make up their minds. To reach a consensus among the generals on the plan of action, a set of rules must be made. This set of rules needs to be Byzantine fault tolerant (or resistant to traitors) and the following conditions need to hold:

A. All loyal generals will decide upon the same plan of action.

    a. The loyal generals will all do what the set of rules says they should, but the traitors may do anything they wish.

b. The algorithm must guarantee condition A regardless of what the traitors do.

B. A small number of traitors cannot cause the loyal generals to adopt a bad plan.

Similarly, in a blockchain network, the consensus algorithm is the set of rules that the nodes (or "generals") have to follow:

A. All good nodes have to agree on the same plan of action (whether a transaction is valid).

a. All good nodes will follow the rules set by the consensus algorithm; check the ledger history to ensure that a transaction is valid before putting on the ledger. Bad nodes can do what they want such as work together to invalidate legitimate transactions or validate double-spent transactions (by invalidating the first transaction).
b. The consensus algorithm must guarantee A no matter what the bad nodes do.

B. As long as the number of bad nodes is small enough, the good nodes will not adopt an invalid transaction.

Lamport, Shostak and Pease (2019) suggest various solutions to the Byzantine Generals Problem. In the oral message version with one general acting as a leader, it is found that a solution will exist for the Byzantine Generals Problem when

$$n \geq 3m + 1,$$

where n is the number of generals in the system and m is the number of traitors (faults). In other words, the algorithm can ensure correct operation only if fewer than one-third of the processes are faulty. If unforgeability of messages is possible, higher fault tolerance is possible.

Patel (2020) explains that Byzantine fault tolerance on PoW networks is 50%, assuming zero network latency (messages can be sent around the network instantaneously). Under actual observed conditions, it is 46% for Ethereum and 49.5% for Bitcoin, but it goes down to 33% if network latency is equal to the block time and reduces to zero as network latency approaches infinity. Thus, under most conditions, a malicious actor needs to control around 50% of the network to successfully launch a Byzantine attack on a PoW network.

In general, there are two fundamental stages to a BFT system:

1. Agreement
2. Execution

The agreement stage is where the nodes agree on what should be done. Each consensus algorithm has its way for the majority of the nodes to reach an agreement. Once the outcome is agreed upon, it moves on to the execution stage and puts the outcome on the ledger.

3.3 Consensus Protocols Used in Blockchain and DLT

Other than PoW, there have been many consensus algorithms that were proposed and implemented onto live blockchain networks. Some of these variations are driven by the need to overcome the shortcomings with PoW by reducing the amount of energy consumed or improving the amount of decentralisation on the network. Others are proposed to overcome scalability issues that Bitcoin is experiencing, aiming to be able to process more transactions per second. Then, there are those that are specifically created for use in permissioned blockchain networks where nodes are considered trusted and there is less need for incentive mechanism to ensure behaviour. Figure 3.2 summarises the consensus algorithms we will cover in this chapter and their type.

3.3.1 *Consensus for Trustless Blockchains*

In trustless blockchains, none of the nodes are considered trusted. We need to rely on the consensus algorithm and the appropriate incentives like mining rewards to ensure that the network members behave in the right way. It is important that the incentives are aligned

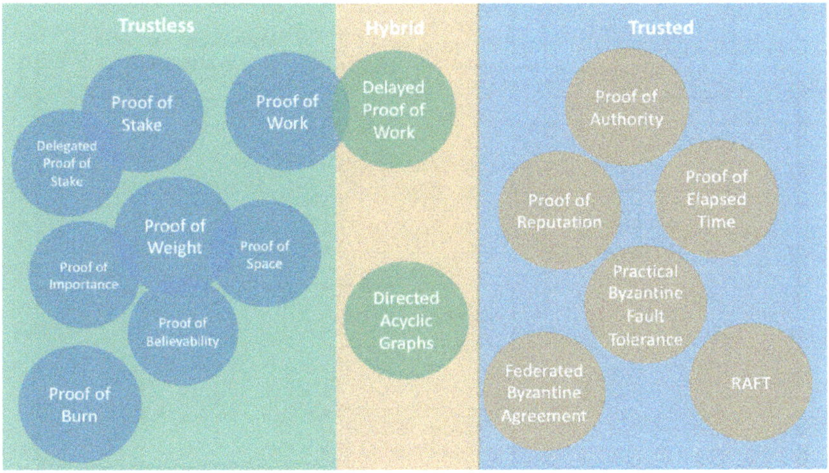

Figure 3.2: Categories of consensus for blockchain and DLT.

to encourage the appropriate actions. Some general guidelines to consider are as follows:

1. Doing the right thing gets rewarded.
2. Rewards from continuing to do the right thing should outweigh the potential net benefits from doing bad things — the costs of doing bad things should be high.

Proof of Work

Proof of Work is the grandparent of trustless consensus in a blockchain. PoW has been tried and tested since 2008 and is working well. Bitcoin, Ethereum, Litecoin and Dodgecoin are some of the cryptocurrency networks that have adopted PoW. Nodes on the network can create blocks in the ledger when they participate in PoW. PoW is competitive in nature as only one node can win the mining reward for each block. The steps in PoW are as follows and are described in Figure 3.3:

1. Receive new broadcasted transactions and check them against the ledger to ensure that they are legitimate (sender has signed the transaction and sender address has enough balance).

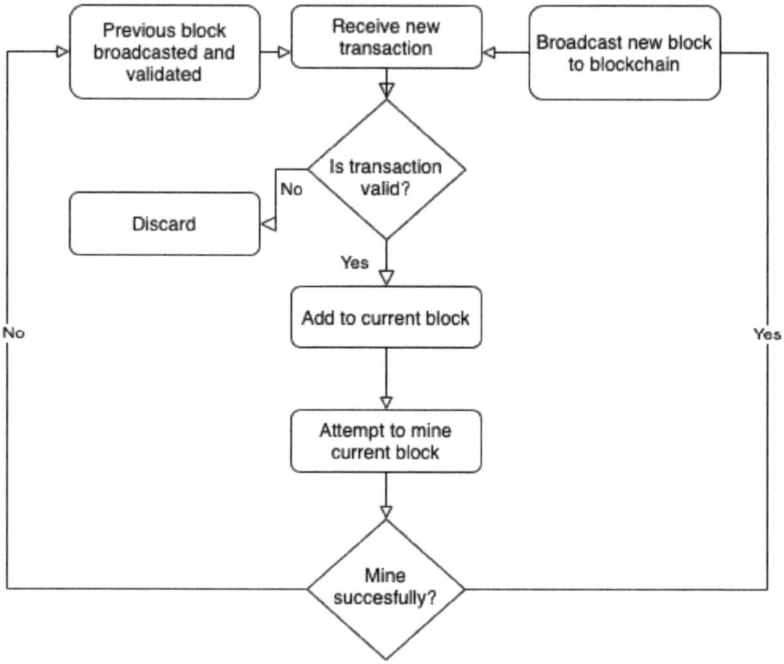

Figure 3.3: Steps in PoW consensus.

2. Discard the transaction if it is invalid.
3. Package legitimate transactions into the current block.
4. Attempt to mine the block.
5. If successful, broadcast the mined block to the network. Start again from Step 1 and mine on top of the block you just created.
6. If not successful (next block is broadcasted before yours), check that the new block broadcasted is valid, go back to Step 1 and mine on top of the new block.

The act of mining is to solve a cryptographic puzzle that requires computation power. The more computation power one has, the more permutations one can try per second and the higher the chance of mining the block. Competition in mining over the years has caused miners to amass large amounts of powerful hardware in order to increase their chances. This tends to favour the resource rich; one miner using a hundred dollars of resources to mine will have higher chances than a hundred miners with a dollar each. This is otherwise known as economies of scale. Mining is also not environmentally friendly and uses a lot of energy. As time is needed to solve the cryptographic puzzle, transactions are not immediate.

Proof of Stake

One of the first proposals as an alternative to address the issues with PoW is Proof of Stake (PoS). One needs to have a stake (or hold some coins) in the system to participate in PoS. In its simplest form, if you own 5% of the total stake, your chance of mining the next block is also 5%. In this way, not much computation (to solve a cryptography puzzle) is needed. PoS is more energy efficient than PoW. PoS is also competitive, only one staker can mine each block.

PoS is also not susceptible to economies of scale; a dollar is a dollar. The chances of mining the block are the same for someone with a hundred dollars' worth of coins and a hundred persons with a dollar each. Attacking a PoS is also more costly than PoW as you will lose your stake if the network detects that you are malicious. In PoW, you do not lose your coins or your mining hardware if you launch a malicious attack.

However, the main issue in PoS is the "nothing at stake" problem. In the event of a fork (where two miners create the next block at the same time), PoW miners have to choose the block they wish to mine on top of as their computing resources are limited. For a PoS miner, there is nothing to lose if they stake on both forks. When a fork occurs, the staker will have coins on both forks, allowing it to stake on both sides. This leads to no resolution on what is the correct chain (see Figure 3.4).

Different projects have made attempts at solving the "nothing at stake" problem. Peercoin[1] is one of the first cryptocurrencies to use PoS. It used checkpoints which prevent a reorganisation of the blockchain beyond the last known checkpoint. This was later made optional as the blockchain network reached a suitable level of

[1] https://docs.peercoin.net/#/proof-of-stake.

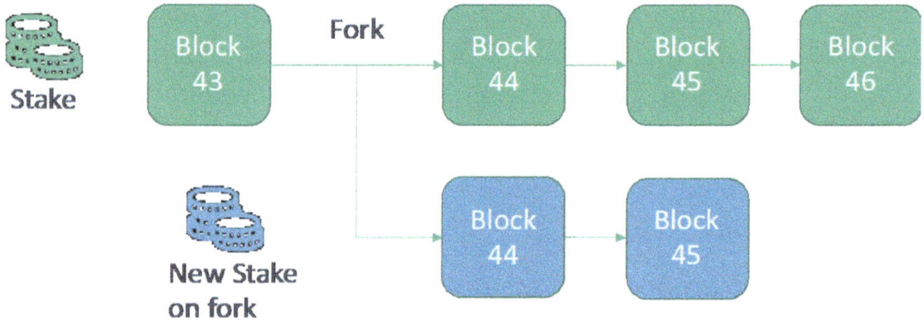

Figure 3.4: The "Nothing at Stake" problem in PoS.

distribution. In the Nxt[2] protocol, only reorganisation of the last 720 blocks is allowed. However, this only contains the problem but does not solve it. Ouroboros[3] is a PoS used by the Cardano blockchain; this method has been mathematically proven to be secure and uses an innovative method to randomly choose the block miner with a secure multiparty implementation of a coin-flipping protocol.

In Ethereum's proposal for switching to PoS, nodes can be "punished" if they stake on top of more than one blockchain branch. As of June 2020, Ethereum is underway to transition to Casper[4] (Ethereum's version of PoS) in two stages. Once implemented, one can become a validator (stake) on the Ethereum blockchain by staking 32 Ethers.

Delegated Proof of Stake

In Delegated Proof of Stake (DPoS), as the name implies, the staking is delegated. Owners of coins (or stake holders) can elect and choose leaders who will stake/vote on their behalf. Since there are fewer stakers to coordinate, this is faster than PoS.

EOS[5] utilises DPoS; 21 leaders (or witnesses) are elected at a time in EOS and there is a pool of standby nodes in case one of the existing

[2] https://nxtdocs.jelurida.com/Nxt_Whitepaper#Nxt.E2.80.99s_Proof_of_Stake_Model.
[3] https://www.cardano.org/en/ouroboros/.
[4] https://docs.ethhub.io/ethereum-roadmap/ethereum-2.0/proof-of-stake/.
[5] https://eos.io/.

witnesses drops out or turn outs to be malicious. The witnesses are paid a fee (that is set by the stake holders) for producing blocks. The 21 witnesses produce blocks one at a time in a round-robin fashion. Thus, a witness cannot produce consecutive blocks, making double-spending attacks by the witness impossible. A witness is skipped if it is unable to produce a block within the allocated time slot. Stake holders can vote out witnesses that continue to miss blocks or publish invalid transactions.

DPoS is collaborative instead of competitive as everyone has a turn. This method allows faster blocks and scales better than PoW or PoS. Other than EOS, Steemit, Bitshares and Lisk also use DPoS. However, this method is also more centralised than PoW and PoS. The control over the network falls mostly on the 21 witnesses. If a stake holder has sufficient coins, it can vote itself in to be a witness and control the entire network.

Proof of Weight

Proof of Weight refers to a large class of consensus algorithms where the chance of being chosen to validate or mine the next block is based on a weighted score. This class of consensus usually aims to make it more costly to lose the acquired weighted score, thus ensuring that validators continue to be good. Proof of Weight is generally energy efficient but incentive mechanism design is important, and it may be hard to ensure that incentives are aligned to the outcomes. Proof of Believability, Proof of Space and Proof of Importance are forms of Proof of Weight.

Proof of Believability

Proof of Believability is used by IOST[6] and utilises several factors to compose a believability score. With Proof of Believability (PoB), IOST aims to encourage decentralisation in the network. Central to this is the reputation-based sub-token system called Servi. Servi tokens serve as a measurement of a user's contribution to the network

[6]https://iost.io/.

and a way to encourage members to contribute to the development of the network. These non-tradable tokens are awarded to good actors within the ecosystem and factor heavily into the process of choosing the next validator. Servi tokens are non-tradable; only the awardee can use the tokens. Once it is used, the balance is cleared; thus, one cannot accumulate the tokens to gain more advantage. All nodes will have a fair chance at validating a block. Its creation and issuance are also embedded into the protocol; a user's account will be credited after certain contributions to the network.

PoB divides all validators into a believable group and a normal group. The believable group validate the transactions in the first phase and the normal group sample and verify transactions in the second phase. The chance to be elected into the believable group is determined by the believability score, which is calculated by multiple factors such as token balance, contributions to the community and reviews. Believable validators are formed into smaller groups (one validator per group) and transactions are randomly distributed to these groups for validation, thus improving the transaction speed.

This poses a security issue if the validator node is malicious. Thus, the normal group samples the transactions in order to detect inconsistencies. A malicious validator is also at risk of losing their believability (including all the tokens and reputation) if detected. The costs of being caught should outweigh the benefits of entering the bad transactions into the ledger. As a believable validator is unlikely to misbehave, the single validator approach for the transactions makes PoB very fast.

Proof of Space

Proof of Space (PoSpace) was first proposed by Dziembowski *et al.* (2015). Also called Proof of Capacity (PoC), it dedicates a certain amount of disk space in order to participate in validating a block. It is similar to PoW as the miner needs to provide a mathematical proof to demonstrate that the resources (computational power or disk space) have been committed. This is implemented through the use of hard-to-pebble graphs. The prover needs to build labelling of a hard-to-pebble graph and commit to the labelling. To verify the commitment, the prover has to open several random locations in the commitment. PoSpace is seen as fairer (disk space is general purpose compared to specialised mining machines) and greener (uses less electricity). PoSpace is also good for preventing spam and denial of service attacks. Burstcoin and Spacemint are projects that utilise PoSpace.

Proof of Importance

Proof of Importance (PoI) is the consensus algorithm adopted by NEM.[7] It pays out to members participating in PoI based on their importance which depends on various factors, such as notoriety (based on purpose-designed framework), balance and the number of transactions made to and from that position. This "importance" calculation aims to measure the "helpfulness" of a network member.

Similar to PoS, to be eligible to participate in PoI, a network member needs to have a minimum stake of coins (10,000 XEM). Importance is calculated using a specific algorithm and determines the chance one will win the PoI reward. It aims to be a fairer system where anyone who contributes to the network gets to be rewarded. Due to its construct, PoI is also resistant to arbitrary manipulation, Sybil and loop attacks.

Proof of Burn

In Proof of Burn, you "burn" your coins by sending them to an address where they are irretrievable. In exchange, you earn a privilege to mine on the system based on a random selection process. In most implementations, you "burn" cryptocurrency from an alternative chain such as Bitcoin. The more you burn, the higher the chance of being selected to mine the next block. Over time, this probability declines, so you will need to keep burning more coins to retain the same chance. Although the network itself does not exhaust much energy to run Proof of Burn, the cryptocurrencies required to be burnt also expand resources. This method also does not address the

[7] https://docs.nem.io/ja/gen-info/what-is-poi.

fairness issue; those with money to "burn" have higher chances of mining. Slimcoin and TGCoin (Third Generation Coin) uses Proof of Burn.

3.3.2 *Consensus for Trusted Blockchains*

In trusted blockchains, all nodes are known, and thus malicious acts can be identified. Since the nodes have been vetted before being allowed on the network, they are generally assumed to be trusted to validate transactions. Thus, consensus for trusted blockchains is focused on preventing crash faults rather than Byzantine faults in general.

Proof of Authority

In Proof of Authority (PoA), validation is done by approved accounts called validators. The validators validate the transactions and blocks that are recorded on the blockchain. Validators run software that automates this process and need not constantly monitor their computers. However, the validators do need to ensure that their computers are not compromised or attacked. The general conditions to approve a node as a validator are as follows:

1. It must be a verified identity that links the node to real world identity. Ideally, this identity can be cross-checked on a publicly available domain. Identity must be formally verified on-chain, with a possibility to cross-check the information in a publicly available domain.
2. It must be difficult to become a validator. This ensures that the right to validate transactions is valuable to the validator. The validator should view this value highly, such that it would not risk losing validator status by acting maliciously. An example is requiring a node to be an authorised notary in order to be a validator.
3. There must be complete uniformity in the checks and procedures for establishing an authority.

By attaching a reputation to identity, validators are incentivised to uphold the transaction process, as they do not wish to have their identities attached to a negative reputation, thus losing the hard-earned validator role. This method is centralised as there needs to be an authority that vets and admits validator nodes. Thus, it is usually used in private and permissioned blockchains. PoA is much faster than PoW as no computation is required. It is used by VeChain, POA Network and the Ethereum testnets Kovan and Rinkeby.

Proof of Reputation

Proof of Reputation (PoR) is similar to PoA; it depends on the reputation of the participants to keep the network secure. A validator risks financial or brand consequences if they attempt to be malicious. Thus, the validator also needs to have a reputation important enough such that the consequences are costly. To be admitted into the network, a potential validator needs to pass verification and prove their reputation. Existing validators may vote on the eligibility of the new entrant or a weighted matrix may be used to decide. Other than the method of choosing the validator, PoR operates like PoA once the validators are admitted into the network. Due to its similar nature to PoA, PoR is also more suitable for trusted and permissioned blockchains. GoChain[8] uses Proof of Reputation.

Proof of Elapsed Time

Proof of Elapsed Time (PoET) was invented in early 2016 by Intel. It is used in permissioned blockchains to decide who gets to mine the next block. It is based on the principle of a fair lottery system where every node is as likely to be the winner. It relies in specialised hardware and this cannot be adopted universally by a public network.

PoET algorithm works as follows:

- Each participating node is randomly assigned a period of time to wait and goes to sleep for the specified period.

---

[8]https://gochain.io/proof-of-reputation/.

- The first node to wake up (with the shortest waiting time) gets to mine the next block and commit it to the blockchain network.
- The same process repeats for the next block.

The PoET network consensus mechanism needs to ensure two important factors:

- First, participating nodes must be given a waiting time that is indeed random and not a shorter duration chosen purposely by the participants in order to win.
- Second, the winner must complete the waiting time.

To achieve this, Intel utilises their SGX technology to execute trusted code in a protected environment. This prevents any attempt to alter the code and also ensures that the results are verifiable by external parties. PoET is used by the Hyperledger Sawtooth project which is led by Intel.

Practical Byzantine Fault Tolerance

Practical Byzantine Fault Tolerance (PBFT) was one of the first solutions proposed for the Byzantine Generals Problem. There is a leader node in a PBFT system, and all other nodes are backup nodes. Every node will communicate with each other to come to agreement on the state of the system using majority voting. For PBFT to work, the number of malicious nodes cannot exceed one-third of the system. There are four phases in a round of PBFT consensus:

- A request to add a transaction to the network is sent to the leader node.
- The leader node broadcasts this to all the other nodes.
- Each node executes the request and sends a reply to the requestor.
- The requestor waits for $n+1$ does returning the same result, where n is the maximum allowable number of malicious nodes.

The leader node is alternated and can be changed if certain amount of time has lapsed or the other nodes determine that the leader node is faulty. PBFT is usually only used in permissioned networks as there is no incentive mechanism to prevent untrusted malicious nodes from joining the network and making up the majority. The benefit of PBFT is that it is fast and scalable. It is used in Hyperledger Fabric V0.6 and Zilliqa (Zilliqa, 2017).

Federated Byzantine Agreement

Federated Byzantine Agreement (FBA) is another class of solutions to the Byzantine Generals Problem used by currencies like Stellar and Ripple. Nodes are known and verified ahead of time. The nodes choose who they trust, and eventually quorums of nodes emerge from decisions made by the individual nodes making up the FBA network. A quorum is the minimum number of nodes required for a solution to be correct. After a quorum forms, the block is validated and included on the blockchain. FBA uses "quorum slices", which are subsets of quorums that can convince specific nodes operating on the network to agree with them. In Ripple's FBA, transactions are grouped into sets and are validated in four rounds starting with 50% agreement and working up to 80% quorum in the fourth round. This ensures that the transactions are not double spend.

RAFT

RAFT[9] is named after Reliable, Replicated, Redundant, and Fault-Tolerant. RAFT is not Byzantine fault tolerant and is usually used in permissioned networks. It is a way to ensure each node in the network agrees upon the same transactions. It arrives at consensus via an elected leader. Nodes in a RAFT network can be leader or a follower. A follower can also be a candidate in the case that the leader becomes unavailable. The leader replicates the ledger to the followers. The followers know that the leader exists from a heartbeat message sent by the leader. If no heartbeat is received in a stipulated amount of time, the follower switches to a candidate and initiates a leader election. RAFT is used in Quorum and in later versions of Hyperledger Fabric.

---

[9] http://thesecretlivesofdata.com/raft/.

3.3.3 *Hybrid Blockchain Networks*

Delayed Proof of Work

Delayed Proof of Work (dPoW) is a hybrid consensus method. It utilises a secondary blockchain's hashing power to provide additional security for the primary blockchain. The primary blockchain can be either a public or a permissioned blockchain.

Komodo[10] makes use of dPoW by attaching itself to the Bitcoin blockchain. A group of notary nodes add data from the primary blockchain to the secondary blockchain. Komodo allows for either PoS or PoW to be run on the primary blockchain and only works for PoW secondary blockchains. To tamper with a transaction on the primary blockchain, one must also change the data on the secondary blockchain. Thus, Komodo can rely on the security of the larger Bitcoin blockchain to keep its data immutable.

There are two types of nodes within the Komodo dPoW system, notary nodes and normal nodes. Sixty four notary nodes notarise and add confirmed blocks from the primary dPoW blockchain to the attached secondary blockchain. Notary nodes are elected by dPoW blockchain stakeholders. The notarisation process requires a majority (33 nodes) to sign the transaction. Notary nodes do this in a round-robin fashion, reducing the competition for rewards. Normal nodes partake in the usual consensus on the primary blockchain such as PoS or PoW. If the secondary blockchain network goes down, the primary network can go on as usual without the additional security of the attached blockchain.

This concept of piggybacking on a stronger network allows for increased security without high-energy usage. It also allows for chains of blockchain to be formed, for example another blockchain network can attach itself to Komodo which is attached to Bitcoin. This allows the Bitcoin blockchain to value add to other dPoS blockchains. It also

[10] https://komodoplatform.com/security-delayed-proof-of-work-dpow/.

creates incentives for other networks to support larger networks like Bitcoin without being entirely reliant on its functionality.

Directed Acyclic Graphs

Directed Acyclic Graphs (DAGs) are generalised forms of blockchain and can be applied to both trusted and trustless networks. The DAG structure allows transactions to be added in a parallel fashion, making it highly scalable; see Figure 3.5 for an example. In most blockchain systems we have looked at with a linear structure, blocks are added one by one to the blockchain. This makes blockchains inherently slow. In DAGs, each block or transaction confirms a number of previous blocks. Although deemed be the next-generation blockchain structure, one of the main issues of DAGs is that smart contracts are usually implemented via oracles and not be directly deployed on chain.

There are a number of variations which depend on the algorithm for choosing which previous blocks to verify, the ordering of transactions and how transaction finality is reached. We introduce three such algorithms below. Other consensus using DAG structure includes Holochain, Block-Lattice, ByteBall and Mokka.

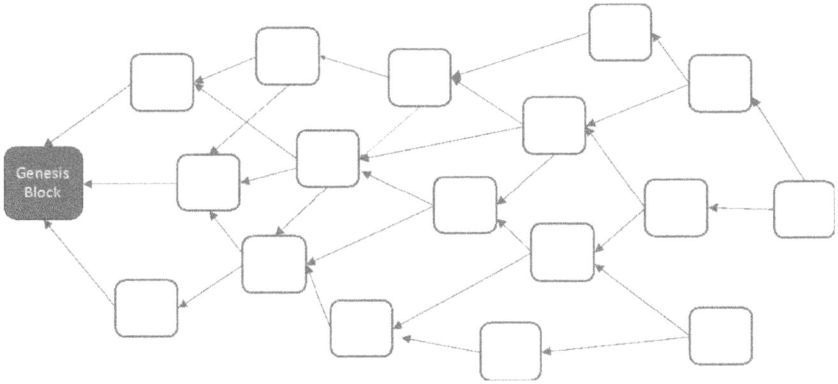

Figure 3.5: Example of directed acyclic graph network.
Note: Arrows are pointing from parent to child.

Tangle

Tangle[11] is the DAG consensus algorithm used by IOTA.[12] Tangle adopts a pay-it-forward type of consensus. In order to send a transaction, one needs to validate two previous transactions. As more transactions are added to the network, the validity of the transactions is strengthened. Technically, if one has the ability to generate one-third of the transactions on the network, it would be able to convince the rest of the network that its invalid transactions are valid. Thus, transaction volume needs to be large enough for it to be infeasible to do so. IOTA has implemented a centralised node called "The Coordinator" to double check all of the network's transactions and will remove it once the network is large enough.

Hashgraph

Hashgraph is a gossip protocol consensus developed by Baird (2016). Known transactions are shared with other nodes at random such that all transactions are eventually gossiped to every node. Hedera Hashgraph[13] is a public blockchain network that combines the hashgraph gossip protocol with a Proof-of-Stake consensus and promises a transaction rate of 10,000 transactions per second. Hashgraph consensus protocol has also been implemented in permissioned distributed ledgers.

SPECTRE

Serialisation of Proof-of-work Events: Confirming Transactions via Recursive Elections or SPECTRE (Zohar, 2016) is a proposal to scale Bitcoin that combines PoW and DAGs. Each block mined in SPECTRE points to multiple parents such that the network can support multiple blocks at the same time. SPECTRE is not implemented yet in reality, but can be an interesting solution to scaling cryptocurrency networks.

---

[11] https://blog.iota.org/the-tangle-an-illustrated-introduction-4d5eae6fe8d4.
[12] https://www.iota.org/.
[13] https://www.hedera.com/.

3.4 Conclusion

Consensus algorithms are an important part of ensuring consistency and accuracy on a blockchain or distributed ledger. Developing an understanding of how the types of consensus algorithms work would give us an appreciation of blockchain-based applications, assets and investments, and allow us to make informed decisions. Ultimately, the choice of consensus depends on what the network implementer wants to achieve. It could be for a decentralised public system which needs to be self-governing or an enterprise consortium blockchain which needs to handle sensitive transactions.

The area of consensus algorithms is still evolving as we learn more about how network participants react to different incentives (especially for cryptocurrencies). With a variety of use cases emerging for blockchain, we would expect as much variety in the type of consensus used. With the multitude of blockchain solutions, any blockchain network may also be required to communicate with several others; interoperability will become a key consideration.

References

Baird, L. (2016). The swirlds hashgraph consensus algorithm: Fair, fast, byzantine fault tolerance. Swirlds, Inc. Technical Report SWIRLDS-TR-2016, 1.

Dziembowski, S., Faust, S., Kolmogorov, V., and Pietrzak, K. (2015). Proofs of space. In Annual Cryptology Conference (pp. 585–605). Springer, Berlin, Heidelberg.

Lamport, L., Shostak, R., and Pease, M. (2019). The Byzantine generals problem. In Concurrency: The Works of Leslie Lamport (pp. 203–226).

Patel, R. (2020). Byzantine Fault Tolerance (BFT) and its significance in Blockchain world. HCLTech. Retrieved from https://www.hcltech.com/blogs/byzantine-fault-tolerance-bft-and-its-significance-blockchain-world#:~:text=Byzantine%20fault%20tolerance%20is%2050,as%20network%20latency%20approaches%20infinity.

Zilliqa (2017). The Zilliqa Design Story Piece by Piece: Part 2 (Consensus Protocol). Retrieved from https://blog.zilliqa.com/the-zilliqa-design-story-piece-by-piece-part-2-consensus-protocol-e38f6bf566e3.

Zohar, A. (2016). SPECTRE: Serialization of Proof-of-Work Events, Confirming Transactions via Recursive Elections. Retrieved from https://medium.com/@avivzohar/the-spectre-protocol-7dbbebb707b5.

Chapter 4

Token Economics and Valuation

4.1 Introduction

DeFi, or Decentralised Finance, has been viewed as the future of finance. Bitcoin and the underlying blockchain technology have made a decentralised, distributed and open system feasible. Bitcoin protocol, the very first form of crypto-token network with mass adoption, has provided a potential solution to the lack of trust problem in the traditional and centralised business world. The token economy is an alternative to the centralised third-party trust economy. The underlying financial instruments that drive the decentralised token economy are crypto-tokens. What exactly is a crypto-token, and what drives the value of these crypto-tokens?

Digital assets, currencies or tokens that use cryptography technology are called crypto-tokens. Cryptocurrency is a form of crypto-token that possesses the monetary circulation property and value measurement function. They can be used as a payment tool, just like a currency. Other crypto-tokens without such features are called non-currencies or non-payment tokens. A crypto-token is not only a digitised representation of an object but it is also a cryptography-generated trust carrier formed with consensus by a group of participants in the peer-to-peer network. Goods and services, time and anything of value can be tokenised. The tokenised objects or tokens can be easily traded, and the value increases with the ability to exchange for other objects with value.

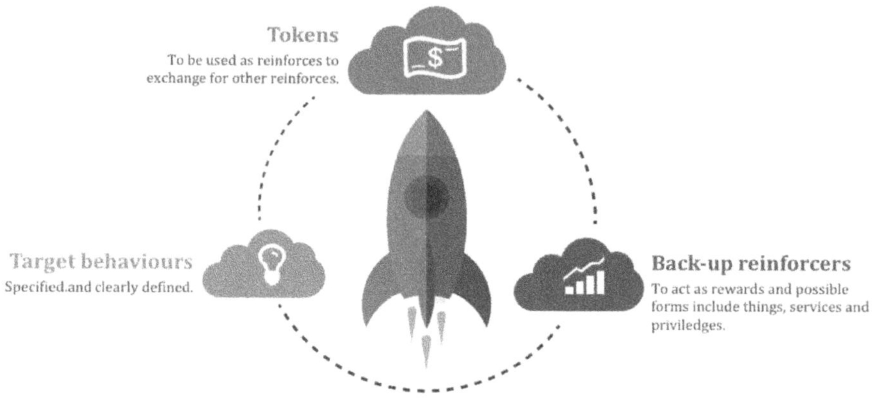

Figure 4.1: Key elements of a successful token economy.

Token economy refers to an innovative decentralised network and system incentivised by the use of crypto-tokens. It was made possible with the emergence of technology such as blockchain, big data, AI, cloud and IoT. Tokens earned are used to exchange for goods or services or certain rights and entitlements. Token economics has to do with the study of human and system behaviour that reinforces good behaviour and reduces bad behaviour so that people will pursue more good behaviour and avoid undesirable behaviour autonomously — in a peer-to-peer decentralised system.

For a token economy to be effective, three elements are necessary: tokens to be used as reinforcers to exchange for other reinforcers, back-up reinforcers that act as rewards and specified target behaviours[1] (see Figure 4.1). In particular, a token is digital or virtual. It may have no intrinsic value on its own and when it is independent of the network or ecosystem. But, once it can be exchanged for other material reinforcers, services or privileges (various forms of back-up reinforcers that act as rewards), the value is released and can be realised. So, the tokens earned when people exhibit good behaviours can have a positive effect in encouraging good behaviours within the network. And as an ecosystem, the

[1]https://en.wikipedia.org/wiki/Token_economy.

- Token economics is a new subject to guide the exploitation of technology after the intersection of blockchain technology, economic theory, and cryptographic algorithms
- Token economics is a new branch of the economy that explains the structure of a particular ecosystem in the blockchain sphere
- Token economy considers the creation and distribution of the value, the consumption, and the circulation

Figure 4.2: Token economics introduction.

alignment of interest further enhances the value of those tokens through the network effect of crowdsourcing resources, wisdom, contribution and momentum. The social scalability impact of a trust-distributed interest-aligned network of incentivised agents driven by tokens, and their value, increases as rewards to form a consensus that fuels further growth.

The success of a token economy rests heavily on the design thinking behind the token economy. The signalling of targeted behaviour needs to be specific and the reward needs to be transparent and clearly defined. Clear and transparent rules of (i) what to do to earn a token; (ii) how many tokens are earned; or (iii) how to redeem rewards (or back-up reinforcers) also should be specified beyond doubt[2] for a token economy to function as intended.

Figure 4.2 gives one definition of token economics. Token economy is the result of further advancement of a token based on blockchain technology (Xu, 2019). Token can be a symbol of value or right. As the symbol of value, the token is the core of the entire economic model, while the token economy considers the creation and distribution of the value, the consumption and the circulation. As a symbol of right, a token represents a kind of incentive, while the token economy considers what type of organisation is suitable, how to create a compelling economics model to embrace partners, suppliers or even competitors and contribute to the whole ecosystem, and what the changes to the governance model are.

[2]https://www.wisegeek.com/what-is-a-token-economy.htm.

The logic underlying token economy is entirely different from that of current tech giants. For Amazon, Google and Facebook, the main operational logic is driven by user traffic and precision of matching with big data. We will discuss the details of several relevant types of economics in the following section.

4.2 Comparison of Token Economy and Others

The prevalence of emerging technologies and digitalisation has witnessed many other new terms such as the (i) digital economy; (ii) Internet economy; (iii) web economy; and (iv) sharing economy. How are they different from the token economy? Let us focus on the digital and sharing economies.

As summarised in the Figure 4.3, the digital economy is playing an increasingly important role in the business world, and people are getting familiar with it. This probably resulted from substantial development that has been made over the past few decades in all three main components of the digital economy as identified by Mesenbourg (2001): (i) e-business infrastructure including the

It refers to an economy that relies much on digital technologies where Internet also plays an important role in conducting businesses (a.k.a. the Internet Economy, Web Economy, or New Economy). Its dependence on data brings lots of opportunities to businesses, but raises issues like data security at the same time.

It depends on the streamlined logistics processes to deliver products, and digitizes transactions (including products, service information and payment methods, etc.) to fully manage transactions by online platforms.

It allows merchants and customers to communicate online, which does not have high requirements for on-site locations. Such light-asset based business model will improve merchants' operating capabilities and make them more cost-effective.

Figure 4.3: Digital economy.

network, human capital, hardware and software; (ii) e-business that refers to how businesses are conducted online; and (iii) e-commerce. In fact, in this era of digitalisation, the differences between the traditional economy and the digital economy are getting unclear as many businesses will inevitably involve the usage of the network.

In addition to the digital economy, the term "sharing economy" is becoming popular, especially with the thriving of companies such as Uber and Airbnb that offer transportation and accommodation solutions by utilising the unused part by sharing. It refers to the economic model where businesses and transactions are conducted in a peer-to-peer way (see Figure 4.4). Such operations include the activity of acquiring, providing or sharing access to goods and services.

However, over recent years, many argue that sharing economy businesses are not so open and inclusive as the name may suggest due to the centralised nature. For example, companies like Uber and Airbnb, although not service providers themselves, control all the transaction and feedback data of all uses, including both the

It is an economic model that utilises peer-to-peer (P2P) transactions based on the Internet. It offers an alternative to traditional business models where business activities start from organisations and the employees hired. In a sharing economy, each individual can be the service provider.

The transactions can either be facilitated by a community-based online platform or a commercial business. The former does not collect any income or profits while the latter gets rewards by providing the resources needed such as an App or online platform.

The Sharing Economy platform acts as a trust authority and allows the traders to make P2P transactions, including B2C, C2C or B2B. As the name suggests, another important feature of Sharing Economy is that it asks the users to share unused values, which can be recycled or reused (e.g. Uber and Airbnb).

Figure 4.4: Sharing economy.

buyers (passengers and guests) and service providers (drivers and hosts). Furthermore, these companies remain in charge of what data to display and make available on the site. The users do not have any decision power over that data, as long as they continue to use the platforms, which will make users dependent on the intermediary and limit both options and profits for users (Trinh, 2018).

Fortunately, the invention of Bitcoin and blockchain technology brings the inspiration of exchange of value in a decentralised manner, solving many of the pain points. Many of the issues in the sharing economy do not exist for the token economy. The idea of decentralisation is achievable, and users can control what to share and what not to share without the need for a third party acting as the intermediary or central authority to validate the peer-to-peer transactions. The similarities and differences between digital economy, sharing economy and token economy are shown in the Figure 4.5 (Liu, 2019).

	Digital economy	**Sharing economy**	**Token economy**
Processed information	Digitalised	Digitalised	Digitalised
Platform	Centralised	Centralised	Decentralised
Business model	B2P2C	C2P2C	P2P
Trusted authority	Yes	Yes	No
Information transparency	No	Some	Yes
Verification cost	Some	Some	Very low
Manual operation	Some	Some	Streamlined

Figure 4.5: Comparison between different economies.

4.3 Tokens and Design Thinking

A crucial component of token economics, just as the name suggested, is token. Token economics aims to address various problems related to tokens, such as its issuance, supply, demand, validation, usage, behaviour and how these matters affect other things in the ecosystem. It studies both broader topics such as the entire ecosystem and the functions and more specific issues such as the technical parameters and individuals. In general, digital tokens would have the functions as shown in Figure 4.6.

When designing a token economy, functions of the tokens need to be thought about thoroughly so that the ecosystem can function seamlessly and can sustain. In a successful token economy, well-developed tokens have the features as shown in Figure 4.7.

Besides the roles of the tokens, the future trend of the token and token values is essential for sustainability. If the tokens have limited use cases, such as (i) unable to be traded freely or in a short period, (ii) susceptible to inflation (issuing too much or too fast), (iii) do not have long-term worth or (iv) unable to meet the legal and technical expectations, users will not be motivated to earn and use tokens, thus making the whole ecosystem unreliable.

The price volatility and stabilisation mechanism of a token are also important matters for any economies, so designers need to

Type	Detail
Transactional	Transactional tokens provide a form of payment
Utility	Utility tokens facilitate transactions, and sometimes mean the ability to use the platform itself
Operation	Token is a determinant of important decisions related to operations in the ecosystem
Profit	Token holders get a portion of revenues or profits, like shares of a company in some sense
Asset-backed	Asset-backed tokens are linked to real-world or virtual assets such as gold, fiat currency or property

Figure 4.6: Functions of digital tokens.
Source: Lee and Teo (2020), Smith + Crown, and authors.

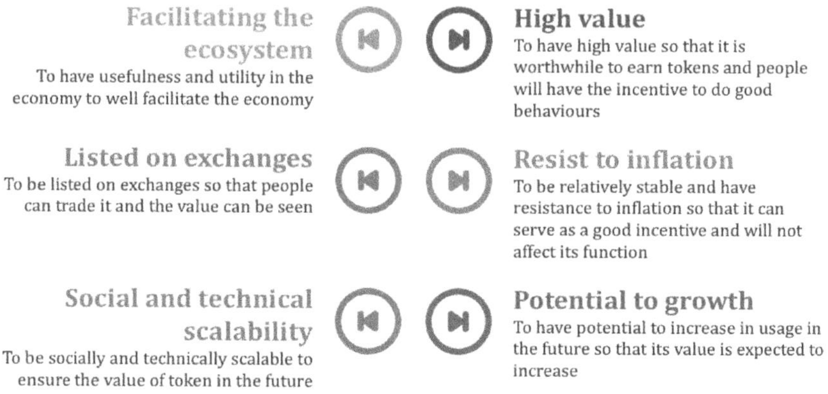

Figure 4.7: Features of tokens.
Source: Hlebiv (2018) and authors.

adopt appropriate monetary policies and have a clear identification of the token's role. In a decentralised economy, we need a consensus algorithm to determine how new tokens are created. An increase in the token supply will cause inflation or the price to decrease. Different measures are used to prevent such occurrences. For example, many cryptocurrencies, bitcoin included, set a limit supply of tokens (21 million for bitcoin). The maximum number of tokens that can ever be created in the ecosystem is fixed a priori to prevent "overprinting" or "inflation".

Token economics is more than just creating the tokens. But, to create an entire ecosystem, the designers need to plan for the future and ensure users are motivated to utilise the platform, with the aid of tokens.

First of all, network effects should be considered. The term refers to the phenomenon that is common in economics and business that growth in the number of users will increase the value of the goods or services. So, in a well-designed token economy, due to its open, peer-to-peer and decentralised nature, users should benefit from the network effects so that the value of the products, services or the platforms can contribute to further growth with more people participating in the ecosystem. Figure 4.8 describes the two types of network effects and two strategies to increase the network effects.

Figure 4.8: Types of network effects.
Source: Tönnissen, Beinke and Teuteberg (2020) and authors.

Figure 4.9: Key elements of token economics.

Careful planning of the tokens used in the system is crucial. Things that may affect the token's value, such as the purpose, the supply and demand, and distribution, have significant impacts on the economy (see Figure 4.9). Developers should design the tokens in such a way that the tokens are worth holding in the foreseeable future and people value it not only for speculative reasons but also for the utilities or benefits in the network or system.

Given the various types and functions of a token, we summarise them into two types of token economy architecture: dual and simple. The former uses two tokens of the same type or the different types, and the latter uses only one token. Although a simple architecture can be successful and have various use cases, there are concerns. In the case of a single token, if people use it to exchange goods or services in the platform or pay the transaction fees so that they can access the platform, the value of the tokens will increase. On one hand, it is desirable for the ecosystem because people would have the incentive to join the network, own the tokens and pursue good behaviours. On the other hand, some token holders, such as investors and speculators who buy or earn the token, not for its utility or function but the potential price increase, may sell the tokens in exchange for profits. This speculative behaviour will cause the price of tokens to drop, thus increasing the price volatility and destabilising the financial utility of the token economy.

Therefore, the dual architecture offers a solution to the problem where two tokens with different roles are introduced in the network. This is to segregate the tokens into different functions and mitigate the effect on the value of tokens. Under this scheme, two tokens are performing different tasks. One example is the payment/utility token that acts as a transaction fee to facilitate transactions and gain platform access or resembles "currencies" that can be exchanged for goods or services. Another token may function like security for the store of value or collateral that can be exchanged with other tokens (Brouwer, 2018). There is no reason to stop at two, and design thinking is the key to solving whatever problems at hand. In the end, the final design must address the pain points to have value acting for payment, utility, security or other functions.

Figure 4.10 shows the main factors to consider when making architecture decisions.

Successful token economics should incentivise not only desirable behaviour but also be able to stabilise the network operation. In contrast, inappropriate token economics may lead to a death spiral if there is a perceived loss of value in the token economy. The following shows both good and bad examples of token economics.

4.3.1 *Good and Bad Examples*

Let us start with the very first decentralised cryptocurrency that still dominates the market today — Bitcoin. It is proven to be

Architecture: Dual or Simple?

Figure 4.10: Key factors affecting the architecture of token economy.
Source: Hlebiv (2018).

a secure and thriving ecosystem that solves the double-spending problem while incentivising nodes to participate in the network without the need for a third party to validate the transactions. Instead, transaction verification is done by nodes. Miners validate transactions following the consensus protocol, and get rewards for the work — the reward of a new block generated plus the transaction fees (all paid in the token, bitcoin). Consequently, more miners will join the network for the return, which makes the network more secure and transactions faster.

Some nodes have more duties, such as miners who validate the transactions and mine new blocks; some participate in the network with lighter duties, such as users that just use bitcoins for transaction purposes. As a result of increasing miners and the associated lower costs, faster transactions and higher security in the network, the ecosystem will attract more and more users with light duties, and more people will value the Bitcoin network and its token, bitcoin. Therefore, the design makes it a win–win–win strategy for all parties: miners get a reward, investors obtain investment returns and developers achieve fame. The network becomes safer and more efficient, while the value of tokens increases. So, there is no conflict of interest among these stakeholders and users, which is a crucial factor that ensures steady growth of the token's value.

The consensus protocol and algorithm in practice involve complicated designs, and there are many additional measures taken to ensure the efficiency of the Bitcoin network. We will not go into too much detail, but we hope to give a good sense of the issues in designing a good token economy. These issues determine success and sustainability. A holistic approach is crucial before any new launch because faulty design leads to undesirable results when implemented. FCoin is one of the most well-known examples of bad token design.

FCoin, a cryptocurrency exchange, was launched in May 2018 and reached a peak daily trading volume of over 10 billion in the following month. Its value was much higher than any of the cryptocurrency exchanges at that time. However, soon after the surge, the trading volume dropped sharply. The exchange eventually went into default in early 2020 with all the unissued FT tokens and those held by the team destroyed and burnt, leaving millions' worth of bitcoins unpaid to its users (Wan, 2020).

The main reason for the failure appears to be the fundamental flaws in its token economics design. "Trans-Fee Mining" is a new model that paid out 80% of the platform's revenue. Trading fees paid by traders and collected by FCoin were distributed to FT holders as dividends (He, 2018). The reward served as a great incentive and seemed appealing at first. But, the value of the coin depended mainly on the trading volume and paying dividends naturally led to a price drop, which in return triggered selling activities of the tokens. The speed of cashing out signified that the token would be losing value and unleashed a vicious cycle. New FT tokens were being mined when these transactions took place, causing the price of the tokens to drop further (consider the supply-and-demand relationship). The value of the token was not inflation proof and lacked price appreciation potential.

A positive correlation between the good business volume of the exchange and the supply of new coins is a bad design in this case with no cap. The unlimited supply of new coins as a reward rapidly increases when business is good. This new supply, in turn, increases the selling volume with no corresponding increase in demand from expectations of price appreciation. Once the selling pressure accumulates, the lower price expectations trigger an even higher selling volume. This volume creates even more supply of new coins and, therefore, more selling pressure. The end story is written even before the launch of the coins. Design fault is a significant reason why many ICOs failed. What makes good token economics? It has to be good design thinking that increases the value of the coin over time. The right question is as follows — what designs lead to good valuation? The answer cannot be explained entirely by traditional valuation methods.

4.4 Token Valuation

4.4.1 *Conventional Valuation Methods*

The following are some of the most commonly used conventional valuation methods for stocks and companies.

a. Discounted cash flow model (DCF)

The discounted cash flow valuation is to assume that the present value of the company can be calculated as the sum of all the future cash flows. In formula, it will be as follows:

$$\text{Value of firm} = \sum_{t=1}^{t=n} \frac{CF_t}{(1+WACC)^t}$$

where n is the life of the asset, CF_t is the cash flow in period t and WACC represents the discount rate used in the model, which is the firm's weighted average cost of capital. This idea can be used for token valuation if the income flow is in another liquid token (e.g., bitcoin or ether) rather than in fiat currencies. However, we can see that if the design leads to a higher token income stream, it does not necessarily mean that the valuation will be higher. The value of FCoin measured in bitcoin or fiat may drop.

b. Dividend discount model (DDM)

While DCF uses future cash flow to estimate the value of a company, the future dividend is used in DDM. So, the value of a company's stocks is assumed to be the present value of the sum of all future dividends paid to its shareholders. Again, FCoin points out the shortcoming of applying this to token valuation.

c. Relative valuation methods

Individual financial ratios are commonly used methods but mostly used for comparison. In relative valuation methods, the value of a company is determined by comparing it to similar or peer companies. The most commonly used ratios include P/E (Price-to-Earnings) and P/B (Price-to-Book). The value of a firm can then be calculated using earnings (book value) multiplied by its peer companies' or industry average P/E (P/B) ratio, which is deemed as a more accurate representation of the firm's profits and value. This market comparison method may be used as one that can compare a token with another. However, as in stocks and shares, these comparative or ranking measures are a function of the entire crypto market. If one is in the crypto world and one is willing to ignore the fiat market, then the method makes sense. That also means that crypto is an alternative class of currencies. If cryptocurrencies or tokens are used frequently for exchange of value, then this method will make some sense. If we think far enough and hold the belief that we are heading towards a barter trade token economics, then it all makes sense. If the token economy has some impact and accounts for a 10–20% of the global economy, these individual financial ratios and comparative valuation methods may make some sense.

However, almost all these popular conventional valuation methods are not applicable to value cryptocurrencies or blockchain startups at this moment. Many of them do not generate predictable future cash flows (most of them do not generate any cash flows or positive earnings at all as they are still at a very early stage of development), nor do they have any accounting data (or at least accounting data are not publicly available for these fintech startups). The lack of underlying assets of cryptocurrencies makes the valuation even more difficult. We need to remind ourselves that we are closer to valuing intellectual property and patents than a legal entity such as security, bond or real estate. Even though it is a piece of software with a business model without a legal entity, it is more than an IP or patent. There is this network effect and the underlying philosophy of tokenised collaborative cooperatives in an autonomous sense. A token is a trusted carrier formed by consensus with little barrier for others to join the network to add more value. The emphasis on strategic importance may be an essential dimension to ponder, and therefore it is worthwhile to focus on strategic valuation.

4.4.2 *Valuation for Cryptocurrencies*

The characteristics of crypto-tokens and the token ecosystem should be considered to analyse the value of a token or a fintech startup. The value of a token and its function in the entire ecosystem play important roles in the value of cryptocurrencies (Cong *et al.*, 2020).

Three main components to value fintech companies are shown in Figure 4.11 (Jain, 2019). The value of a fintech business depends on (i) the nature of the problem that it solves, which will affect the demand of the company's products or services; (ii) the potential increase of scale (for example, people from all around the world can buy and hold the cryptocurrencies or tokens); and (iii) the lower cost (e.g., decentralised network). These unique factors of fintech startups call for new valuation methods.

Figure 4.12 summarises the following potentially feasible methods for fintech startups. Relative methods do not work, but the more flexible scorecard method may be applied using customised parameters to compare the company with its peer or a benchmark company. Other approaches to assess companies at a relatively early stage include the Berkus method, a quick and easy way to evaluate

- The nature of the **problem that it solves** (something that wasn't possible earlier purely due to a breakthrough in technology).
- The ability to **rapidly scale up** across vast geographies without having the need to set up physical presence and infrastructure.
- **The lower cost** due to lean structures that no longer needs vast physical IT infrastructure and manpower required by conventional banks.

Figure 4.11: Components of fintech valuation.
Source: Jain (2019), https://www.toptal.com/finance/valuation/how-to-value-a-fintech-startup.

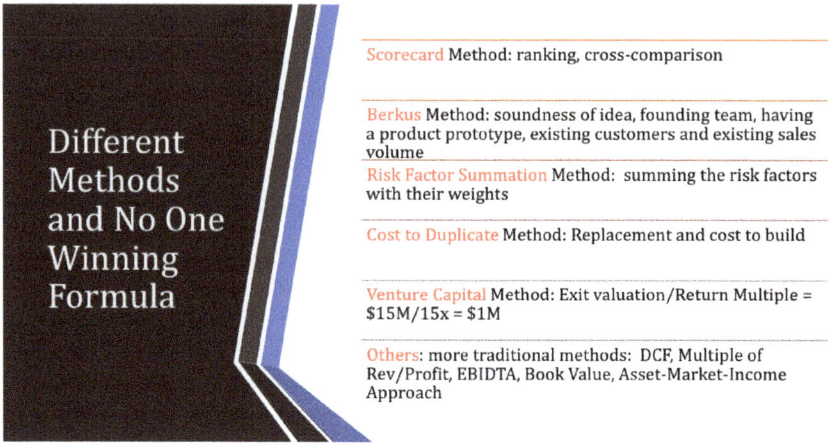

Figure 4.12: Possible methods to value fintech startups.
Source: Jain (2019) and the authors.

a startup, the risk factor summation method, the cost to duplicate method and the venture capital method. While some of the examples are using bitcoin for easy expositions, we can easily substitute the word bitcoin with token.

a. PESTLE

The PESTLE model proposed by Aguilar (1967) is a possible method for blockchain startups. It stands for political, economic, social, technology, legal and environmental factors and details are shown in Figure 4.13. These are the points which business owners must first consider before establishing their company.

Yuneline (2019)[3] highlighted the importance of economics, social and legal factors for cryptocurrency. Each of them affects the cryptocurrency's role as a medium of exchange, society's acceptance and legal restrictions in respective countries. What stood out in Yuneline (2019) was his attempt to discuss Sharia Law's acceptance of cryptocurrency as a form of money. His example carries widespread social implications for cryptocurrency as it affects whether members

[3]https://www.emerald.com/insight/content/doi/10.1108/JABES-12-2018-0107/full/html.

P	E	S	T	E	L
- Government policy - Political stability - Corruption - Foreign trade policy - Tax policy - Labour law - Trade restrictions	- Economic growth - Exchange rates - Interest rates Inflation rates Disposable income - Unemployment rates	- Population growth rate - Age distribution - Career attitudes - Safety emphasis - Health consciousness - Lifestyle attitudes - Cultural barriers	- Technology incentives - Level of innovation - Automation - R&D activity - Technological change - Technological awareness	- Weather - Climate - Environmental policies - Climate change Pressure from NGOs	- Discrimination laws - Antitrust laws - Employment laws - Consumer protection laws - Copyright and patent laws - Health and safety laws

Figure 4.13: PESTEL model.

of the Islamic faith will accept cryptocurrencies as forms of payment. Earlier in April, the US Congressional Research Service (2020)[4] had surfaced economics and legal issues raised by the 116th Congress. These include the economic role of cryptocurrency as a medium of exchange and store of value. Besides, legal aspects concerning money laundering, risks and cross-border transactions are raised with relevant bills passed by Congress to regulate cryptocurrencies. In essence, it is essential to note that different PESTLE forces affect cryptocurrencies differently for different countries. There is no fixed and fast rule, but PESTLE is extremely important in determining the ability to grow and sustain for crypto markets, or even to exist and operate. We can only view it from a strategic viewpoint for valuation.

b. Store of Value

Under the Store of Value (SOV) approach, the value of a digital asset can be determined by its ability to act as SOV, which represents the potential or ability to be valuable while maintaining purchasing power over a prolonged period (Yuneline, 2019). An everyday use case of this theory is gold. It is widely accepted as a form of payment

[4]https://fas.org/sgp/crs/misc/R45427.pdf.

with a relatively stable level of value over the years. The value of gold may be due to gold's naturally limited supply, which provides gold with the ability to have intrinsic value that does not diminish over time.

Cryptocurrencies often have finite supplies by design, such as in the case of Bitcoin, where computer codes predetermined the upper boundary of 21 million bitcoins. Hence, in terms of capping of supply, Bitcoin may be akin to gold and it probably fulfils SOV in theory. It was not surprising that bitcoin was a follow-through from bitgold proposed by Nick Szabo (2005).[5]

The fair value of cryptocurrencies could be derived by calculating the fair value of the price of the currency with SOV, by assuming that the cryptocurrency would ultimately replace gold as the go-to store of value for investors (Leilacher, 2019). For example, the value of bitcoin could be derived by factoring the value of global gold bullion and the ultimate number of bitcoins in circulation.

$$\text{Value of bitcoin} = \frac{\text{Total Global Gold Value}}{\text{Total number of Bitcoin}}$$

$$\$380,000 \text{ per bitcoin} = \frac{\$8 \text{ trillion}}{21 \text{ million BTC}}$$

There is no reason why cryptocurrencies cannot replace a portion of the commodity market. In that case, one can add to the denominator by the number of potential cryptocurrencies that will be liquid as well as just taking a percentage of the commodity market that will be replaced.

$$\text{Value of } a \text{ token} = \frac{\text{Total Global Commodity Value}}{\text{Total number of liquid tokens}}$$

$$\$x \text{ per token} = \frac{\$20 \text{ trillion} * 0.2}{y \text{ billion tokens}}$$

c. TAM SAM SOM

The TAM, SAM and SOM analysis (shown in Figure 4.14) is a method used to better understand a business's relationship with the

[5]https://nakamotoinstitute.org/bit-gold/.

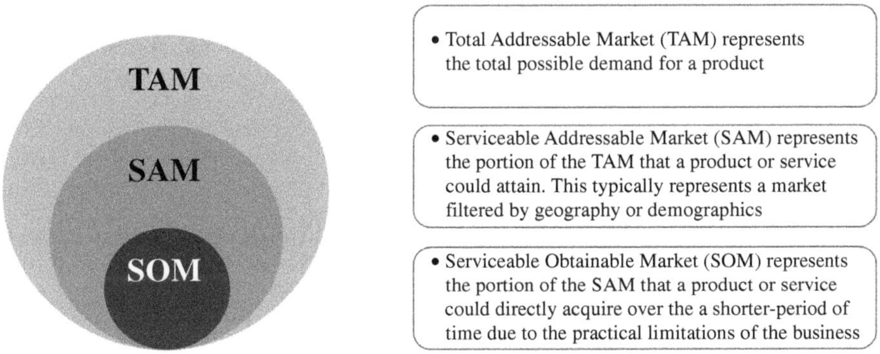

Figure 4.14: TAM, SAM, SOM model.

market (Denault, 2018). The usual way of deriving the values of this model is through a top-down market approach, where one starts at the top of a macro-set and logically filters the data to arrive at an intended market subset (Graham, 2017). Ultimately, deriving the values for a business's TAM, SAM and SOM would demonstrate both a solid understanding of the market as well as one's comprehension of the business limitations. This method may apply to digital assets and blockchain startups that have a revenue model. Again, business judgement is key to this strategic valuation method.

d. Token velocity

Wang (2014) proposes the token velocity theory to derive a value of Bitcoins according to the fundamental macroeconomic equation of exchange: $MV = PQ$. Specifically, P (price) was set to 1, resulting in M being the total market capitalisation of the crypto asset, while Q was defined as the amount of value that is transferred across the network. V remains as the velocity. Substituting M by the market capitalisation gives us the following equation:

$$p_b = \frac{Q}{n_b V}$$

where $M = n_b p_b$, where $n_b =$ number of coins circulating, $p_b =$ price of a coin.

Subsequently, Wang (2014) further assumes that V can be expressed as a linear function of Q,[6] which gives us the following equation:

$$p_b = \frac{1}{n_b * l_t * v_t}$$

where l_t represents the likelihood of bitcoin being transacted and v_t is the velocity of bitcoins being spent.

The velocity of transaction and the total number of bitcoins circulating remain constant. This leaves only the likelihood of transaction, l_t, being inversely proportional to the price of bitcoin, p_b. Following this model, we are now able to model the price of bitcoin by accessing the likelihood of bitcoin transaction — the higher the likelihood of bitcoin being transacted, the lower its price.

e. INET model

The INET model was developed by Burniske (2017) to illustrate the price of a fictional cryptocurrency asset, INET, using the J-curve.

The J-curve is commonly used in economics to illustrate different cash flows over time. However, in the cryptocurrency context, a J-curve represents the change in two forms of single cryptocurrency asset value: The Current Utility Value (CUV) and the Discounted Expected Utility value (DEUV). The CUV represents the value of the cryptocurrency asset that is driven by utility and usage today, while the DEUV represents the present value of an expected utility value that happens in the future (Lannquist, 2018). We derive the DEUV by dividing expected utility value in future, with an appropriate discount rate, akin to our PV formula.

---

[6]Wang (2014) assumed that velocity is proportional to the amount of bitcoins that are saved and transacted, the likelihood of bitcoin saved being l_s and the likelihood of bitcoin transacted being l_t. As such, the velocity for bitcoins saved and spent is expressed as v_s and v_t, respectively. Another assumption made by Wang (2014) was that the velocity of bitcoin transacted is significantly larger than the velocity of bitcoin saved, $v_t \gg v_s$, resulting in the value of v_s being equal to 0. The final assumption then states that velocity can be expressed as a linear function of $Q : V = l_t * v_t * Q$.

As time advances, CUV and DEUV will take turns to drive the price of cryptocurrency. This process works in this manner. Initially, during the launch of the cryptocurrency asset, anticipation drives up DEUV, causing it to be higher in relative percentage terms to CUV. As time progresses, the initial anticipation dies down, while the cryptocurrency asset delivers its true value. During this time, CUV will be in a higher relative percentage to DEUV. Eventually, the market cycle would be reached where both the CUV and the DEUV are expanding. This process allows us to model and estimate the value of a cryptocurrency asset to that of its maturity in a product life cycle.

It is worth highlighting that various factors, such as the velocity, size of asset base, discount rate, adoption rate and supply of tokens, are key considerations when factoring in the model for the utility token INET (Burniske, 2017). As such, previous critics against velocity still stand for the INET model.

f. Network value to transaction (NVT) ratio

The NVT is a valuation metric that attempts to study the relationship between the price of a cryptocurrency and its fundamentals (Leilacher, 2019). NVT is very similar to the Price Earning (P/E) ratio, which is typically used in traditional finance. The P/E ratio provides a measuring stick for comparing if a stock is over or undervalued at any point in time (Elmerraji, 2020), by comparing the valuation of a company to their actual earnings.

While cryptocurrency does not have any earnings (some do have yields from mining or staking) for measurement, one could argue that a suitable fundamental proxy could be derived by assessing the transaction volume of the particular cryptocurrency (Kalichkin, 2018). The principle behind NVT operates similarly as outlined in the following formula:

$$NVT = \frac{\text{network value}}{\text{daily transaction volume}}$$

Therefore, a high NVT for a cryptocurrency would suggest that the cryptocurrency might be overvalued, hinting that the network could be entering a bubble, or simply that the network is experiencing a high growth phase.

g. Metcalfe's Law

Metcalfe's Law highlights that each user in a network can communicate with $(n - 1)$ users, which would theoretically form a network of connectivity. This network of connectivity is subsequently found by various researchers to have the potential to evaluate cryptocurrencies. Zhang *et al.* (2015) find empirical evidence that supports Metcalfe's Law using data from Tencent and Facebook. Alabi (2017) also concludes that Metcalfe's Law modelled Bitcoin, Ethereum and Dash reasonably well.

Under the network effect theory, the value of a network is the square of the users' base with respect to Metcalfe's Law. In other words, as shown in Figure 4.15, the value of a digital currency network can be calculated as the market capitalisation divided by the square number of active daily users. Hence, under such circumstances, cryptocurrencies sharing similar comparables could still stand to thrive together within the cryptocurrency market.

Metcalfe's Law in describing connectivity among users can be better explained with a simple example: If there are three students in a room, there could be a total of $2 + 1 = 3$ connections, and if one imagines a room with 100 students, there could be a total of 4,950 different connections. The example demonstrates the phenomenon of a network's value growing in a nonlinear fashion as more people join

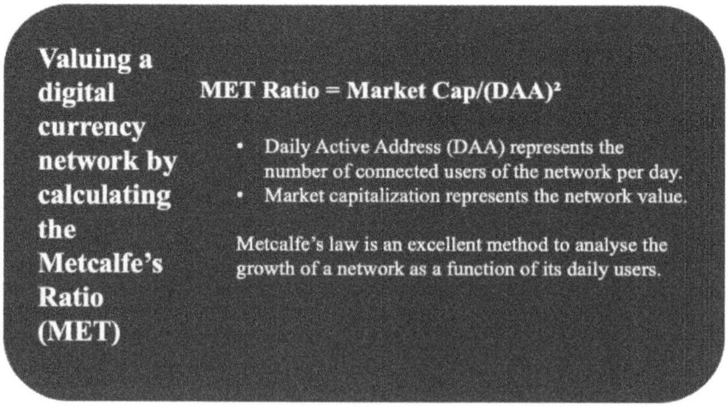

Figure 4.15: MET ratio.

the network. As such, the value of a network of size n would be equal to

$$\frac{n(n-1)}{2}$$

Metcalfe's Law was initially intended to identify the break-even n, where the total network costs are considered with proportionality factor (A), which might decline over time. Therefore, the equation could be best represented as

$$c \cdot n = M = A\frac{n(n-1)}{2}$$

h. Economics and finance of cryptocurrencies

Lee and Teo (2020) propose the mining model that affects the value of cryptocurrencies and discuss a few other factors that affect the economics and finance of cryptocurrencies. In distributed networks, a consensus protocol acts as the incentive mechanisms to ensure a well-functioning token economy. It also controls the creation of new tokens, or the supply of new coins, and thus has a significant impact on the price of the cryptocurrencies. As the consensus protocol is predetermined as part of the programming codes, it is difficult to change and usually has set a cap for the maximum supply, so it creates scarcity of cryptocurrencies. Therefore, the new tokens created are just one factor of the market supply. The scarcity issue will encourage users to hold more coins and drive the price up. Also, the price volatility driven by speculative investors in the cryptocurrency market and the fragmented cryptocurrency exchange industry make the arbitrage and speculation phenomenon even worse.

On the demand side, when people have low trust in the financial system, such as the 2018 Venezuela hyperinflation, the demand of cryptocurrencies increases. Other crypto-specific factors, such as the utility of the token and cost of production, affect cryptocurrency's demand as well. Hayes (2016) and Hayes (2019) document that the marginal cost of production plays an essential role in explaining prices of Bitcoin. Thus, we may expect that during periods of excess demand (or when price bubbles appear), either the market price will fall and/or the mining difficulty will increase to resolve the discrepancy (Lee and Teo, 2020).

From a broader scale, the popularity of cryptocurrencies (or investor attention), cryptocurrency market sentiment and factors related to the associated blockchain networks such as incentives, social scalability, consensus, utility and governance influence the price of the tokens. There is no doubt that token valuation methods will evolve with new designs beyond the income from mining, staking, hedging against loss of trust, option for future payments, etc. Many of the modified quantitative ideas from traditional finance will be applicable with some ingenious twist and understanding of the philosophy underlying the blockchain community. Below are some qualitative methods that are compatible with scoring and ranking valuation methods.

4.4.3 *More Considerations for Token Valuation*

On top of the aforementioned valuation methods, below are some key conceptual frameworks that are also important when valuing the tokens and token economies. Quantitative methods can be developed along those ideas mentioned here.

a. 4Es

The 4Es refer to Economies of Scale, Economies of Scope, Economies of Integration and Economies of Convergence, which are four important aspects when considering the value of fintech companies (see Figure 4.16). It may be very different from valuing services and products provided by fintech companies and traditional companies as the tokens and products are digital, which have entirely different cost and production relationships. In particular, the marginal costs of an additional unit of products are minute. The fourth E (Economies of Convergence) becomes vital as the convergence of technology brings a convergence of profit and social objectives, which is also why the leapfrog economies may have mass adoption before others.

Economies of Scale

- It refers to the ability to produce a product for less cost the higher level of production. This helps scale the product as you are spending less money per unit to produce more.

Economies of Scope

- In the crypto world, it can be defined as the benefits to scaling when the product is extended to different industries. For example, Ethereum can be said to have higher economies of scope than Bitcoin as the programming language allows for more varied smart contracts compared to Bitcoin's limitations to largely financial functions.

Economies of Integration

- If any resource can be used for multiple purposes, it can be said to have economies of integration. A real life example would be electricity derived from burning fossil fuels. Heat generated from this process is used to turn a steam turbine which in turn produces more electricity. This is also known as co-generation. If the resource generated from using cryptocurrencies can be used back into the cryptocurrency system (such as tokens that serve as mining reward), it creates a positive cycle of generation results.

Economies of Convergence

- Emphasis and rapid development of any emerging technology will promote the development and innovation of other technologies. Companies that put great emphasis on technology will likely be the leading ones that benefit from the technology convergence trend, which will also lead to the convergence of profits and social goals.

Figure 4.16: 4Es.

b. 3Cs

The 3Cs describe characteristics of an environment (geological or institutional) that are ideal nurturing grounds for successful fintech companies, and by extension, cryptocurrencies.

Community

The concept of clustering in economics describes how companies who that in the same industry tend to gather together in geographical concentrations. This increases the general productivity of the industry as a whole as it fosters productive competition among the industry peers. Similarly, a strong community has a high tolerance for failure and encourages innovative thinking which is extremely important for a technology company or product like cryptocurrency to succeed.

Compassion

Another factor that spurs innovations in technologies is their compassion to failure. The mindset of people within these communities is that failure is not the end of the world but rather a valuable lesson for the next attempt. Such a mindset is important in the world of fintech startups and especially for the cryptocurrency market where the competition is steep and failure rate high. Empathy is another compassion factor that helps with social scalability in the sense that a sticky customer base grows exponentially in a short time.

Creativity

With the first two traits, it then comes as no surprise that creativity can be fostered in such a community as innovation is not just encouraged verbally but also backed by economic action.

c. LASIC principles

Outlined in the LASIC principles are five characteristics that the cryptocurrencies should have to maximise the chances of success and minimise the risk of government or social media resistance. So, they are important factors to consider for token valuation.

Low Margins

Low margins are meant to prevent competition and to attract users to achieve critical mass in terms of a sticky user base. With low margins, economies of scale can take place and monetisation becomes easier. For fintech companies and cryptocurrencies, low margin is a key feature, compared to conventional businesses.

Asset Light

Asset light companies are able to keep fixed costs low and stay nimble and flexible. Scaling a company that is asset light is also much easier in this case.

Scalable

As mentioned above, a product's ability to scale directly impacts the product's future profitability. The number of sticky users is a key factor in monetising the product and estimating the value of the product. For example, cryptocurrencies that can scale well will be able to handle more business transactions and will thus enhance the value of token economy.

Innovative

Similar to creativity in the 3Cs rules, businesses should remain innovative, so should their products. It is important to tap into the future trend to remain competitive. Another way is to lead the trend, as in the case of Apple and Bitcoin and its blockchain technology.

Compliance Easy

Finally, providing services or products that are compliance easy will minimise the risk of regulating bodies restricting their use and jeopardising the prospects for a fintech startup. Changes in the regulatory environment and compliance process may have major influences on the costs of fintech companies and thus affect their profitability and value.

d. 6Ds

The First Industrial Revolution involved steam and coal power to operate machinery. The Second used electricity. The Third involved electronics and information technology to automate production. Currently, we might be in the midst of the Fourth Industrial Revolution, which aims to use AI and IOT technology to transform the physical and digital world further. This transformation will take the form of 6Ds: Digitalisation, Disintermediation, Democratisation, Decentralisation, Diminishing Oneself and Data Privacy Protection (see Figure 4.17).

- **Digitalisation** involves the usage of digital technologies to change a business model. We see how firms are beginning to explore advertising opportunities using social media and increase their customer base through e-commerce. Cryptocurrency can tokenize assets to bring physical assets into the digital space for transactions and secure ownership.
- **Disintermediation** refers to the removal of the middlemen in transactions to reduce costs on the transacting parties and increase efficiency. Ethereum is an example of a cryptocurrency with potential disintermediation applications with its smart contract capabilities.
- **Democratisation** is the process in which digital technology allows people who are currently underserved or unserved to have access to the technology at an affordable cost to them. With cryptocurrency, micro insurances and micro lending can be secured and provided for customers with risk profiles that may be deemed as too risky for traditional financial institutions.
- **Decentralisation** refers to the process where control is distributed amongst the users without any centralised third parties to control the network. Cryptocurrencies like Bitcoin and Ethereum are by nature decentralised.
- **Diminishing Oneself** refers to the process of having the creators of the coin to step down from a leading role in the continued development of the product. The purpose of this factor is to allow creators to function like a facilitator instead to minimise single points of failure. Satoshi Nakamoto, the creator of Bitcoin, is the premier example of this trait as he faded away after he published the paper on the cryptocurrency.
- **Data Privacy Protection** refers to the growing emphasis on privacy in an increasingly transparent world where information is stored for eternity on servers and is accessible by anyone everywhere.

Figure 4.17: 6Ds.

First, the discussion of the digital economy is inextricable from the concept of "Digitisation". Digitisation and digitalisation are sometimes used interchangeably, but the meanings are completely different. Digitisation is the process of converting information from a physical format to a digital format and the vector and form of information changes. The change of physical conversion into numbers can be understood as information digitisation, that is "digitisation".

When information exists in digital form, there will be "qualitative" changes in our way of work and workflow. Therefore, the use of digital information to improve business processes and even change business and business models is called digitalisation. That is the digitalisation of business processes and business models, namely digitalisation. There is a big difference between digitisation and digitalisation. Digitalisation will have a significant impact on the economy and can solve many current economic imbalances.

At the same time, in the virtual world, once such a trust has been attacked by invasions or illegal control, the loss will be incalculable. Therefore, in the long run, we advocate sequential, gradual "decentralisation" to promote the establishment of distributed trust mechanisms. The gradually appropriate distribution of trust is the most important foundation to achieve sustainability and stability. Decentralisation and data privacy are vital to the digital economy. In addition to the technology, one must abandon self-centred thinking — that is diminishing oneself.

In general, to make things available for the general public, many of the e-commerce or fintech companies have done the first 3Ds, but not the fourth — decentralisation. The diminishing is also important as this may not create an extra barrier when bringing the services and products abroad. But, the most valuable companies are the ones that can accomplish the last 3Ds (to protect the users).

e. 7Ws

The 7 Dimensions or 7Ws (维度) refer to seven key characteristics that a fintech company has that can make it highly valued: Open, Altruistic, Global, Crowdsourcing Wisdom, Crowdsourcing Contribution,

Encompassing Interest of All and Beneficial to All. The idea was first mentioned by Shen (2015).

Open

Openness refers to how open a project or company is. For example, if the source code is open and publicly available, like Python and Bitcoin, it becomes easier for developers to implement the codes, build additional layers on it, revise it and develop it. Stakeholders such as users and investors can also be more assured about the design and function of the network.

Altruistic

The founding team and managing team of fintech companies should also be altruistic. If they think only about themselves, it is difficult to see if the stakeholders' interests will be valued in the long run, thus limiting the value of the firms.

Global

As mentioned earlier, the user base plays an important role in any business's success, more so for fintech companies. Digital services or products that typical fintech companies provide do not have many geographical restrictions as traditional ones, making going global an easier target to achieve. The security and reliability of the system depend on the number of people that use it, and the more, the better. Hence, fintech companies should consider catering to a global audience instead of merely focusing on their local jurisdiction.

Crowdsourcing Wisdom

Crowdsourcing wisdom will utilise the wisdom of the crowd or the network. A little breakthrough from multiple sources will result in a huge breakthrough when brought together.

Crowdsourcing Contribution

Similar to the above, a decentralised cryptocurrency can crowdsource contributions to attain supercomputers like processing speeds and power. Mesh technology, for example can lower average costs if more

4Es	3Cs	LASIC	6Ds	7Ws
- Economies of Scale - Economies of Scope - Economies of Integration - Economies of Convergence	- Community - Compassion - Creativity	- Low Margin - Asset Light - Scalable - Innovative - Compliance Easy	- Digitalisation - Disintermediation - Democratization - Decentralisation - Diminishing Oneself - Data Privacy Protection	- Open - Altruistic - Global - Crowdsourcing Wisdom - Crowdsourcing Contribution - Encompassing Interest of All - Beneficial to All

Figure 4.18: Summary of conceptual valuation frameworks.

people contribute to the network. The crowdsourcing concept is crucial in a token economy to enjoy the economies of scale.

Encompassing Interest of All

It is important to consider every stakeholder group. In particular, for a peer-to-peer network, every stakeholder is important as they play key roles in the development of the project and determine whether a token economy can function well.

Beneficial to All

In addition to ensure the interest of all stakeholders are aligned, it is important to make sure all players can benefit from the services, products, or behaviors.

Figure 4.18 summaries the discussed conceptual frameworks to consider when valuing fintech companies.

4.5 Conclusion

To better understand the value of a token, the overall ecosystem and underlying blockchain design thinking cannot be neglected. From a business perspective, we can look at the governance, economic incentives and scalability dimensions to continuously distribute trust and increase the cost of hacking. Looking at one project or company is not enough, as out of 100, 95 may just be loss ladders to build the capabilities for the entire ecosystem. Without the ladder projects, the ecosystem can never be built and so we may need to consider the value of the entire ecosystem — something that traditional bankers and fund managers find difficult to reconcile and explain to shareholders and investors when an individual or too many projects fail before the last few succeed. One would have been fired long before the supernormal returns are obtained.

The collapse of projects like FCoin could have been avoided with a better design of the token economics — that is why factors such as the role and functions of the tokens, the architecture and the monetary policy discussed here are so important. If there is no token, the winner likely takes all. That is why we need tokens and token economics. The company, platform provider or developer will have control of all the data and earn most of the profits, which is not what we aim to do. Traditional economics has already covered many of the topics. Token economics is just an expansion to include the knowledge of the cryptocurrencies and tokens as well as the new business models. We are anticipating a variety of token economics applications, a more inclusive ecosystem and the emergence of widely accepted and effective valuation methods for tokens.

In future, the majority of companies will likely use tokens to raise funds, similar to what ICOs did before but with different schemes and/or names. Many blockchain startups failed with ICO because they treated tokens as securities or financing instruments without thorough considerations about the token utilities and economics. Tokenisation is a process and an alternative that can be much more powerful — it accords "affordable" legal status to those things that do not have a clear ownership structure and legal status previously, such as livestock. For instance, previously, only the ownership of a cow had legal status and transactions of the cow possible. Investors can purchase a fraction of a cow or exchange for other things. It bypasses the expensive step of forming a company to own the cow. The token itself defines the property right and can fractionalise the livestock without having to deal with the shares of the company. Tokenisation provides solutions to tackle many pain points in the businesses today and helps achieve an inclusive and ultimate goal of maximising the value for all. Also, the value of the tokens and stocks shall not compete with each other, but supplement each other to increase the values of both. In fact, shares that define voting rights can be now tokenised as a governance token. How this can be achieved is what we should focus on in the future and experiment in DeFi, also known as decentralised finance, distributed finance or simply as open finance.[7]

References

Aguilar, F. J. (1967). *Scanning the Business Environment.* Macmillan.

Alabi, K. (2017). Digital blockchain networks appear to be following Metcalfe's Law. *Electronic Commerce Research and Applications*, 24, 23–29.

Brouwer, A. J. (2018). The dual token structure thesis. Retrieved from https://blog.goodaudience.com/the-dual-token-structure-thesis-c3a43ef54537.

Burniske, C. (2017). The crypto J-curve. *Medium.* Retrieved from https://medium.com/@cburniske/the-crypto-j-curvebe5fdddafa26.

Cong, L. W., Li, Y., and Wang, N. (2020). Tokenomics: Dynamic adoption and valuation (No. w27222). *National Bureau of Economic Research.*

Denault, J. F. (2018). The handbook of marketing strategy for life science companies: Formulating the roadmap you need to navigate the market. Routledge.

Elmerraji, J. (2020). 5 Must-Have metrics for value investors. *Investopedia.* Retrieved from https://www.investopedia.com/articles/fundamental-analysis/09/five-must-have-metrics-value-investors.asp.

Graham, A. (2017). TAM methodology: An explanation and example of total addressable market analysis. *Toptal.* Retrieved from https://www.toptal.com/finance/market-sizing/total-addressable-market-example.

Hayes, A. (2016). Decentralised banking: Monetary technocracy in the digital age. In *Banking Beyond Banks and Money* (pp. 121–131). Springer, Cham.

Hayes, A. S. (2019). Bitcoin price and its marginal cost of production: Support for a fundamental value. *Applied Economics Letters*, 26(7).

He, H. (2018). The Death of FCoin: A tale of bad token design. Retrieved from https://hackernoon.com/the-death-of-fcoin-a-tale-of-bad-token-design-261d64a8116f.

Hlebiv, O. (2018). What Is Token Economics. Retrieved from https://applicature.com/blog/blockchain-startups/what-is-token-economics.

Jain, N. (2019). How to Value a Fintech Startup. Retrieved from https://www.toptal.com/finance/valuation/how-to-value-a-fintech-startup.

[7]https://fintechnews.sg/37725/blockchain/how-defi-is-building-a-new-financial-system/.

Kalichkin, D. (2018). Rethinking Network Value to Transactions (NVT) Ratio. *Medium.* Retrieved from https://medium.com/cryptolab/https-medium-com-kalichkin-rethinking-nvt-ratio-2cf810df0ab0.

Lannquist, A. (2018). Today's crypto asset valuation frameworks. *Medium.* Retrieved from https://medium.com/blockchain-at-berkeley/todays-crypto-asset-valuation-frameworks-573a38eda27e.

Lee, D. K. C. and Teo, E. G. S. (2020). The new money: The utility of Cryptocurrencies and the need for a New Monetary Policy. Working Paper. Retrieved from https://papers.ssrn.com/sol3/papers.cfm?abstract_id=3608752.

Leilacher, A. (2019). What the network value to transactions ratio can tell about crypto. *Cryptonews.* Retrieved from https://cryptonews.com/exclusives/what-the-network-value-to-transactions-ratio-can-tell-about-3156.htm.

Lielacher, A. (2019). Digital asset valuation: Top 7 metrics for valuing bitcoin, altcoins, and cryptocurrencies. *Bitcoin Market Journal.* Retrieved from https://www.bitcoinmarketjournal.com/digital-asset-valuation/.

Liu, K. (2019). Token economics #2: Comparison review of token economy. Retrieved from https://hackernoon.com/token-economics-1-why-do-we-need-token-economics-2c0006098aea.

Mesenbourg, T. L. (2001). Measuring the digital economy. U.S. Bureau of the Census.

Shen, B. (2015). Blockchain Economy: 7W's. Retrieved from https://www.ccvalue.cn/article/78508.html

Szabo, N. (2005). *Bit Gold.* Satoshi Nakamoto Institute. Retrieved from https://nakamotoinstitute.org/bit-gold/

Tönnissen, S., Beinke, J. H., and Teuteberg, F. (2020). Understanding token-based ecosystems — a taxonomy of blockchain-based business models of startups. *Electron Markets.* Retrieved from https://link.springer.com/article/10.1007/s12525-020-00396-6.

Trinh, L. (2018). Sharing economy vs token economy: You Decide. Retrieved from https://kambria.io/blog/sharing-economy-vs-token-economy-you-decide/.

Wan, C. (2020). Cryptocurrency exchange Fcoin expects to default on as much as $125 M of users' bitcoin. Retrieved from https://www.theblockcrypto.com/post/56191/cryptocurrency-exchange-fcoin-expects-to-default-on-as-much-as-125m-of-users-bitcoin.

Wang, J. C. (2014). A simple macroeconomic model of bitcoin. *Working Paper.* Retrieved from https://ssrn.com/abstract=2394024.

Xu, M., Li, J., and Wang, M. (2019). *Token Economics* (1st edition). CITIC Press Corporation.

Yuneline, M. H. (2019). Analysis of cryptocurrency's characteristics in four perspectives. *Journal of Asian Business and Economic Studies*, 26, 206–219.

Zhang, X. Z., Liu, J. J., and Xu, Z. W. (2015). *Tencent and Facebook Data Validate Metcalfe's Law.* Springer Link.

Chapter 5

Cryptocurrency as an Alternative Investment Class

Jointly written with Guo Li*

5.1 Introduction

The surge of Bitcoin's price and emerging applications of blockchain technology had prompted heated discussions over cryptocurrencies. Over 1,000 cryptocurrencies had been launched until early 2018, and that number has gone up to over 7,000 during the past two years, according to *CoinGecko.com* (see Figure 5.1). Hundreds of billions worth of total market capitalisation (see Figure 5.2) indeed poses great investment opportunities for investors, with one third, or around US$90 billion, consisting of altcoins (cryptocurrencies other than bitcoin; see Figure 5.3).

In a nutshell, the cryptocurrency market has the following features: (i) attracting a large amount of funds, (ii) increasing number of altcoins and (iii) altcoins playing an increasingly important role. However, constructing an investment portfolio using cryptocurrencies and how it performs compared to the mainstream asset classes such as stocks, bonds and other alternatives (e.g., commodities and REITs) are under-examined. Investing in cryptocurrencies means

---

*Assistant Professor, Fudan University; Academic Researcher, Shanghai Institute of International Finance and Economics, Shanghai, People's Republic of China.

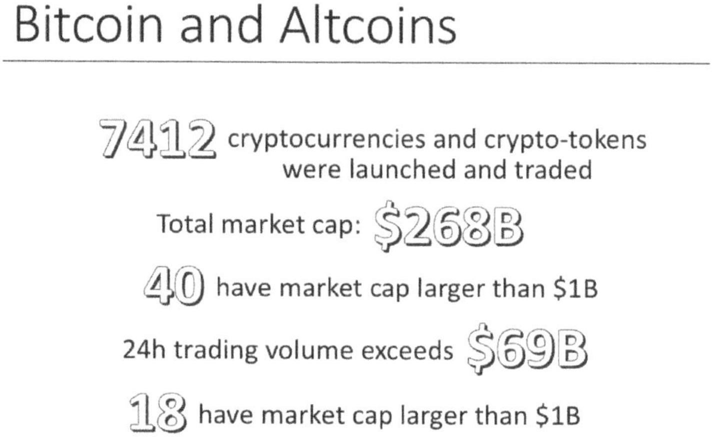

Figure 5.1: Cryptocurrency market overview.
Source: https://www.coingecko.com/en.

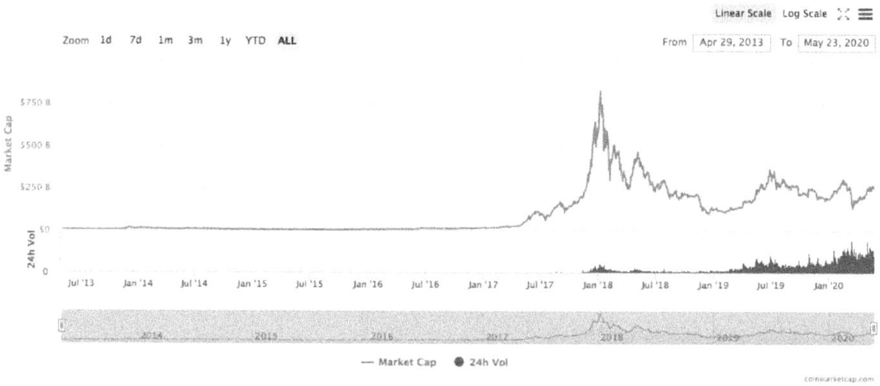

Figure 5.2: Total market capitalisation.

more than simply investing in Bitcoin alone as there are many other choices (i.e., altcoins). As a result, the cryptocurrency market generates many investment opportunities and is worth studying.

In our paper, titled "*Is cryptocurrency a new investment opportunity?*", we analyse the diversification effect of cryptocurrencies (Lee *et al.*, 2017). Then, we perform sentiment analysis and based on the

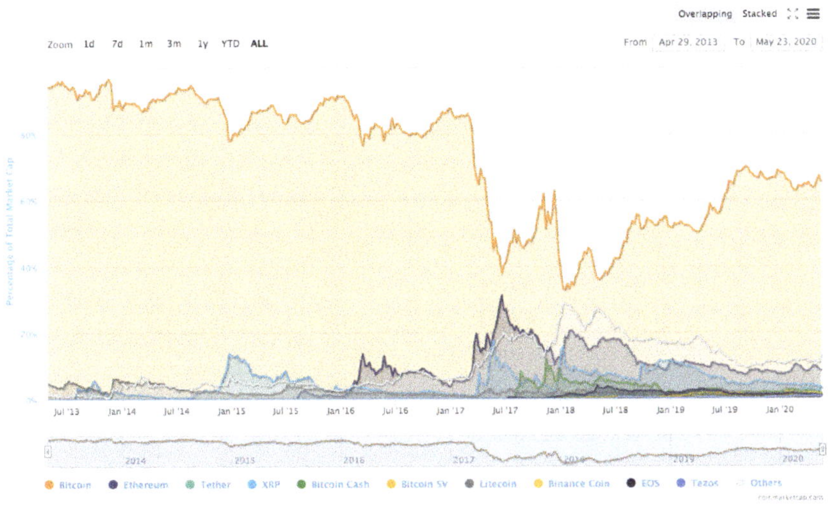

Figure 5.3: Market capitalisation dominance.

results, we construct a portfolio which has generated a significant alpha.

5.2 Data

We collect cryptocurrency data from *CoinGecko.com* and data for other traditional asset classes from Bloomberg. The whole sample period spans from August 2014 to March 2017. Here, we use CRIX (CRypto IndeX[1]) as a proxy for cryptocurrency market performance, like S&P 500 for the stock market. It was established as early as 2014 and incorporated various numbers of constituents that can best reflect the whole cryptocurrency markets based on both liquidity and market value rules (Trimborn and Härdle, 2018). For the analysis, we included the top ten cryptocurrencies that had been included most frequently in the CRIX index, shown in Figure 5.4.

For the traditional assets, we include S&P 500, Gold, S&P GSCI Commodity Index, Oil futures, private equity and REITs. If we plot the cumulative returns of CRIX and traditional asset class, we can

[1]https://thecrix.de/.

Number	Cryptocurrency	Symbol	Times Being Included in CRIX
1	Bitcoin	BTC	32
2	Ethereum	XRP	32
3	Litecoin	LTC	31
4	Dash	DASH	29
5	Dogecoin	DOGE	28
6	Monero	XMR	26
7	Bitshares	BTC	26
8	MaidSafeCoin	MAID	25
9	Nxt	NXT	24
10	Bytecoin	BCN	24

Figure 5.4: Top 10 cryptocurrencies included in the CRIX.

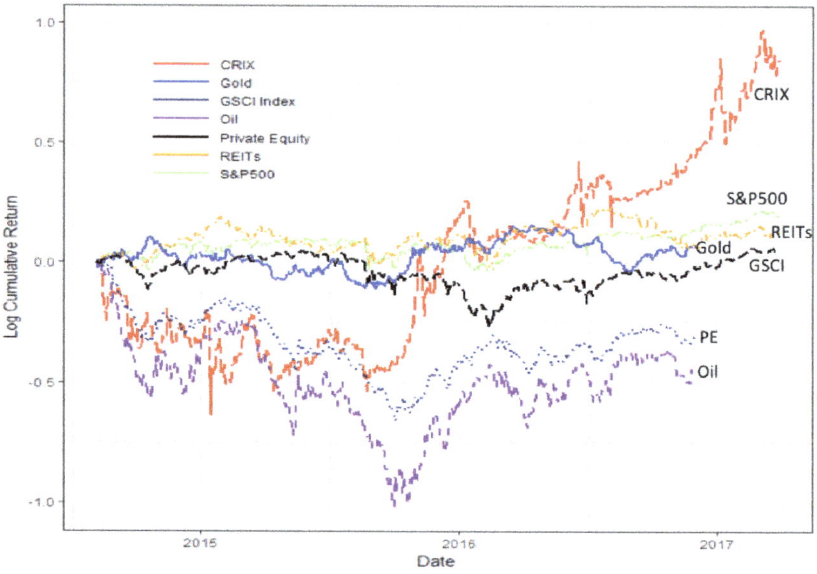

Figure 5.5: Cumulative returns of assets.

see that the return of the CRIX index had increased a lot from 2015 to 2017, much higher when compared to the rest of the asset classes (Figure 5.5). But, it seemed much more volatile than the others in the meantime.

	Mean	SD	Skew	Kurt	Min	Max	Rho
CRIX	0.0012	0.0326	−1.0375	12.8923	−0.2264	0.1932	0.0135
BTC	0.0008	0.0388	−0.5274	10.3023	−0.2518	0.2014	−0.0059
XRP	0.0009	0.0515	1.1100	10.1929	−0.1958	0.3286	0.1357
LTC	0.0041	0.0794	−0.0954	36.5501	−0.8635	0.7619	−0.1126
DASH	0.0027	0.0766	0.6470	9.7346	−0.3740	0.5476	−0.0489
DOGE	0.0005	0.0589	1.7617	17.5638	−0.2752	0.4802	0.0183
XMR	0.0033	0.0839	1.6386	16.0059	−0.3363	0.7203	0.0315
BTS	−0.0008	0.0730	1.4375	12.7584	−0.2933	0.5252	0.0572
MAID	0.0040	0.1210	3.7434	55.4465	−0.4900	1.6675	−0.1411
NXT	−0.0019	0.0724	2.0406	20.3759	−0.3636	0.6999	−0.0794
BCN	−0.0008	0.0577	−0.5688	23.7415	−0.5472	0.3744	−0.0451

	Mean	SD	Skew	Kurt	Min	Max	Rho
T-Note	4.95E-06	6.54E-06	0.9694	2.7994	0	2.00E-05	0.989
S&P 500	0.0003	0.0084	−0.3068	5.6039	−0.0402	0.0383	0.0095
Gold	0.0001	0.009	0.3896	5.998	−0.0338	0.0459	−0.0446
Oil	−0.0006	0.0258	0.1879	4.5863	−0.1079	0.1015	−0.1287
GSCI	−0.0004	0.0138	0.0958	4.5697	−0.0659	0.0526	−0.0872
REITs	0.0002	0.0097	−0.5848	4.7931	−0.0486	0.0284	0.0332
PE	7.26E-05	0.0087	−0.7855	7.6016	−0.05	0.0327	0.1888

Figure 5.6: Summary statistics of assets.

From the summary statistics, we can see that cryptocurrencies outperformed the traditional asset class in terms of average daily return (see Figure 5.6). For example, the daily return of CRIX is 0.12%, four times higher than that of S&P 500. However, this outperformance comes with a high degree of volatility, in other words, a higher risk.

5.3 Diversification Analysis

We then look at how cryptocurrencies improve the performance of a portfolio that consists of traditional assets. We first evaluate the comovement between cryptocurrencies, including the CRIX index as the market representative and ten major cryptocurrencies, and traditional assets by studying the correlation coefficients (Chen *et al.*, 2016). We apply a static correlation model and a dynamic conditional

❑ Static Correlation

	CRIX	BTC	XRP	LTC	DASH	DOGE	XMR	BTS	MAID	NXT	BCN
S&P 500	0.036	0.038	0.22	0.013	0.102	−0.001	0.084	0.044	0.058	0.057	0.044
T-Note	−0.02	0.017	−0.01	0.006	−0.013	−0.037	−0.011	−0.04	0.058	−0.072	−0.035
Gold	0.036	0.069	−0.064	0.045	0.045	0.01	−0.053	0.02	0.018	0.041	0.047
Oil	−0.065	−0.075	−0.006	−0.076	−0.03	−0.094	0.032	0.005	0.009	−0.021	−0.025
GSCI	0.015	0.03	0.004	0.031	0.043	0.029	−0.01	−0.033	0.028	0.003	−0.015
REITs	−0.014	0.004	0.003	0.043	−0.025	−0.016	−0.045	−0.058	0.011	−0.036	−0.052
PE	−0.037	−0.007	−0.02	−0.029	−0.039	−0.017	−0.02	−0.094	0.024	−0.079	−0.012

❑ Dynamic Conditional Correlation (DCC)

	Mean	SD	Min	Q25	Median	Q75	Max
S&P 500	−0.0182	0.0250	−0.0810	−0.0357	−0.0193	−0.0007	0.0697
Gold	0.0233	0.0494	−0.1326	−0.0081	0.0231	0.0531	0.2442
Oil	−0.0951	1.64E-07	−0.0951	−0.0951	−0.0951	−0.0951	−0.0951
GSCI	0.0330	4.60E-08	0.0330	0.0330	0.0330	0.0330	0.0330
REITs	−0.0263	2.29E-07	−0.0263	−0.0263	−0.0263	−0.0263	−0.0263
PE	−0.0279	7.42E-09	−0.0279	−0.0279	−0.0279	−0.0279	−0.0279

Figure 5.7: Correlation between CRIX and the rest.

correlation (DCC) model (Engle, 2002). Almost all correlations, between that of the CRIX and traditional asset classes, are less than 0.1 (see Figure 5.7). For example, the correlation between CRIX and the S&P 500 is 0.036. In fact, according to the first row, a majority of cryptocurrencies we studied have correlations with the stock market that are less than 0.05. These very low correlations reinforce our statement that cryptocurrencies may be a promising investment class in terms of hedging the risk of mainstream assets.

If we look at the dynamic correlation, instead of average correlation, cryptocurrencies still show good diversification potential over the whole sample period as even the largest, 0.2442, is still considered quite low. The persistence of low comovement with mainstream assets further suggests good investment opportunities in cryptocurrency as an alternative asset class.

We then examined the performance after adding the CRIX index into a portfolio that originally consists of traditional assets such as S&P 500, private equity, REITs and Gold. From the efficient frontier in Figure 5.8, we can see the return and standard deviation of CRIX and six common investments. CRIX has the highest return and it is the only one that lies on the efficient frontier, while the return of Oil is the lowest with a relatively high level of risk. In other words, CRIX

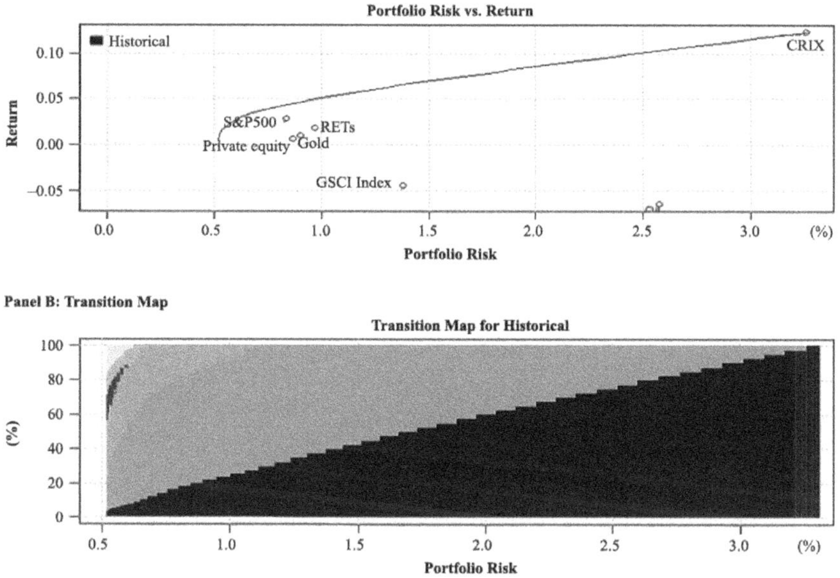

Figure 5.8: Efficient frontier and transition map.

seems to provide the best performance for a risk-averse investor who can take a high risk.

According to transition map of our portfolio performance, S&P 500 and CRIX dominate the portfolio, while the other investments only contribute to the portfolio when the portfolio risk is low. Moreover, for any risk-averse investor who is willing to tolerate daily volatility above 2%, the transition map suggests investing more than half of his or her initial wealth into CRIX.

The efficient frontier figure, Figure 5.9, plots the market efficient frontiers of the mainstream portfolio with and without CRIX. The inclusion of CRIX shifts the efficient frontier upwards. This means that under the same level of risk, a portfolio with CRIX has a higher return than the portfolio consisting of only mainstream assets.

5.4 Sentiment Analysis and Portfolio

5.4.1 *Sentiment Analysis*

We further investigated the sentiment effect in the cryptocurrency market, using the average return in the past ten trading days as

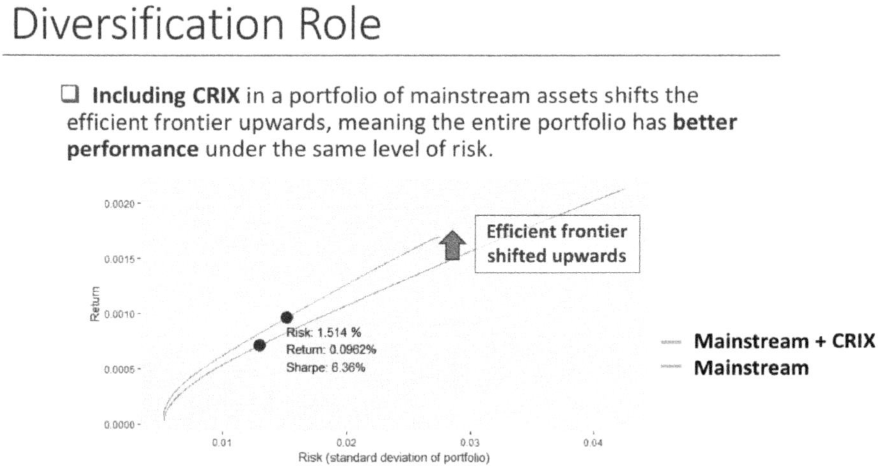

Figure 5.9: Efficient frontier and optimal portfolio.

the proxy of investor sentiment for each cryptocurrency. Extant literature suggests that sentiment-induced overnight returns are reversed during the trading day because rational investors will come into the market to correct the mispricing, investors will buy (sell) the assets with high (low) past returns and then a strong return reversal will be observed later (Berkman *et al.*, 2012).

To examine whether this effect exists in the cryptocurrency market, we select the top 100 cryptocurrencies that have been included in CRIX over the whole sample period. The average return in the past 10 trading days is used as the proxy of investor sentiment for each cryptocurrency in our analysis. After sorting them into three groups according to the sentiment level (high, median and low) for each trading day, we defined the day that a certain crypto falls into the high (low) sentiment group as its high (low) sentiment event day. Each cryptocurrency may have multiple event days (see Figure 5.10).

As shown in Figure 5.11, the results suggest that return cryptocurrencies with high (low) past return/sentiment will drop (increase) in the following day. So, investor sentiment strongly affects the cryptocurrency market as there is an obvious return reversal for both high and low sentiment groups. The reason may be that cryptocurrencies, unlike other traditional asset classes, do not have

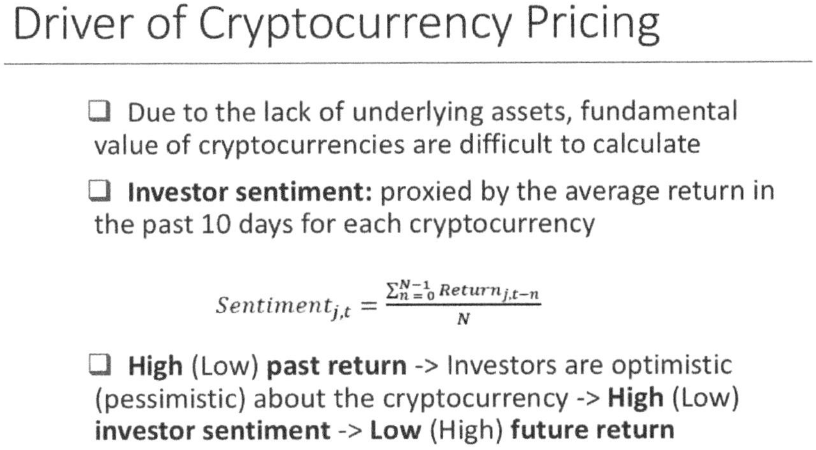

Figure 5.10: Sentiment in cryptocurrency market.

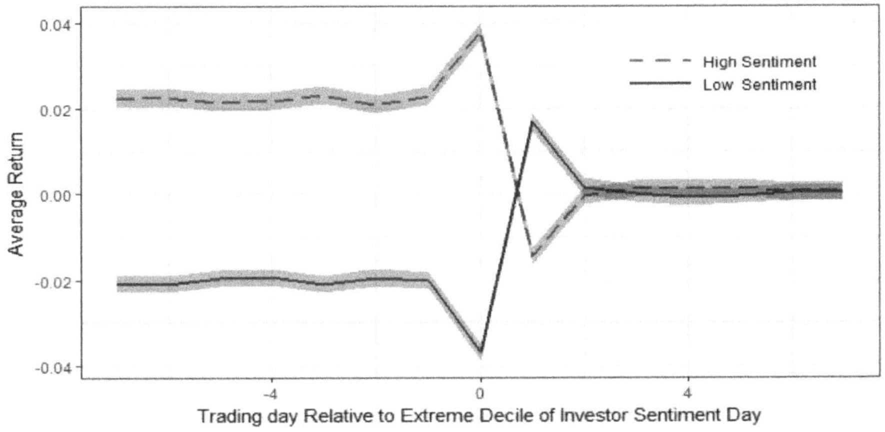

Figure 5.11: Sentiment effect of cryptocurrency market.

real underlying assets and their fundamentals are hard to understand. So, without fundamental support, investor sentiment will affect the market.

5.4.2 *Sentiment Portfolio*

Since we have observed a confirmed reversal effect in the returns of cryptocurrencies, next we will try to explore this investment

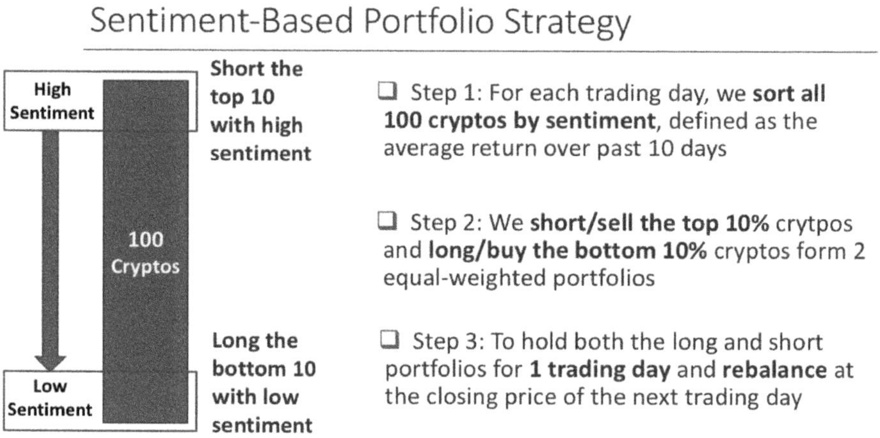

Figure 5.12: Sentiment-based portfolio strategy.

opportunity by constructing a long–short portfolio based on our sentiment measure. In other words, we would act like rational investors, who enter the market to correct the mispricing, and form a portfolio strategy based on sentiment information to gain positive risk-adjusted profits (see Figure 5.12).

We construct the sentiment portfolio based on the strategy of buying low-sentiment and selling high-sentiment cryptocurrencies[2] for the whole sample period using the top 100 cryptocurrencies included in CRIX. We also include an equally weighted portfolio that invests equally in all 100 cryptocurrencies. The trading costs have been ignored for research purposes.

Figure 5.13 shows that the cumulative returns of the sentiment portfolio are over 20 times the initial investment after 2016, much higher than that of CRIX and the equal-weighted portfolio.

According to the portfolio cumulative return for each sentiment group, low-sentiment groups have highest cumulative returns and the high-sentiment groups have the lowest return (see Figure 5.14). This result serves as strong evidence supporting the fact that investor sentiment plays a very important role in the cryptocurrency market.

The distribution of average monthly abnormal return of the sentiment portfolio may provide additional information about the

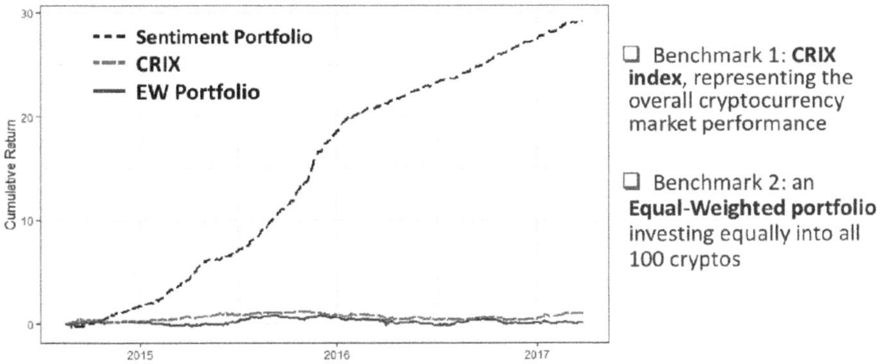

Figure 5.13: Sentiment portfolio performance.

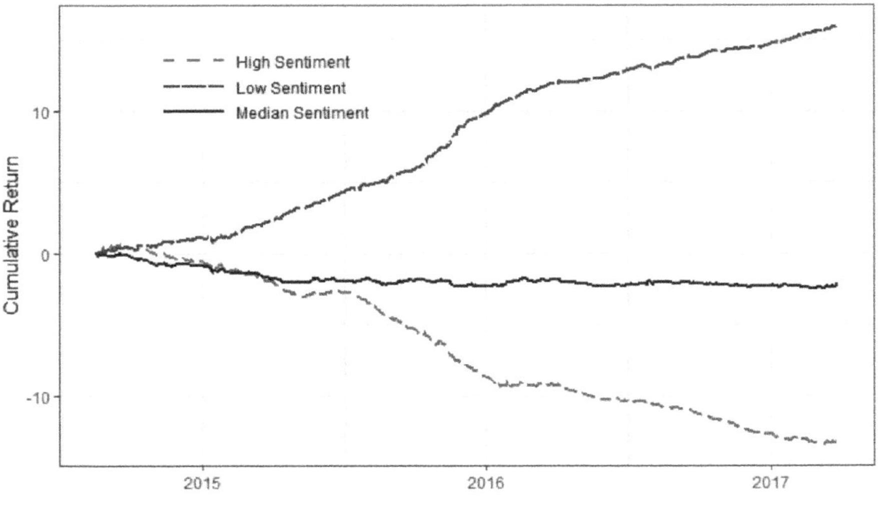

Figure 5.14: Sentiment portfolio performance of different levels.

portfolio's performance. We can clearly see the frequency at which average monthly abnormal return occurs (in bins) during the whole sample periods. Each frequency bin stands for a range of abnormal returns. The daily abnormal return is calculated as stock returns minus CRIX index returns to adjust for cryptocurrency market risk. We can see that the portfolio's average abnormal return falls between 50% and 100% for the most months, followed by 100% and 200%.

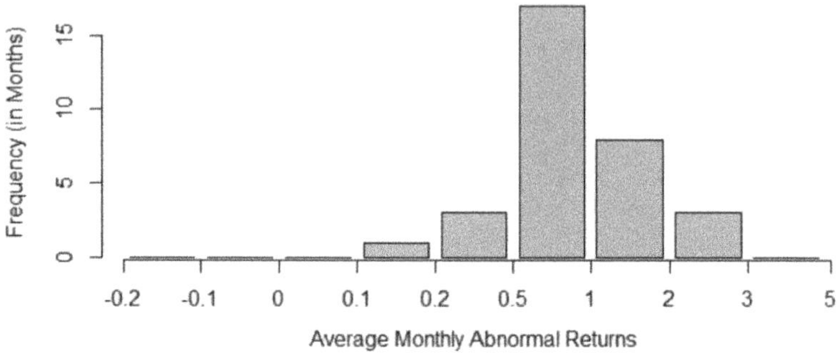

Figure 5.15: Portfolio monthly return distribution.

Notably, none of average monthly returns are negative. Thus, the sentiment-based strategy has outstanding performance, indicating a good arbitrage opportunity (see Figure 5.15).

In addition, we compared the performance of sentiment portfolio with other investment assets, including traditional investment tools and other cryptocurrencies, using several risk-adjusted return measures. For the information ratio, S&P 500 is used as the benchmark.

We find that of all investment classes, the sentiment-based cryptocurrency portfolio has the highest average return, 2.34% daily (see Figure 5.16). In terms of risk-adjusted returns such as the Sharpe ratio and information ratio, it also significantly outperforms the others. Therefore, it is safe to conclude that our sentiment portfolio provides very good risk arbitrage return to investors.

5.4.3 *Robustness Check*

Considering that previous results do not account for transaction costs, we further analyse the portfolio performance in a more practical way. Namely, we conduct the following robustness checks: one with an assumption of non-zero transaction costs and the other with different sentiment formation periods.

Results show that performance of our sentiment portfolio does not vary much with different trading costs (see Figure 5.17). For example, in the cases of an extreme trading cost of 10 bps, the sentiment-based trading strategy still generates a high annual return (11.22 times) with a t-value of 15.50. So, the sentiment portfolio is insensitive

	Mean Return	Volatility	Sharpe Ratio	Information Ratio	Maximum Drawdown
S&P 500	0.0003	0.0084	0.0354		-4.02%
Sentiment Portfolio	0.0234	0.0382	0.6106	0.5929	-15.59%
Equal-Weight Portfolio	5.96E-05	0.0287	0.0021	0.0141	-17.89%
CRIX	0.0008	0.0316	0.0268	0.0274	-22.64%
Gold	0.0001	0.0090	0.0109	-0.0158	-3.38%
Oil	-0.0006	0.0258	-0.0239	-0.0336	-10.79%
GSCI Index	-0.0005	0.0139	-0.0325	-0.0484	-6.59%
REITs	0.0002	0.0098	0.0189	-0.0144	-4.86%
PE	0.0001	0.0087	0.0093	-0.0338	-5.00%
BTC	0.0008	0.0390	0.0213	0.0134	-25.18%
XRP	0.0008	0.0516	0.0157	0.0098	-19.58%
DASH	0.0039	0.0796	0.0491	0.0451	-86.35%
MAID	0.0026	0.0768	0.0333	0.0295	-37.40%
DOGE	0.0008	0.0589	0.0130	0.0078	-27.52%
XMR	0.0032	0.0840	0.0381	0.0344	-33.63%
BTS	-0.0007	0.0733	-0.0099	-0.0138	-29.33%
BCN	0.0040	0.1214	0.0329	0.0303	-49.00%
NXT	-0.0017	0.0725	-0.0234	-0.0271	-36.36%
LTC	-0.0008	0.0578	-0.0130	-0.0180	-54.72%

Figure 5.16: Sentiment portfolio performance and other asset classes.

	Whole Sample Period		Before 2016		After 2016	
Trading Cost (bps)	Raw Annualized Return	t-value	Raw Annualized Return	t-value	Raw Annualized Return	t-value
1	11.58	15.97	13.76	11.77	9.22	11.38
2	11.54	15.91	13.72	11.73	9.18	11.33
3	11.50	15.86	13.68	11.70	9.14	11.29
4	11.46	15.81	13.64	11.67	9.10	11.24
5	11.42	15.76	13.60	11.63	9.06	11.19
6	11.38	15.71	13.56	11.60	9.03	11.15
7	11.34	15.65	13.52	11.57	8.99	11.10
8	11.30	15.60	13.48	11.53	8.95	11.06
9	11.26	15.55	13.44	11.50	8.91	11.01
10	11.22	15.50	13.39	11.47	8.87	10.96

Figure 5.17: Sentiment portfolio performance with different transaction costs.

to transaction costs, which implies a relatively low turnover of our strategy.

In addition, we test whether the selection of the formation period will have any great impact on the portfolio's performance. Previously,

	Whole Sample Period		Before 2016		After 2016	
Formation Period (day)	Raw Annualized Return	t-value	Raw Annualized Return	t-value	Raw Annualized Return	t-value
11	11.53	16.00	13.57	16.00	9.28	16.00
12	11.62	16.95	13.66	16.95	9.33	16.95
13	11.27	16.14	13.73	16.14	8.42	16.14
14	11.21	15.53	14.25	15.53	7.58	15.53
15	11.53	15.64	14.42	15.64	7.93	15.64
16	12.01	16.52	14.77	16.52	8.44	16.52
17	11.60	15.42	14.41	15.42	7.80	15.42
18	11.44	15.08	13.91	15.08	7.93	15.08
19	11.21	15.00	13.59	15.00	7.62	15.00
20	11.22	14.99	13.32	14.99	7.87	14.99

Figure 5.18: Sentiment portfolio performance with different sentiment formation periods.

a formation period of 10 trading days was used to average the daily returns. So, in the robustness check, we adopt various periods (from 11 days to 20 days) as the formation periods. From the table below, we can see that the portfolio performance is insensitive to the selection of formation periods. In particular, when we use 20 days as the formation period, the annualised portfolio return is 11.22 with a t-value of 14.99, suggesting a consistent sentiment effect on the cryptocurrency market (see Figure 5.18).

This strategy may encounter some obstacles in practice. For example, we cover 100 cryptocurrencies that have been most frequently included in the CRIX; sort them based on the investor sentiment to find the portfolio group to short and long; hold for 1 day and rebalance the next day; and repeat the strategy every day. Also, the short positions of cryptocurrencies are not feasible. However, evidence that investor sentiment affects the cryptocurrencies still provides valuable information about the prices of cryptocurrencies.

5.5 Conclusion

The cryptocurrency market has large investment potentials as it brings many new investment opportunities. We have thousands of cryptocurrencies to choose from with a total market value of hundreds of billions. It outperforms many mainstream asset classes in terms of risk-adjusted return, has generally very low correlations with existing investment tools and plays an important role in the diversification of portfolios. In further investigation of sentiment, we find that it largely affects the cryptocurrency market. A portfolio strategy based on cryptocurrency investor sentiment generates significant excess returns.

References

Berkman, H., Koch, P. D., Tuttle, L., and Zhang, Y. J. (2012). Paying attention: Overnight returns and the hidden cost of buying at the open. *Journal of Financial and Quantitative Analysis*, 47(4), 715–741.

Chen, S., Chen, C., Härdle, W. K., Lee, T. M., and Ong, B. (2016). A first econometric analysis of the CRIX family. Working Paper.

Engle, R. (2002). Dynamic conditional correlation: A simple class of multivariate generalized autoregressive conditional heteroskedasticity models. *Journal of Business & Economic Statistics*, 20(3), 339–350.

Lee, D. K. C., Guo, L., and Wang, Y. (2017). Cryptocurrency: A new investment opportunity? *Journal of Alternative Investments*, 20(3), 16–40.

Trimborn, S. and Härdle, W. K. (2018). CRIX an Index for cryptocurrencies. *Journal of Empirical Finance*, 49, 107–122.

Chapter 6

A Look at Security and Privacy: Bitcoin, Cryptocurrencies and Blockchain Networks

Ernie Teo*

6.1 Security of Blockchain Networks

The design of Bitcoin and its blockchain ensured that the data stored in the ledger are very hard to change and tamper with; the use of cryptography in blockchain ensures this. Incentive mechanisms embedded in the consensus protocol help to align all validators to be good. The distributed network checks the validity of the transactions to ensure that no fraudulent transaction goes through.

The security of the blockchain network comes with its decentralisation and distribution. As these features diminish, someone could gain control of the network and be able to compromise the security of the network. Some common network attacks are hard to execute on a blockchain network.

Take, for example, a Sybil attack, where someone attempts to take over a network by creating multiple accounts on the system. This would mean running multiple nodes on a blockchain network. If the

*Adjunct Senior Lecturer, National University of Singapore; Co Vice-Chairman, Blockchain Association Singapore, Singapore.

attacker can get access to enough nodes, he can block transactions (from other users) and disconnect you from the public network. By separating you from the main network, he can double spend or block your transactions.

Consensus algorithms make it hard to carry out a Sybil attack; one usually has to expand resources (such as computer power or tokens) in order to become a node on the blockchain network. This makes it expensive and difficult. Miners have a strong incentive to keep mining honestly as a large number of resources are needed to mine coins. However, this sort of attack is known to happen in real life to weaker/smaller blockchain networks. In really large-scale Sybil attacks, where the attackers manage to control the majority of the network computing power or hashrate, they can carry out a 51% attack.

6.1.1 *The 51% Attack*

In blockchain networks running Proof-of-Work (PoW) consensus, nodes are usually programmed to look for the blockchain with the most blocks as the correct version of history. Miners with more than 50% of the network hashing power can take advantage of this. This miner (let us call it Miner X) can send funds to one address (Wallet A) on the main chain, and double spend the same funds to another address on a forked copy of the blockchain that it is secretly mining with more hashing power than the main chain.

Other miners will continue to mine on the "Main Chain" while the secret fork is not revealed (see Figure 6.1). Thus, they will recognise

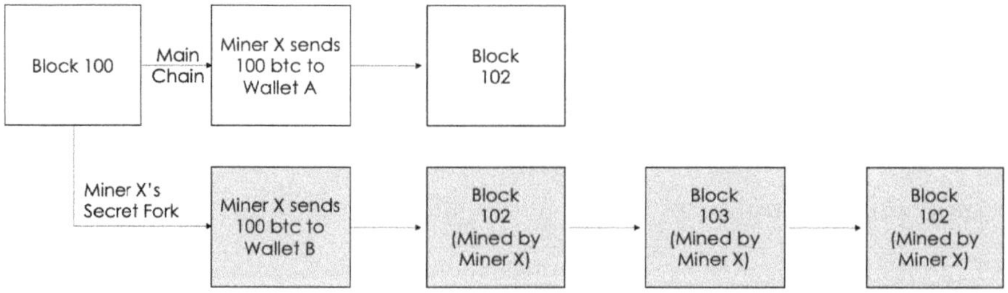

Figure 6.1: Mining process, forks and creation of chains.

the 100 btc transferred to Wallet A as valid. Cryptocurrency exchanges may pay out in fiat currency as a result.

Miner X with more hashing power can mine faster on the secret fork. Once it has more blocks than the main chain, Miner X can reveal it. The rest of the miners will mine on the longer fork when it is revealed. The secret fork will be recognised as the main chain and the 100 btc in Wallet A will become invalid. However, if someone (like an exchange) has paid out fiat money or goods and services based on the receipt of the 100 btc in Wallet A, this may not be recoverable. This is also known as a "double spend" attack.

Ethereum Classic (ETC) fell victim to a 51%-attack on January 5, 2019.[1] This went on for three days, finally halting on January 8, 2019, with estimated losses of US$ 1.1 million. On January 7, digital asset exchange Coinbase reported that its systems had detected unusual activity on the Ethereum Classic blockchain. As a result of the suspicious activity, the trading platform suspended all ETC trades in order to protect user funds.

According to Mark Nesbitt (the security engineer at Coinbase),[2] the platform's systems had detected this activity as early as January 5, a couple of days before the reports began in the media. At that time, ETC developers contended that the unusual activity detected by Coinbase could be attributed to the testing of new mining machines and denied any double spends or any losses stemming from the activity.

However, more reports and evidence began to trickle in from blockchain analysis firms as well as other digital asset trading platforms. Gate.io was the first exchange to corroborate Coinbase's findings.[3] Gate.io research confirmed that the ETC 51% attack happened successfully. In the analysis, they detected seven rollback transactions (invalid transfers due a block becoming invalid).

---

[1]https://cointelegraph.com/news/ethereum-classic-51-attack-the-reality-of-proof-of-work.

[2]https://bravenewcoin.com/insights/etc-51-attack-what-happened-and-how-it-was-stopped.

[3]https://www.gate.io/article/16735.

Four of them were created by the attacker and in total 54,200 ETC was transferred. Gate.io further corroborated Coinbase's findings that the attack was not just an innocent deep-chain reorganisation.[4]

Revealing the attacker's wallet addresses as well as other information pertinent to the malicious transactions, Gate.io also explained the attack had resulted in losses amounting to US$40,000 for the exchange. However, the exchange said it would not pass on the losses to its users. It also raised the confirmation number for ETC transactions and called on the ETC developers to change the consensus mechanism for the blockchain in order to avoid another attack. Following the Gate.io revelation, more exchanges began to either limit ETC trading activity on their platforms or increase the confirmation limit. Some of these include CoinCheck and Bitflyer as well as the mining pool Etherchain. Concurrently, ETC developers finally confirmed the presence of a 51% attack, referencing a report that a single party had been able to acquire over 50% of the network's hashrate.

On January 9, SlowMist published a report with in-depth analysis of the attack.[5] The firm found that the first attempted malicious transaction was carried out on the trading platform, Bitrue. The attacker executed a double spend worth US$14,000. Appearing to confirm Coinbase's estimate of US$1.1 million lost as a result of the attack, Slow Mist said that the attacker halted its activities due to the actions of exchange. "Based on continuous tracking, we found that, in view of the increase in block confirmations and the ban on malicious wallet addresses by exchanges, the attacker's 51% attack on ETC has stopped after that."

Coinbase was able to protect its users by halting trading of ETC. Given that ETC was one of the top 20 digital assets by market capitalisation, the 51% attack reverberated throughout the cryptocurrency community. It was easy for machines mining ETH to

---

[4]This can happen in certain circumstances as the blockchain network is asynchronous and some machines mine faster than others.

[5]https://medium.com/@slowmist/the-analysis-of-etc-51-attack-from-slowmist-team-728596d76ead.

PoW 51% Attack Cost

This is a collection of coins and the theoretical cost of a 51% attack on each network.

Learn More | Tip

Name	Symbol	Market Cap	Algorithm	Hash Rate	1h Attack Cost	NiceHash-able
Bitcoin	BTC	$168.34 B	SHA-256	84,879 PH/s	*$307,813*	0%
Ethereum	ETH	$22.97 B	Ethash	168 TH/s	*$121,370*	4%
BitcoinCashABC	BCH	$4.30 B	SHA-256	2,555 PH/s	*$9,265*	13%
Litecoin	LTC	$2.85 B	Scrypt	204 TH/s	*$16,304*	6%
EthereumClassic	ETC	$750.08 M	Ethash	8 TH/s	*$5,808*	85%
Dash	DASH	$700.61 M	X11	5 PH/s	*$1,897*	5%
Zcash	ZEC	$433.18 M	Equihash	5 GH/s	*$12,011*	4%
BitcoinGold	BTG	$154.92 M	Zhash	2 MH/s	*$411*	18%

Figure 6.2: PoW 51% attack cost (same as footnote 5).

switch to mining ETC as ETC uses the same mining algorithm as Ethereum. Since the ETC network was much smaller than ETH's, it was easy to gain the majority hashrate. The rise of cloud-based mining has made "hashrate for hire" a norm in the industry. And, for blockchain networks that are relatively small, it became attractive for bad actors to launch such attacks. Crypto 51[6] lists the estimated costs of renting the necessary hash power for some popular cryptocurrencies. It is surprising how low the costs of launching such attacks were. Figure 6.2 is a snapshot taken from Crypto 51.

An hour-long attack on Ethereum Classic, for example, could be done for around US$6,000. A Litecoin hijack would cost around US$16,000 an hour; even Ethereum could be attacked at a cost of around US$120,000 an hour.

[6]https://www.crypto51.app/.

In May 2018, Bitcoin Gold (a Bitcoin fork) was also attacked.[7] Bitcoin Gold's hashrate was significantly lower than that of Bitcoin, making it vulnerable to attacks. The cost of the attack on Crypto 51 was only US$400. In Figure 6.3, we compared the number of nodes on both networks in February 2019. Bitcoin Gold's nodes make up less than 2% of Bitcoins. Thus, we can see that a blockchain network is more vulnerable to 51% attacks if the network size is small. Larger networks like Bitcoin and Ethereum enjoy more resilience to such attacks as the costs make it harder to achieve both monetarily as well logistically (see Figure 6.4 for number of nodes in the Bitcoin network). This factor needs to be considered for anyone looking to invest in cryptocurrencies or to run their applications on their blockchain networks.

6.1.2 *Denial-of-Service Attacks*

A Denial-of-Service (DoS) attack aims to make a system or network inaccessible to its users. This is done by constantly sending traffic or information to the target, causing it to crash. A DoS attack blocks legitimate users from accessing the service. High-profile organisations are usually susceptible to these attacks, like financial institutions, media or government organisations. DoS attacks usually do not result in loss of information or assets, but the down time it causes can be costly as well. For example, if a bank gets attacked, it may not be able to process financial transactions.

The decentralised nature of blockchain makes for strong protection against DoS attacks. If certain nodes on the network had gone offline, the blockchain network can continue to validate transactions and create blocks. When the nodes come back online, they can sync up with the network and resume from the current block. However, in blockchain networks with distributed computing such as Ethereum, DoS attacks are possible if there are vulnerabilities in the code.

---

[7] https://qz.com/1287701/bitcoin-golds-51-attack-is-every-cryptocurrencys-nightmare-scenario/.

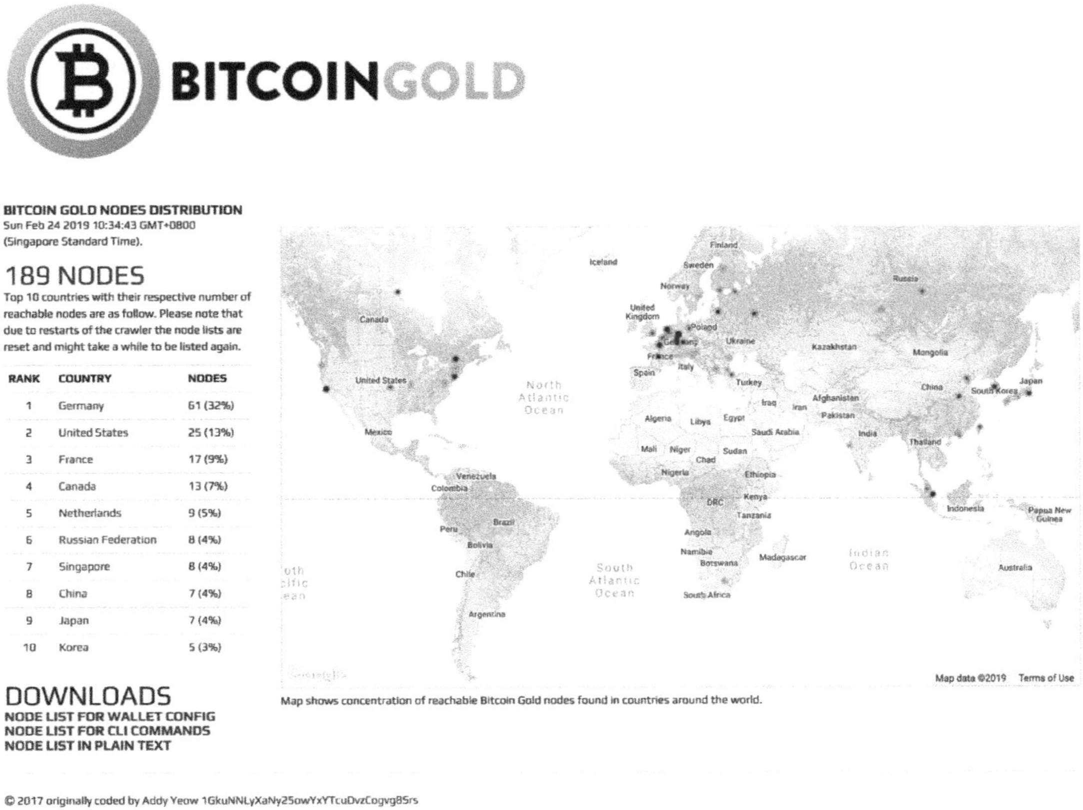

Figure 6.3: Number of nodes in Bitcoin Gold.
Source: https://status.bitcoingold.org.

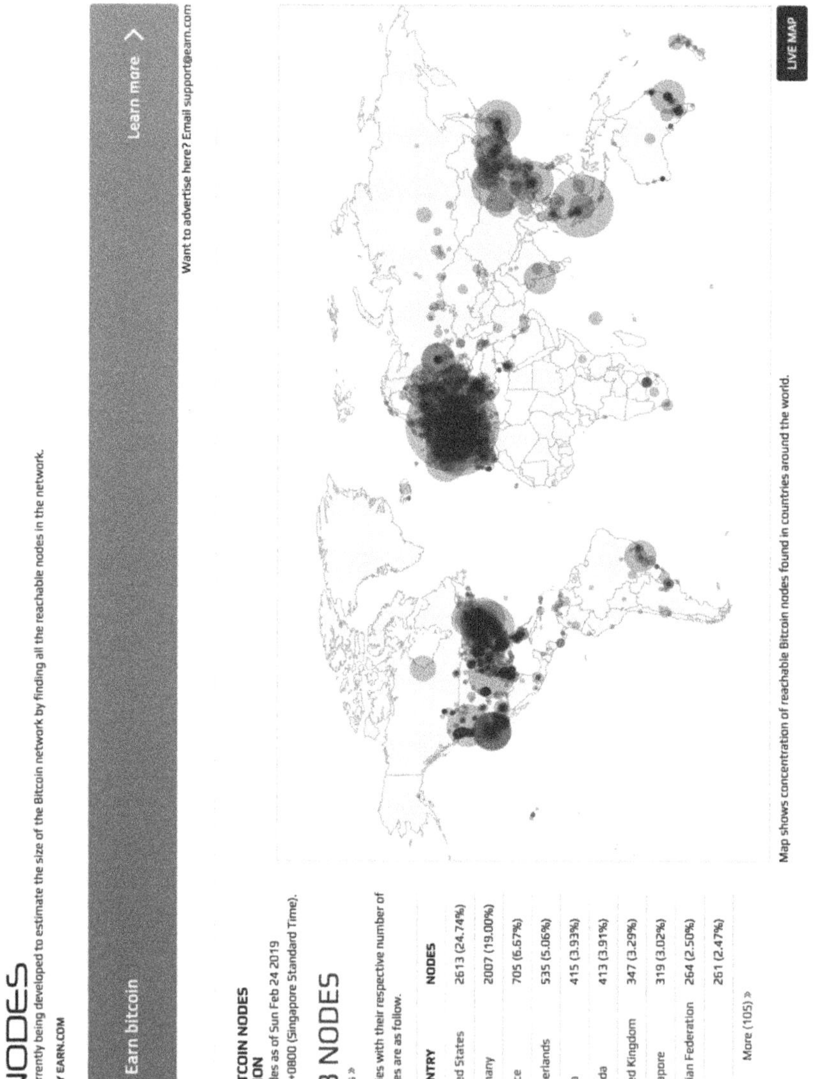

Figure 6.4: The number of nodes in Bitcoin.

Source: https://bitnodes.earn.com.

In 2016, the Ethereum network experienced such an attack.[8] On 22nd September, the first day of Devcon (Ethereum foundation's annual conference), nodes running the Geth client started to crash due to lack of memory. The crash only affected clients that were based on the Go language, and Ethereum created a hotfix the next day to address it.

Vitalik Buterin (Ethereum's founder) released a statement[9] in the post-mortem. The underlying problem involved Ethereum's EXTCODESIZE attribute, which is included in each transaction by design. An attacker could use this attribute to ask for additional checks against the Ethereum network database, up to 50,000 at a time. This caused the clients to crash as they ran out of memory; it caused a two to three times reduction in the rate of block creation. As stated by Vitalik, there was no consensus failure, and neither the network nor any client at any point fully halted.

6.1.3 *Software Flaws*

Although the flaw (which allowed the DoS attack) in the Ethereum was patched, this event also revealed the vulnerability of more complex blockchain networks. In particular, networks that have applications or smart contracts running on them are susceptible to flaws in the code or bugs. Smart contracts are only as good as the humans who write them, and code bugs or oversights can lead to unintended adverse actions being taken. Smart contracts on blockchain are meant to be immutable; this means that when the code gets exploited, there is no easy way to prevent this. Various software bugs have been found in decentralised apps (dApps) or smart contracts, which has led to tens of millions in damages over the years.

One of the first large incidents with smart contracts was the DAO (Decentralised Autonomous Organisation) hack.[10] "The DAO" was

---

[8]https://cointelegraph.com/news/ethereum-is-under-ddos-attack-miners-are-alerted.

[9]https://blog.ethereum.org/2016/09/22/transaction-spam-attack-next-steps/.

[10]https://blockgeeks.com/guides/ethereum/.

a project run by a team behind a startup called Slock.it. The aim was to create a decentralised venture capital firm where investors can make decisions to invest through smart contracts. It was funded through a token sale that raised US$150 million dollars. Shortly after the fund raise was completed in 2016, the DAO was hacked by an unknown attacker who stole US$50 million worth of ether. This was possible because of a backdoor in the code.

As a large amount of money was involved, the Ethereum foundation got involved and the community voted to roll back the blockchain and execute a hard fork. ETC (Ethereum Classic) was a result of this, being the original blockchain where the hack happened. ETH (Ethereum) was where the majority agreed to rewrite a small part of the blockchain and return the stolen money to the owners. Both blockchains are identical up to the point where the fork was implemented. This move was intensely debated and controversial. A blockchain network in principle is meant to be immutable. By executing the rollback, a dangerous precedent has been set which goes against the spirit of blockchain.

As such, any smart contracts that are to be deployed into a blockchain network should go under intense review and testing. Smart contracts and code should be reviewed and audited by external parties. The application should undergo penetration testing. It is advisable to have good security practices in place as flaws may remain hidden for a while. No matter how experienced the programmer, mistakes can be made.

6.1.4 *Cryptocurrency Exchange Hacks*

The final blockchain security issue is not an issue with the actual blockchain network and its technology; it is to do with cryptocurrency exchanges. Exchanges are very attractive to hackers as they hold massive amounts of cryptocurrencies and sometimes do not have very good security practices. Most exchanges operate in a centralised manner and thus they do not have the benefits of the decentralised blockchain. Private keys and wallets containing the cryptocurrencies of investors were not well protected, allowing hackers to steal these keys and transfer the assets out of the wallets.

The most famous exchange hack was that of Mt. Gox in 2014[11] where around 850,000 bitcoins, worth US$470 million (at that time), were stolen by a hacker. Mt. Gox was the industry leader at that time; they process about 70% of all bitcoin transactions. All the affected users were unable to get their money back. Exchange hacks were still prevalent, and hundreds of millions were stolen by hackers. It is always good practice to transfer your crypto holdings to self-managed secure wallets (such as a hardware device). If you have large amounts of cryptocurrencies, consider using a custodian service with high levels of security.

Although blockchain networks are secure by design, they can still be vulnerable to bad actors such as in situations described above. The risk of such attacks needs to be considered when trading in cryptocurrencies and deploying a blockchain network. However, security considerations go beyond hackers. In the next section, we look at protecting user data privacy.

6.2 Ensuring Privacy of Users on Blockchain Networks

Owners of bitcoins enjoy some amount of anonymity when they transact on the Bitcoin blockchain as they are only identified by their public addresses. However, all transactions are transparent on the blockchain. Forensic analysis can bundle addresses and find patterns. When you transact with exchanges, regulation requires that the exchange collects your identity and information. Even if you transact on a peer-to-peer basis only, your IP address can be logged in nodes and be linked to your bitcoin address. When you purchase something online with bitcoin, your physical address and other information can also be linked to your bitcoin address. This means that a bitcoin user's privacy is not entirely protected when they transact on blockchain. Privacy is an important element when it comes to digital payments. With paper money, you have the freedom to use it without being tracked.

[11]https://www.wired.com/2014/03/bitcoin-exchange/.

6.2.1 *Ensuring Privacy of Cryptocurrencies*

The crypto community has been working to improve the privacy aspects of cryptocurrencies. Figure 6.5 provides an overview of the technologies.

One commonly used method is coin mixing. Coin mixing services prevent users' addresses from being tracked by mixing coins from multiple senders before they are sent to the recipients. The ownership of coins is obfuscated with coin mixing. Some examples are Mixcoin, CoinJoin, SharedCoin and CoinShuffle. The solutions differ in the amount of security they provide.

Another method is to anonymise signatures. The two most commonly used signature schemes to achieve this are "group signatures" and "ring signatures". Group signature is a cryptography scheme proposed in the 1990s. With this scheme, any member of a group can sign a message for the group using her own secret key. The digital signature can be validated by the group public key. The verifier can only know that the signature came from the group but not the identity of the actual signer. The group signature scheme requires an administrator or authority to add and remove group members. By the nature of its design, this is suitable for consortium blockchains.

The ring signature scheme also achieves anonymity with a group of users. However, a group administrator is not required. With ring signatures, one cannot determine who the actual signer within the group is. The group can be arbitrarily formed by any users

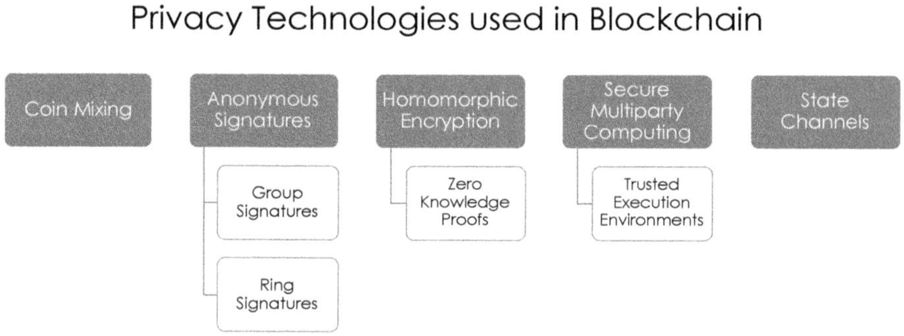

Figure 6.5: Privacy technologies used in blockchain.

without any additional setup. Thus, such schemes are good for public blockchains. Examples of public blockchains with ring signature schemes are Monero and Ethereum.

Another important method to protect data privacy is homomorphic encryption. It is a cryptography method that allows certain operations to be performed on encrypted data. This means one can perform a calculation without having to decrypt the data. For example, one can determine if a wallet has sufficient amount for a transfer without knowing the actual amount of funds in the wallet. This technique can be used to store data on blockchain without having to change the properties of the blockchain. It allows public blockchains to operate without having to store transactional data publicly. Ethereum smart contracts can provide homomorphic encryption on data stored on the Ethereum blockchain. Zero Knowledge Proofs are one form of homomorphic encryption and are used by blockchains such as ZCash.

Another widely discussed type of privacy protection technique is Secure Multi-Party Computation (SMPC). This technique allows multiple parties to each compute part of the input data in a way which does not compromise on the privacy of the input. Many real-world problems (where inputs need to remain anonymous) such as voting and bidding can be solved with SMPC. SMPC eliminates the need for a trusted authority to count votes or check bids. In 2015, a decentralised (blockchain-based) SMPC platform called Enigma was proposed. Enigma provides autonomous control and protection of personal data while eliminating the necessity and dependency of a trusted third party.

Enigma utilises a Trusted Execution Environment (TEE). TEE is an isolated computing environment, where other applications within the machine will not be able to access or tamper with the computation. One notable type of TEE technology is the Intel Software Guard eXtensions (SGX). It forms the basis for secure and privacy-preserving smart contracts on Enigma. One use case is for a decentralised credit-scoring algorithm. Multiple inputs for a person's credit score such as account information, transactions, payments and credit history can be stored in an encrypted manner on the blockchain. When required, the credit score is calculated within the TEE and only the credit score is returned to the requestor (without exposing the raw data). Blockchain provides additional trust for the encrypted raw data as it cannot be tampered with once stored.

Another method of ensuring privacy on a permissioned blockchain is the use of state channels.

These are private channels between two or more users. These users exchange the signed transactions between each other without broadcasting to the blockchain. We can imagine state channels as mini blockchains within the main blockchain network. State channels can be configured to have a limited lifespan and the channel can be closed by updating the latest state of transactions to the blockchain.

6.2.2 *Privacy Considerations and Design for Blockchain Applications*

Privacy on blockchains extends beyond cryptocurrency transactions. In many business applications, sensitive business data are involved. These data need to be shared appropriately with the members on the blockchain network. Global regulations around user privacy are also evolving rapidly and becoming stricter. The implementation of the EU's General Data Protection Regulation (GDPR) in May 2018 changed the landscape of technology. When personal data are collected, companies have to indicate what it will be used for and cannot use it for anything else. They need to minimise the amount of data they collect and keep, limiting it to only what is necessary for the purpose intended. When requested, companies have to be able to tell users what data they hold and alter or delete the data.

The largest causes of data leaks are human related (see Figure 6.6).

Thus, privacy is not just about the technology but also its design and policies that restrict what humans are able to do. Data privacy is concerned with the proper handling of data. There are three key considerations: consent, notice and regulation. Specifically, practical data privacy concerns often revolve around the following:

- whether or how data are shared with third parties;
- how data is legally collected or stored;
- regulatory restrictions such as GDPR and PDPA.

Most government regulations include obligations in terms of where data processing can take place, also known as "transfers of personal data" to third countries. The Indonesian data protection bill guarantees that the data pertaining to the personal data of Indonesians will exist only within Indonesia and will be protected by the government. The GDPR specifies that personal data can generally only be transferred to third countries if they are deemed "adequate". This presents an interesting problem for decentralised blockchain networks. It may be necessary to border off the blockchain network to ensure that the data do not leave the geographical constraints of the country.

Another consideration is how the data are being stored; some amount of processing could increase the privacy of the data. Various techniques can be used to fulfil this purpose. Pseudonymisation can be used to hide personal data by replacing information that links the data to particular individuals with artificial identifiers.

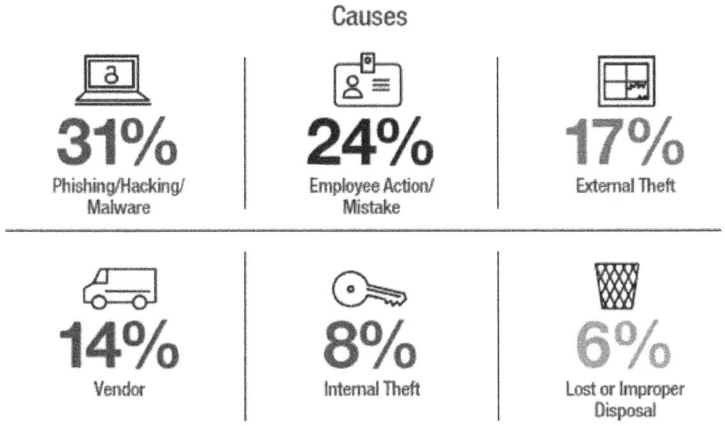

Figure 6.6: Causes of data leaks.
Source: https://www.dataprivacymonitor.com/cybersecurity/deeper-dive-human-error-is-to-blame-for-most-breaches/.

One can mask the data by hiding parts of the data by replacing it with random characters or other data. Data blurring is one form of pseudonymisation. Pictures and videos containing faces can be blurred out to protect the identity of individuals captured by the camera. In pictures of identity documents such as passports, the sensitive information can also be blurred out.

Encryption converts data to another form which is only readable to someone who has access to a key or password. There are two categories of encryption, symmetric and asymmetric. In symmetric encryption, there is only one password and anyone with the password can decrypt the data. In asymmetric encryption, there are sets of key pairs (public and private key). The key pairs are required to encrypt and decrypt the data. Asymmetric encryption is widely used in the design of blockchain systems. Data should be encrypted while being moved and also while in storage.

As data in a blockchain can be read by its network, we need to consider two types of risks when storing sensitive data on a blockchain. "Reversal risks" are the likelihood that the data can be decrypted, such as when someone is able to gain access to the keys. Reversal risks exist as long as the keys exist. Many encryption techniques may one day be cracked. Thus, it is not sufficient to just store encrypted data. "Linkability risks" occur when one can link the data to an individual by analysing patterns.

Hashing techniques that are used in blockchain applications are non-reversible. Whether personal data are hashed is widely debated. It also comes down to whether there are potential reversibility and linkability risks. It may be possible to reverse a hash using brute force if the data come from a known set of possibilities (e.g., numbers from one to a million). This can be mitigated by salting or peppering the data, where extra data (that is only known to the generator of the hash) is added before creating the hash. Transactional data on blockchain may be linkable if you use an application to perform actions on your behalf which is linked to your address. This can be mitigated by using the anonymous signature schemes described above.

When designing a blockchain network which will store user data, one needs to consider the following points (see Figure 6.7).

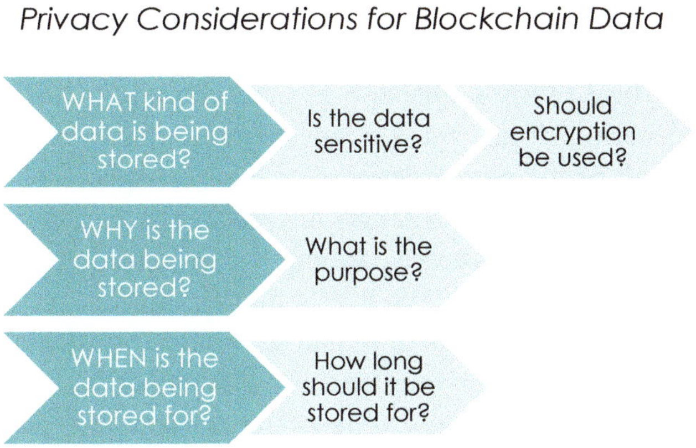

Figure 6.7: Privacy considerations for blockchain data.

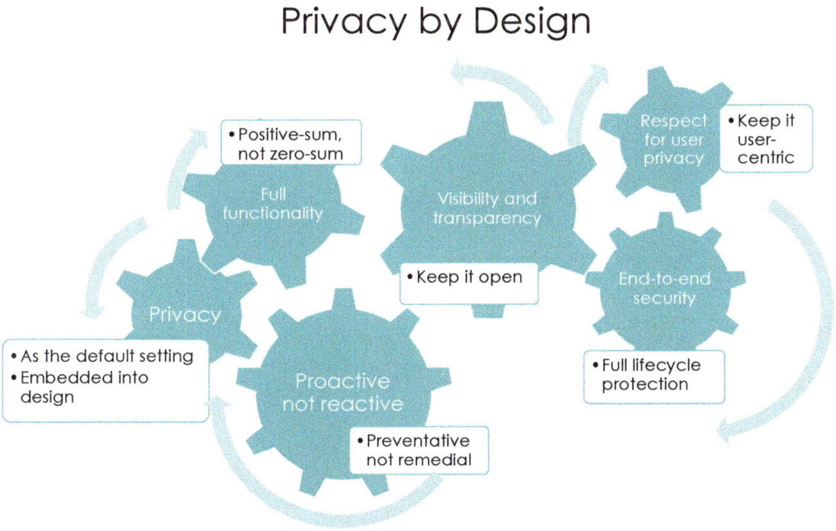

Figure 6.8: Privacy by design principles.

One should pick the appropriate techniques and apply them to the design of the network. "Privacy by Design" is an approach to systems engineering which requires privacy to be taken into account throughout the whole engineering process. It is based on seven "foundational principles" (see Figure 6.8).

In the current data economy, many services like social media or messaging platforms are offered free to users in return for the use of their data. This landscape is now changing due to increase in user protection from various governments. However, this does not mean that users cannot choose to share aspects of their data in return for free services. Blockchain networks can potentially be used to help manage users' consent with regard to their data. New developments in applied mathematics around cryptography, blockchains and machine learning can allow for data-driven business models. By solving the privacy concerns, we may be able to create a decentralised data economy where the market can all share and trade data. With tools like secure multiparty computing and zero knowledge proofs, data can be used to train machines learning algorithms without revealing the raw data. Users can contribute to their data and get paid for it. Data from humans, devices, applications and algorithms can be agglomerated and analysed.

Chapter 7

Introduction to Blockchain Smart Contracts and Programming with Solidity for Ethereum

Ernie Teo*

7.1 Introduction

The concept of smart contracts was first discussed in Nick Szabo's (1997) paper, "The Idea of Smart Contracts". He proposed smart contracts as a means to embed contractual clauses into digital assets.

For smart contracts to be useful for digital assets, there needs to be transparency and trust between the contractual parties. The emergence of Bitcoin reignited the discussion of smart contracts as an application for blockchains. It serves as a system that aids trustworthy execution of smart contract. They run exactly as programmed without any possibility of downtime, censorship, fraud or third-party interference. Instead of recording transfers of bitcoin on the blockchain, smart contracts are stored (see Figure 7.1).

*Adjunct Senior Lecturer, National University of Singapore; Co Vice-Chairman, Blockchain Association Singapore, Singapore.

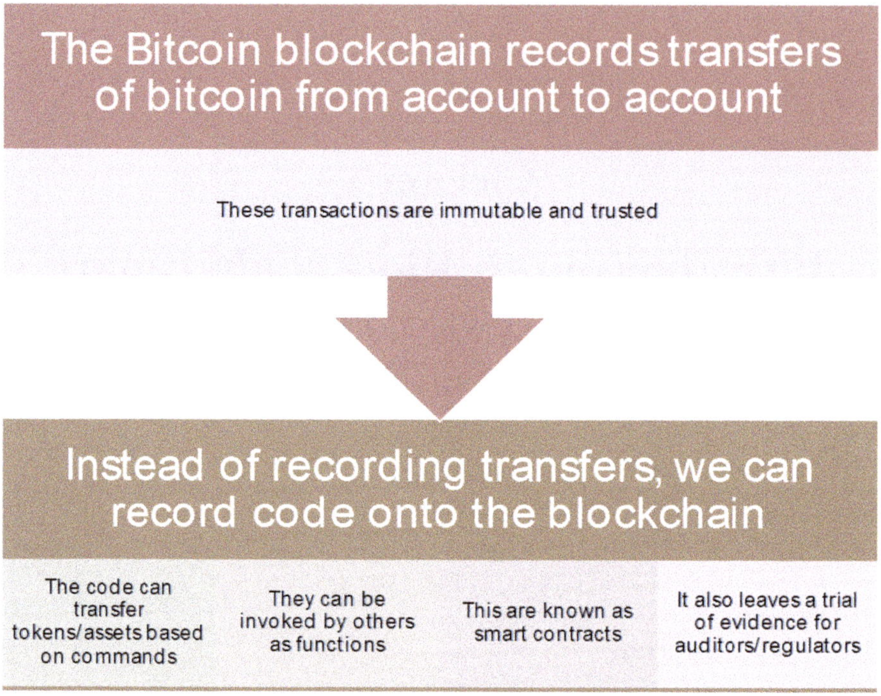

Figure 7.1: Characteristics of smart contracts.

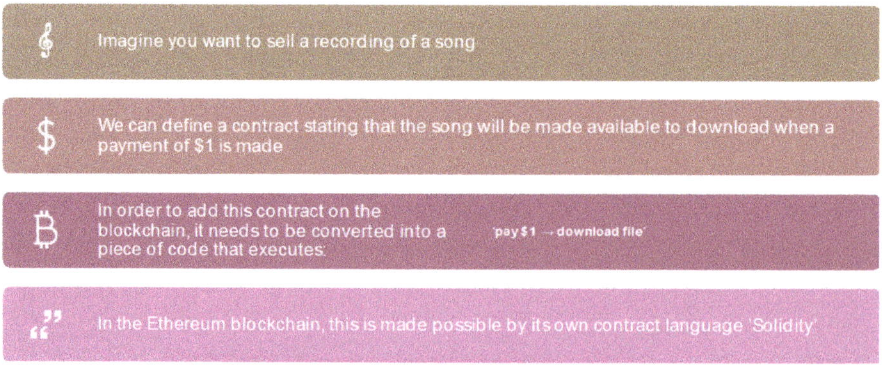

Figure 7.2: Smart contract for music.

Take, for example, the sale of original music online (see Figures 7.2 and 7.3).

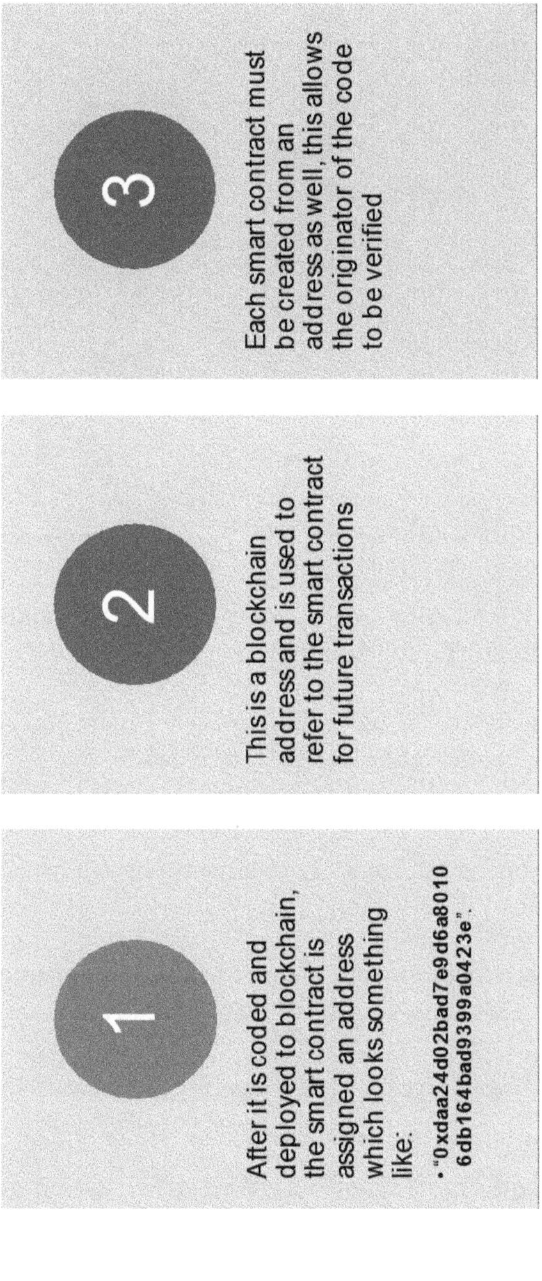

Figure 7.3: Assignment of smart contract to blockchain address.

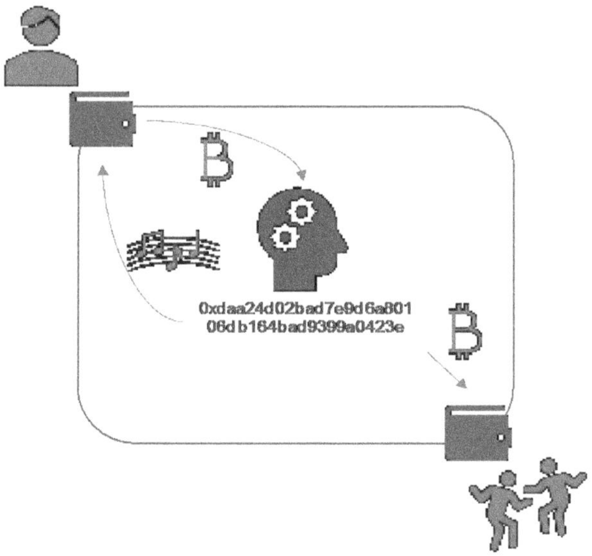

Figure 7.4: Buying a song via a smart contract on blockchain.

Suppose Billy wants to buy a song. Using the smart contract, Billy will go through the following steps (see Figure 7.4):

1. He sends US$1 from his blockchain wallet to the smart contract.
2. The song will be available for Alice to download.
3. The smart contract assigns the rights to download the song to Billy's wallet.
4. US$1 is distributed to the song creators (the smart contract can even keep part of it as a fee).

There is no middleman (like a record label or a music platform) in the above process. The smart contract will always action as it is programmed.

Other ways that smart contracts are used on blockchain include the following:

1. **Issuing of tokens.** Tokens can represent virtual currency or physical assets. These tokens can be used for fund raising; Initial Coin Offerings (ICOs) are a good example. Other types of assets

that can be tokenised include property, gold or even fiat currencies like the USD.

2. **Ecommerce.** This reduces the need for middlemen for the sale of virtual goods such as the music in the example in Figure 7.2. Another great use case for ecommerce is escrow contracts. Escrows hold custody of payment between a buyer and seller until the transaction is completed. Instead of having a trusted middleman (such as Paypal) to hold the payment, a smart contract holds the funds (in token form) instead.
3. **Lotteries.** A smart contract can act as a lottery. Users can buy the lottery by sending funds into the contract. After the results are determined, the smart contract will be paid out to the winners. The process is transparent and cannot be changed.

7.2 Ethereum

Ethereum's global computer (or the Ethereum virtual machine) processes code in a decentralised way, relying on the resources of the nodes on the blockchain network (see Figure 7.5). Invented in 2013, the first version of Ethereum was released in 2016 (see Figure 7.6).

Before Ethereum was conceptualised, blockchains had limited ability to process code. Ethereum is different; rather than giving a set of limited operations, it allows developers to create whatever operations they want. This means developers can build thousands of different applications that go way beyond anything we have

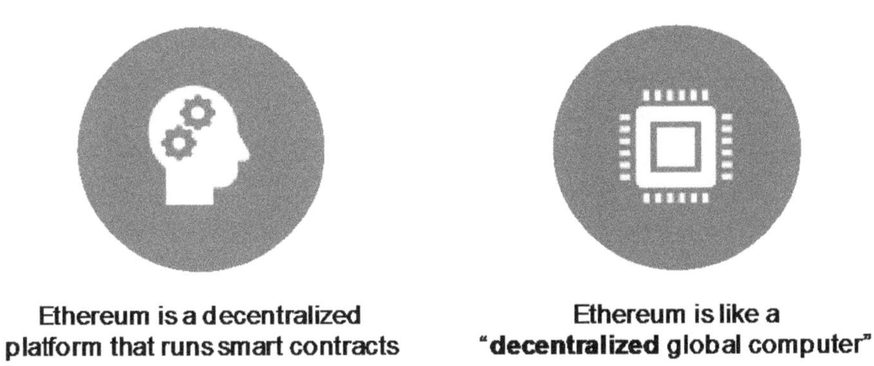

Figure 7.5: Characteristics of Ethereum.

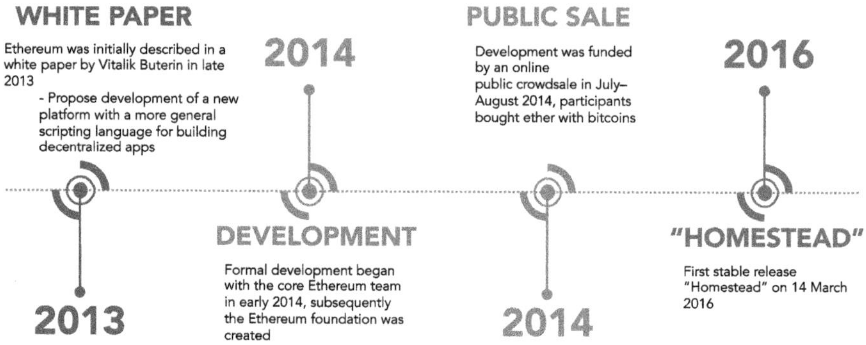

Figure 7.6: Ethereum's timeline.

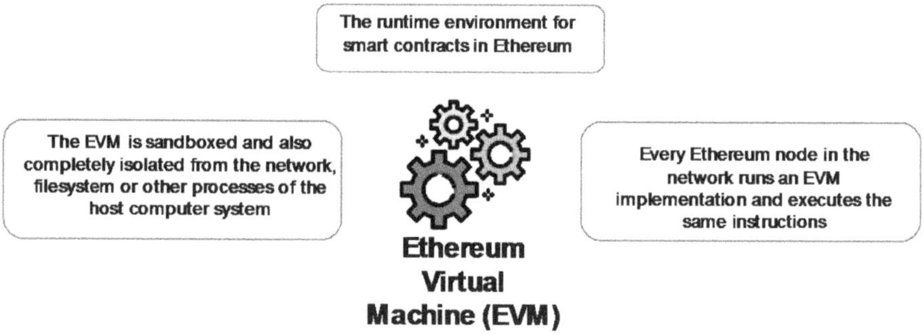

Figure 7.7: Ethereum Virtual Machine.

seen before. Ethereum aims to be "Turing complete"; anything that can be mathematically represented can be programmed and put into a smart contract. Ethereum is a decentralised global computer that processes smart contracts.

The Ethereum Virtual Machine (EVM) is software that runs on every computer on the Ethereum network (see Figure 7.7). This allows one to run any program, regardless of the programming language given enough time and memory. The EVM makes the process of creating blockchain applications much easier and more efficient than ever before. Rather than building and deploying a new blockchain for each application, Ethereum allows for the development of potentially thousands of different applications all on one platform.

In Ethereum, smart contracts are stateful decentralised applications that are stored in the Ethereum blockchain for later execution by the EVM. One pays the network for executing the instructions embedded in Ethereum contracts with ether (or more technically "gas"). Ether or ETH is the native currency on the Ethereum Blockchain (similar to how bitcoins or BTCs are native on the Bitcoin blockchain); it is used to pay for transactions including deployment and invocation of smart contracts. Smart contracts on Ethereum can be implemented in a variety of Turing complete scripting languages.

7.3 Tools for Ethereum Smart Contract Development

Figure 7.8 describes high-level architecture for Ethereum Smart Contract (ESC); it includes the front end, the development platform and the blockchain network. Figures 7.9–7.14 provide descriptions of the various applications described in Figure 7.8 and their applications in creating ESC.

Some useful links for setting up the development tools:

1. Metamask Wallet
   (a) https://metamask.zendesk.com/hc/en-us/articles/360015489531-Getting-Started-With-MetaMask-Part-1-.
2. Truffle Framework
   (a) https://truffleframework.com/.

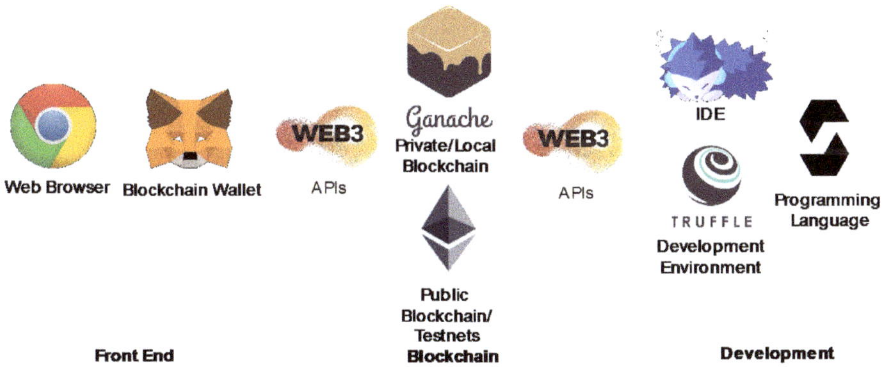

Figure 7.8: Overview of Ethereum smart contract architecture.

Tools for Ethereum Smart Contract Development

- Solidity is an object-oriented, high-level language for implementing smart contracts
- Smart contracts are programs which govern the behaviour of accounts within the Ethereum state
- Solidity was influenced by C++, Python and JavaScript and is designed to target the Ethereum Virtual Machine (EVM)

Figure 7.9: Solidity for Ethereum smart contract development.

Tools for Ethereum Smart Contract Development

- MetaMask is an web wallet that lets you connect to an Ethereum blockchain
- It can manage, transfer, receive Ethers and and ERC20 tokens on the Ethereum blockchain
- It also allows you interact with Dapps

Figure 7.10: MetaMask for Ethereum smart contract development.

Tools for Ethereum Smart Contract Development

- Remix IDE is an IDE for Solidity decentralised App (dApps) developers, powered by Remix
- Remix is a suite of tools that helps smart contract development, compilation, testing & deployment

- https://remix.ethereum.org

Figure 7.11: Remix IDE for Ethereum smart contract development.

Tools for Ethereum Smart Contract Development

A world class development environment, testing framework and asset pipeline for blockchains using the Ethereum Virtual Machine (EVM), aiming to make life as a developer easier

With Truffle, you get:

- Built-in smart contract compilation, linking, deployment and binary management
- Network management for deploying to many public & private networks

Figure 7.12: Truffle for Ethereum smart contract development.

Tools for Ethereum Smart Contract Development

- web3.js is a collection of libraries which allow you to interact with a local or remote Ethereum node, using an HTTP, WebSocket or IPC connection

Figure 7.13: web3.js for Ethereum smart contract development.

Tools for Ethereum Smart Contract Development

- A personal blockchain for Ethereum development you can use to deploy contracts, develop your applications, and run tests
- It is available as both a desktop application as well as a command-line tool (formerly known as the TestRPC)

Figure 7.14: TestRPC for Ethereum smart contract development.

3. Solidity
   a. https://solidity.readthedocs.io/.
4. Web3
   a. https://web3js.readthedocs.io/.
   b. http://www.dappuniversity.com/articles/web3-js-intro.

7.4 Writing Your Own Ethereum Smart Contracts with Remix

To get started, you should have a Metamask wallet set up (https://metamask.io/). You will also need some testnet tokens; we will use the Rinkeby network. Visit https://faucet.rinkeby.io/ for RETH. We will use the Remix IDE (https://remix.ethereum.org) to develop and deploy our smart contracts.

7.4.1 *Getting Started*

After opening the Remix IDE in your browser, choose "New File". Name your contract "myfirstcontract.sol". You will see a blank document. To start, we use "version pragma" to declare the version of Solidity compiler we are using; all Solidity codes start with it. It helps to prevent issues with future compiler versions. You can declare a specific version or a range, for example,

```
pragma solidity ∧ 0.5.16;
pragma solidity >= 0.4.0 < 0.6.0;
```

Next, create your contract by typing

```
contract MyFirstContract {

}
```

Do the following to compile the contract (see Figure 7.15). If there are errors in the code, the contract will fail to compile. If you cannot find the Solidity compiler, add it with the Plugin Manager.

A contract contains the code (functions) and data (state) that reside at a specific Ethereum address. Let us start with a simple "Hello world" code to get acquainted with Solidity contracts.

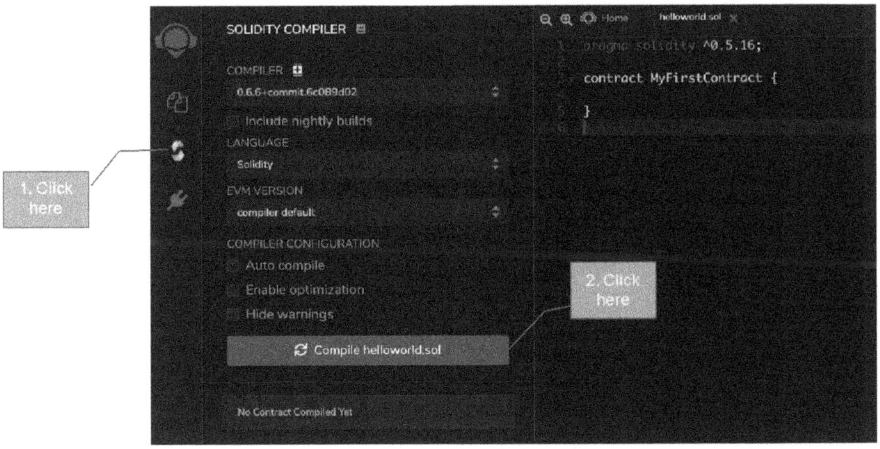

Figure 7.15: Contract compilation.

We start by defining a state variable called "message" which will be the string type. The Get function will return the value of the variable "message". The Set function will assign a new value to the variable "message".

To define the function, we start with the reserved word **function**, followed by the name of a particular function, then the parameters and finally the ⟨visibility specifiers⟩. The contract will look like this:

```
pragma solidity ^0.5.0;

contract MyFirstContract {
  string message;

  function get() public view returns(string memory) {
    return message;
  }

  function set(string memory _message) public {
    message = _message;
  }
}
```

Functions can be public or private. Public functions can be called outside of the contract. Private functions can only be called from its current contract (by some other function).

Function Visibility Specifiers:

- public: visible externally and internally
- private: only visible in the current contract
- external: only visible externally (only for functions)
- internal: only visible internally

Functions can also be pure, view or payable. If a function does not write any data on blockchain, it is recommended to be view, because view functions do not cost any gas.

Function Modifiers:

- pure: Disallows modification or access of state
- view: Disallows modification of state
- payable: Allows them to receive Ether together with a call

If the function returns some value, you will need to specify that with the reserved word **returns** and then in regular brackets to specify which type does function returns. In this case, it will be string (because we return our variable message which is string). If the function does not return any value, there is no need for returns statement. It is common practice to write function arguments with underscore syntax (_message). This convention came from JavaScript, where private methods and variables start with _.

Next, we test the contract. We compile (as described previously) and deploy. To deploy, choose the Deploy and Run module (add the module if it is not there). Choose JavaScript VM as the environment; we are deploying the smart contract in your computer memory (see Figure 7.16).

After deployment, you will see the deployed contract below where you can test the functions. We can now see methods from our contract (see Figure 7.17).

There are two buttons (get & set) for our two public functions (private cannot be seen here).

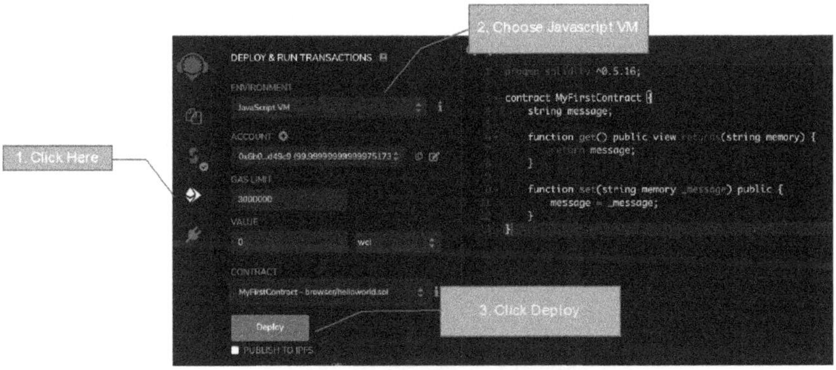

Figure 7.16: Deploy and Run.

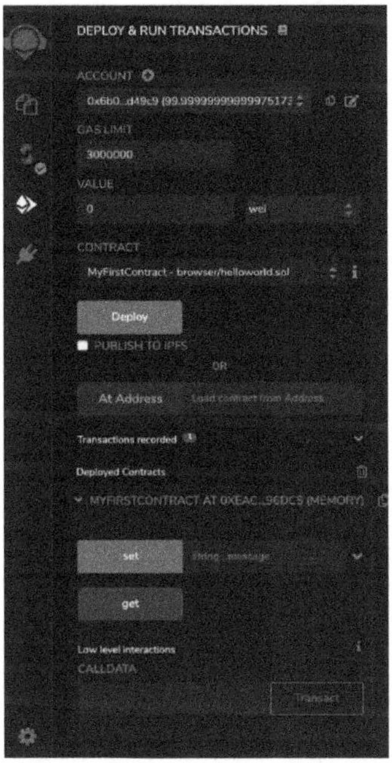

Figure 7.17: Execution of function.

Click the Get button for the EVM to execute the function. You will see an empty string returned. Now, type a message in the "set" field and click the Set button. Click the Get button again, and your message will be returned.

However, it does not say Hello world; we can initialise the message with a constructor. You can write constructor in Solidity with

```
constructor() public {
  // do something...
  }
```

We update the code to the following:

```
pragma solidity ^0.5.0;

contract MyFirstContract {
   string public message;

   constructor() public {
      message = "Hello world!";
   }

   function set(string memory _message) public {
      message = _message;
   }
}
```

We have made the message public and removed the Get function. If we make the state variables public, one can claim their values from outside the contract. Solidity will make for each public state variable a method with the same name which can be called as a regular function. We do not need the get function once we do this. This will reduce the size of the code and make it cheaper to deploy.

You can compile, deploy and test the updated code. A message button now replaces the Get function; it will return the value of message.

Next, we will create an ERC-20 contract. The token contract consists of the following:

- ERC-20 Interface — The token rules or standard
- SafeMath Library — Add-on arithmetic operations
- Your customised token contract

ERC-20 tokens follow a list of rules so that they can be shared, exchanged for other tokens or transferred to a crypto-wallet; these are defined in the ERC-20 Interface. The ERC-20 standard consists of three optional rules and six mandatory rules. If you include certain functions in the token's smart contract, you are ERC-20 compliant.

Mandatory rules:

- totalSupply
- balanceOf
- transfer
- transferFrom
- approve
- allowance

Optional rules:

- Token Name
- Symbol
- Decimal (up to 18)

Below is an ERC-20 Interface contract:

```
pragma solidity ^0.5.0;
contract ERC20Interface {
 function totalSupply() public view returns (uint);
 function balanceOf(address tokenOwner) public view returns
(uint balance);
 function allowance(address tokenOwner, address spender) pub-
lic view returns (uint remaining);
 function transfer(address to, uint tokens) public returns (bool
success);
 function approve(address spender, uint tokens) public returns
(bool success);
 function transferFrom (address from, address to, uint tokens)
public returns (bool success);
 event Transfer(address indexed from, address indexed to, uint
tokens);
 event Approval(address indexed tokenOwner, address indexed
spender, uint tokens);
}
```

The Safe Math Library is needed to correctly implement some functions. Arithmetic operations in Solidity wrap on overflow; this can easily result in bugs. Safe Math restores this intuition by reverting the transaction when an operation overflows. Using this library instead of the unchecked operations eliminates an entire class of bugs, so it is recommended to use it always.

The code for the Safe Math Library is the following:

```
contract SafeMath {
  function safeAdd(uint a, uint b) public pure returns (uint c) {
    c = a + b;
    require(c >= a);
  }
  function safeSub(uint a, uint b) public pure returns (uint c) {
    require(b <= a); c = a - b; }function safeMul(uint a, uint b) public
pure returns (uint c) {c = a * b; require(a == 0 ||c / a == b); }function
safeDiv(uint a, uint b) public pure returns (uint c) {require(b >0);
    c = a / b;
  }
}
```

In Solidity, inheritance is pretty similar to classic oriented object programming languages. For example,

```
contract baseContract {
  // base contract code...
}

contract inheritedContract is baseContract {
  // inherited contract code...
}
```

When a contract inherits from multiple contracts, only a single contract is created on the blockchain, and the code from all the base contracts is copied into the created contract. Our main token contract will inherit the ERC-20 Interface and the Safe Math Library:

```
contract CoinContract is ERC20Interface, SafeMath
```

In our token contract, we define the three optional rules:

- Name — gives your token an identity
- Symbol — usually three letters
- Decimals — defines the lowest possible value of the token. The maximum number of decimal places allowed is 18. Eighteen decimals is the strongly suggested default; avoid changing it.

```
string public name;
string public symbol;
   uint8 public decimals;
   uint256 public _ totalSupply;
```

_totalSupply has a uint256 data type and decimals uint8. Solidity is a statically typed language, which means that the type of each variable (state and local) needs to be specified at compile time. Solidity provides several elementary types which can be combined to form complex types. Integers can be int or uint: signed and unsigned integers of various sizes. An unsigned integer is an integer that can never be negative; signed, on the contrary, can be both negative and positive. We will use only uint in our contract.

Our token also needs an initial supply, and a record of all balances. In constructor, we will initialise our contract, including the initial supply tokens to the creator of the contract (that is msg.sender). You can set your own name and symbol.

```
constructor() public {
  name = "TokenName";
  symbol = "XYZ";
  decimals = 18;
  _ totalSupply = 1000000000000000000000000000;

  balances[msg.sender] = _totalSupply;
}
```

To store balances, we use mappings. Mapping types are declared as mapping(_KeyType => _ ValueType). We can mark mappings public and have Solidity create a getter. The _KeyType will become a required parameter for the getter and it will return _ValueType. The _ValueType can be a mapping too. The getter will have one parameter for each _KeyType, recursively. We map address (that is a data type also) to uint:

```
mapping(address => uint) balances;
mapping(address => mapping(address => uint)) allowed;
```

The blockchain contains transactions within blocks, and each transaction contains log entries. These log entries represent results of events coming from a smart contract. In the Solidity source code, to define an event, you mark it thus by preceding it with the event keyword (similar in usage to the function keyword). For example, you can find the following in the ERC-20 Interface contract:

```
event Transfer(address indexed from, address indexed to, uint
tokens);
```

You then call the event in the body of whatever function you wish to cause to generate the event. You can do so using the emit keyword:

```
emit Transfer(address(0), msg.sender, _ totalSupply);
```

The token contract now looks like this:

```
contract CoinContract is ERC20Interface, SafeMath {
   string public name;
   string public symbol;
   uint8 public decimals;

   uint256 public _totalSupply;

   mapping(address => uint) balances;
   mapping(address => mapping(address => uint)) allowed;
```

```
    constructor() public {
        name = "TokenName";
        symbol = "XYZ";
        decimals = 18;
        _totalSupply = 1000000000000000000000000;

        balances[msg.sender] = _ totalSupply;
        emit Transfer(address(0), msg.sender, _ totalSupply);
    }
}
```

We also need to add code for the six mandatory functions in our main token contract:

1. totalSupply
   Identifies the total number of ERC 20 tokens created. The purpose of this method is to determine the total number of tokens floating around the ecosystem.

   ```
   function totalSupply() public view returns (uint)
   {
     return _ totalSupply - balances[address(0)];
   }
   ```

2. balanceOf
   Returns the number of tokens that a particular address has in their account.

   ```
   function balanceOf(address tokenOwner) public view returns
   (uint balance)
   {  return balances[tokenOwner];
   }
   ```

3. allowance
   In order to carry out a transaction, one of the most important data that the contract should know is the balance of the user. If the user does not have the minimum required number of tokens, the function cancels the transaction.

```
function allowance(address tokenOwner, address spender)
public view returns (uint remaining)
{
  return allowed[tokenOwner][spender];
}
```

4. approve
   To give approval to the user to collect the required number of tokens from the contract's address. The approve function also checks the transaction against the total supply of tokens to make sure that there are none missing or extra. It makes sure that counterfeiting or double spending is impossible.

```
function approve(address spender, uint tokens) public returns
(bool success)
{
  allowed[msg.sender][spender] = tokens;
  emit Approval(msg.sender, spender, tokens);
  return true;
}
```

5. transfer
   This function lets the owner of the contract send a given amount of the tokens to another address just like a conventional cryptocurrency transaction.

```
function transfer(address to, uint tokens) public returns (bool
success)
{
  balances[msg.sender] = safeSub(balances[msg.sender],
tokens);
  balances[to] = safeAdd(balances[to], tokens);
  emit Transfer(msg.sender, to, tokens);
  return true;
}
```

6. transferFrom
   transferFrom() allows you to automate payment transfers to a specific account.

```
function transferFrom (address from, address to, uint tokens)
public returns (bool success)
{
  balances[from] = safeSub(balances[from], tokens);
  allowed[from][msg.sender] = safeSub(allowed[from][msg.
     sender], tokens);
  balances[to] = safeAdd(balances[to], tokens);

      emit Transfer(from, to, tokens);
  return true;
}
```

The final code looks like the following:

```
pragma solidity ^0.5.0;
// ------------------------------------------------------------------
// ERC Token Standard #20 Interface
//
// ------------------------------------------------------------------
contract ERC20Interface {
  function totalSupply() public view returns (uint);
  function balanceOf(address tokenOwner) public view returns
(uint balance);
  function allowance(address tokenOwner, address spender)
public view returns (uint remaining);
  function transfer(address to, uint tokens) public returns (bool
success);
  function approve(address spender, uint tokens) public returns
(bool success);
  function transferFrom(address from, address to, uint tokens)
public returns (bool success);
```

```
  event Transfer(address indexed from, address indexed to, uint
tokens);
  event Approval(address indexed tokenOwner, address indexed
spender, uint tokens);
}
// ----------------------------------------------------------------
// Safe Math Library
// ----------------------------------------------------------------
contract SafeMath {
  function safeAdd(uint a, uint b) public pure returns (uint c) {
    c = a + b;
    require(c >= a);
  }
  function safeSub(uint a, uint b) public pure returns (uint c) {
    require(b <= a); c = a - b; }function safeMul(uint a, uint
b) public pure returns (uint c) {c = a * b; require(a == 0 ||c /
a == b); }function safeDiv(uint a, uint b) public pure returns
(uint c) {require(b >0);
    c = a / b;
  }
}

contract CoinContact is ERC20Interface, SafeMath {
  string public name;
  string public symbol;
  uint8 public decimals; // 18 decimals is the strongly suggested
default, avoid changing it


  uint256 public _totalSupply;

  mapping(address => uint) balances;
  mapping(address => mapping(address => uint)) allowed;

  /**
  * Constructor function
```

```
    *
    * Initializes contract with initial supply tokens to the creator
of the contract
    */
    constructor() public {
        name = "TokenName";
        symbol = "XYZ";
        decimals = 18;
        _totalSupply = 1000000000000000000000000000;

        balances[msg.sender] = _totalSupply;
        emit Transfer(address(0), msg.sender, _totalSupply);

    }
function totalSupply() public view returns (uint) {
        return _totalSupply - balances[address(0)];
    }
    function balanceOf(address tokenOwner) public view returns
(uint balance) {
        return balances[tokenOwner];
    }
    function allowance(address tokenOwner, address spender)
public view returns (uint remaining) {
        return allowed[tokenOwner][spender];
}
    function approve(address spender, uint tokens) public returns
(bool success) {
        allowed[msg.sender][spender] = tokens;
        emit Approval(msg.sender, spender, tokens);
        return true;
    }
    function transfer(address to, uint tokens) public returns (bool
success) {
```

```
        balances[msg.sender] = safeSub(balances[msg.sender],
tokens);
        balances[to] = safeAdd(balances[to], tokens);
        emit Transfer(msg.sender, to, tokens);
        return true;
    }
    function transferFrom(address from, address to, uint tokens)
public returns (bool success) {
        balances[from] = safeSub(balances[from], tokens);
        allowed[from][msg.sender] = safeSub(allowed[from][msg.
sender], tokens);
        balances[to] = safeAdd(balances[to], tokens);
        emit Transfer(from, to, tokens);
        return true;
    }
}
```

You can now compile, deploy and test your contracts. The next step is to deploy to the testnet. To do so, change the environment to "Injected Web3" (see Figure 7.18).

Before you click Deploy, make sure that your Metamask wallet is set to a testnet wallet with enough token balance (If your Metamask wallet is connected to the Main Ethereum Network instead, your wallet will be charged real ETH and the contract will be deployed into the live network). Once you click Deploy, Metamask will prompt you to approve the payment for the transaction fee (see Figure 7.19).

Once the transaction is complete, you can see a green tick in the console box. You can also click on the link to check the transaction on Etherscan (an Ethereum blockchain explorer). You can find your wallet address (creator), the smart contract address and the token details on Etherscan (see Figure 7.20).

Clicking on the token link will bring you to the Token page (see Figure 7.21).

You can add the token to your Metamask wallet by following the steps below (see Figure 7.22).

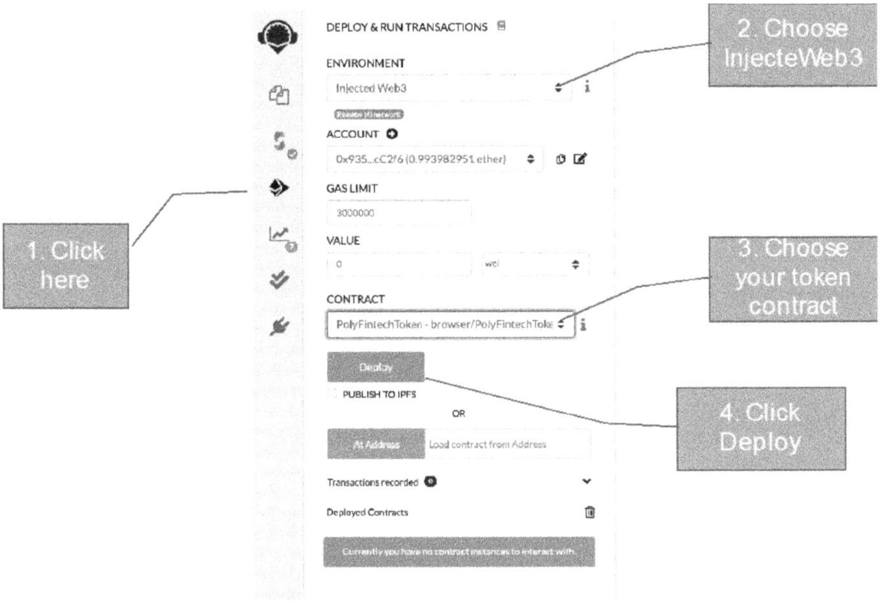

Figure 7.18: Deploying Testnet.

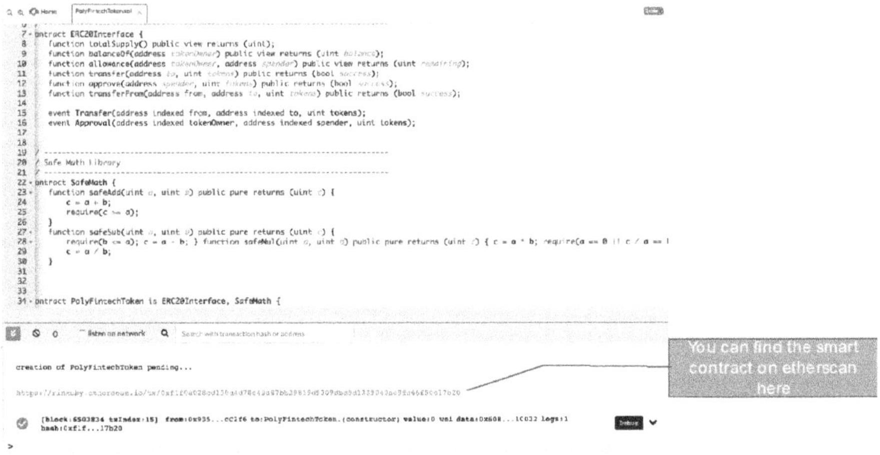

Figure 7.19: Approval of payment by Metamask wallet.

Congratulations! You have created an ERC-20 token on the Ethereum testnet.

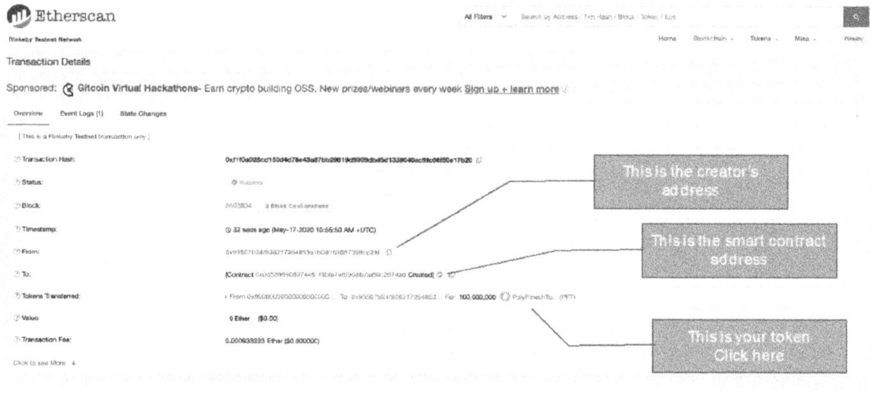

Figure 7.20: Checking transaction on Etherscan.

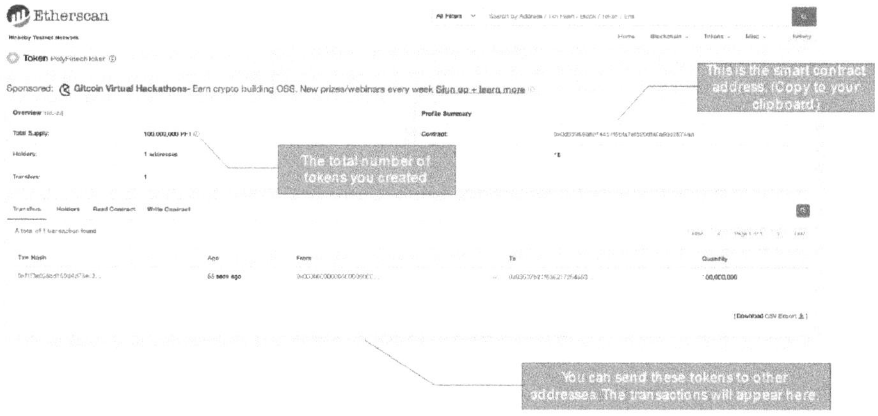

Figure 7.21: Token page.

7.5 ERC-20

The key use of the ERC-20 contracts has been for raising funds through a mechanism called ICOs. Thus, Ethereum is also known as the ICO crowdfunding machine. One of the easiest applications of Ethereum's smart contract system is to create a simple token which can be transacted on the Ethereum blockchain instead of ether. This kind of contract was standardised with ERC-20. Ethereum became the host of a wide scope of ICOs.

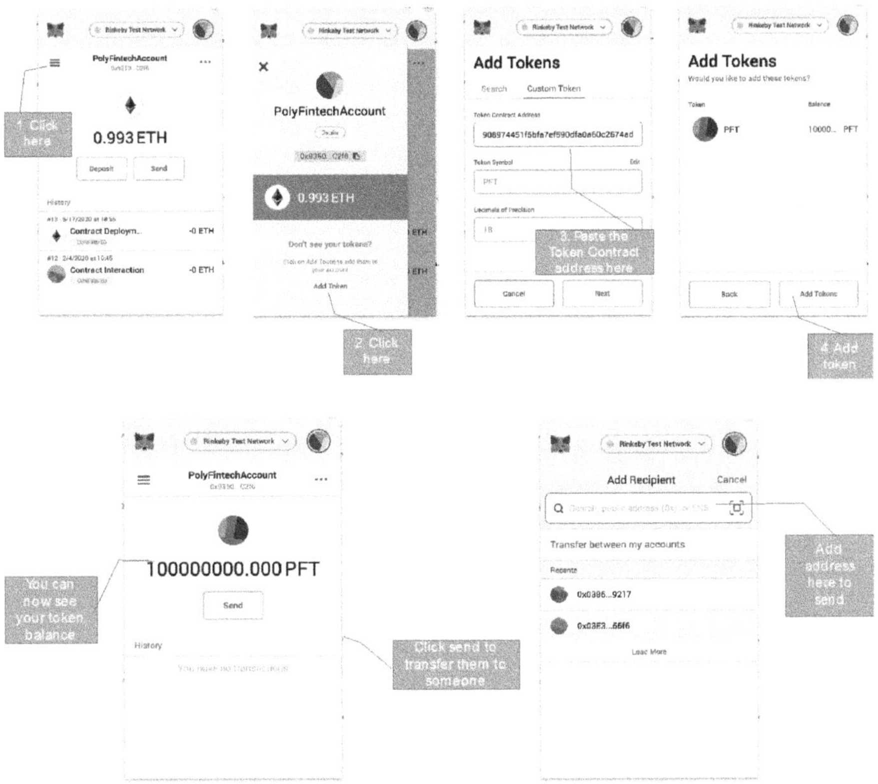

Figure 7.22: Adding token to Metamask.

The concept of funding projects with a token on Ethereum became the blueprint for a new and highly successful generation of crowdfunding projects. To invest in tokens on top of Ethereum, you simply transfer ETH to the ICO smart contract from your wallet. The tokens appear in your account and you are free to transfer them as you want. There are a set of smart contracts written specifically for this purpose termed "Token Sale" contracts.

In "ERC-20", ERC stands for Ethereum request for comments and 20 stands for a unique ID number to distinguish this standard from others. A token on Ethereum is basically just a smart contract that follows some common rules — it implements a standard set of functions that all other token contracts share, such as transferFrom(address_from, address_to, uint256_tokenId) and balanceOf(address_owner). So, basically, a token is just a contract that keeps track of who owns how much of that token and some functions, so those users can transfer their tokens to other addresses. Since all ERC-20 tokens share the same set of functions with the same names, they can all be interacted with in the same ways.

An application that is capable of interacting with one ERC-20 token is also capable of interacting with any other ERC-20 token. More tokens can be added to the App (one example is the Metamask wallet) in the future.

Another example of this would be an exchange. When an exchange adds a new ERC-20 token, really it just needs to add another smart contract it talks to. The exchange only needs to implement this transfer logic once; then, when it wants to add a new ERC-20 token, it is simply a matter of adding the new contract address to its database. The ERC-20 standard can also be used to represent physical assets, for example, a piece of property. This allows the physical asset to be fractionalised and traded.

7.6 What's Next

Now that you have a basic understanding of Solidity smart contracts, you can start writing contracts for your own use cases. To make your application complete, you will also need to connect your smart contract to a front-end application. Given below are some resources to follow to find out more:

- https://www.dappuniversity.com/articles/the-ultimate-ethereum-dapp-tutorial.
- https://www.moesif.com/blog/blockchain/ethereum/Tutorial-for-building-Ethereum-Dapp-with-Integrated-Error-Monitoring/.
- https://medium.com/coinmonks/ethereum-land-marketplace-dapp-tutorial-part-1-create-and-deploy-a-smart-contract-351bc0d62be2.
- https://www.trufflesuite.com/tutorials/pet-shop.

Chapter 8

Hands-On Lab with MultiChain

Roy Lai* and Yu Yinghui†

8.1 From Bitcoin Blockchains to MultiChain

8.1.1 *Double-Spending Problem and Byzantine Generals Problem*

The term "blockchain" originally refers to the underlying technology used in implementing the Bitcoin protocol and network in Satoshi Nakamoto's paper "Bitcoin: A Peer-to-Peer Electronic Cash System" in 2008. As the paper title indicated, blockchain technology has been used to solve the Double-Spending Problem.

In the digital world, data such as photos and emails can be easily copied and replicated (see Figure 8.1). Preventing double-spending problems (see Figure 8.2) is the key to create an effective digital proof of IOU ("I owe you").

In the real world, people use fiat money and double spending is not an issue, as the physical cash transactions are managed by a centralised trusted third party (the bank).

In a decentralised digital world, to solve the double-spending problem without the need for a trusted third party, another problem needs to be solved first. It is called the Byzantine Generals Problem (Lamport *et al.*, 1982; see Figure 8.3).

*Founder, Sentinel Chain.
†School of Business, Singapore University of Social Sciences, Singapore.

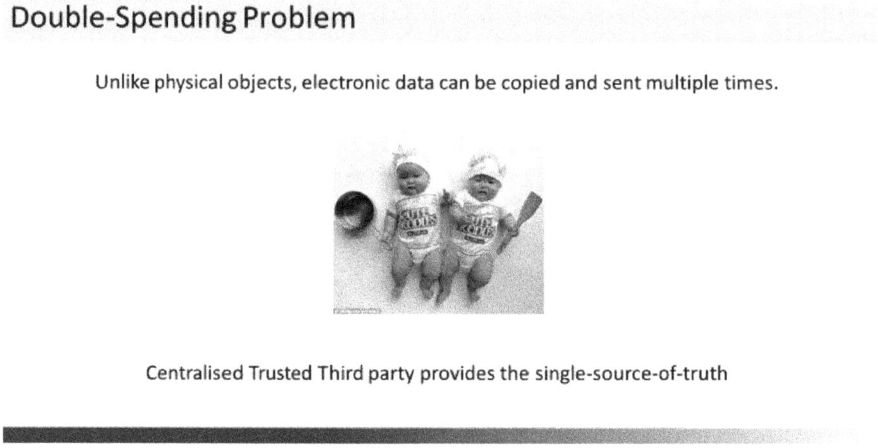

Figure 8.1: Duplication in the physical vs digital world.

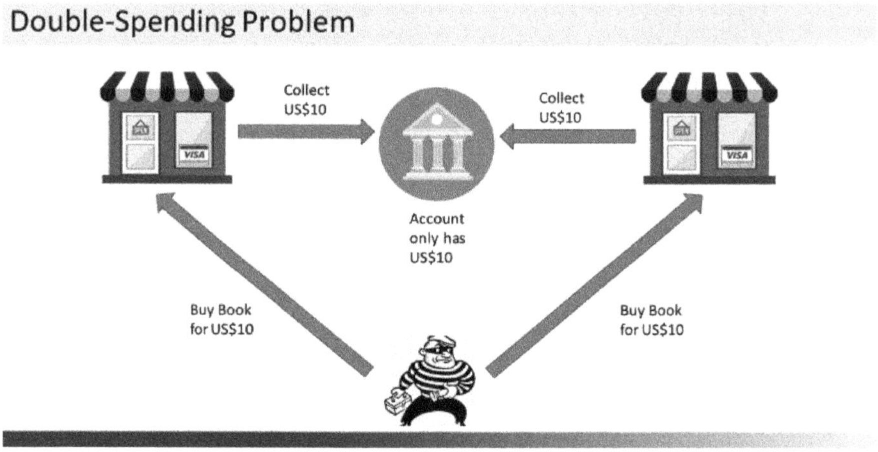

Figure 8.2: Double-spending problem illustration.

As a continuation of the ancient Roman Empire in its eastern provinces, the Byzantine Empire ruled most of Eastern and Southern Europe throughout the Middle Ages.

The Byzantine Generals Problem describes a scenario where several divisions of the Byzantine army were camped outside an enemy fort and trying to take the fort down (see Figure 8.4). Each

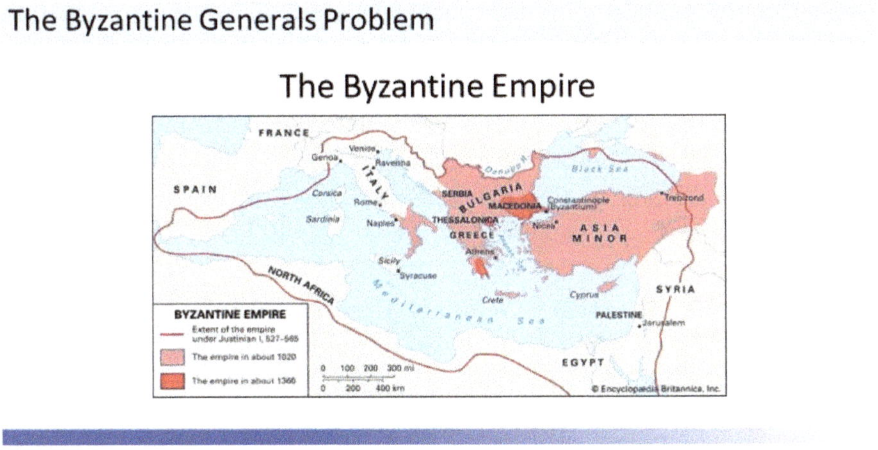

Figure 8.3: Byzantine Generals Problem.

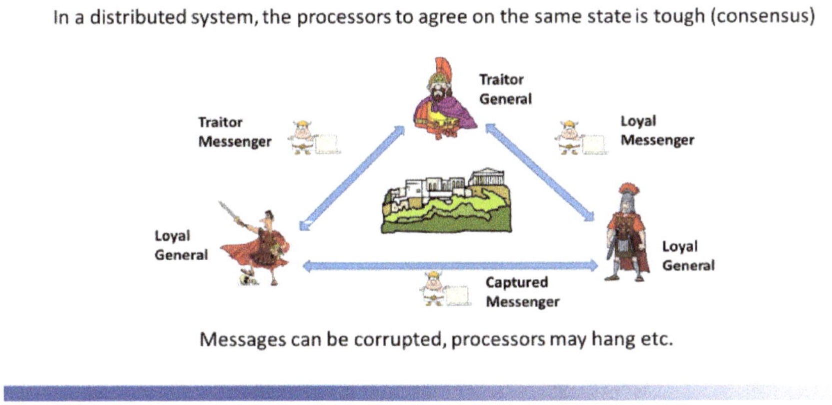

Figure 8.4: Consensus process and effects of Byzantine Generals Problem.
Note: Lamport *et al.* (1982). The Byzantine Generals Problem.

division was commanded by its own general, and all the generals could communicate with one another only by messenger. The generals needed to have a coordinated plan of action in order to take down the enemy fort. However, some of the generals could be traitors and they would try to present an agreement to be reached. The generals must have an algorithm to guarantee that (A) all loyal generals decide upon the same plan of action, and (B) a small number of traitors cannot cause the loyal generals to adopt a bad plan.

The Byzantine Generals Problem assumes that there will be an unknown number of participants that are expected to misbehave and attempt to subvert the network; hence, it is often used as an analogy in computer science to describe the challenges faced by distributed systems in achieving consensus over unreliable communication links.

Solving the Byzantine Generals Problem requires complicated algorithms, and such algorithms did not exist until the 1970s. They only worked in lab-like environments, however, and they can only be deployed in large-scale and expensive developments, such as Boeing airplanes or submarines, where every component within the entire system has to work with a very tight margin of error (see Figure 8.5).

Bitcoin and Boeing 777 share the similarity that both solve the Byzantine Generals Problem, but Bitcoin solves it with cheap hardware. The trade-off is that the confirmation in the Bitcoin (or some other cryptocurrencies) network takes place in a different way: the network needs time to collect votes and reach consensus. In essence, time is the price (or rather, a unique feature) that the Bitcoin network pays to reach consensus in a decentralised setup.

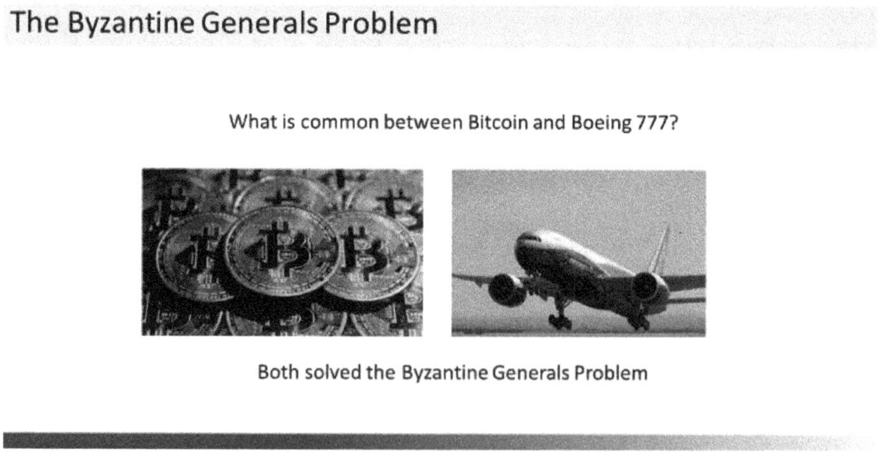

Figure 8.5: Byzantine Generals Problem in reality.

8.2 Bitcoin Concepts

8.2.1 *Bitcoin and Blockchain*

Bitcoin ("B" as upper case) refers to the protocol used to secure bitcoin currency and govern how nodes in the network communicate with each other, whereas bitcoin ("b" as lower case) refers to the cryptocurrency traded, which is essentially just numbers built in the blocks within the network (Figure 8.6).

The technology that is used to implement this protocol is called blockchain.

8.2.2 *Peer-to-Peer Network Protocol*

There are a few ways to design a network (Figure 8.7). In a centralised network, there is a decision-making authority. A decentralised network means that there is no single authority and that multiple nodes on the network are involved in decision-making. A distributed network means operating loads are shared across all nodes. It is usually a decentralised network taken to the extreme (note that a centralised but distributed network may be possible). Bitcoin network is a decentralized network of distributed Bitcoin nodes.

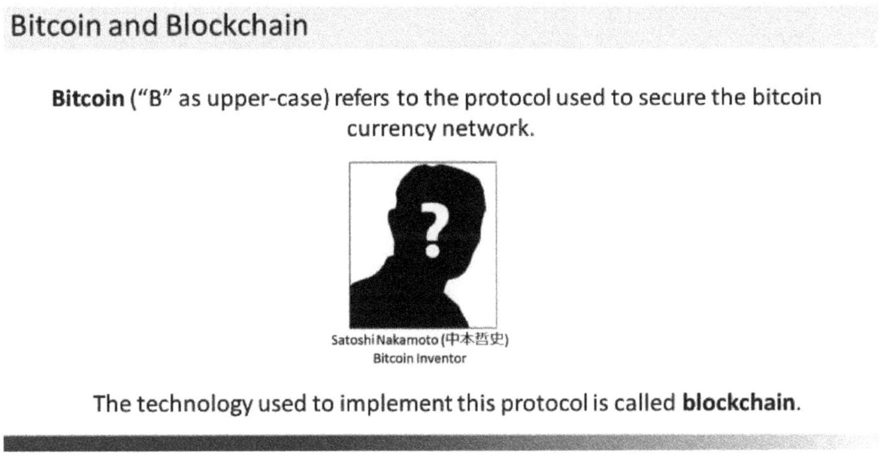

Figure 8.6: Bitcoin and blockchain.

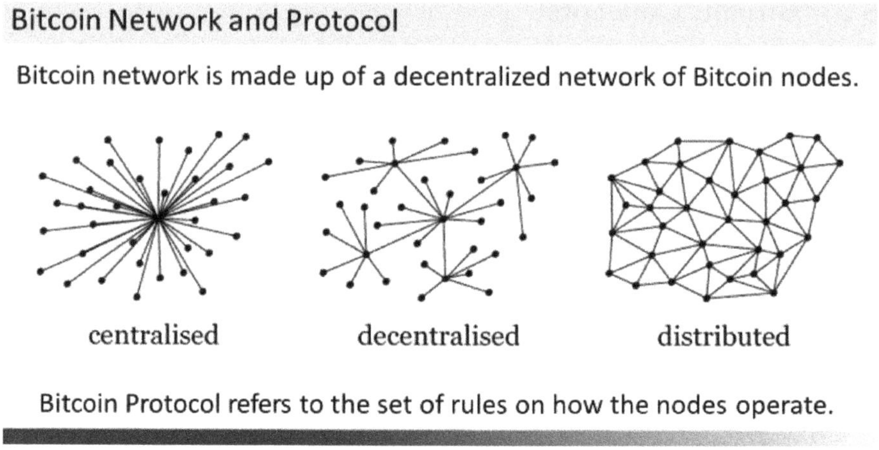

Figure 8.7: Bitcoin network and distribution protocol.

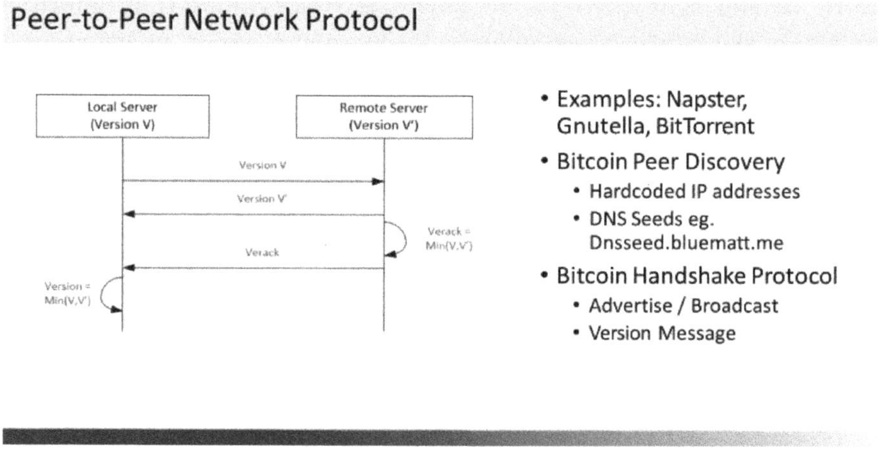

Figure 8.8: Peer-to-Peer network protocol.

In this public decentralised network, the distributed nodes need to discover other nodes with the same software installed (see Figure 8.8). Similar to applications like BitTorrent, this peer-to-peer discovering process is described as a "handshake", which refers to the process that two nodes establish a connection with each other and start to exchange version and verack messages, in order to ensure compliance

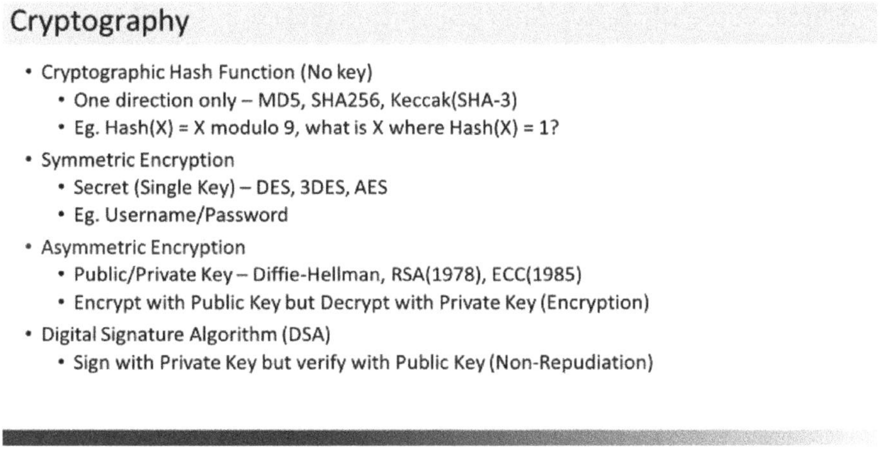

Figure 8.9: Cryptography.

between peers. Other metadata will also be passed on, such as block size and configuration of time needed to arrive at consensus.

8.2.3 *Cryptography*

A hash function is a function that maps data of arbitrary size to fixed-size values, and it is in one direction only. Symmetric cryptography means the same key is used for verifying the authenticity of data. Asymmetric cryptography is used extensively in blockchain, and it involves using pairs of related keys — a public key to process the data and a private key to validate it. On the contrary, in the Digital Signature Algorithm (DSA), data are signed with a private key but can be verified with the public key. Public keys may be disseminated widely, but private keys are known only to the owners.

One type of the asymmetric cryptography is elliptic-curve cryptography (ECC), an approach based on the algebraic structure of elliptic curves over finite fields (see Figure 8.9).

8.2.4 *Elliptic Curve Digital Signature Algorithm (ECDSA)*

The equation of an elliptic curve follows the formula $y^2 = x^3 + ax + b$, and Bitcoin uses a particular set of parameters called secp256k1, the

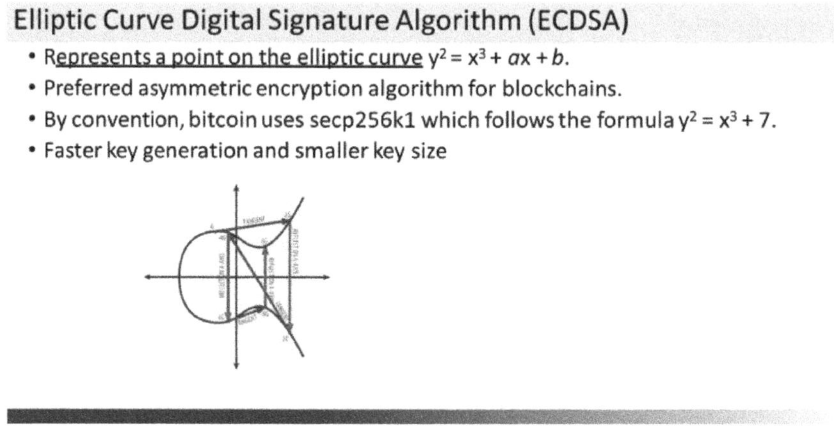

Figure 8.10: Elliptic Curve Digital Signature Algorithm.
Note: "A (relatively easy to understand) primer on elliptic curve cryptography", Nick Sullivan.

formula being $y^2 = x^3 + 7$, in its Elliptic Curve Digital Signature Algorithm (ECDSA) (see Figure 8.10). Secp256k1 has the desired feature of efficient computation and is able to generate keys of smaller size and at a speed 30% faster than other curves.

8.2.5 *Bitcoin Private Key*

Every bitcoin wallet has a private key. The Bitcoin private key is essentially a 256-bit number, and it is generated in a random way, and hence it is only known to the user who generates it.

In the Bitcoin network, a sender signs data using his private key and the receiver can verify the legitimacy of the data using the sender's public key (the public key can be seen by everyone in the network).

In the multichain context, a private key serves three purposes:

- For you to send native currency or native assets to other addresses.
- For you to prove ownerships to items published on streams.
- For you to assign permissions and get authorisations.

The Bitcoin private key can be stored either as

- A hexadecimal number (see Figure 8.11), or

- A Base58 encoded string also known as Wallet Interchange Format (WiF), as shown in Figure 8.12.

Losing a private key will grant others access to your currency, assets, streams and permissions; hence, private keys should be managed independently and externally, for instance, by HSM (Hardware Security Modules), and used only when required to sign transactions (see Figure 8.14).

8.2.6 *Bitcoin Public Key*

- The Bitcoin public key is derived from the Bitcoin private key, but not vice versa.
- A public key can be used by others to verify your signature without knowing your private key.
- A public key is represented by the following:

Figure 8.11: Hexadecimal number.

Figure 8.12: Wallet interchange format.
Note: Two encoding systems are used here — hexadecimal and Base58. Base58 is a group of binary-to-text encoding systems used to represent large integers as alphanumeric text, introduced by Satoshi Nakamoto for use with Bitcoin. It consists of the twenty-six letters of both upper cases and lower cases and numbers 0–9, while excluding 0 (zero), O (capital o), I (capital i) and l (lower case L) to avoid confusion to human eyes. Figure 8.13 exemplifies how decimal numbers are represented by the two encoding systems.

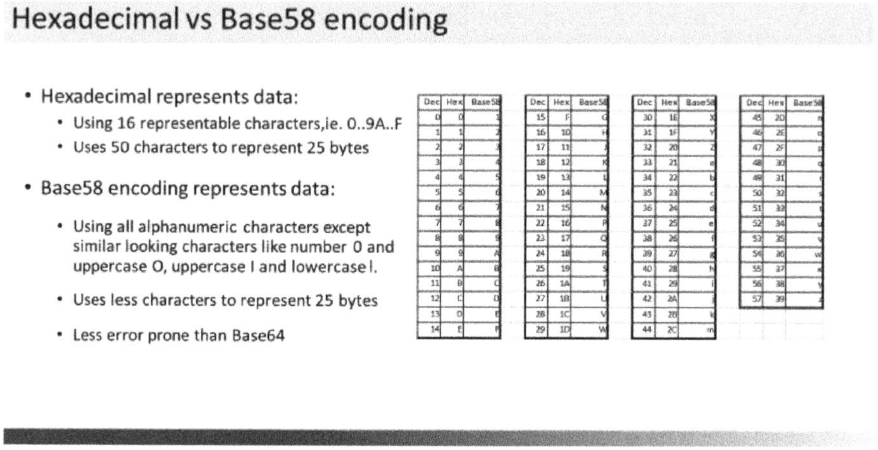

Figure 8.13: Representation of numbers in the two encoding systems.

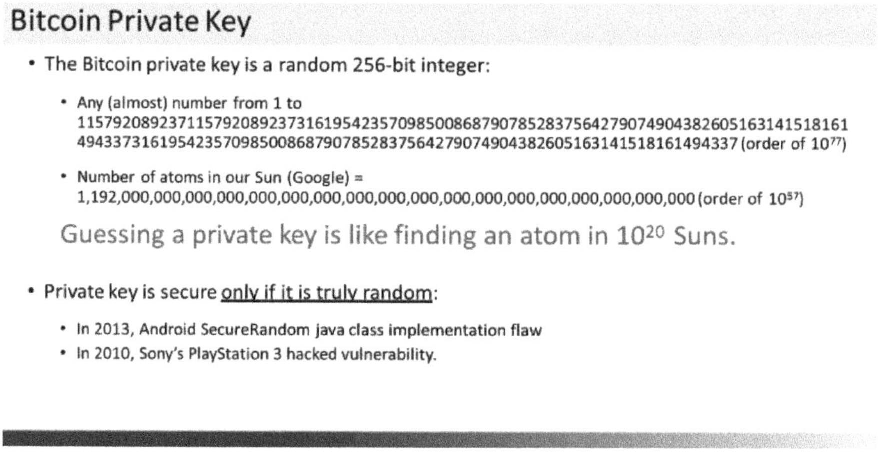

Figure 8.14: Bitcoin private key.

- A 65-byte hexadecimal number that starts with a 4 (old uncompressed format), or
- A 33-byte hexadecimal number that starts with a 2 or 3 (new compressed format).

The Bitcoin wallet address is derived from a public key, but not vice versa (see Figure 8.15). A wallet address is used

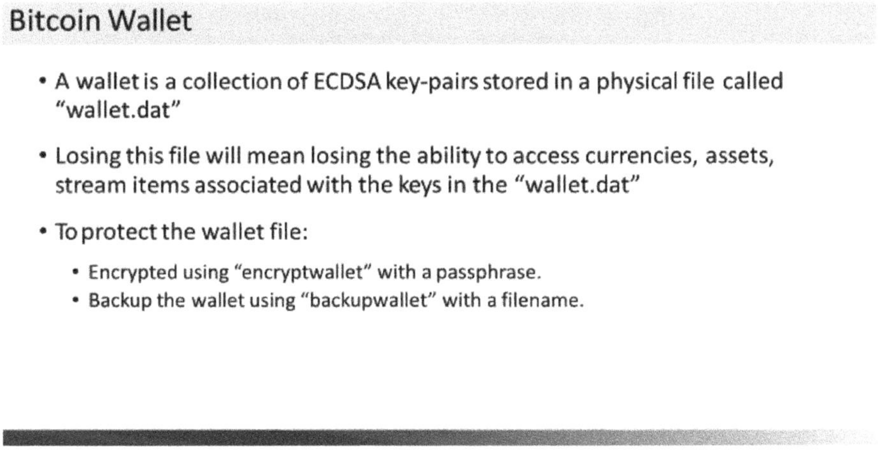

Figure 8.15: Bitcoin wallet.

Figure 8.16: Wallet address.

- By others to send you native currency or native assets on blockchain.
- By others to verify your ownership of items published on blockchain.
- By the blockchain to verify your permissions.

A wallet address looks as shown in Figure 8.16.
But, it is stored internally as shown in Figure 8.17.

- 25 bytes for Bitcoin
- 28 bytes for MultiChain (see Figure 8.18).

As the address indicates, multichain is extended based on the Bitocoin blockchain and it is essentially a fork of Bitcoin Core (the Bitcoin software). There are well-selected features and enhancements

Figure 8.17: Bitcoin wallet storage.

Figure 8.18: MultiChain address.

in multichain that enable users to launch a customised private blockchain that is easy to configure and can be used by organisations for financial transactions. This chapter discusses these features and enhancements of multichain, by comparing Bitcoin blockchain and multichain in details.

There are two types of Bitcoin addresses (Figure 8.19). An address that begins with "1" is based on the hash of a public key. Hence, such an address belongs to and represents the public key owner, i.e., a human being. This is the most common type of address on the Bitcoin network. Addresses that begin with "3", on the contrary, are based on the hash values of Bitcoin scripts. They represent special programs on the network. Users send transactions to such addresses when certain conditions need to be fulfilled in order for bitcoins to be received, e.g., for escrow purposes.

One example is a multi-signature address, which is essentially a script to make sure that enough signatures are received before a transaction can go through (see Figure 8.20).

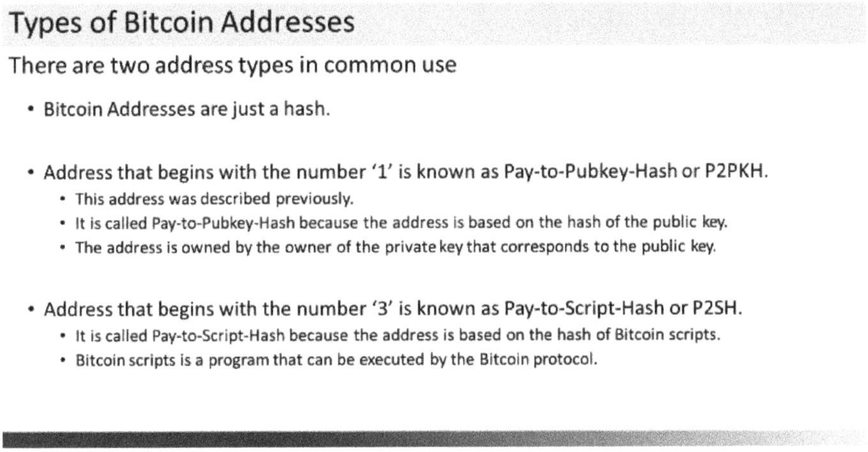

Figure 8.19: Types of Bitcoin addresses.

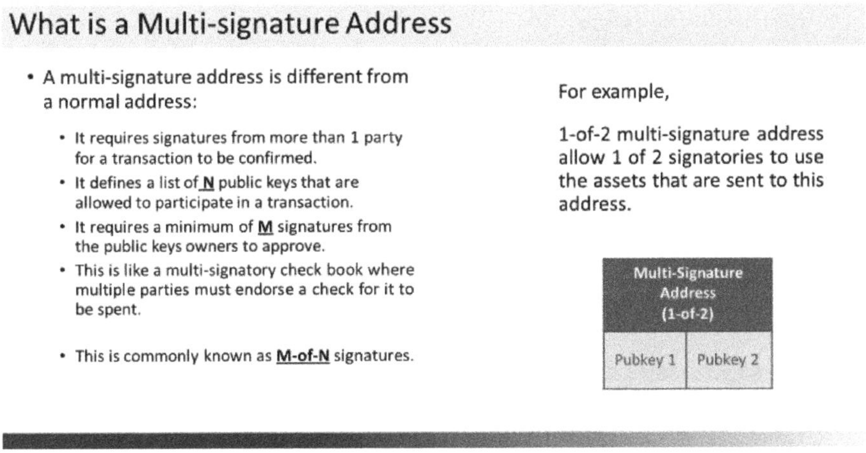

Figure 8.20: Multi-signature address.

8.2.7 *Bitcoin Block Structure*

A blockchain data structure is a linked list (hence the term "chain") of data blocks (see Figure 8.21). Each block contains the hash value of the preceding block, and this serves as a link to the preceding block and establishes the order throughout the chain of blocks.

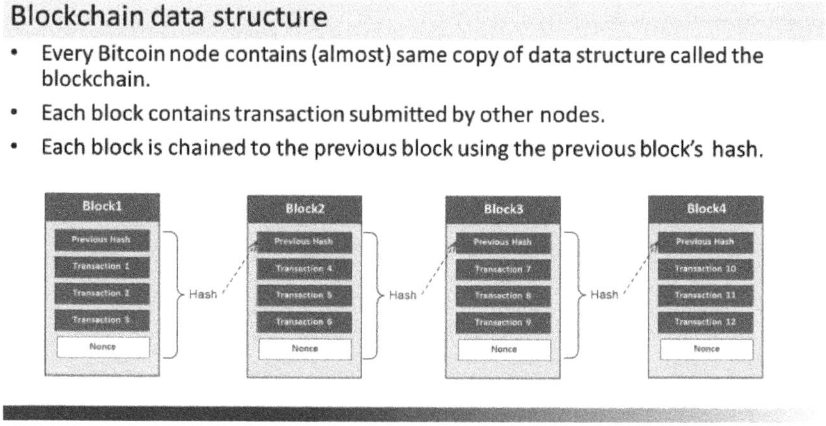

Figure 8.21: Blockchain data structure.

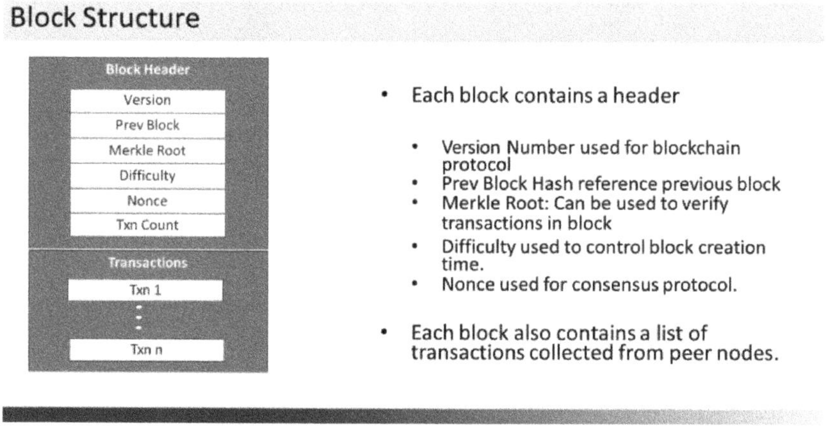

Figure 8.22: Block structure.

A block primarily contains two parts: the list of transactions collected from all other nodes and the block header (see Figure 8.22).

The block header contains a few fields:

- *Version*: Users have to use the same version of the protocol. A block generated using a different version will not be accepted
- *Hash of the Preceding Block*: It is also the transaction ID of the preceding block. If there is any slight change in the transaction

details in the preceding block, then the hash value will be completely different from what is stored in the next block, and the chain will be broken.

If someone would like to change transaction details in an existing block, then he needs to regenerate all the blocks that have been linked after that block. It is extremely difficult due to the proof-of-work process involved in generating blocks.

- *Merkle Root*: It is the hash of all the hashes of all the transactions in the block. It is the top hash (or root hash) of a tree structure (called Merkle Tree), where transactions are hashed in pairs, then the obtained hash values are concatenated in pairs and hashed again. The Merkle Root is a short yet unique fingerprint of all the transactions and helps to verify if a transaction belongs to this block. To verify if a single transaction is included in the block, not all the transactions in the data are needed. Instead, one only needs to know the hash values along the path (from the bottom transaction up till the Merkle Root). This process is called Merkle Proof.
- *Difficulty Level*: It measures how many hashes (statistically) should be generated to find a valid solution to solve (hence generate) the Bitcoin block and earn the mining reward. It is set to be "inefficient" in a sense, in order to stipulate enough time for all the nodes to synchronise. Difficulty is adjusted from time to time to make sure that on average it takes 10 minutes to generate a block.
- *Nonce*: A 32-bit (4-byte) field whose value is randomly regenerated by miners, until the hash of the block is less than or equal to the current target of the network.

8.2.8 *Proof-of-Work Consensus Algorithm*

The block-generating process is like a lottery held every 10 minutes on average (see Figure 8.23). The node who finds an eligible nonce value first has the privilege to attach this block to the blockchain and receive the mining reward.

When a miner successfully generated a hash value that is smaller or equal to the target, this hash value is called Proof of Work

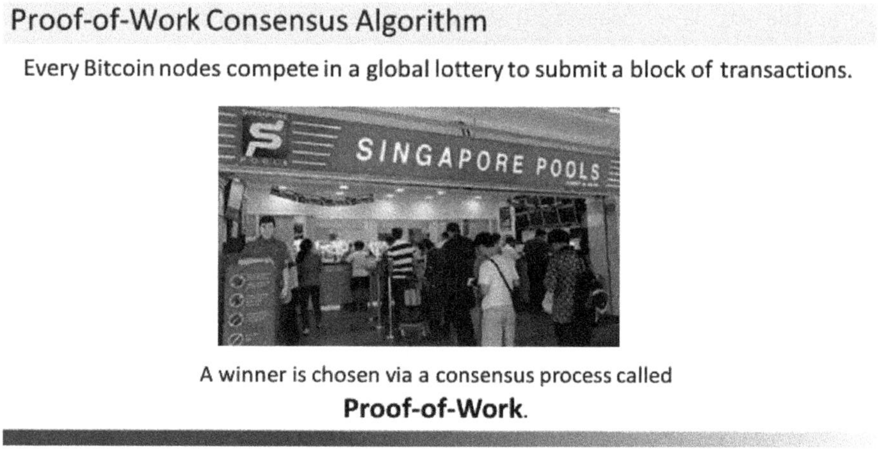

Figure 8.23: Proof-of-Work "lottery".

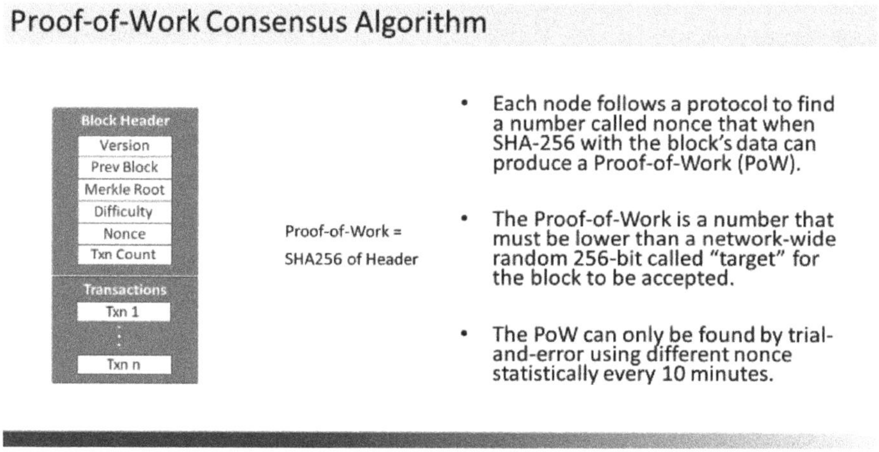

Figure 8.24: Proof-of-Work algorithm.

(PoW). PoW also refers to this consensus algorithm where miners keep generating nonce and calculating hash values in order to hit the jackpot, i.e., generating the next block (see Figure 8.24). Hashing is regarded as "work", and statistically, it all comes down to the computing power a node owns.

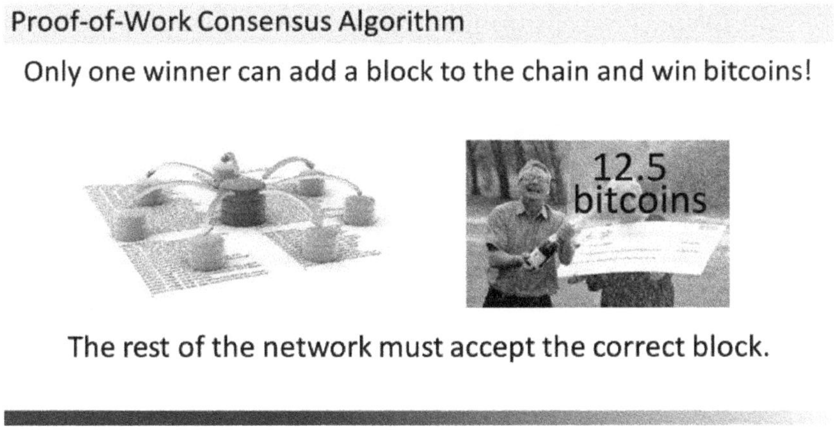

Figure 8.25: Proof-of-Work winner takes all.

As part of the consensus mechanism, once a miner submits his Proof of Work, the rest of the network must accept his block (see Figure 8.25).

A Sybil attack is a kind of security threat to a system where one person tries to take over the network by creating a large number of pseudonymous identities and uses them to gain a disproportionately large influence. The Proof-of-Work consensus algorithm means the ability of a node (or a group of nodes) to create blocks must be proportional to the total processing power. This renders Sybil attacks economically impractical, since a party that tries to launch a Sybil attack needs to actually own the computing power (imagine 51% of all the mining machines in the world) to keep creating new blocks (Figure 8.26).

Changing previous blocks on the Bitcoin network is also very difficult based on the same logic. Under the PoW consensus algorithm, all nodes accept the longest chain and work on the next block based on the longest chain. If a node changes a previous block, he will have to create new blocks to attach to the changed block, and at a faster speed than the rest of the world so that his chain will outgrow the original one. One will need to own 51% of the computing power of the whole network in order to do that (see Figure 8.27).

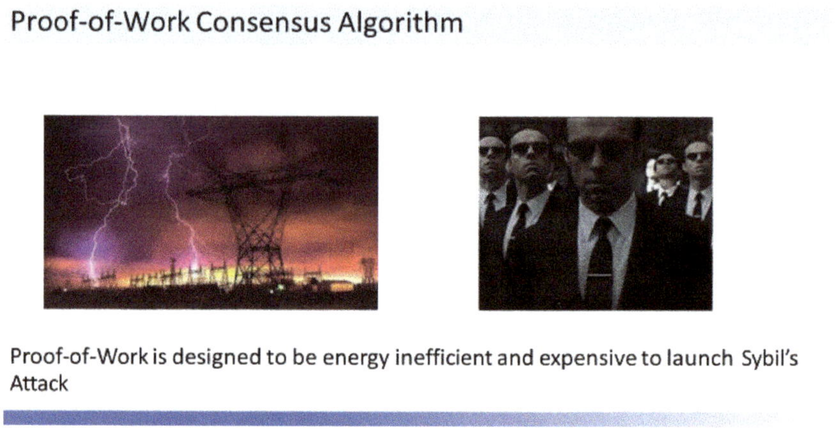

Figure 8.26: Proof-of-Work protection against Sybil attack.

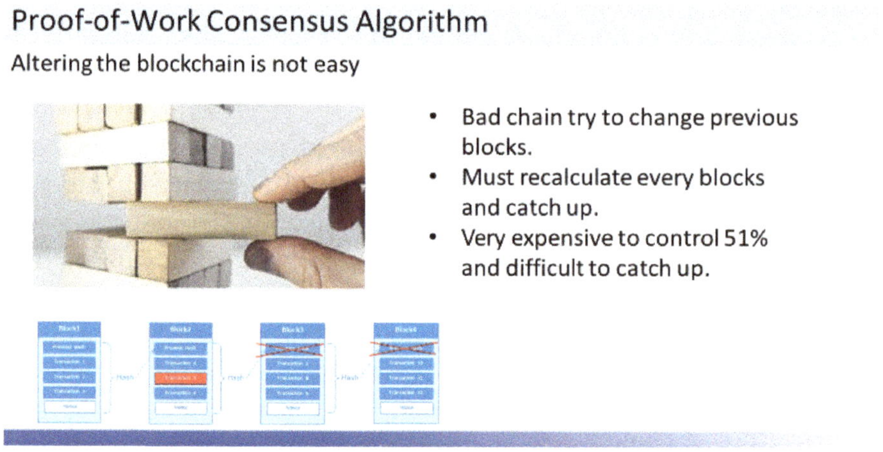

Figure 8.27: Proof-of-Work protection immutability.

8.2.9 *Blockchain Fork*

A fork can happen on the blockchain due to two correct blocks being generated at the same time, and the network accepts the longer chain (see Figure 8.28). To be secure against such a fork (double spending), a transaction should not be considered as confirmed until it is a certain number of blocks deep. On Bitcoin blockchain, usually six

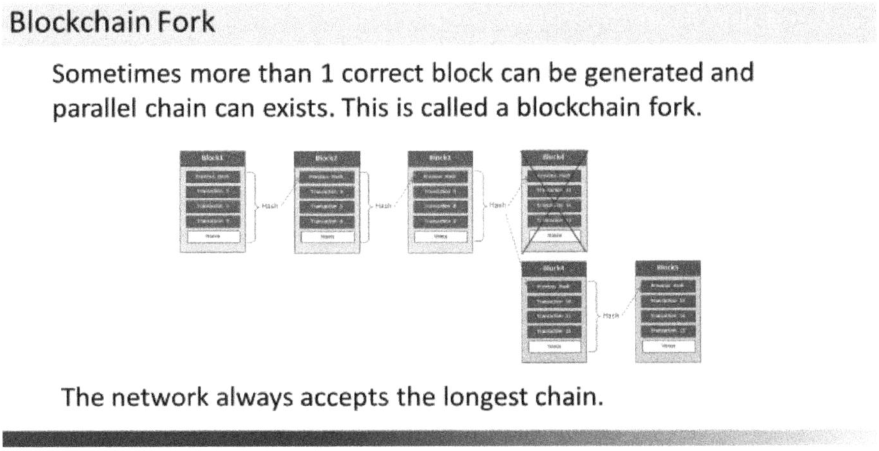

Figure 8.28: Blockchain fork.

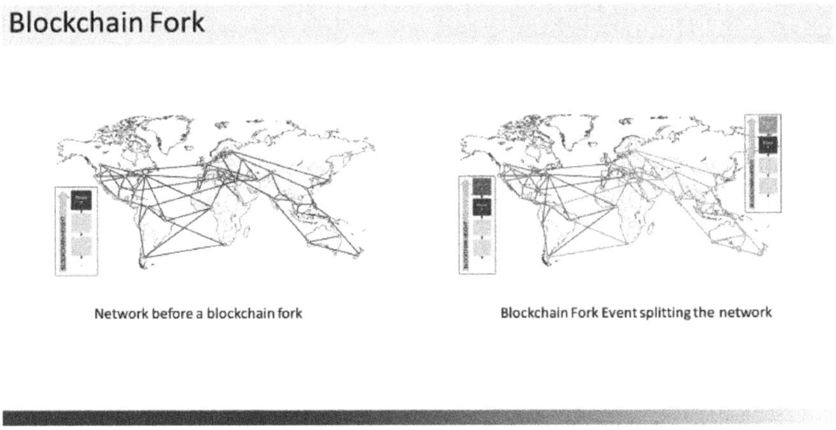

Figure 8.29: Forks across different geography.
Source: Mastering Bitcoin by Andreas M. Antonopoulos.

new blocks need to be generated after a transaction, in order to consider that transaction as confirmed.

Such forks sometimes happen in different geological areas — where physical proximity makes a slight difference in the speed of synchronisation (see Figure 8.29).

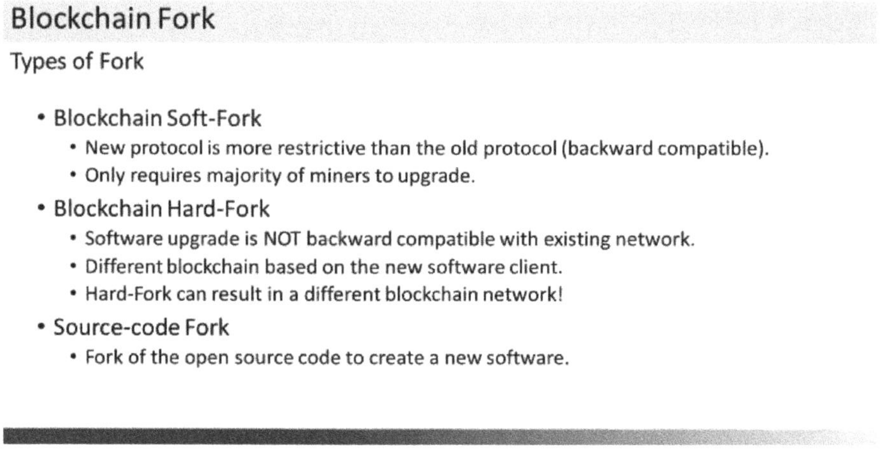

Figure 8.30: Types of intentional forks.

There are three types of (intentional) forks. A soft fork refers to a change of the blockchain protocol which is backward-compatible. Non-updated nodes are still able to process transactions and generate blocks, so long as they do not break the new protocol rules (see Figure 8.30).

A hard fork is a change of protocol which is incompatible with the previous versions. When a hard fork is planned, nodes voluntarily upgrade their software to follow the new rules, leaving the old versions behind. The ones who do not update are left mining on the old chain, which very few people will be doing.

If a fork is controversial, it means there is disagreement within the community about the upgrade, and the protocol is usually forked into two incompatible blockchains, hence two different cryptocurrencies.

A source code fork is not a fork in the blockchain, but rather a change in the source code which might result in new software.

8.2.10 *Bitcoin Transactions*

Before going into the details of bitcoin transactions, one thing to note is that unlike the transactions in the real world where money or cash is passed around, bitcoin transactions are analogous to handling the recipient a key, which can be used to unlock the bitcoins from

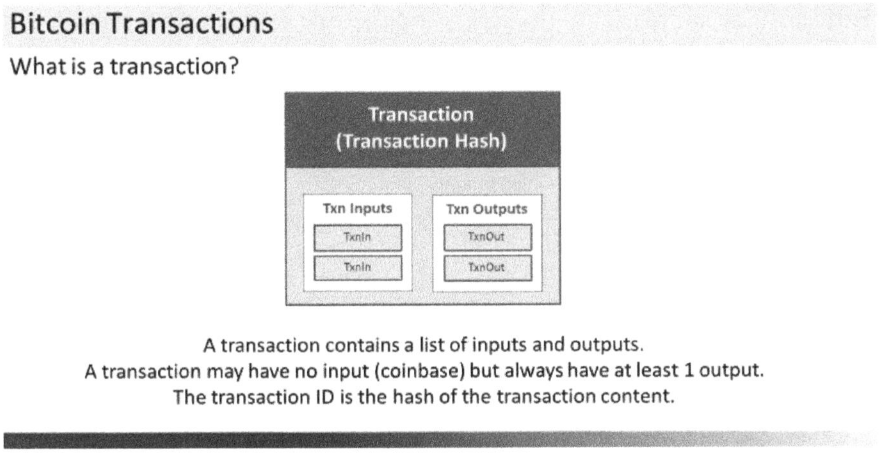

Figure 8.31: Explaining bitcoin transactions.

a previous transaction, and hence represent the ownership of these bitcoins.

A transaction contains two parts: inputs and outputs (Figure 8.31). Total value of the outputs will be equal to or smaller than the total value of inputs; the difference is the mining fee.

A transaction input is made of the following (see Figure 8.32):

- *Previous transaction's ID*: The ID is a hash of a previous transaction.
- Previous transaction's output.
- *ScriptSig*: ScriptSig is the short form for signature script. It is the first half of a script (the other half is scriptPubKey) and it is the unlocking script that satisfies the conditions placed on the previous output by the scriptPubKey, and it is what allows it to be spent.

A transaction output is made of the following (Figure 8.33):

- A single value of cryptocurrency (note that it is smaller than the total value of inputs).
- *ScriptPubKey*: ScriptPubKey is the second half of a script (the first half is scriptSig) and it is a locking script placed on the output of a Bitcoin transaction that requires certain conditions to be met in order for a recipient to spend the bitcoins.

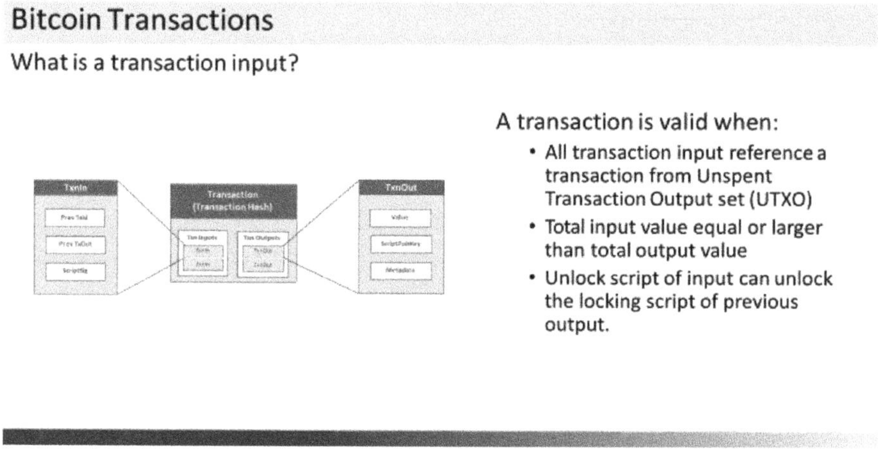

Figure 8.32: Bitcoin transaction input.

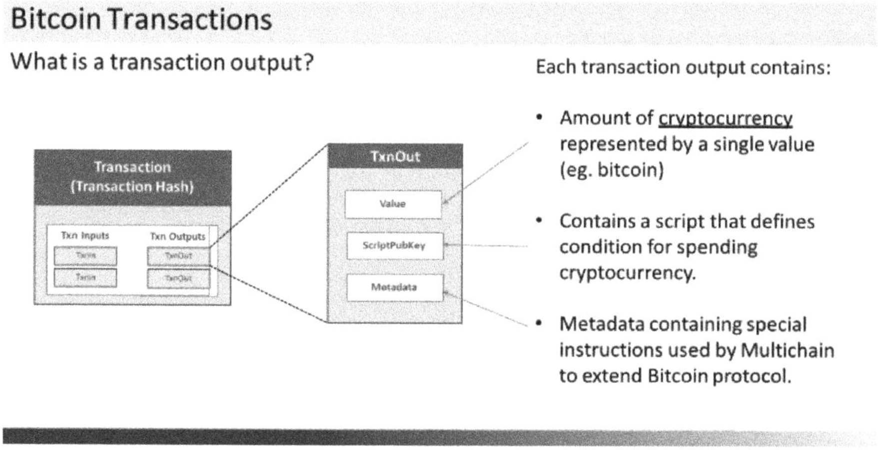

Figure 8.33: Bitcoin transaction output.

- *Metadata*: Metadata are not relevant to the transaction itself, and are usually used to extend Bitcoin protocol. They can be used to contain special instructions to certify and transfer the ownership of a variety of assets beyond cryptocurrency, or just save arbitrary pieces of data which do not affect transfers of bitcoins.

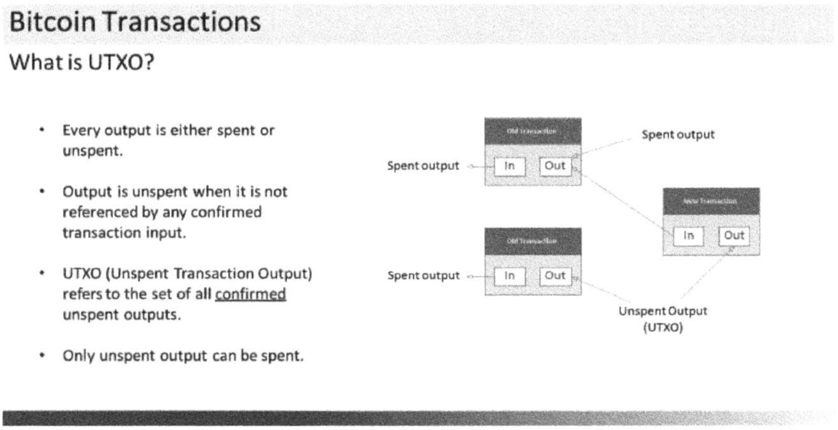

Figure 8.34: Unspent Transaction Output (UTXO).

A transaction output can only be referenced by confirmed transaction input ONCE. Before the reference, it is called Unspent Transaction Output (UTXO), and after the reference it is output spent (see Figure 8.34).

A transaction is valid if all inputs reference UTXOs and if the scriptSig in each input can unlock the scriptPubKey of the respective previous output, i.e., it satisfies the conditions placed on the output by scriptPubKey (Figure 8.35).

Wallet balance is the sum of all UTXO that has been sent to this wallet address (but not spent yet; see Figure 8.36).

8.2.11 *Bitcoin Script Language*

Bitcoin Script language is a rudimentary, stack-based programming language that enables processing of the transactions on the Bitcoin blockchain, and it is not a Turing complete language (see Figure 8.37). Turing Completeness is a mathematical concept and is a measure of the computability of a programming language. A non-Turing Complete language basically means that the language is designed without complex constructs such as loops and conditions which limit its ability to create general purpose programs. In Bitcoin's case, this is by design as it avoids the risks of bad

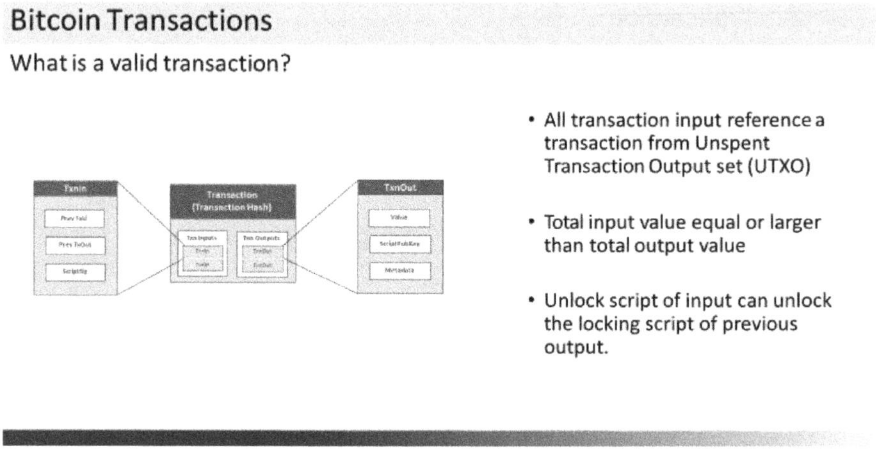

Figure 8.35: Valid transaction.

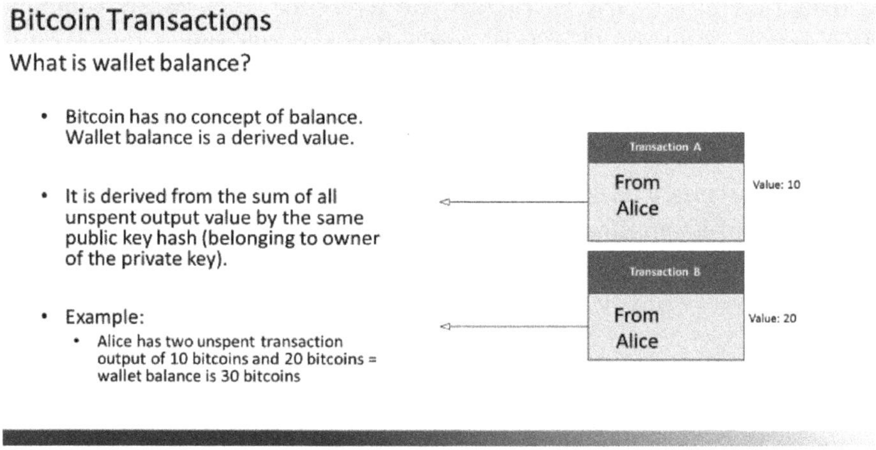

Figure 8.36: Wallet balance.

programming such as infinite loop from bringing down the entire network.

Script expressions use Reverse Polish Notation (RPN) and are processed using stacks and a postfix algorithm (see Figure 8.37). RPN, also known as postfix notation, is a method of placing the

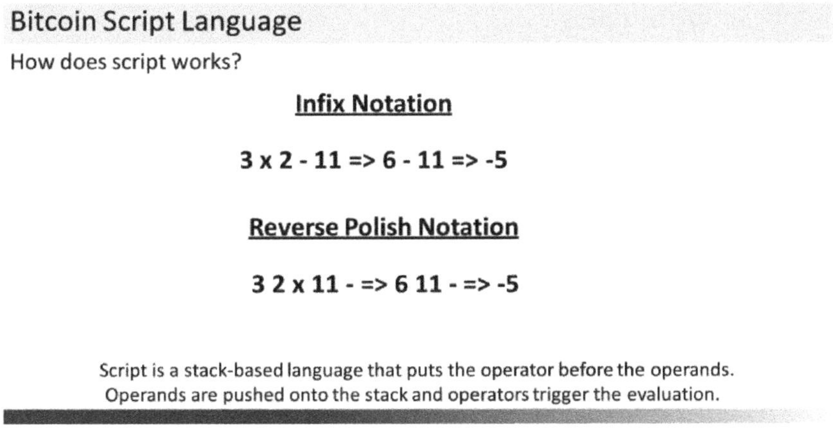

Figure 8.37: Bitcoin script language.

operation function at the end of a sentence. For example, adding 5 and 6 in Script must be written as "5 6 +" rather than "5 + 6".

A stack is a data structure that is linear and can be thought of as a real physical stack or pile. Items at the top of the stack can be added (pushed) or removed (popped) in a "Last In, First Out (LIFO)" order. Using RPN, Bitcoin script pushes operands onto the stack first, followed by the operator which triggers the evaluation. Specifically, the operator will be popped out of the stack, followed by the operands, and the expression gets calculated, and the result will be pushed back onto the stack.

In a bitcoin-spending transaction, output can only be spent in discrete value (Figure 8.38). For example, Alice wants to send 25 units to Bob. Assume Alice only received two transactions previously, where she received 10 bitcoins in one transaction, and 20 bitcoins in the other. The outputs of these two previous transactions (the two UTXOs) will be referenced as inputs for the new transaction to Bob. The new transaction to Bob will have two outputs: one is to send Bob 25 bitcoins, and the other is to send the balance of 5 bitcoins (or slightly less than 5 if we consider transaction fee) back to Alice herself.

From an earlier discussion, we also know that for Alice to successfully spend the UTXOs, she will need to provide ScriptSig (the

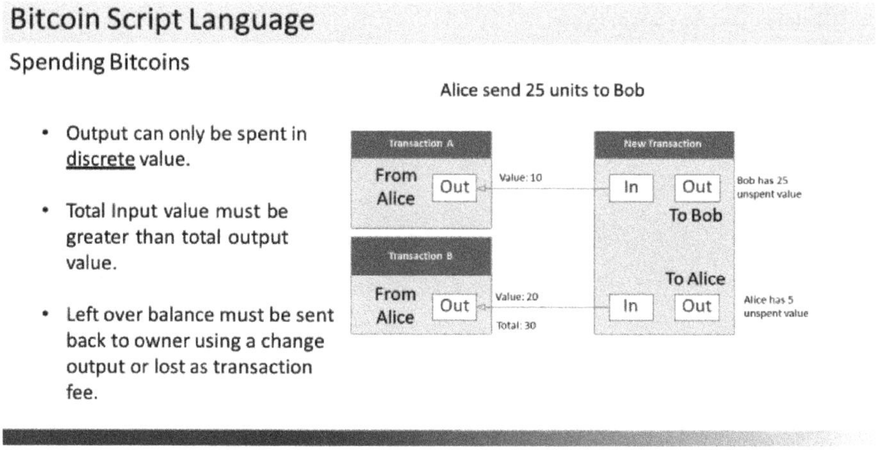

Figure 8.38: Spending bitcoins.

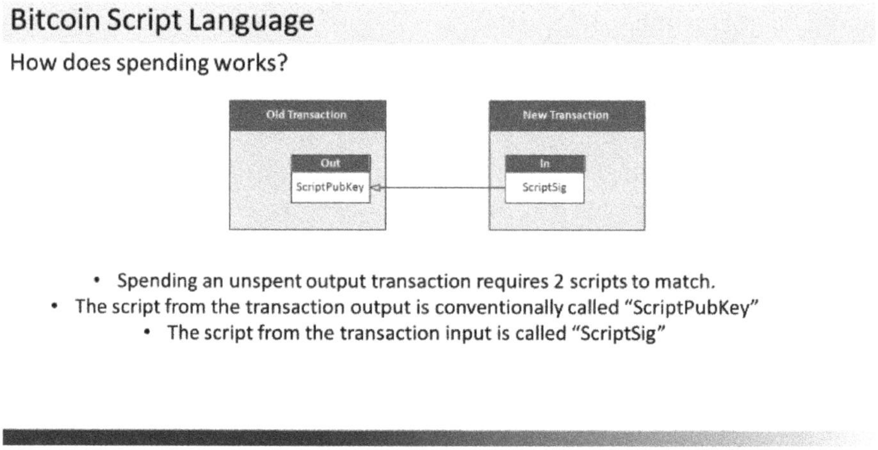

Figure 8.39: Verifying expenditure of UTXOs.

unlocking script, based on her private key) in the new transaction (see Figure 8.39). This ScriptSig is combined with the ScriptPubKey (the locking script, based on her public key) in the previous transactions and executed. If the returned result is TRUE, it proves that Alice does indeed own the private key paired with the public key, and the spending is successfully executed.

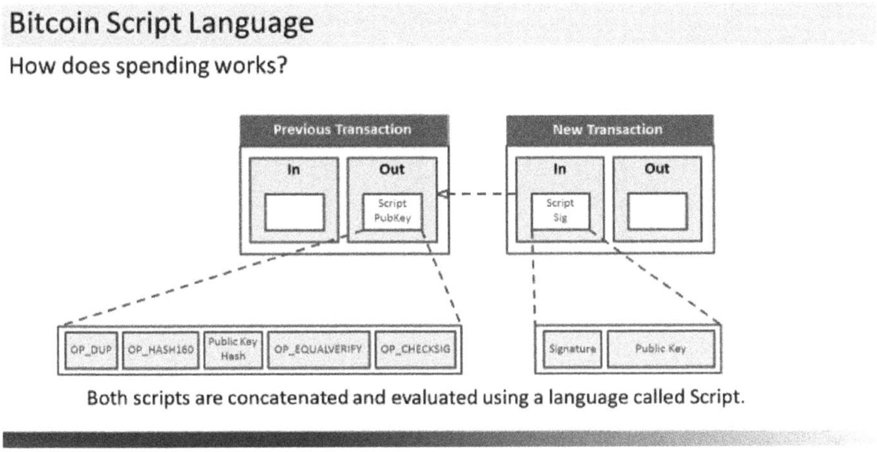

Figure 8.40: Spending bitcoin at the script level.

Now, we look at how spending is executed at the script level.

ScriptPubKey consists of five components as shown in Figure 8.40.

(1) OP_DUP
(2) OP_HASH160
(3) ⟨pubkeyHash⟩
(4) OP_EQUALVERIFY
(5) OP_CHECKSIG

ScriptSig contains two components: Signature and Public Key.

(1) ⟨sig⟩
(2) ⟨pubkey⟩

When ScriptPubKey and ScriptSig are combined, the two components from ScriptSig are appended at the front of ScriptPubKey's components (i.e., in front of OP-DUP), and they are pushed onto the stack in turn for calculations (see Figures 8.41 and 8.42).

Step 1: Signature is pushed onto the stack (see Figure 8.41).
Step 2: Public Key is pushed onto the stack.

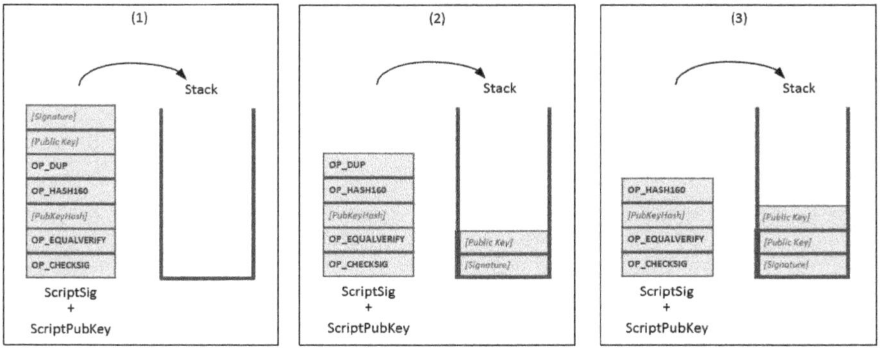

Figure 8.41: Stacking of components of ScriptSig and ScriptPubKey.

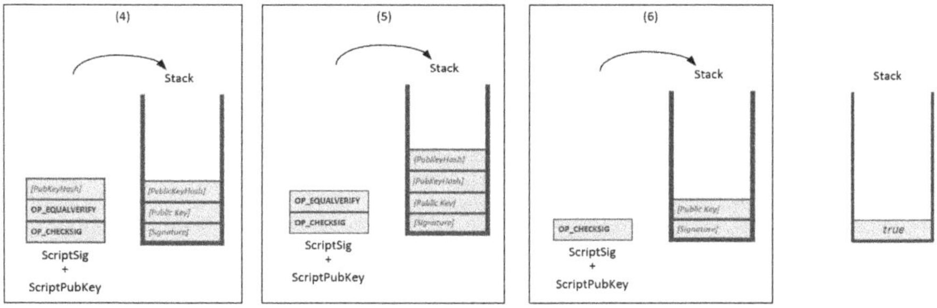

Figure 8.42: Stacking and execution of spending.

Step 3: Operator of Duplicate [OP_DUP] is pushed on the stack: duplication operation is triggered and results in two [Public Key]s on the stack.

Step 4: Operator of Hash160 is pushed onto the stack: This operation returns the 20-byte hash value of the public key [PubKey-Hash] (see Figure 8.42).

Step 5: [PubKeyHash] from the scriptPubKey is pushed onto the stack.

Step 6: The operator [OP_EQUALVERIFY] is pushed on the stack, and it verifies if the two [PubKeyHash] currently on the stack are the same. Note that the first one [PubKeyHash] is from scriptSig, and the second is from scriptPubKey.

Word	Opcode	Hex	Description
NA	1-75	0x01-0x4b	The next opcode bytes is data to be pushed onto the stack
OP_PUSHDATA1	76	0x4c	The next byte contains the number of bytes to be pushed onto the stack.
OP_NOP	97	0x61	Does nothing.
OP_VERIFY	105	0x69	Marks transaction as invalid if top stack value is not true.
OP_RETURN	106	0x6a	Marks transaction as invalid. A standard way of attaching extra data to transactions is to add a zero-value output with a scriptPubKey consisting of OP_RETURN followed by exactly one pushdata op. Such outputs are provably unspendable, reducing their cost to the network. Currently it is usually considered non-standard (though valid) for a transaction to have more than one OP_RETURN output or an OP_RETURN output with more than one pushdata op.
OP_DROP	117	0x75	Removes the top stack item.
OP_DUP	118	0x76	Duplicates the top stack item.
OP_EQUAL	135	0x87	Returns 1 if the inputs are exactly equal, 0 otherwise.
OP_VERIFYEQUAL	136	0x88	Same as OP_EQUAL, but runs OP_VERIFY afterward.
OP_RIPEMD160	166	0xa6	The input is hashed using RIPEMD-160.
OP_SHA256	168	0xa8	The input is hashed using SHA-256
OP_HASH160	169	0xa9	The input is hashed twice: first with SHA-256 and then with RIPEMD-160.
OP_CODESEPARATOR	171	0xab	All of the signature checking words will only match signatures to the data after the most recently-executed OP_CODESEPARATOR
OP_CHECKSIG	172	0xac	The entire transaction's outputs, inputs, and script (from the most recently-executed OP_CODESEPARATOR to the end) are hashed. The signature used by OP_CHECKSIG must be a valid signature for this hash and public key. If it is, 1 is returned, 0 otherwise.
OP_CHECKSIGVERIFY	173	0xad	Same as OP_CHECKSIG, but OP_VERIFY is executed afterward.
OP_CHECKMULTISIG	174	0xae	Compares the first signature against each public key until it finds an ECDSA match. Starting with the subsequent public key, it compares the second signature against each remaining public key until it finds an ECDSA match. The process is repeated until all signatures have been checked or not enough public keys remain to produce a successful result. All signatures need to match a public key. Because public keys are not checked again if they fail any signature comparison, signatures must be placed in the scriptSig using the same order as their corresponding public keys were placed in the scriptPubKey or redeemScript. If all signatures are valid, 1 is returned, 0 otherwise. Due to a bug, one extra unused value is removed from the stack.
OP_CHECKMULTISIGVERIFY	175	0xaf	Same as OP_CHECKMULTISIG, but OP_VERIFY is executed afterward.

Figure 8.43: List of commonly used script Opcodes.

Step 7: Once Step 5 returns true, the last operator [OP_CheckSig] will be pushed onto the stack. It verifies if the public key is generated by the private key which is used to sign the signature.

If the returned result from Step 6 is true, the spending is successfully executed.

A list of commonly used script opcodes are shown in Figure 8.43. With these opcodes, functions other than spending can be achieved. For example, instead of sending a transaction to a wallet address, one can publish a transaction on the network and send bitcoins to anyone who can return a certain hash value. Any user who can return such a hash value will be able to unlock the transaction and receive the bitcoins.

8.3 Purposes and Differences of Public and Private Blockchains

Bitcoin blockchain is a public permissionless blockchain (Figure 8.44). Anyone from the public Internet can join or leave the blockchain network without any need for providing any forms of identification or asking for permission.

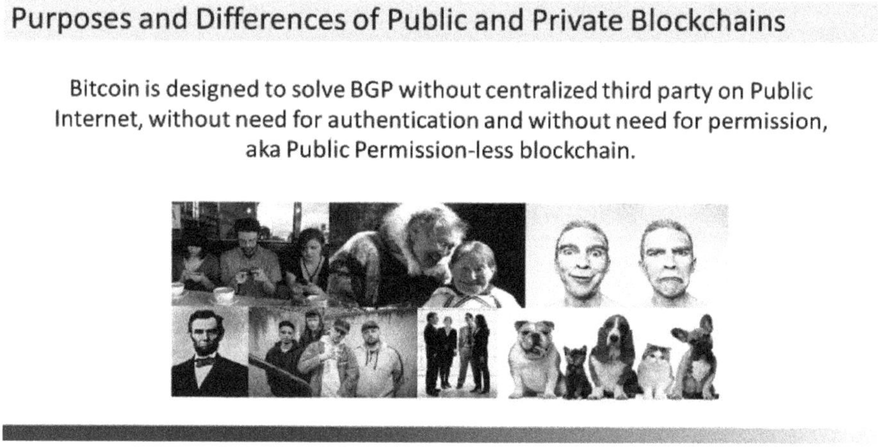

Figure 8.44: Public permissionless blockchain.

For a public blockchain, most classical distributed systems algorithms that require nodes to be known ahead of time will not work, since authentication is not used. As the environment is assumed to be public Internet and anonymous, a public blockchain is susceptible to Sybil attacks, and consensus protocols that cannot handle Byzantine failures are not applicable.

A private blockchain on the contrary provides a more sanitised environment (Figure 8.45). Figure 8.46 further lists the differences between public and private blockchains, as well as the pros and cons for turning to a private blockchain.

A private blockchain assumes that all actors on the network are known and trusted, belonging to a controlled membership. These actors can be individuals such as employees and customers or organisations such companies or departments within companies. A central authority (or group) may be required to perform the identity verification and approval of membership.

Since all members are known and access is permissionable, use of token mining to create an intrinsic incentive model is not required; therefore, solution can achieve better performance.

The public blockchain and private blockchain are examples of the blockchain trilemma, which suggests it is not possible to achieve all

Purposes and Differences of Public and Private Blockchains

What if blockchain is used in more sanitized environment?

Figure 8.45: Private permissioned blockchain.

Purposes and Differences of Public and Private Blockchains

Conditions	Bitcoin Protocol	Corporate Environment
Centralization	Peer-to-Peer	~~Peer-to-Peer~~ Organisation-to-Organisation
Types of Faults	Byzantine	Byzantine
Authentication	Not-Authenticated	~~Not-Authenticated~~
Permissions	Permission-less	~~Permission-less~~
Synchrony	asynchronous	asynchronous

Except
- Immutability
- Transaction Confidentiality

Gain
- Latency / Resiliency / Scalability
- Authentication / Authorisation
- More efficient Consensus Model
- Token-less / No Proof-of-Work Rewards

Figure 8.46: Comparing public and private blockchains.

three preferable features: decentralisation, security and performance. Bitcoin blockchain is regarded as having high decentralisation, high security, but not so much on the performance. A private blockchain can achieve security and performance, while sacrificing decentralisation.

8.4 Introduction to MultiChain

MultiChain is a private blockchain platform based on a fork of Bitcoin Core. It is a new and special form of high-resilience database that allow shared control across organisational boundaries.

MultiChain has the well-structured features of being lightweight and easy to configure. It is used by prominent companies and software (see Figure 8.47).

Setting up a private blockchain on multichain follows four steps (see Figure 8.48):

Step 1: Install the multichain software.
Step 2: Configure the first node, i.e., the admin node.
Step 3: Use the first node to configure the permission of other nodes.
Step 4: Connect with other nodes.

On the bitcoin blockchain, the assets (bitcoins) are issued by the protocol itself, while on the multichain, the owner can issue his/her owner assets, similar to a central bank printing its own money if it is permissioned to do so (Figure 8.49).

On multichain, streams can be used for data storage (Figure 8.50).

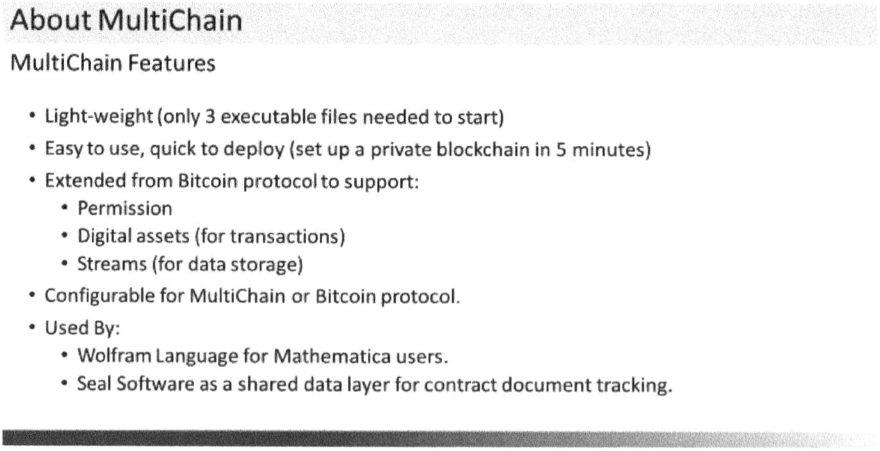

Figure 8.47: Features of multichain.

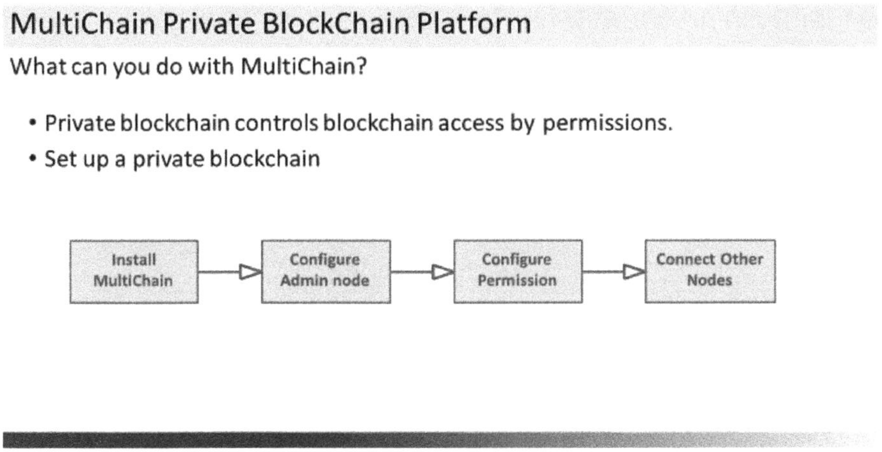

Figure 8.48: Steps to set up private blockchain on multichain.

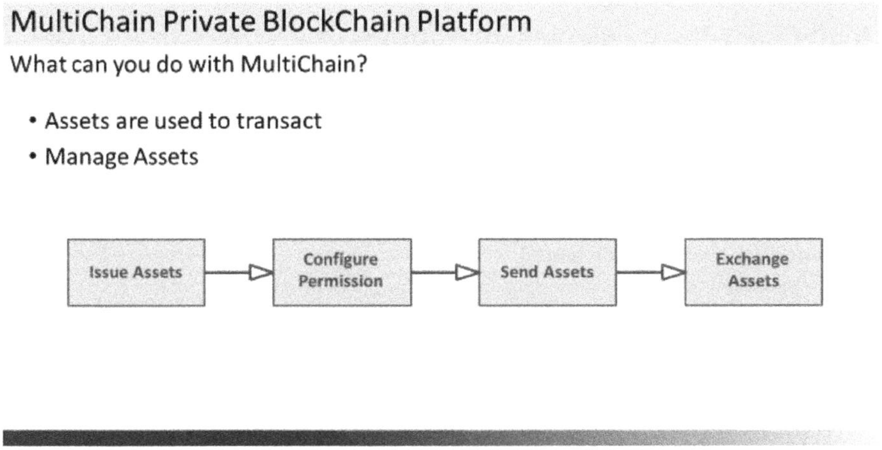

Figure 8.49: Issuance of assets on multichain.

Given in Figure 8.51 are the three executable files needed during the setup and use of multichain. The two main configuration files should be set before the chain is created and running. Some hidden folders will be created while setting up the blockchain.

Multichain-util is used to create a blockchain and kick off the process (see Figure 8.52).

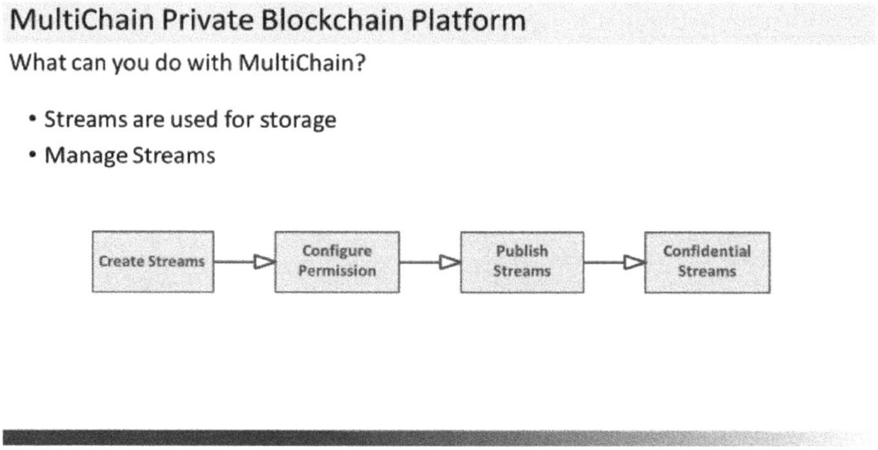

Figure 8.50: Data storage on multichain.

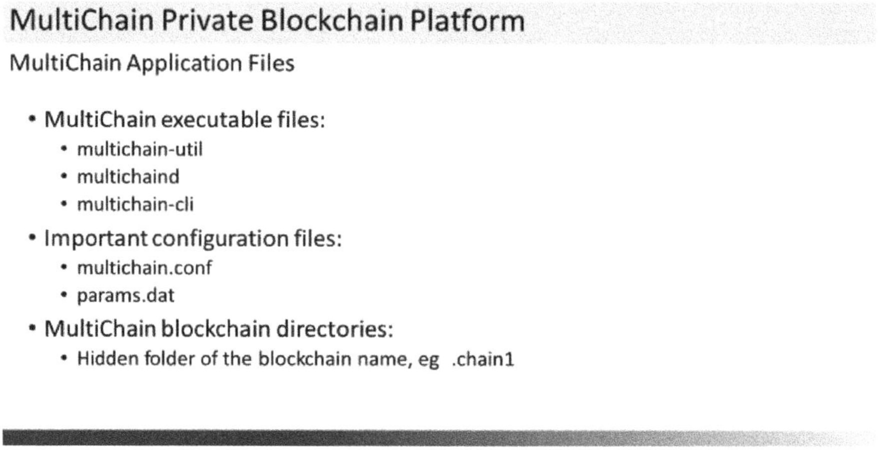

Figure 8.51: Executive files needed for multichain.

Multichaind is the service running on the nodes (see Figure 8.53).

Multichain-cli is the command line tool to issue command lines to the nodes (see Figure 8.54).

The multichain.conf file contains parameters for the specific node. "rpcuser", "rpcpassword" and "rpcallowip" are the three fields that

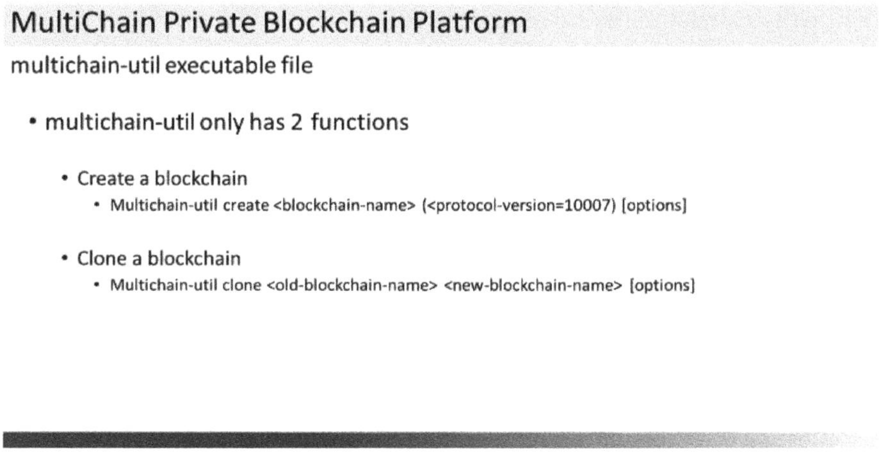

Figure 8.52: Multichain-util.

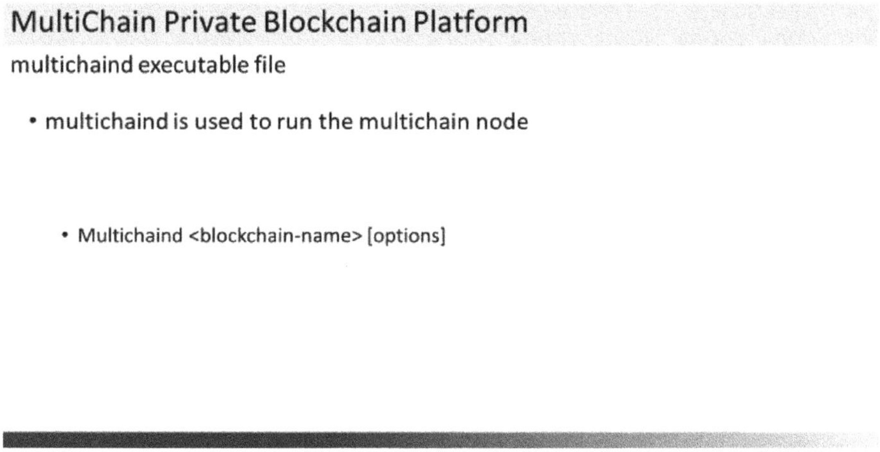

Figure 8.53: Multichaind.

need to be changed in the configuration file, which enables the user to talk to the blockchain nodes remotely (see Figure 8.55).

The params.dat file contains parameters for the multichain, which are the same for every node (see Figure 8.56). The parameters cannot be changed once the blockchain is initialised.

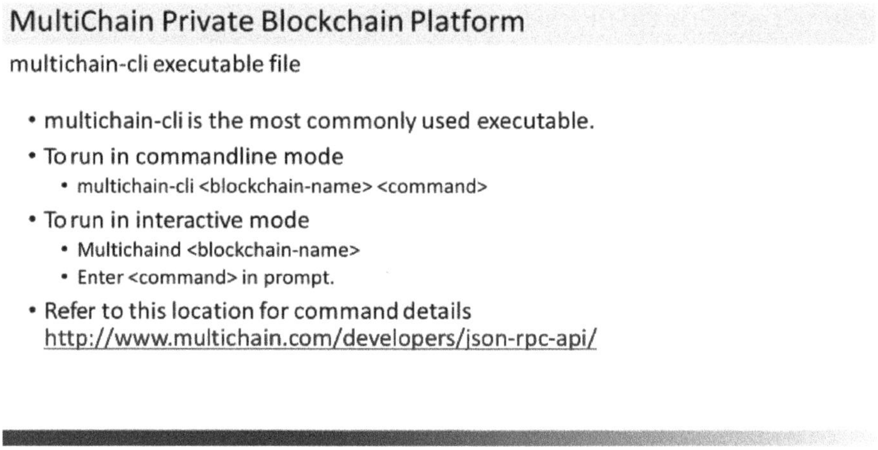

Figure 8.54: Multichain-cli.

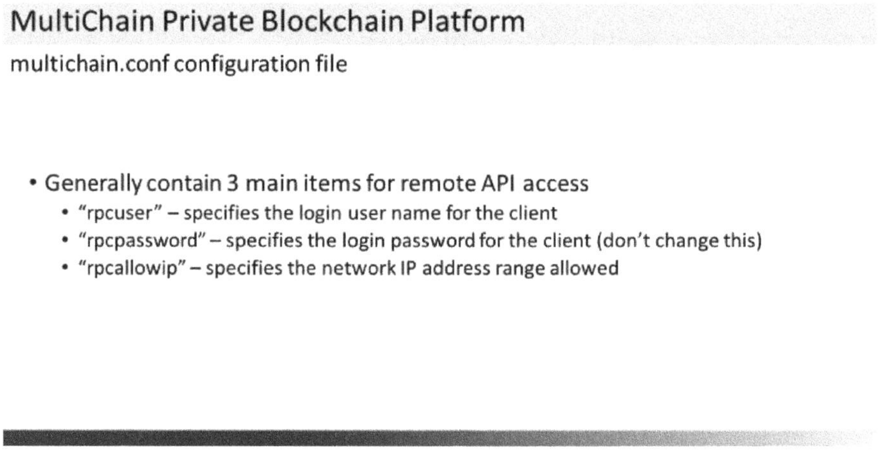

Figure 8.55: Multichain.conf.

8.4.1 *MultiChain Permissions*

MultiChain allows permissions to be assigned according to wallet addresses (see Figure 8.57). Low-level permissions include whether a node can connect to the other nodes, and whether a node can send or receive assets. Medium-level permissions include the capability to issue assets and create streams. Operators can mine or change the

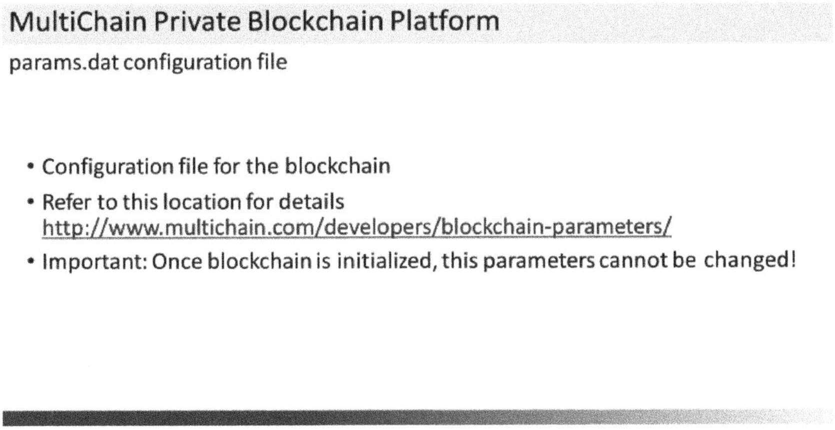

Figure 8.56: params.dat configuration file.

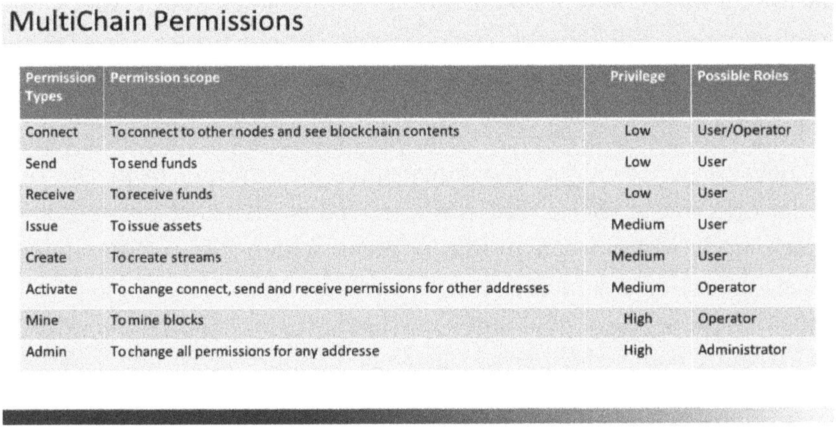

Permission Types	Permission scope	Privilege	Possible Roles
Connect	To connect to other nodes and see blockchain contents	Low	User/Operator
Send	To send funds	Low	User
Receive	To receive funds	Low	User
Issue	To issue assets	Medium	User
Create	To create streams	Medium	User
Activate	To change connect, send and receive permissions for other addresses	Medium	Operator
Mine	To mine blocks	High	Operator
Admin	To change all permissions for any addresse	High	Administrator

Figure 8.57: MultiChain permission types, scope and relevant information.

permissions for other nodes, and the administrator has the highest power to change all permissions for any address.

8.4.2 *Peer-to-Peer Handshaking Protocol on MultiChain*

As the configuration of nodes on multichain is a bit more complicated than that of the Bitcoin blockchain (for example, various multichain

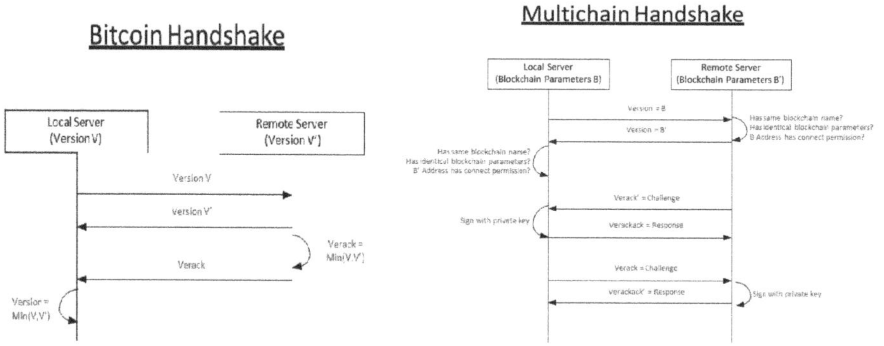

Figure 8.58: Bitcoin handshake vs multichain handshake.

nodes might have different permissions), the handshake between nodes on multichain is also more complicated; the entire configuration file needs to be sent to each other (see Figure 8.58). Specifically, three messages will be sent, version, verack and verackack, and they perform the following additional functions:

- Check that both peers are on a blockchain with the same name.
- If necessary, download the blockchain parameters from the other side; otherwise, check that both are using identical parameters.
- Each node identifies a public address which has connection permissions and for which it has the private key.
- Each node sends a challenge message to the other node which it must sign using the private key corresponding to the address it presented.

As there are different levels of permissions on multichain (especially since an admin role has the most powerful permissions), a consensus governance model is applied. More than one admin node exists on the network, and it takes certain number of votes from admin nodes in order to reach consensus.

For example, a decision needs to be made regarding whether to grant admin role to a new node. If the admin-consensus-admin parameter is set at 0.6, then confirmations from more than 60% of the existing admin nodes are needed in order to reach consensus and grant the new node the admin role (see Figure 8.59).

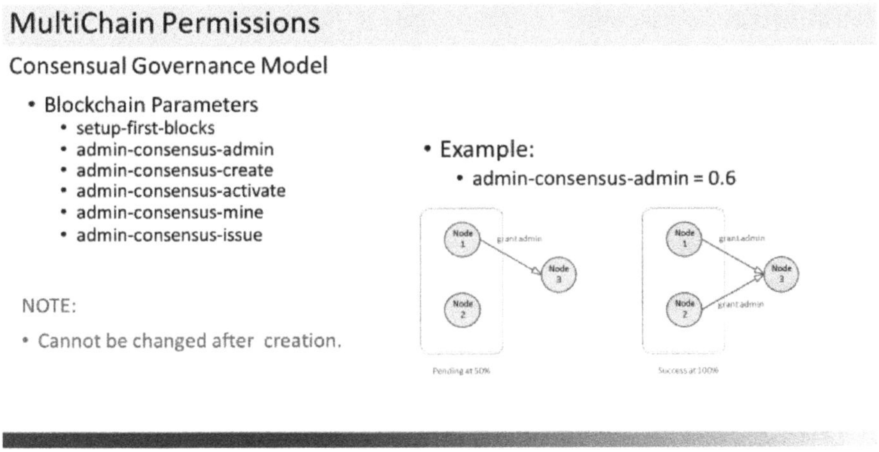

Figure 8.59: Granting of permission on multichain.

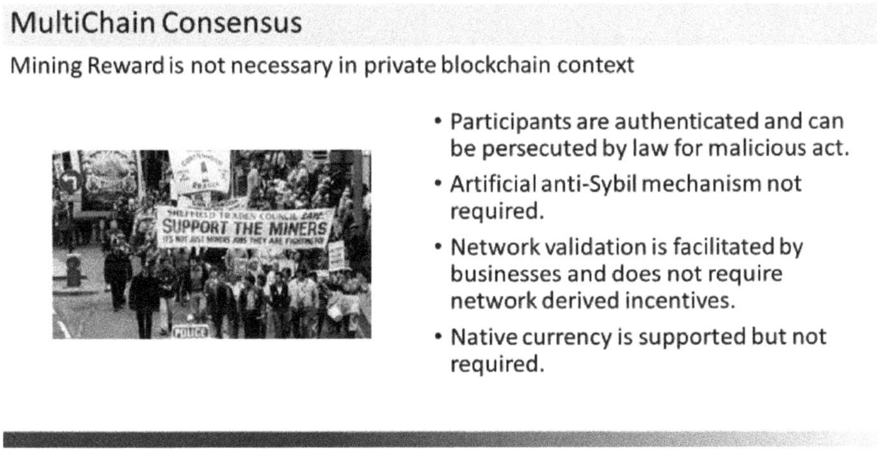

Figure 8.60: Incentive for mining.

8.4.3 *MultiChain Consensus*

As discussed earlier, the mining reward is not necessary in the private blockchain context such as multichain (see Figure 8.60).

One dilemma posed by private blockchains is that one participant could monopolise the mining process. MultiChain solves this dilemma

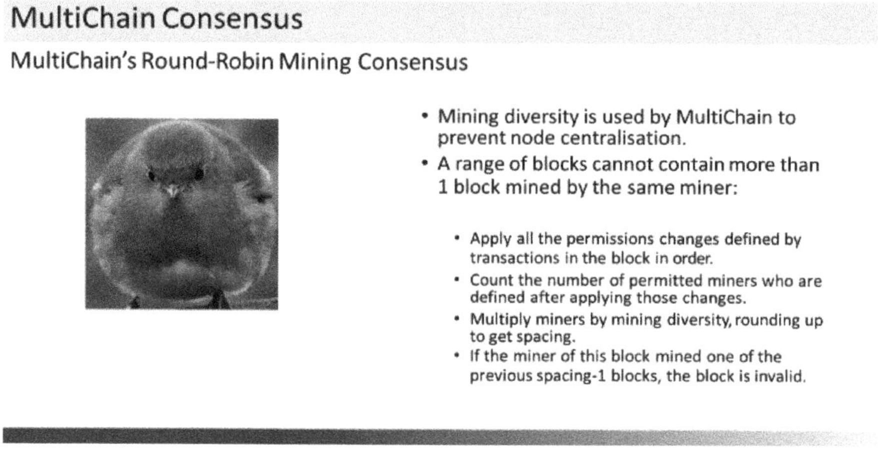

Figure 8.61: MultiChain consensus protocol.

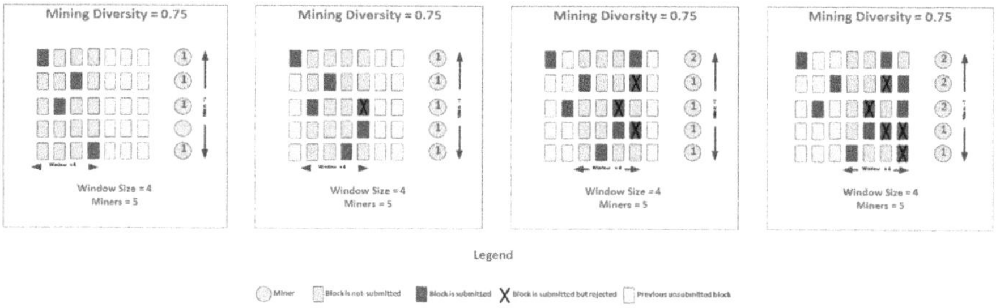

Figure 8.62: Effect of mining diversity = 0.75.

by applying a constraint on the number of blocks which may be created by the same miner within a given window (see Figure 8.61).

To implement a round-robin schedule (where the permitted miners must create blocks in rotation), a parameter called "Mining Diversity" is set up with the constraint $0 \leq$ Mining Diversity ≤ 1.

The number of permitted miners on the blockchain is multiplied by the Mining Diversity, and the result is rounded up to get an integer called spacing. If the miner of a block has mined one of the previous spacing-1 blocks, the block is invalid.

Figure 8.62 illustrates the effect of setting Mining Diversity to 0.75.

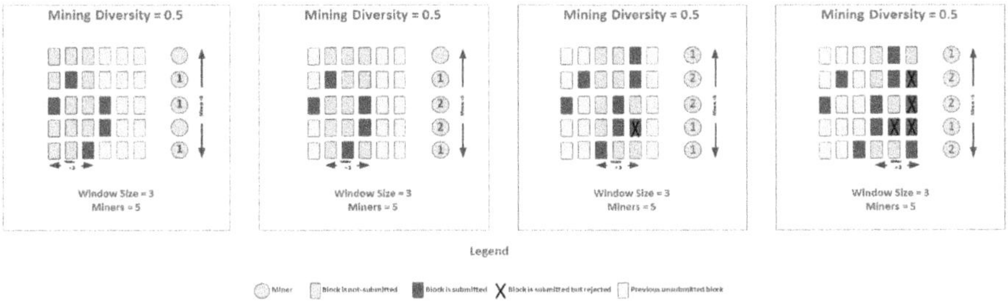

Figure 8.63: Effect of mining diversity = 0.50.

There are five permitted miners in this example. Hence, spacing (i.e., the window size) is calculated as $5 \times 0.75 = 4$, which means that a miner cannot mine two or more blocks in any four consecutive blocks. A miner who had mined a block needs to wait for three blocks to be mined by other miners before he can generate a block again. Otherwise, his block will be rejected when he submits it to the network.

The higher the Mining Diversity is, the more the miners will be involved in the block generation. The possible downside is that the whole blockchain freezes up if some miners become inactive.

Figure 8.63 illustrates what might happen if the Mining Diversity is set at 0.5.

Spacing (i.e., the window size) is calculated as 3 (i.e., 5 multiplied by 0.5 and then rounded up). A miner who has mined a block needs to wait for only two blocks to be mined by other miners before he can generate block again. As the spacing is shorter now compared to when the diversity was set at 0.75, there is a higher chance that multiple miners are generating blocks simultaneously.

Figure 8.64 illustrates what might happen if the Mining Diversity is set at 0.25.

Spacing (i.e., the window size) is calculated as 2 (i.e., 5 multiplied by 0.25 and then rounded up).

Figure 8.65 illustrates what might happen if the Mining Diversity is set at 0.

For Mining Diversity set at 0, there is no restriction at all, and every permitted miner can mine blocks at any time.

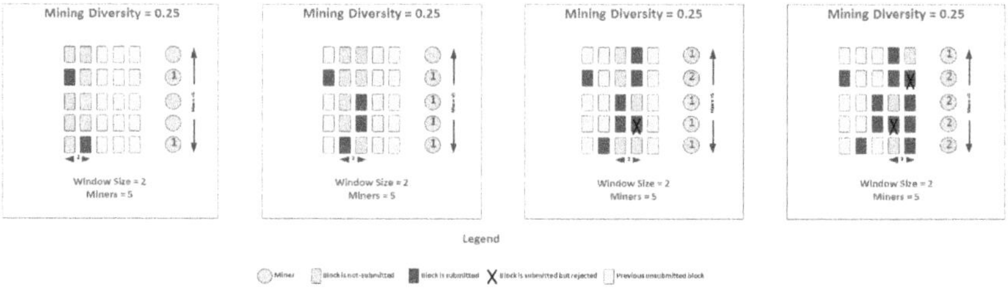

Figure 8.64: Effect of mining diversity = 0.25.

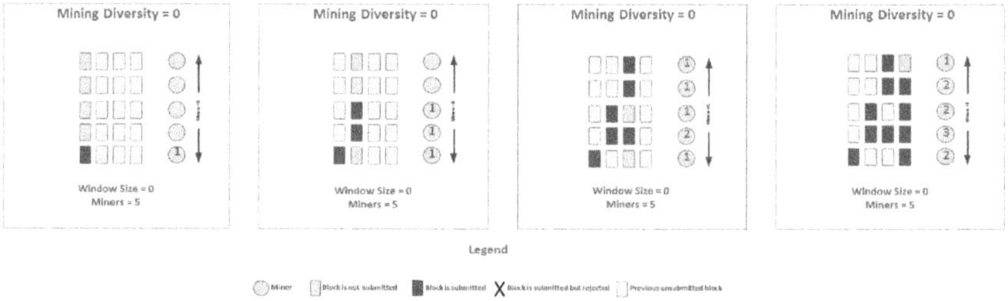

Figure 8.65: Effect of mining diversity = 0.

The concentration risk is higher in that one miner is generating more blocks than others, and in that it takes fewer miners to collude in order to undermine the network.

In summary, the Mining Diversity parameter defines the strictness of the round-robin scheme, i.e., the proportion of permitted miners who would need to collude in order to undermine the network. A value of 1 ensures that every permitted miner is included in the rotation, whereas 0 represents no restriction at all. In general, higher values are safer, but a value too close to 1 can cause the blockchain to freeze up if some miners become inactive. Usually, a value of 0.75 is regarded as a reasonable compromise. To conserve resources, nodes will not attempt to mine on a chain in which they had already mined one of the previous spacing-1 blocks.

8.4.4 *MultiChain Asset*

Native currency on a blockchain is generically generated by the protocol, such as Bitcoin and Ethereum (see Figure 8.66). Native

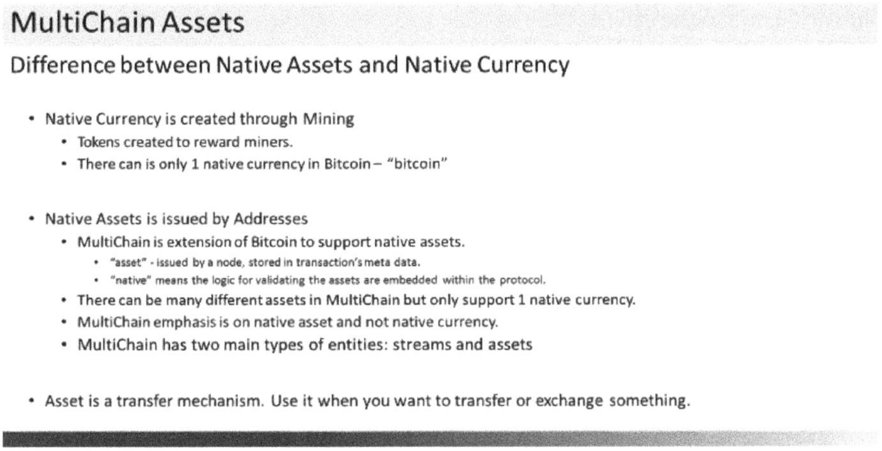

Figure 8.66: Difference between native assets and native currency.

assets are issued by addresses, and the word “native” means that the logic for validating such assets is embedded within the protocol. There can be many different assets in multichain, but only one native currency.

Bitcoin 2.0 is a concept that refers to leveraging the Bitcoin protocol above and beyond its native currency bitcoin, such as securing and validating external transactions that do not originate on the main chain (see Figure 8.67). A related term is “colored coins”, which describes a class of methods for representing and managing real-world assets on top of the Bitcoin blockchain. Earlier, we discussed that the Bitcoin Script language allows it to store small amounts of metadata on the blockchain, which can be used to represent such asset manipulation instructions. However, the presence of such non-native assets encoded in the metadata is not subjected to network-level verification, because Bitcoin nodes cannot read the metadata and also because neither Bitcoin nodes nor Bitcoin tracks such non-native assets. The only way to validate the balance of such non-native assets is to download the full history of bitcoin transactions.

MultiChain assets, on the contrary, are built into the protocol and validated at the network level (Figure 8.68). It encodes the identifiers

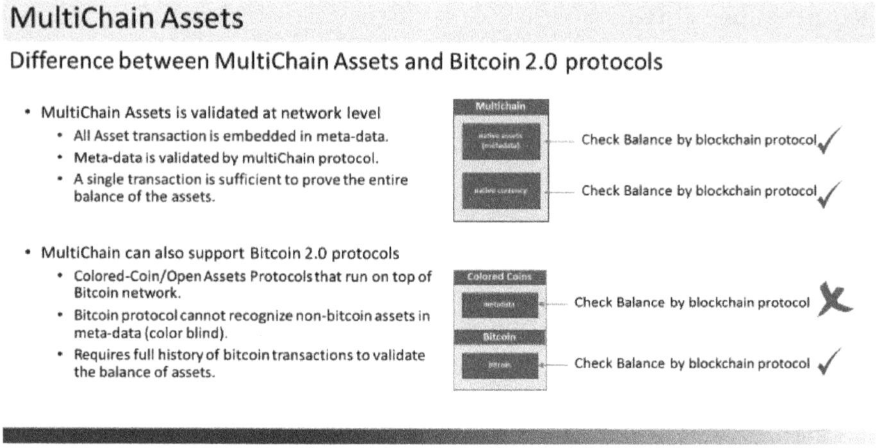

Figure 8.67: Difference between multichain assets and bitcoin 2.0 protocols.

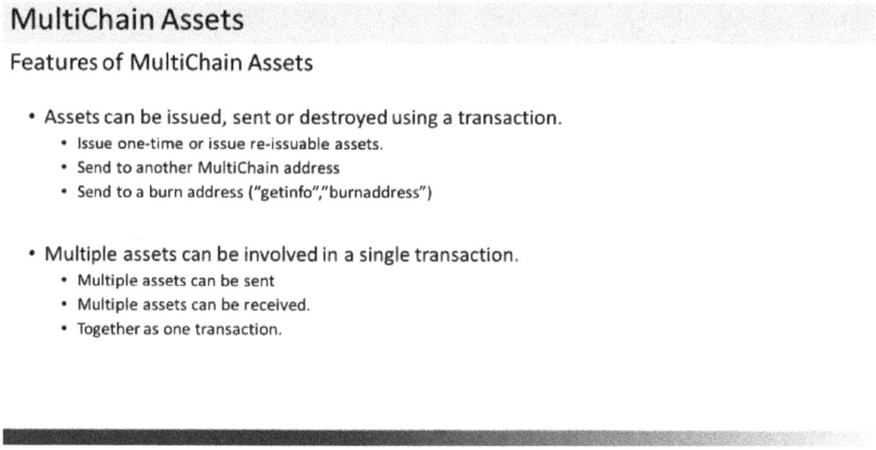

Figure 8.68: Features of multichain assets.

and quantities of all assets into each transaction output, using an extension provided by bitcoin's scripting language.

The rule for validating transactions is extended to verify that the total quantities of all assets in a transaction's output are exactly matched by the total in its inputs (this equality requirement is stricter than the constraint for the native currency, in which the

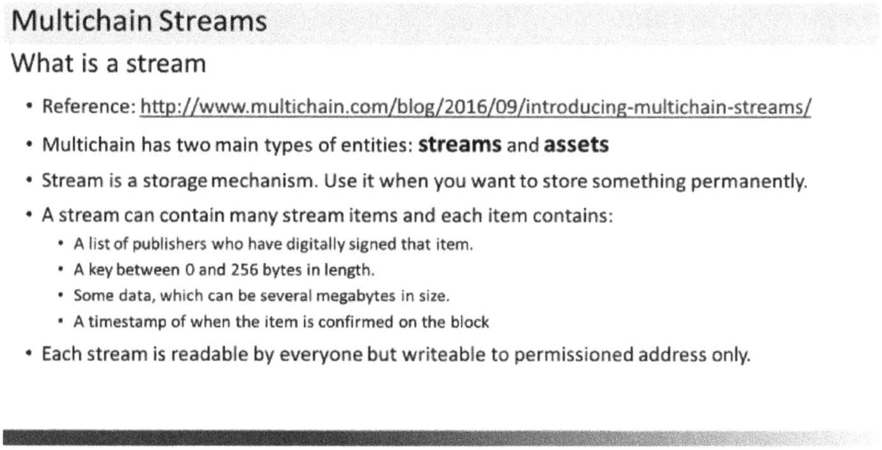

Figure 8.69: Definition of a stream.

output may be less than the input, with the difference collected as a fee by miners).

8.4.5 *MultiChain Streams*

A stream is a set of data storage functionality introduced to multichain in 2016. It is mainly for general data retrieval, timestamping and archiving, rather than the transfer of assets between participants (Figure 8.69).

Steams can be used to implement three different types of databases on a chain (see Figure 8.70):

1. A key–value database or document store, in the style of NoSQL.
2. A time series database, which focuses on the ordering of entries.
3. An identity-driven database where entries are classified according to their author.

8.5 Hands-On Lab with MultiChain

This section introduces how a hands-on lab session with multichain is done, where participants set up a private blockchain, set up permissions, create and issue native assets and make transactions.

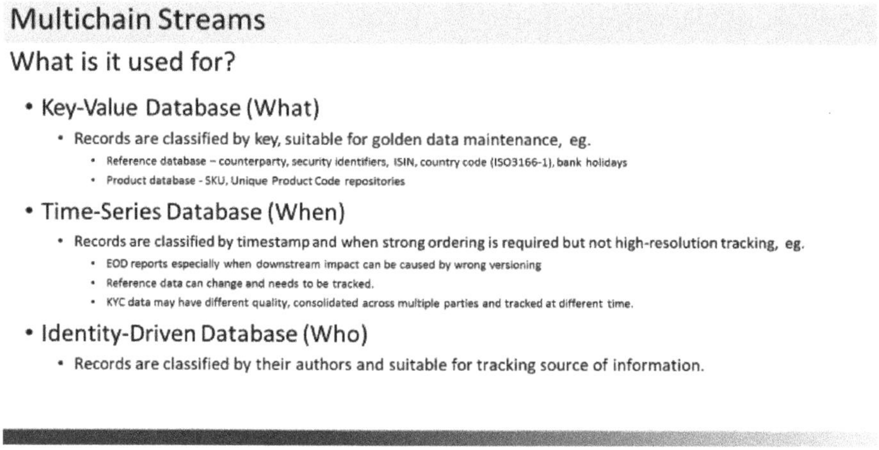

Figure 8.70: What, When and Who of multichain streams.

8.5.1 *MultiChain Installation*

A Microsoft Azure account[1] and Putty are needed for this session.

Initially, create virtual machine on Ubuntu server in Azure (see Figure 8.71).

Then, connect to the virtual machine using Putty (see Figure 8.72).

Next, download the latest version of multichain community from https://multichain.com/download-community/ (see Figure 8.73).

Note that there need to be at least three participants in this session, so they can set up Server 1, 2 and 3 following the abovementioned steps. In later sessions, they will act as three different nodes on multichain.

8.5.2 *Setup a MultiChain Private Blockchain Network*

The participants form into groups of 3 members, and in each group they identify each member as Node 1, Node 2 and Node 3.

[1]https://azure.microsoft.com/.

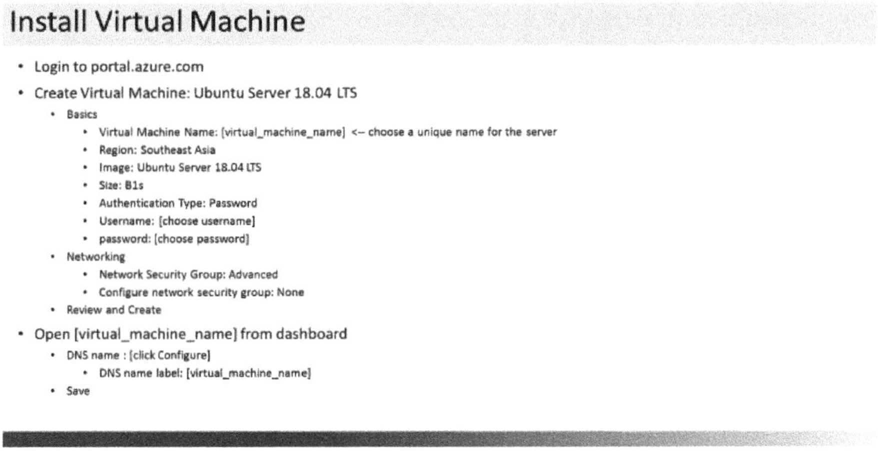

Figure 8.71: Creation of virtual machine on Ubuntu.

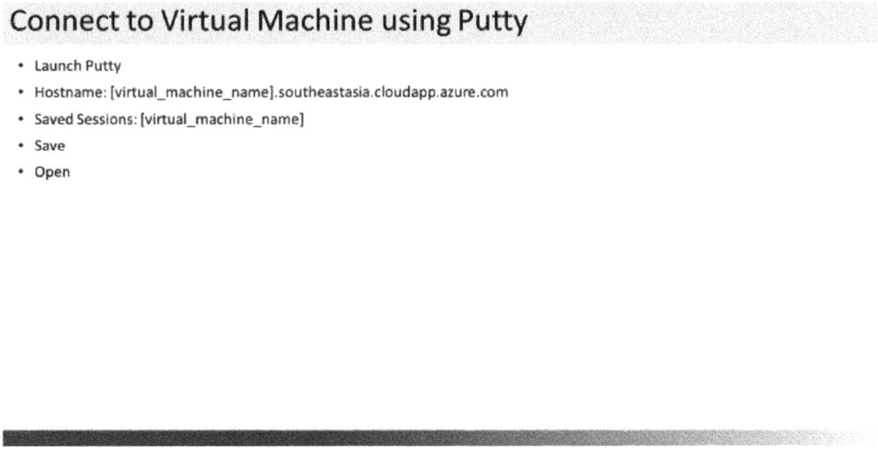

Figure 8.72: Connect to virtual machine using Putty.

Overview

Below are the steps for setting up Node 1 and Node 2 and establishing a connection (see Figure 8.74):

Step 1: Node 1 runs *multichain-util create chain1* to create the first node, which is also the admin node.

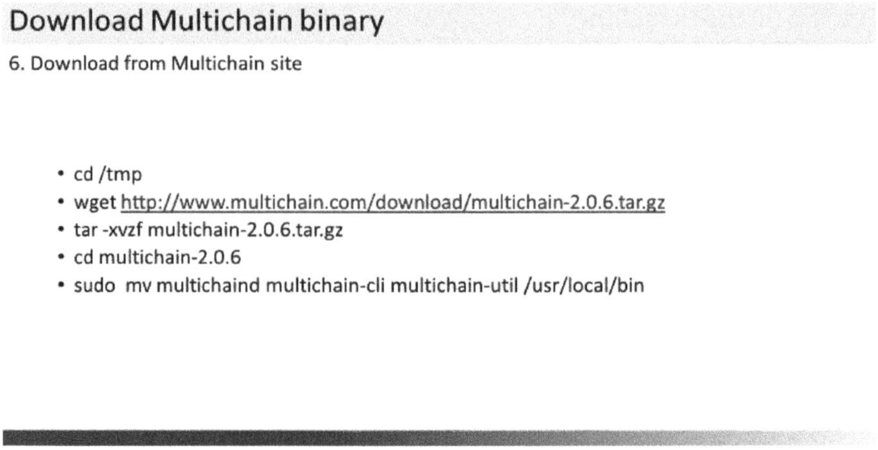

Figure 8.73: Download multichain community.

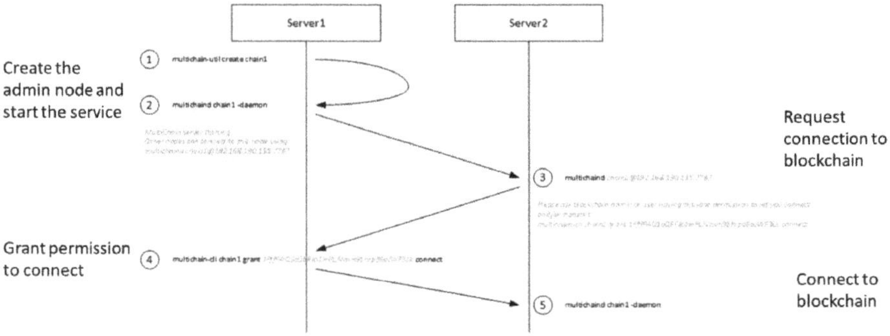

Figure 8.74: Steps 1–4, establishing connections between Node 1 and Node 2.

Step 2: Node 1 then runs *multichaind chain1 -daemon* to start running multichain as a service from this node.

Step 3: Node 2 sends a request to connect to Node 1, by running *multichaind chain1@<IP address of Node 1> :<port number>*. As this is the first time Node 2 tries to connect, it will be automatically rejected, but Node 1 will receive notification.

Step 4: Node 1 grants permission to connect to Node 2 by running *multichain-cli chain1 grant <wallet address of Node 2> connect.*

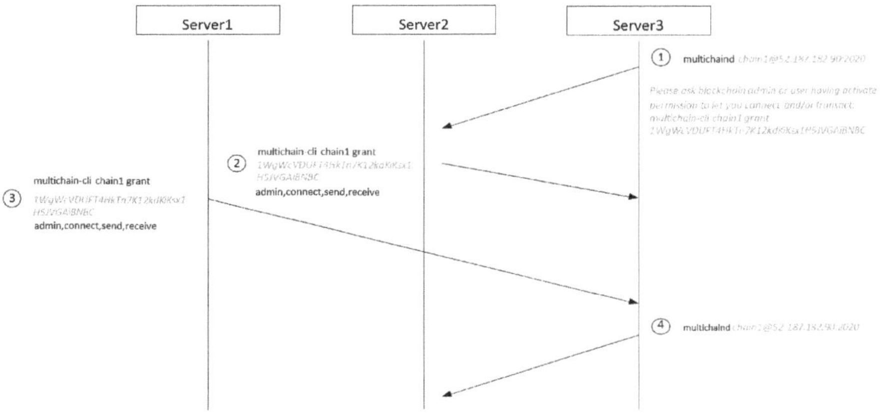

Figure 8.75: Steps 1–3, establishing connections with Node 3.

Node 1 needs to let Node 2 know that the permission has been granted, then Node 2 repeats the 2nd step to connect.

Step 5: Node 2 runs *multichaind chain1 -daemon* to start running multichain.

Setting up a third Node and connecting it to Node 1 and Node 2 works in a similar way (see Figure 8.75):

Step 1: Node 3 sends a connect request to Node 1 or Node 2, by running *multichaind chain1@< IP address of Node 1 or Node 2>:<port number>.*

Step 2: Node 2 or Node 1 can grant permission by running *multichain-cli chain1 grant < wallet address of Node 3> connect.*

Other permissions such as admin, send and receive can also be granted.

Step 3: Node 3 repeats Step 1 to connect.

Detailed Steps and Execution

Node 1 runs *multichain-util create chain1* and creates a blockchain called "chain1". Node 1 then should be able to see the folder called ".multichain" (see Figure 8.76).

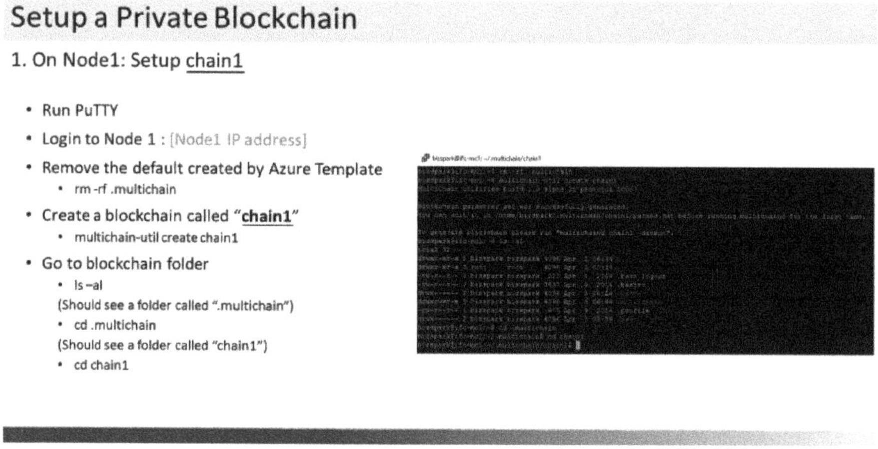

Figure 8.76: Set up chain 1.

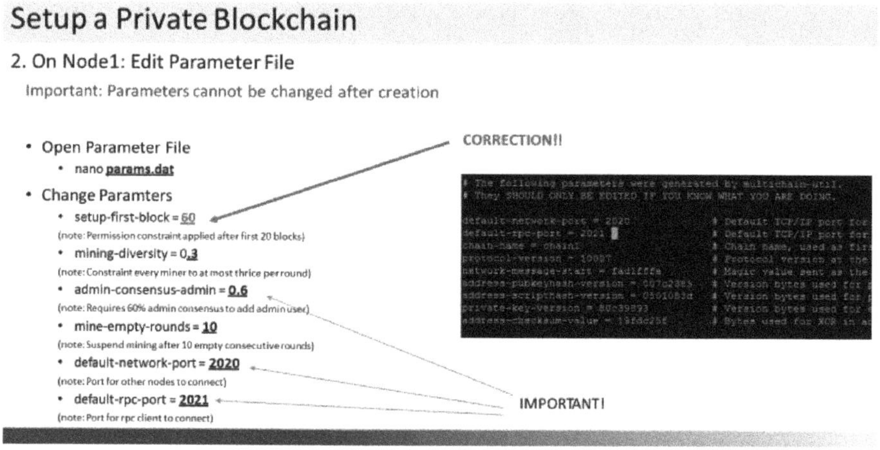

Figure 8.77: Edit parameter file.

Enter the folder ".multichain", and further enter the subfolder "chain1"; Node 1 will see two files: "multichain.conf" and "params.dat".

Node 1 should then immediately change the parameters, as these parameters cannot be changed once he starts to run the multichain (see Figure 8.77).

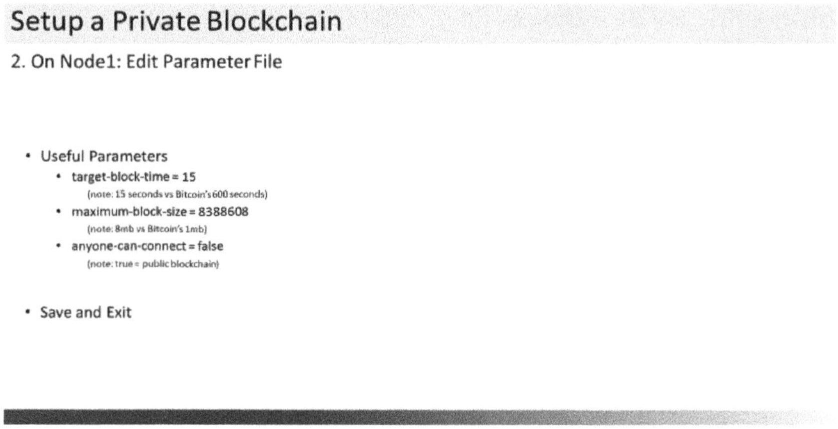

Figure 8.78: Other useful parameters.

The default-network-port is for node-to-node connection and will be used later by other nodes to connect to the blockchain. Rpc-port is for programming purposes. In this example, we changed the network port to 2020 and rpc-port to 2021.

The parameters discussed previously such as Mining Diversity and admin-consensus-admin should be decided and updated now. In this example, we changed admin-consensus-admin to 0.6.

Some other useful parameters (see Figure 8.78) that should also be considered and updated are *target-block-time* (the average time to generate a block), *maximum-block-size* (the maximum size of a block) and *anyone-can-connect* (if anyone can connect to this blockchain. If it is set to "Yes", then it becomes a public blockchain).

When Node 1 runs the daemon command, the blockchain called chain1 will officially start running. Note that daemon can be run in the background, so that Node 1 can still operate in the console (Figure 8.79).

Node 2 runs *multichaind chain1@<IP address of Node 1>:<port number>*to connect to Node 1, and he will be able to see the wallet address of Node 1 from the output (see Figure 8.80).

Node 1 grants Node 2 permissions to admin, connect, send and receive. It is important to have another admin node in the network (see Figure 8.81).

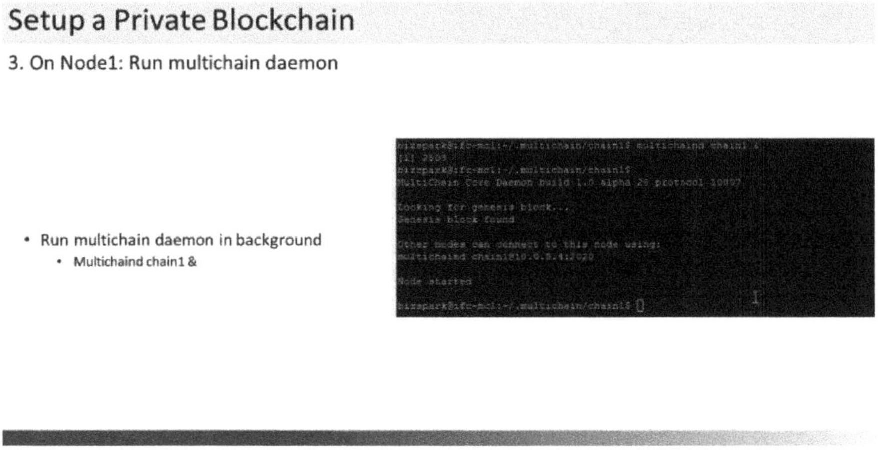

Figure 8.79: Run multichain daemon.

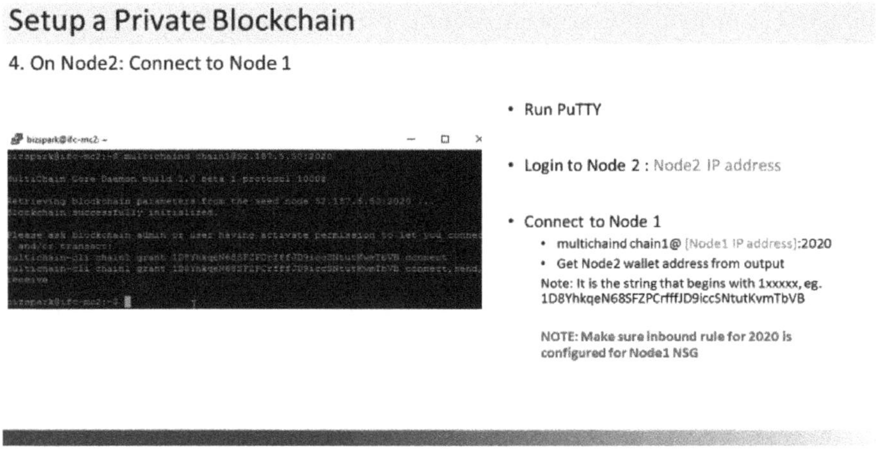

Figure 8.80: Connecting Node 2 to Node 1.

Node 2 connects to Node 1 again and this time it should be successful (see Figure 8.82).

Node 3 will request to connect to Node 2 in a similar way (Figure 8.83).

Node 1 and Node 2 can view the permissions and it is important that both should be admin nodes (see Figure 8.84).

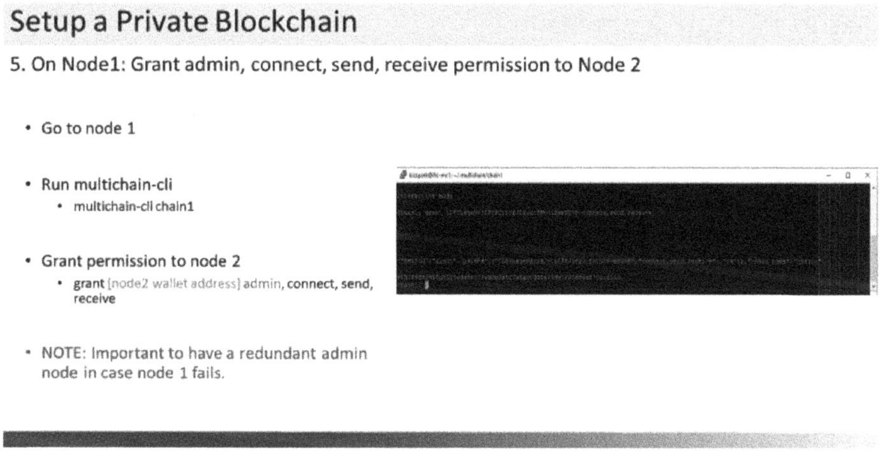

Figure 8.81: Granting permission on Node 1.

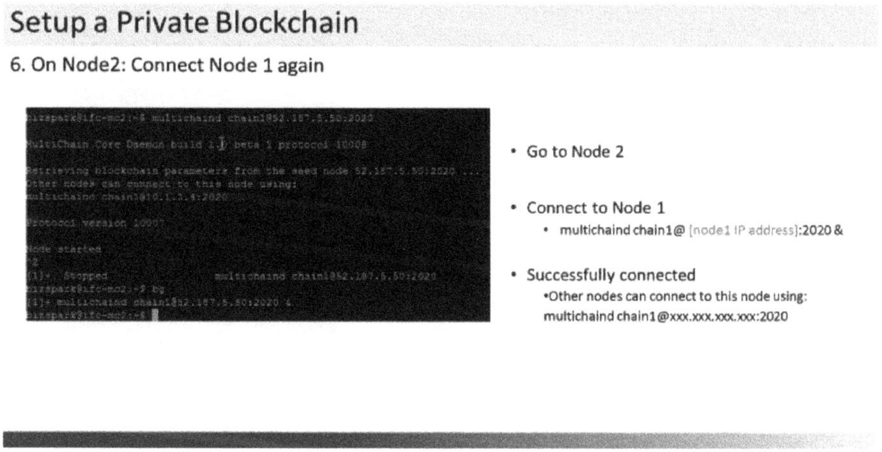

Figure 8.82: Connecting Node 2 to Node 1 again.

Admin nodes verify the value of admin-consensus-admin. In this example, we set the parameter to 0.6, which means 60% of the admin nodes are needed to reach consensus. This means both Node 1 and Node 2 need to grant permission to Node 3 in order for the permission to be effective (see Figure 8.85).

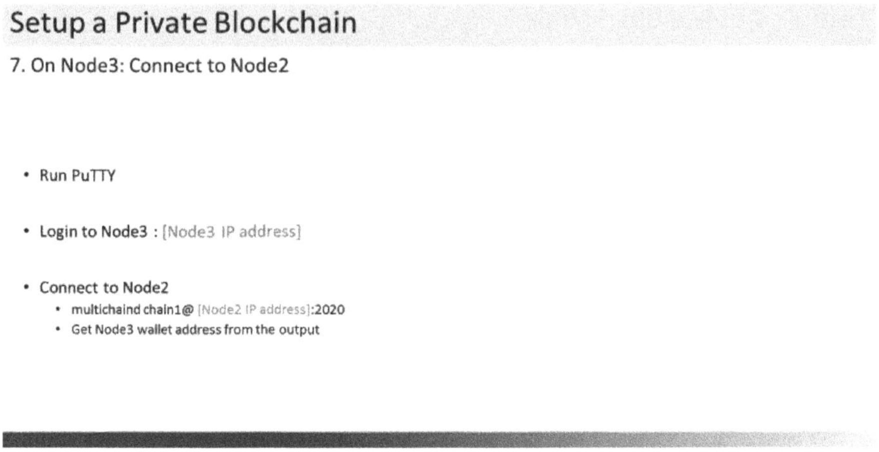

Figure 8.83: Connecting Node 3 to Node 2.

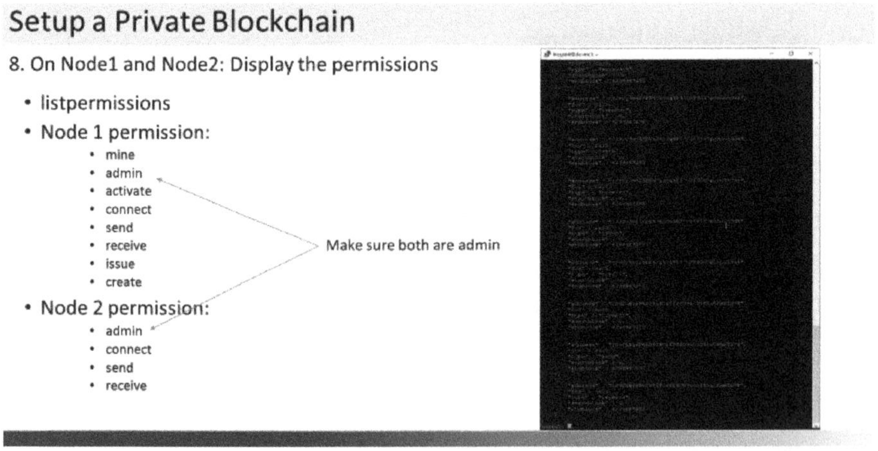

Figure 8.84: Assessing permissions on Node 1 and Node 2.

Node 1 grants permission. It is equivalent to a 50% admin vote (there are two admins in total), hence the permission status is still pending (see Figure 8.86).

Node 2 also grants permission. It is equivalent to a 100% admin vote (there are two admins in total), hence the permission is approved (see Figure 8.87).

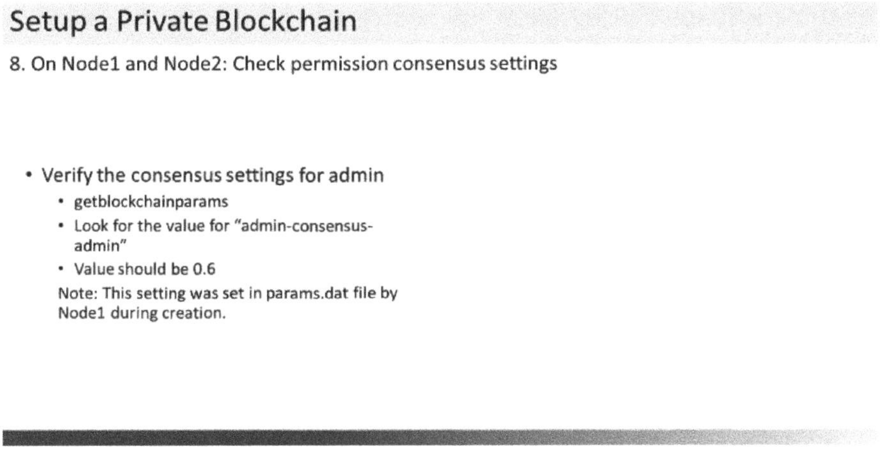

Figure 8.85: Verify consensus settings for admin on Node 1 and Node 2.

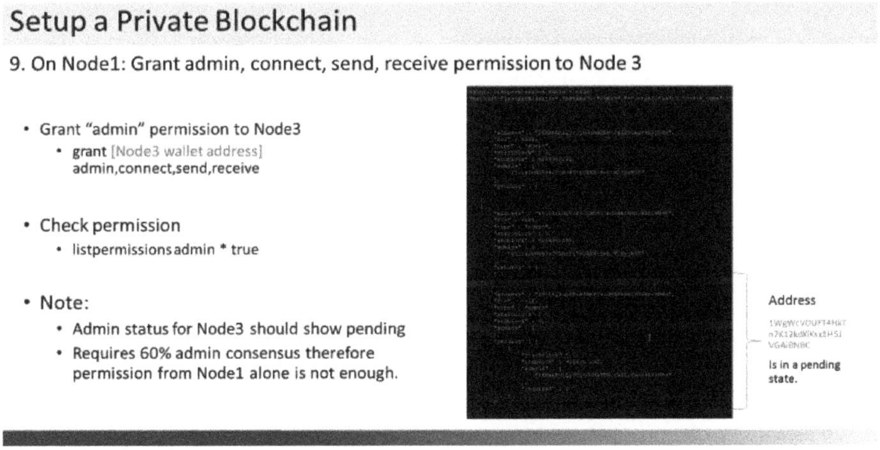

Figure 8.86: Granting permission on Node 1.

Node 3 now can connect to Node 2 (see Figure 8.88).

8.5.3 *Use MultiChain API with Multichain-cli*

API (Application Programming Interface) is a computing interface to a software component or a system, which defines how other components or systems can use it. It can be regarded as a software

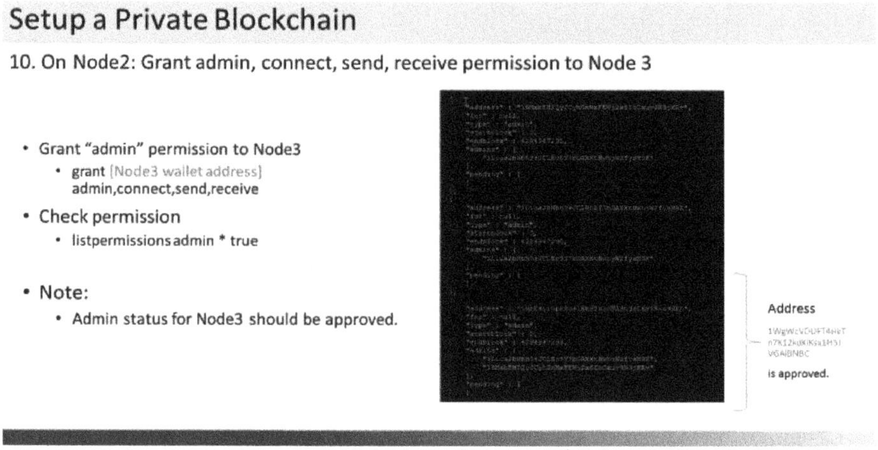

Figure 8.87: Granting permission on Node 2.

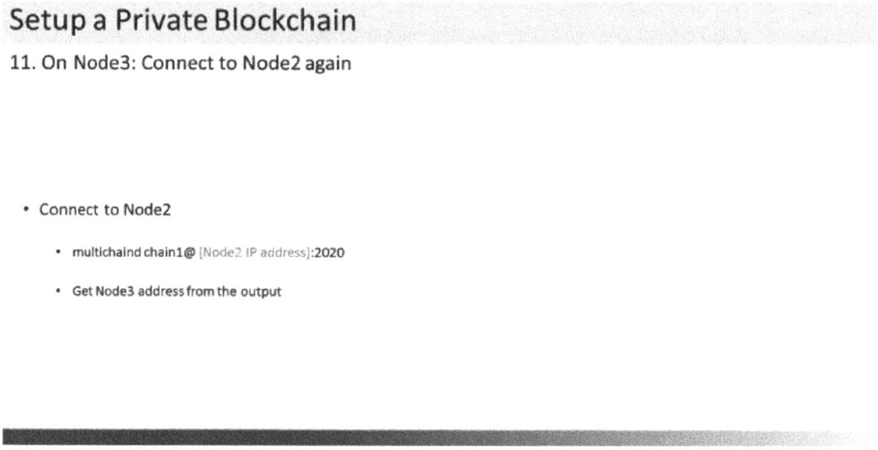

Figure 8.88: Connect to Node 2 again.

intermediary and is designed for external applications to talk to the service and issue commands. In this session, we illustrate how to use multichain API to issue commands and control how the multichain operates (note that MultiChain is compatible with any API library developed for Bitcoin Core).

We will focus on accessing API via *multichain-cli* command-line tool (alternatively, it can be done via the other JSON-RPC client; see Figure 8.89).

The latest updates of the API commands are available at https://www.multichain.com/developers/json-rpc-api/(see Figure 8.90).

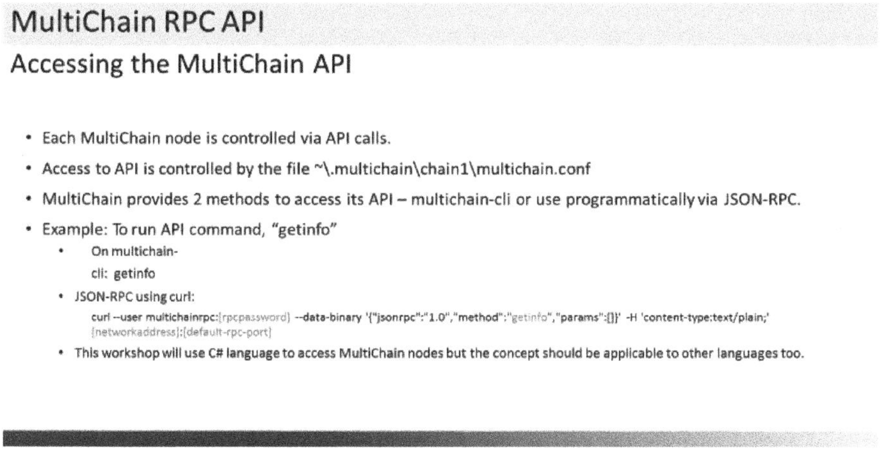

Figure 8.89: Accessing multichain API.

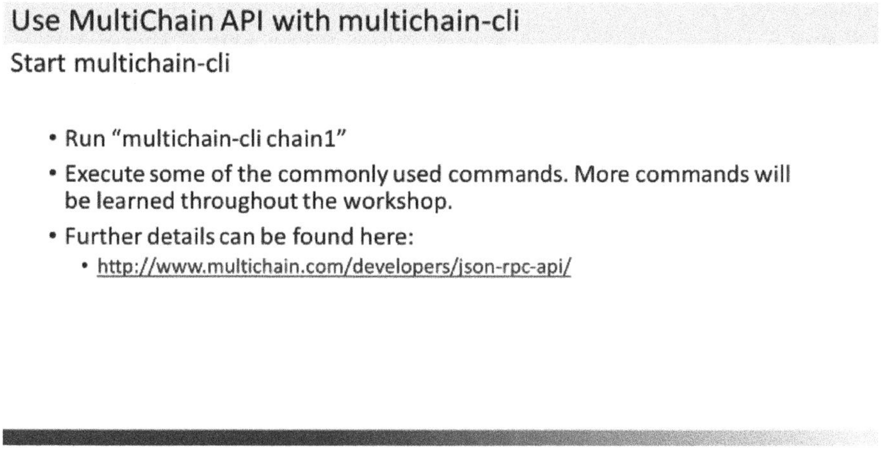

Figure 8.90: Run multichain-cli.

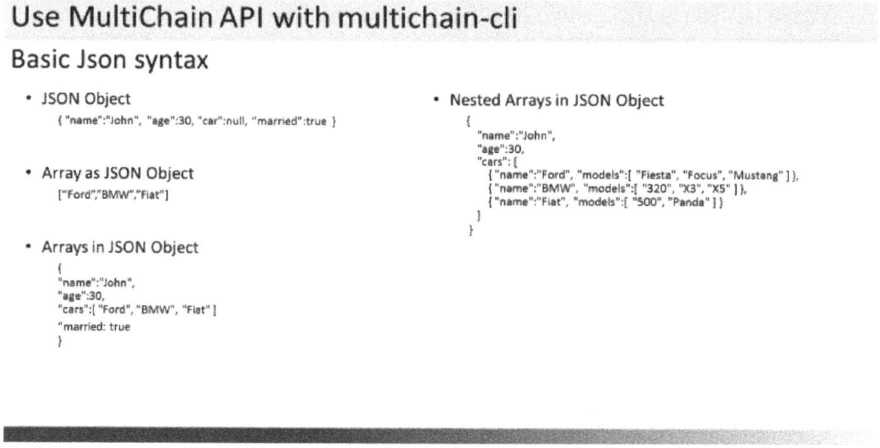

Figure 8.91: Basic JSON syntax.

JavaScript Object Notation (JSON) is an open standard, language-independent file format and data interchange format that uses human-readable text to store and transmit data objects consisting of attribute–value pairs and array data types. It is a very concise data format and easy to transfer through the network. Figure 8.91 provides some examples of the paired JSON objects and arrays objects (nested arrays means that some arrays are nested within other arrays).

Figure 8.92 provides some of the most used API commands.

getinfo returns general information about this node and blockchain. There are five attributes (highlighted in blue), namely "protocolversion", "protocol", "port", "blocks" and "connections", that the node can compare against other nodes and understand if the node is connected to the other nodes properly. For example, all nodes should have the same protocol, same protocol version, same port number and the same number of blocks (if they are well in sync).

getpeerinfo returns information about the other nodes to which this node is connected. For MultiChain blockchain, handshake and handshakelocal fields are also available, showing the remote and local addresses used during the handshaking for that connection (see Figure 8.93).

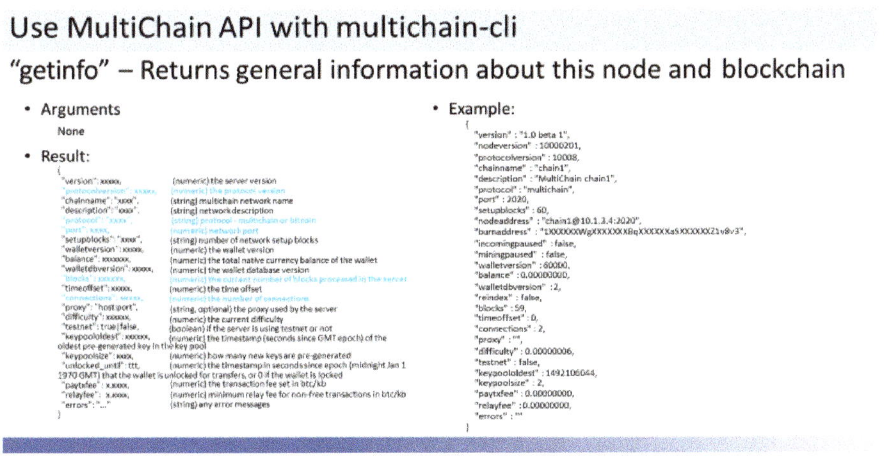

Figure 8.92: Utilising getinfo.

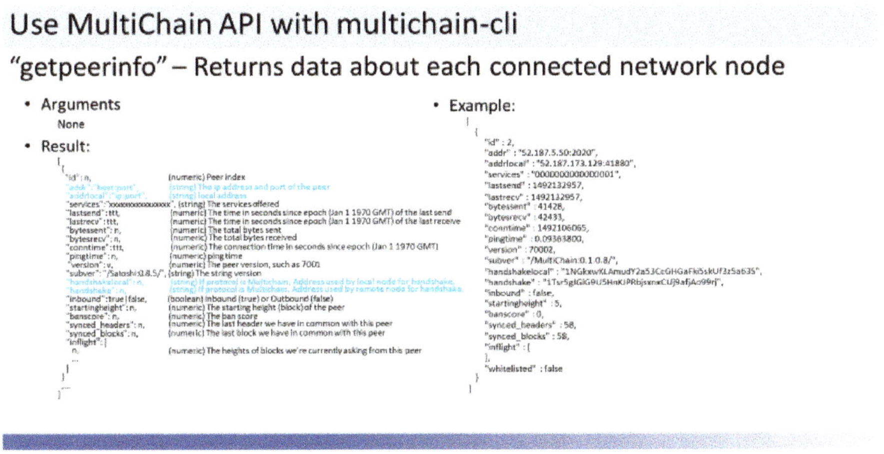

Figure 8.93: Utilising getpeerinfo.

getblockchaininfo returns information about the blockchain. The *blocks* (number of current blocks on the chain) and *bestblockhash* (hash value of the most recent block) can be compared across nodes to check if they are perfectly synchronised (see Figure 8.94).

getblock returns information about the block with the given hash or at the given height in the active chain (see Figure 8.95).

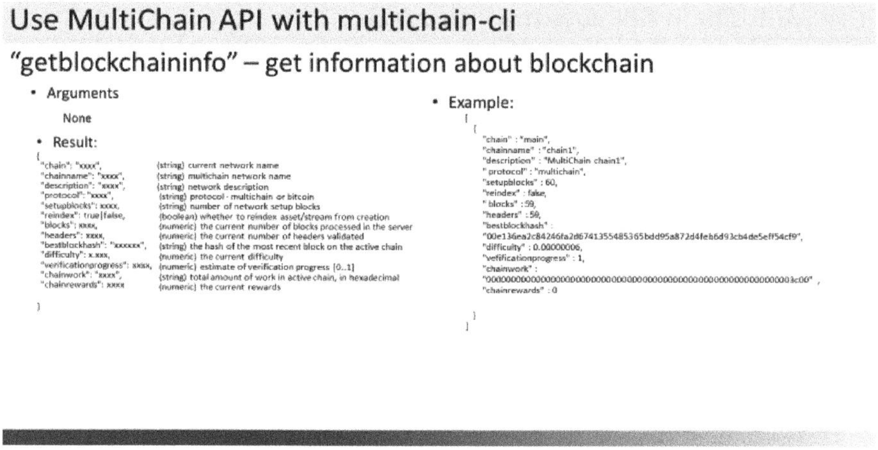

Figure 8.94: Utilising getblockchaininfo.

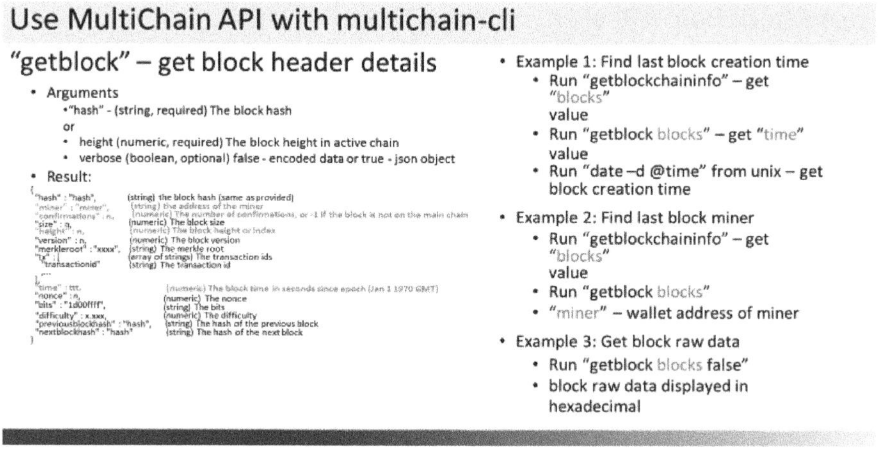

Figure 8.95: Utilising getblock.

In the returned attributes, the term "confirmations" means the number of confirmations (new blocks) since that block was mined; hence, it is a measure of how deep the given block is in the blockchain.

getblockchainparams returns a list of values of this blockchain's parameters. These values are stored in the file params.dat (see Figure 8.96).

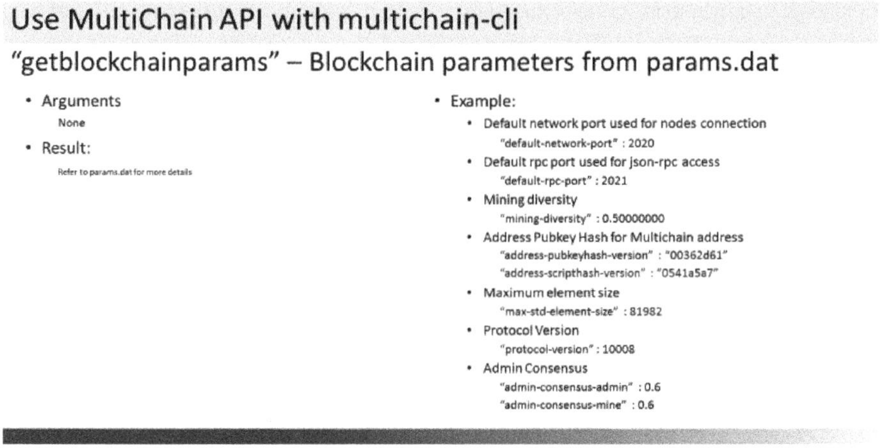

Figure 8.96: Utilising getblockchainparams.

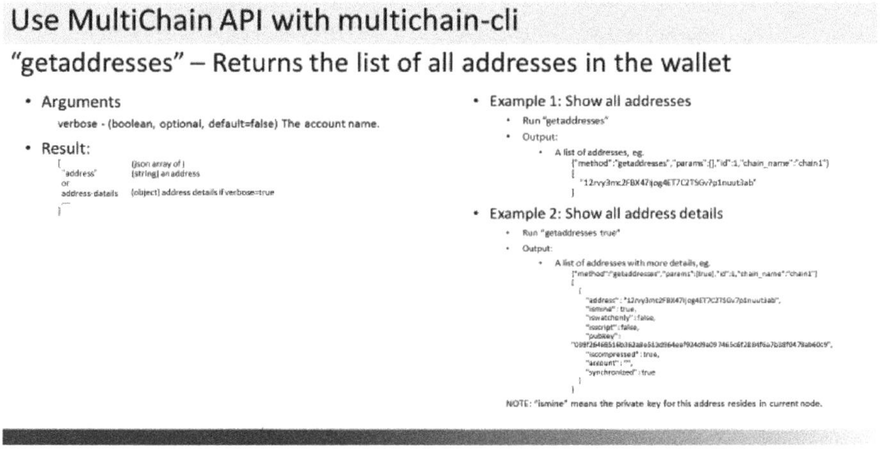

Figure 8.97: Utilising getaddresses.

getaddresses returns a list of addresses in this node's wallet. Set *verbose* to *true* to get more details about each address. If an address has the attribute "ismine" set as *true*, then this address resides with the current node (see Figure 8.97).

listpermissions returns a list of all permissions which have been explicitly granted to addresses. It can also list all addresses with a certain permission. For example, *listpermissions admin* will return addresses of all the admin nodes (see Figure 8.98).

grant is used to grant permissions to an address or a comma-separated list of addresses. For global permissions, set *permissions* to one of *connect, send, receive, create, issue, mine, activate, admin* or a comma-separated list thereof (see Figure 8.99).

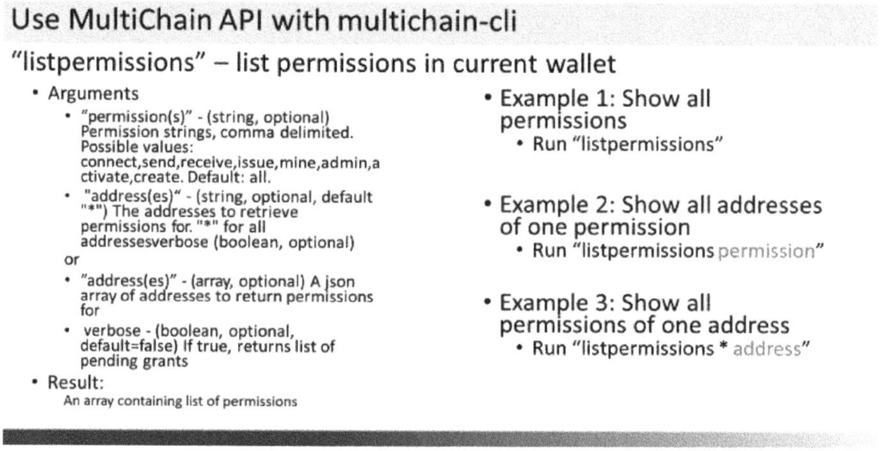

Figure 8.98: Utilising listpermissions.

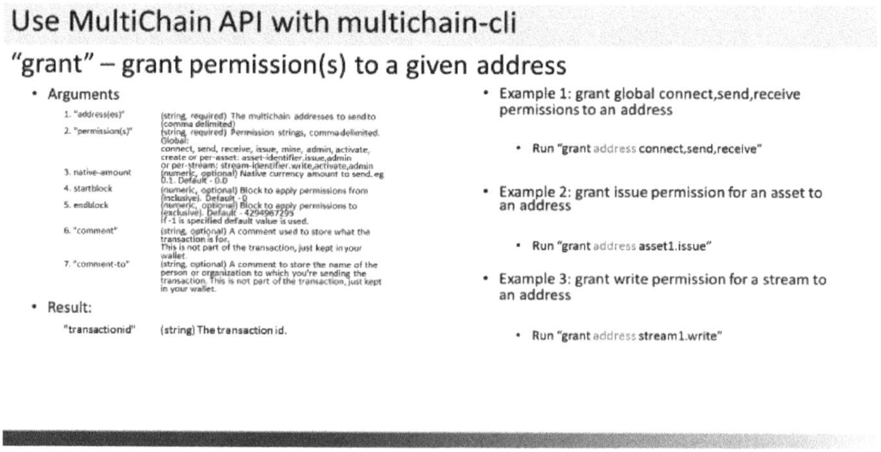

Figure 8.99: Utilising grant.

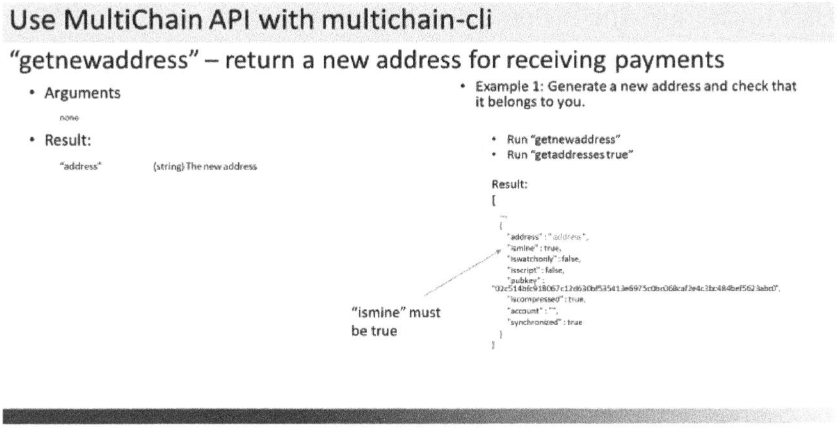

Figure 8.100: Utilising getnewaddress.

For per-asset or per-stream permissions, use the form *asset.issue, send, receive, activate, admin* or *stream.write, read, activate, admin* where *asset* or *stream* is an asset or stream name, ref or creation txid (transaction ID).

Only admin nodes can run the *grant* command. This command returns the txid of the grant transaction sent.

getnewaddress returns a new address whose private key is added to the wallet. If multiple users are using a single multichain node's wallet, call *getnewaddress* to get a different address for each user (Figure 8.100).

importaddress is used to add an address (or an array of addresses) to the wallet, without the associated private keys. This creates one or more watch-only addresses, whose activity and balance can be retrieved via various APIs (e.g., with the includeWatchOnly parameter), but whose funds cannot be spent by this node (see Figure 8.101).

The more addresses a node chooses to watch, the slower the node becomes, as it monitors more transactions coming in.

8.5.4 *Manage Native Assets Using Multichain-cli*

This section illustrates how to create and manage native assets on MultiChain.

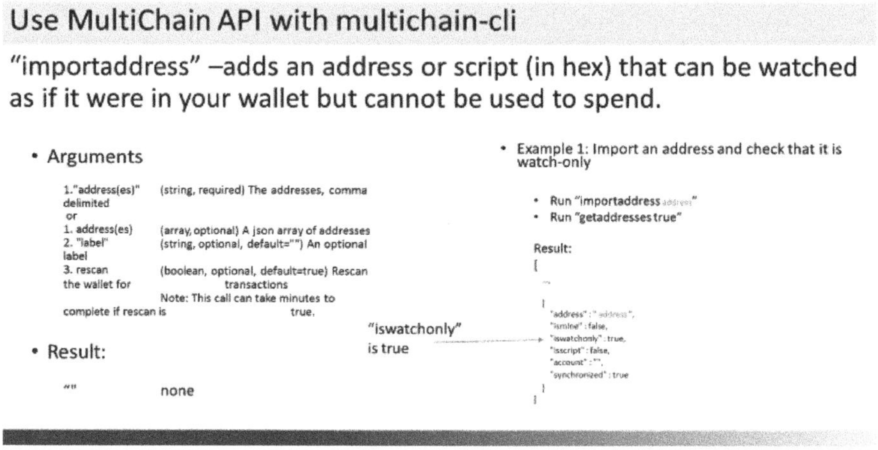

Figure 8.101: Utilising importaddress.

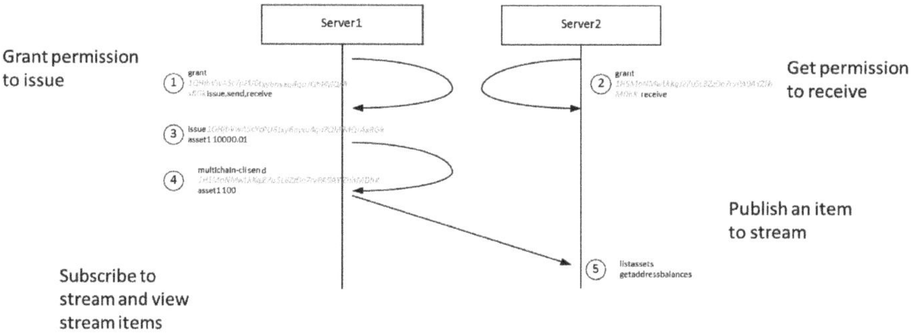

Figure 8.102: Steps 1–4 in issuing Asset 1.

Overview: Issue Native Assets using Multichain-cli

Figure 8.102 summarises the steps to issue a native asset called "asset1" using multichain-cli:

Step 1: Node 1 grants itself the permission to issue, send and receive.
Step 2: Node 2 grants itself the permission to receive.
Step 3: Node 1 issues an asset called "asset1" to its own wallet; the total quantity is 10,000, and the smallest denomination is 0.01.
Step 4: Node 1 sends a quantity of 100 asset1 to Node 2.

Step 5: Node 2 runs *listassets* and *getaddressbalances* to check if asset1 is received. Node 1 can run the same commands and check the balance (which should be 9,900 now).

Commands Used for Issuing Assets

It is recommended to check a developer's webpage for the latest updates of the commands (see Figure 8.103).

issue is used to create a new asset on the blockchain, sending the initial quantity units to the address specified (Figure 8.104).

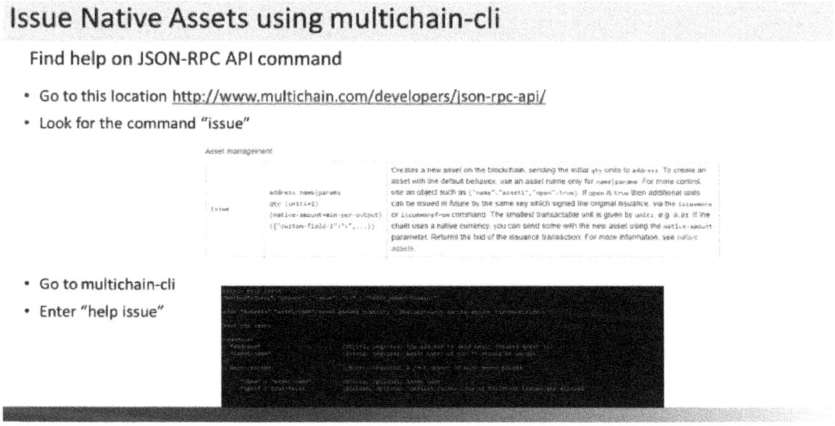

Figure 8.103: Developer's page.

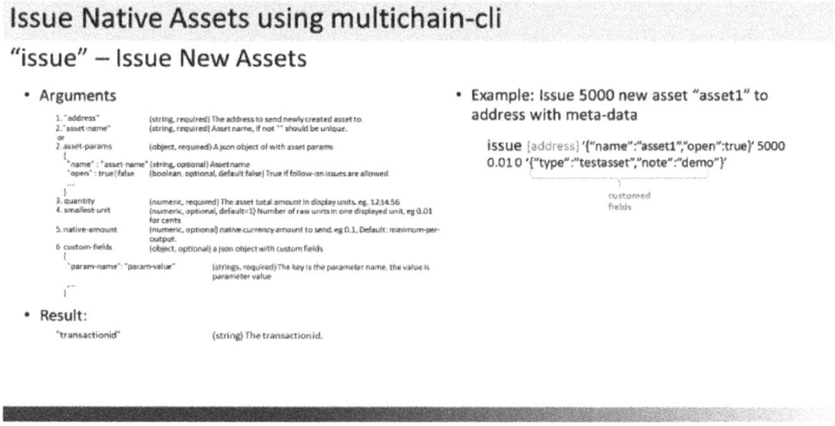

Figure 8.104: Issue new assets.

sendasset is used to send the specified quantity of the asset to the address, returning the txid (see Figure 8.105).

getaddressbalances returns a list of all the asset balances for an address in this node's wallet (see Figure 8.106). Argument *minconf* can be used to specify a minimum number of confirmations that have

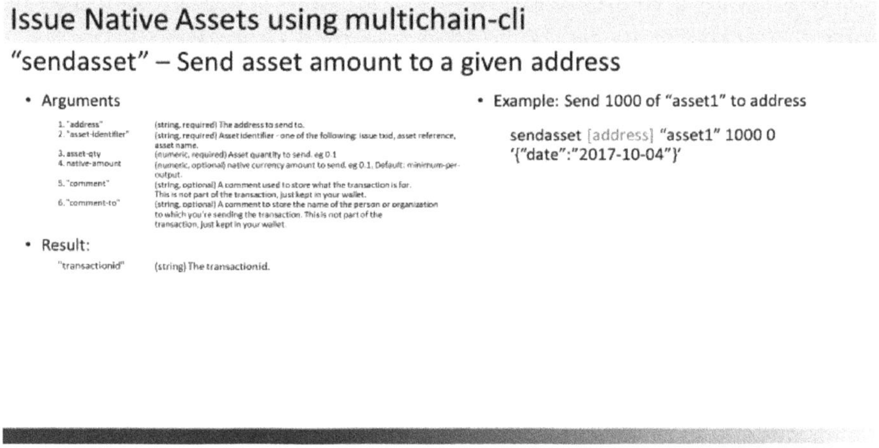

Figure 8.105: Send asset to given address.

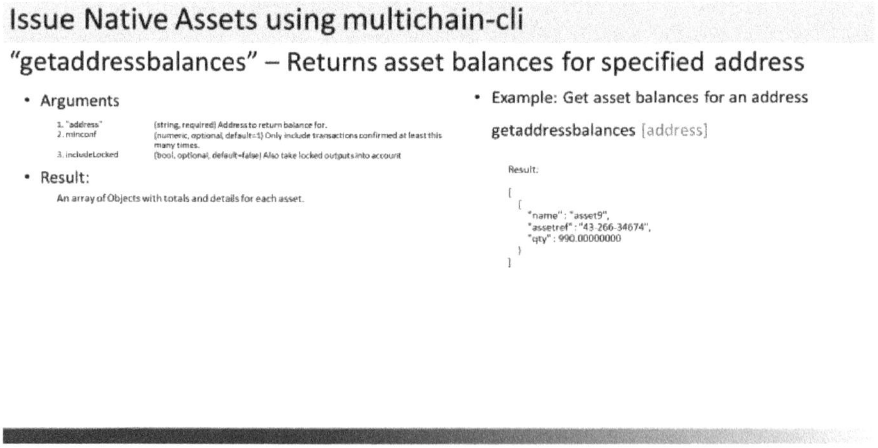

Figure 8.106: Return asset balances for specified address.

to be satisfied. *includeLocked* can be set to true to include unspent outputs which have been locked, e.g., by a call to *preparelockunspent.*

listassets returns information about assets issued on the blockchain (see Figure 8.107).

Detailed Steps and Execution

Admin nodes grant permissions to other nodes, so that they can issue their own assets (see Figure 8.108).

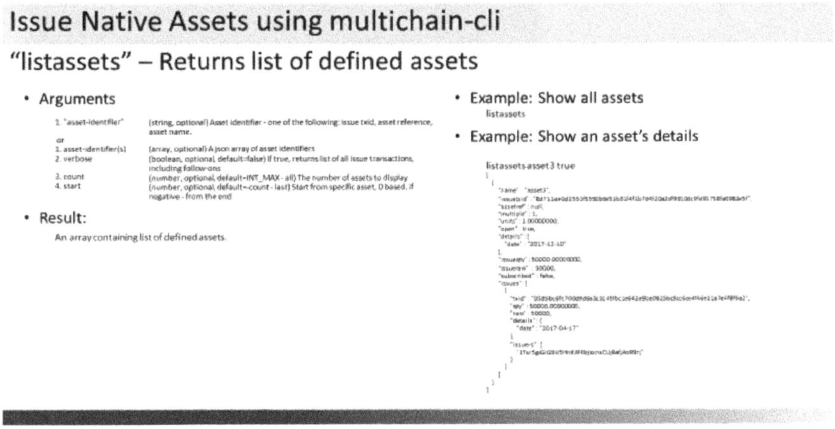

Figure 8.107: Return list of defined assets.

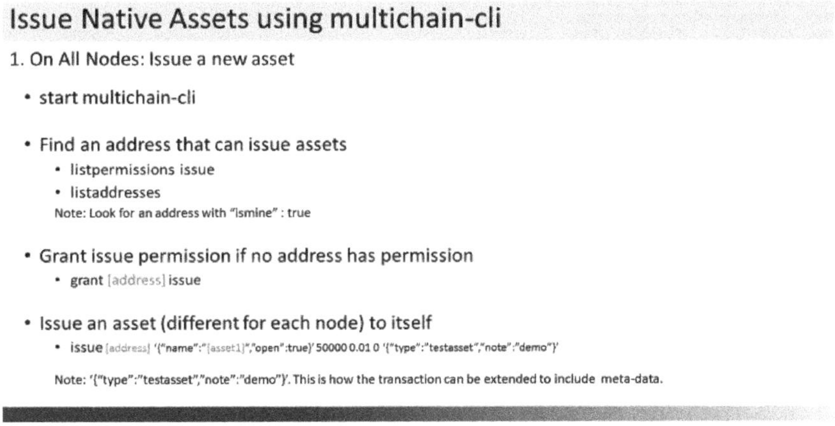

Figure 8.108: Admin nodes granting permissions.

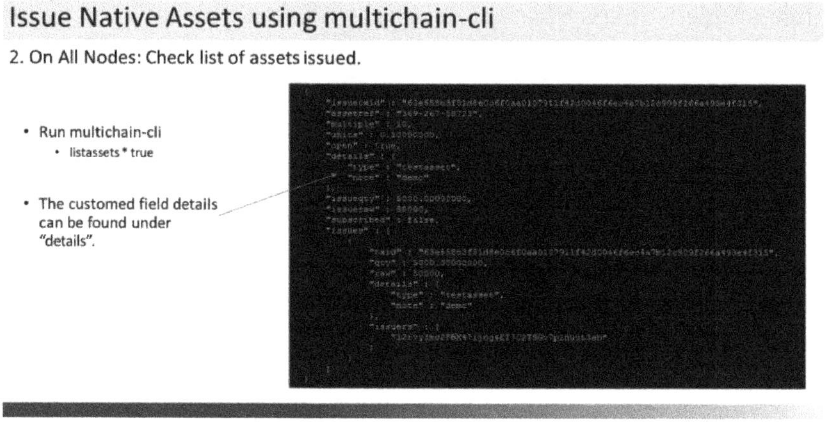

Figure 8.109: CheckList of assets issued.

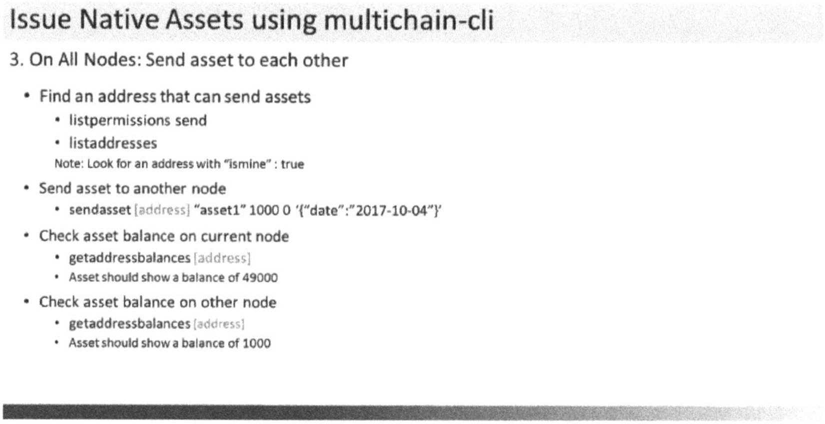

Figure 8.110: Send asset to each other.

Check if the assets are issued successfully (see Figure 8.109).

All nodes send assets to each other (see Figure 8.110) and check asset balances to verify if the transactions have gone through (see Figure 8.111).

8.5.5 *Manage Stream Using Multichain-cli*

This section illustrates how to create and manage streams on MultiChain.

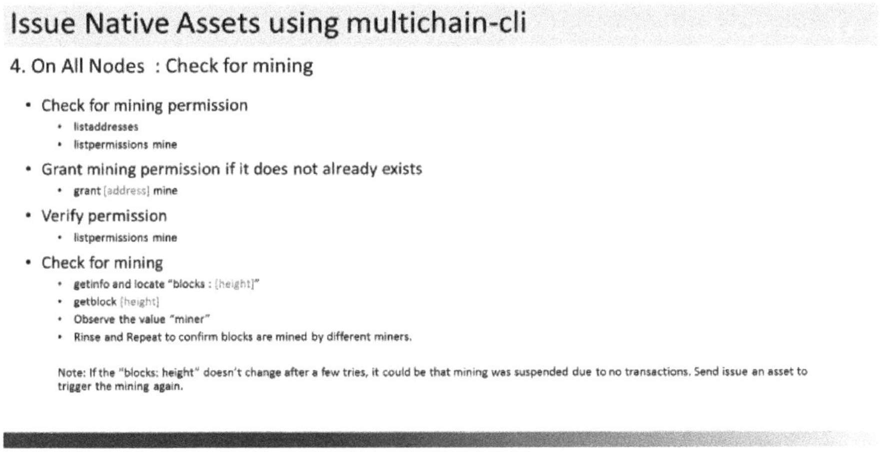

Figure 8.111: Checking for mining.

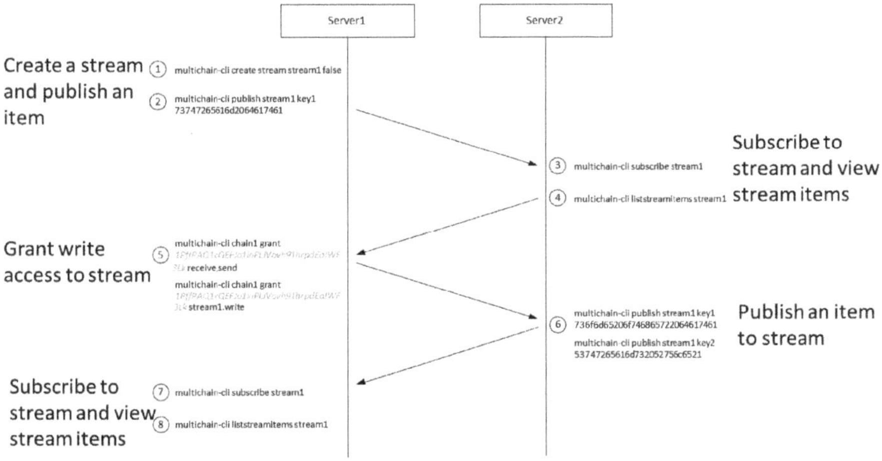

Figure 8.112: Steps 1–8 in creating stream 1 using multichain-cli.

Overview: Create stream using Multichain-cli

Figure 8.112 summarises the steps to create a stream called "stream1" using multichain-cli:

Step 1: Node 1 creates a stream named "stream1". He sets the parameter *open* to *false*; hence, anyone who wants to write in this stream needs to get permission first.

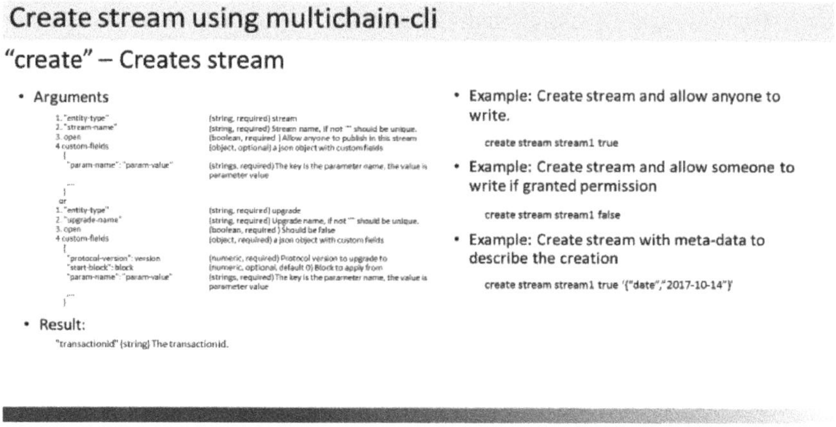

Figure 8.113: Create a new stream.

Step 2: Node 1 publishes an item (including a key and hexadecimal data) in the stream.
Step 3: Node 2 subscribes to stream1.
Step 4: Node 2 calls a querying command to view the items on stream1.
Step 5: Node 1 grants permission to Node 2 to send, receive and write into stream1.
Step 6: Node 2 publishes an item onto the stream.
Step 7: Node 1 subscribes to stream1.
Step 8: Node 1 can view the items on stream1.

Commands Used for Creating Stream

create is used to create a new stream on the blockchain (see Figure 8.113). The parameter *type* should be set to "stream", followed by the name of the stream to be created. The node who calls this command can set the parameter *open* to *true* if he allows anyone to write in the stream, or false if he prefers other nodes to get permission first in order to write in the stream.

The command returns the transaction ID for the creation.

publish is used to publish an item in a given stream (see Figure 8.114). The parameters required are *stream-identifier*, *key* and *data-hex*. The *stream-identifier* can accept stream name, stream

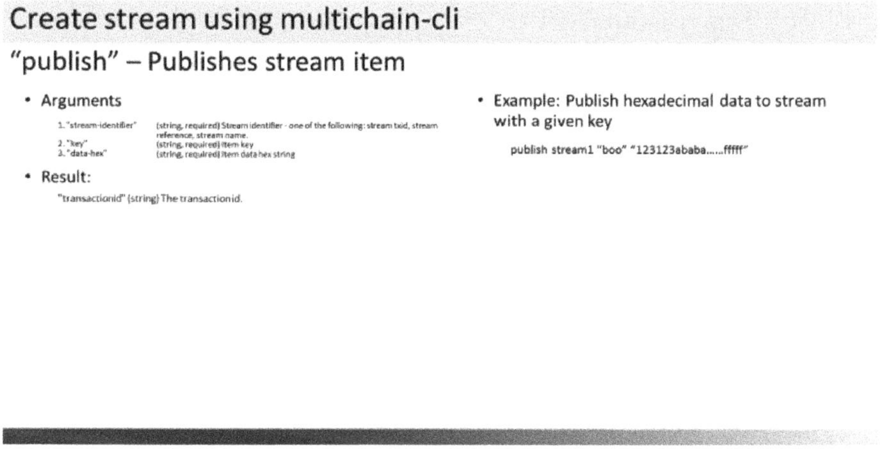

Figure 8.114: Publish a stream item.

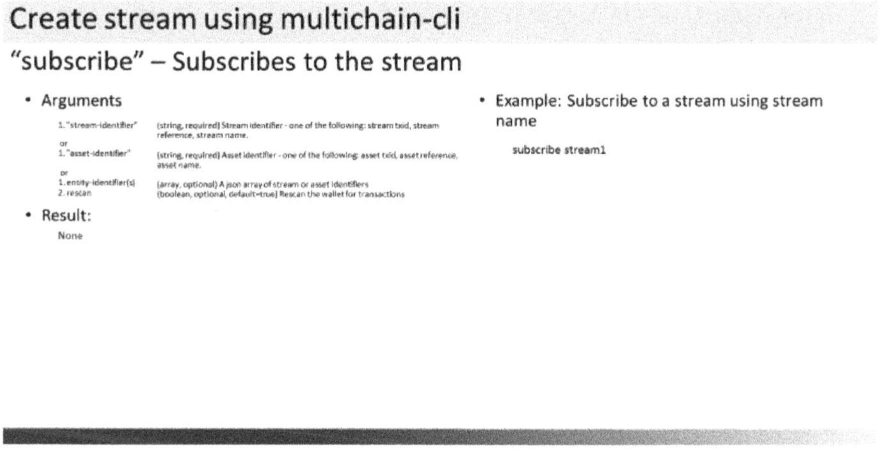

Figure 8.115: Subscribe to the stream.

reference or creation txid. The *key* parameter can accept a single textual key or an array, and the *data-hex* parameter can accept raw hexadecimal data.

A node calls *subscribe* to subscribe (start tracking) to a stream using stream name, stream reference or creation txid (see Figure 8.115). The command can also be used to subscribe assets.

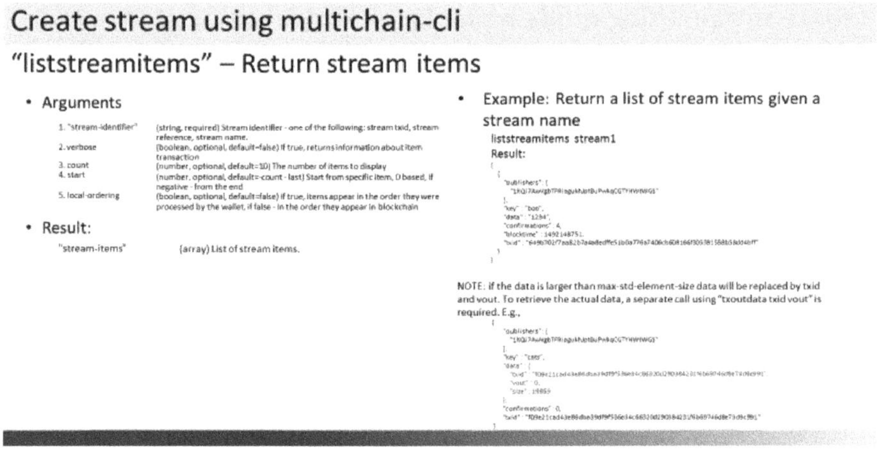

Figure 8.116: Return stream items.

liststreamitems is a command used to query subscribed streams (see Figure 8.116). It returns the list of items in the stream. Set *verbose* to true for additional information about each item's transaction. Parameters *count* and *start* can be used to retrieve part of the list only, with negative *start* values indicating the most recent items.

liststreamkeyitems is another command for querying subscribed streams (see Figure 8.117). It returns the list of items with the given key only.

liststreampublisheritems is another command for querying subscribed streams (see Figure 8.118). It returns the list of items with the given address only.

Detailed Steps and Execution

Node 1 creates a new stream called stream 1, and sets parameter *open* to *false*. He then can verify the permissions on stream 1, by calling *listpermissions* (see Figure 8.119).

It was discussed previously that when calling this function, specific permissions can be listed (such as in the form of *stream.write,read,activate,admin*), or * can be passed to list all permissions.

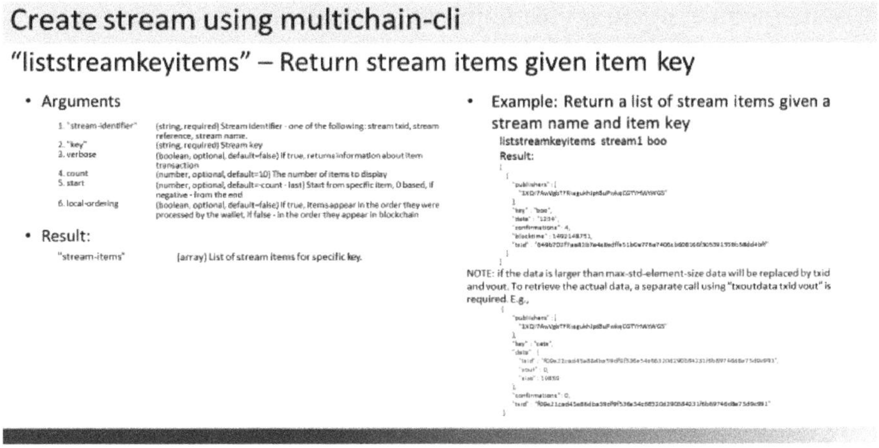

Figure 8.117: Return stream items using given key items.

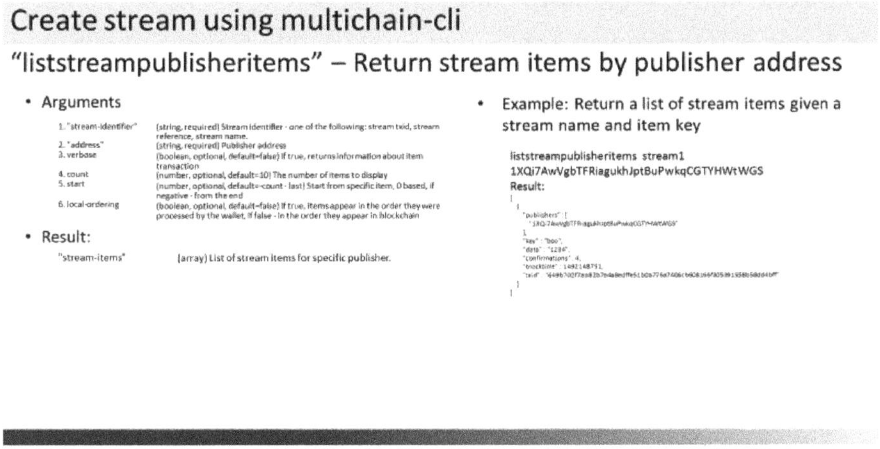

Figure 8.118: Return stream items by publisher's address.

Note that node1 should only have "write" permission at the moment.

Node 1 calls *publish* to publish an item on stream1. The item includes a key and certain data in hexadecimal format (see Figure 8.120).

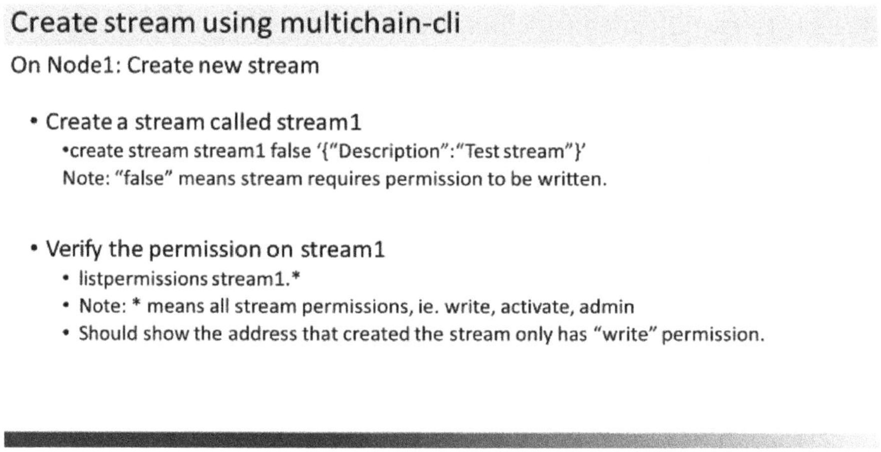

Figure 8.119: Create stream 1 on Node 1.

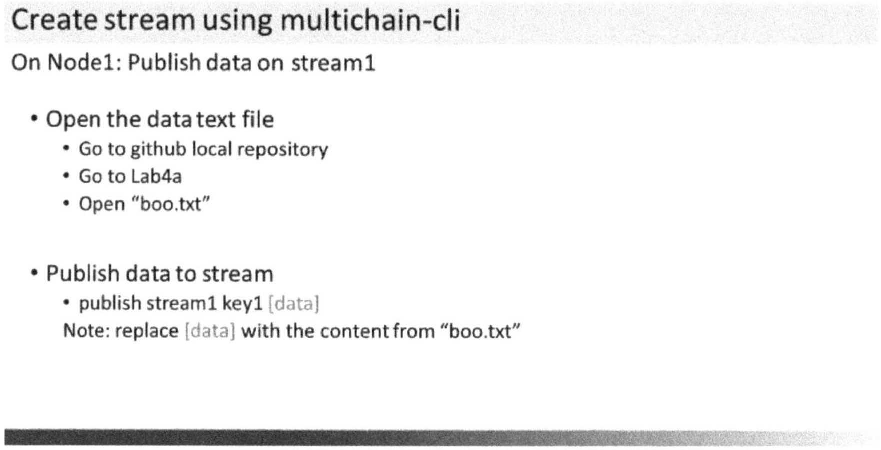

Figure 8.120: Publish data on stream 1.

Node 2 verifies if the stream has been created properly (see Figure 8.121). He calls *liststreams* and checks if the stream named "stream1" can be seen. Note that Node 2 currently does not have permission to view the content.

liststreams returns information about streams created on the blockchain. Specify a stream name, stream reference or creation txid

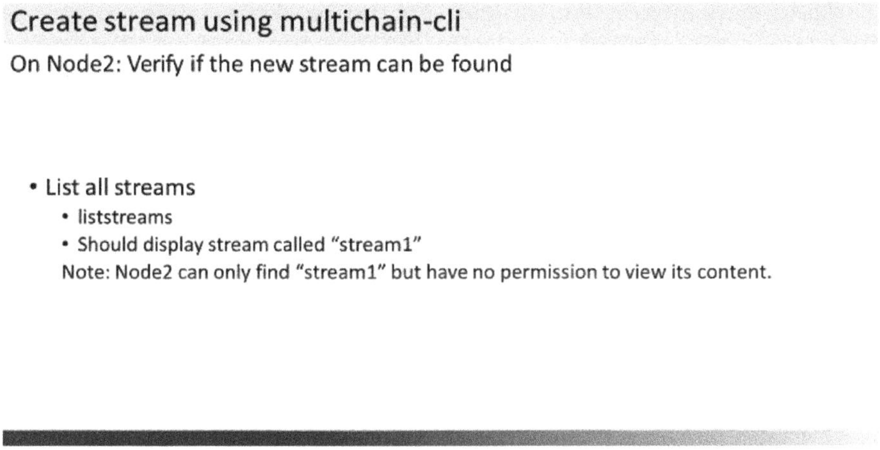

Figure 8.121: Verify the new stream.

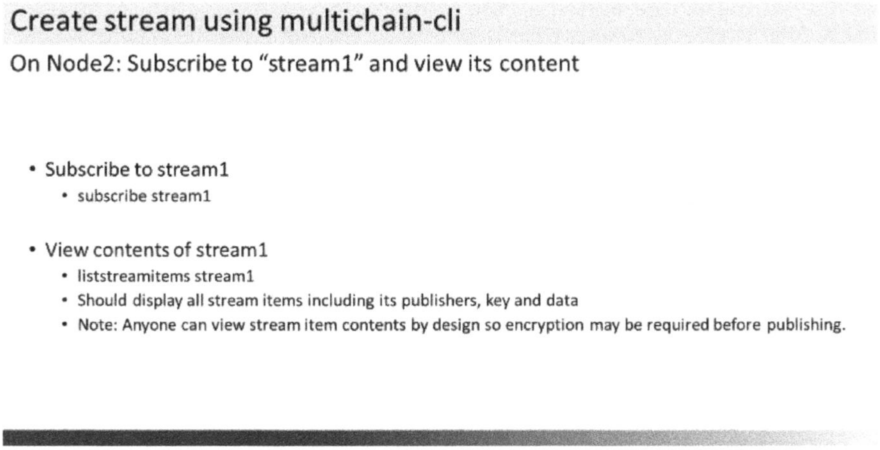

Figure 8.122: Subscribe and view stream 1.

to retrieve information about one stream only, an array thereof for multiple streams or * for all streams.

Node 2 subscribes to "stream1", and then calls *liststreamitems* to view the items such as publishers, key and data on the stream (see Figure 8.122).

Note that anyone can do this on the blockchain; hence, stream item content is available to everyone by design. A publisher can choose to encrypt the data before publishing.

Data are encrypted and decrypted off-chain, usually with symmetric cryptography (see Figure 8.123).

Node 1 grants permission to Node 2 to publish to stream1 (Figure 8.124).

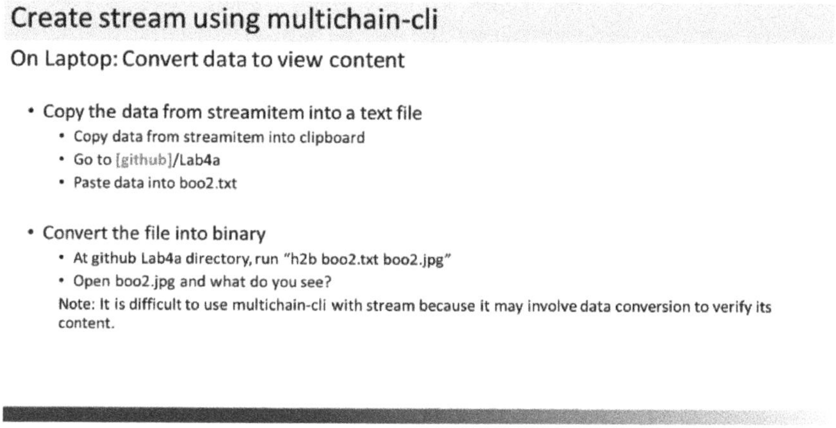

Figure 8.123: Subscribe and view stream 1.

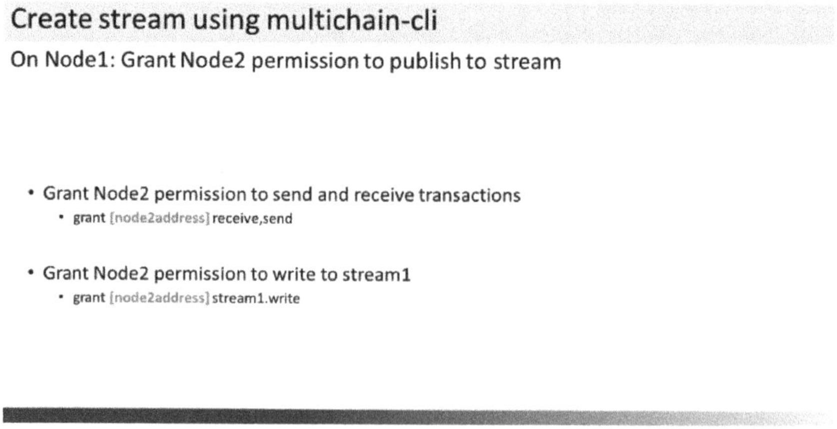

Figure 8.124: Grant Node 2 permission to publish to stream.

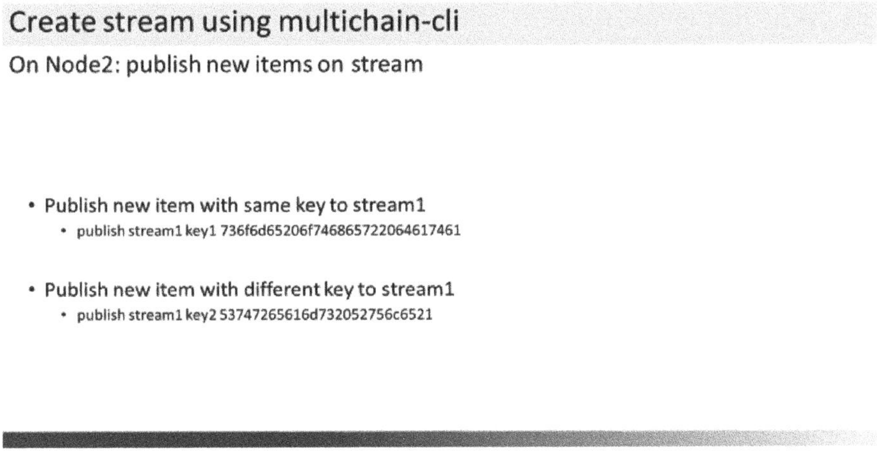

Figure 8.125: Publish new items on stream for Node 2.

Node 1 needs to call *grant* twice to grant such permission. It is called for the first time to grant permissions, such as to receive and to send, and it is called the second time to grant per-stream permissions, such as to write onto the stream.

Now, Node 2 can publish items onto the stream. He can publish a new item with the same key or a different key (Figure 8.125).

8.5.6 *Manage Atomic Exchange Transactions Using Multichain-cli*

This section discusses how to make atomic exchange transactions on MultiChain.

Earlier examples demonstrated sending of transactions in one direction, but a trade happens in both directions. One-direction transaction will not work in a trade due to counterparty risks.

In financial markets, many products are traded in the OTC (over-the-counter) market. The counterparties sign contracts with each other without an intermediary and each assumes the risk that the counterparty might default (see Figure 8.126).

In such bilateral trades, when one party defaults (for example, the Lehman Brothers during the Global Financial Crisis), the other

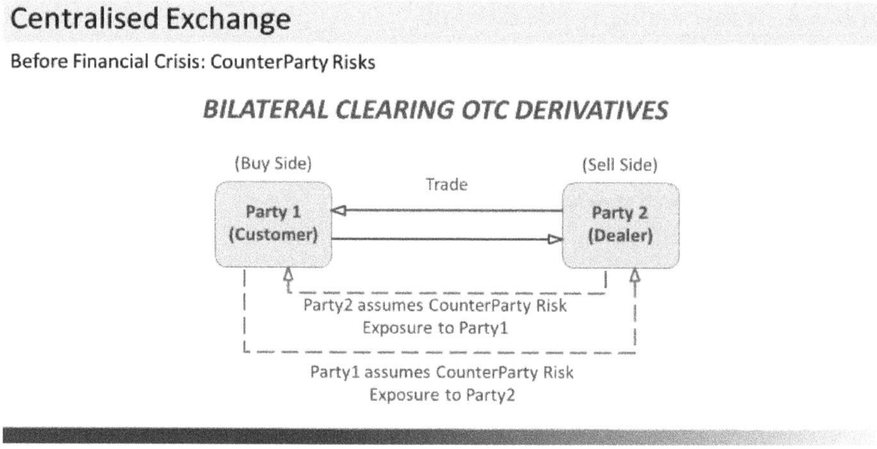

Figure 8.126: CounterParty risks with over-the-counter market.

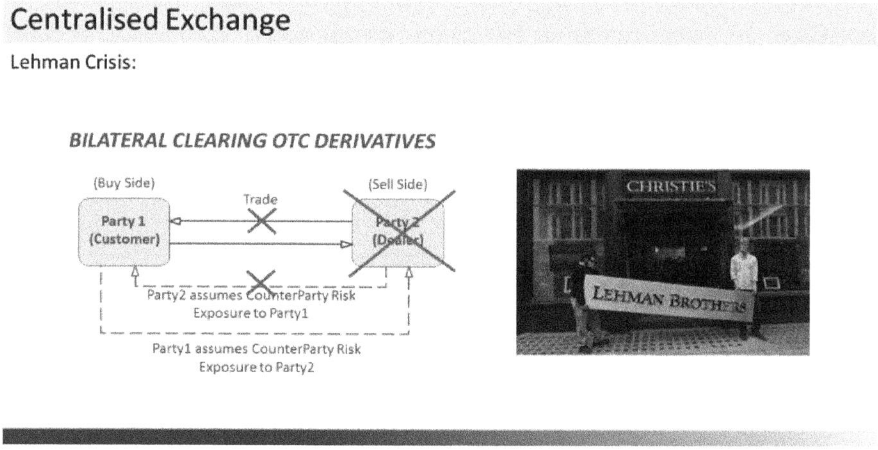

Figure 8.127: Lehman Brothers crisis explained.

party will suffer a loss and it could also cause a chain of effects (see Figure 8.127).

For exchange-traded products, there is a trusted third party (clearing house) to lower the counterparty risks among participants, but concentration risk is significantly increased (see Figure 8.128).

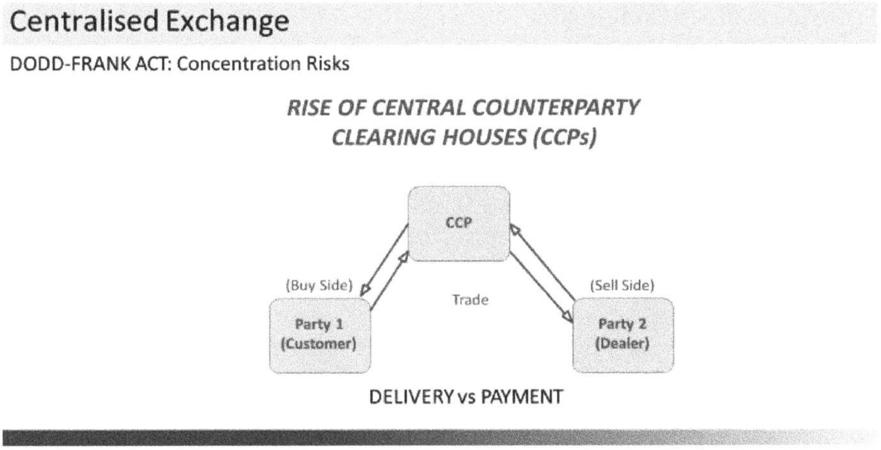

Figure 8.128: Dodd-Frank Act CCP establishment.

What if there is a technology that can do away with the third party? Is it possible for Party 1 and Party 2 to enter a trade without a middleman, and the exchange can be completed if, and only if, both parties receive what they want? Such a trade structure is called atomic exchange, a computer science term for "all or nothing" (see Figure 8.129).

This section explains how atomic exchange can be executed in MultiChain.

Overview of Atomic Exchange Transaction

Figure 8.130 summarises the steps to execute atomic exchange:

Step 1: Node 1 owns asset5 and he prepares to offer 1 unit of asset5.

Step 2: Node 1 creates a raw exchange where he offers 1 unit of asset5 to Node 2, and asks for 1 unit of asset2.
In this step, Node 1 sends over a script that is essentially a locking script. In order to complete the exchange, Node 2 not only needs to provide an unlocking script based on his private key but also needs to own 1 unit of asset2 that Node 1 had asked for.

Step 3: Node 2 prepares to offer 1 unit of asset2.

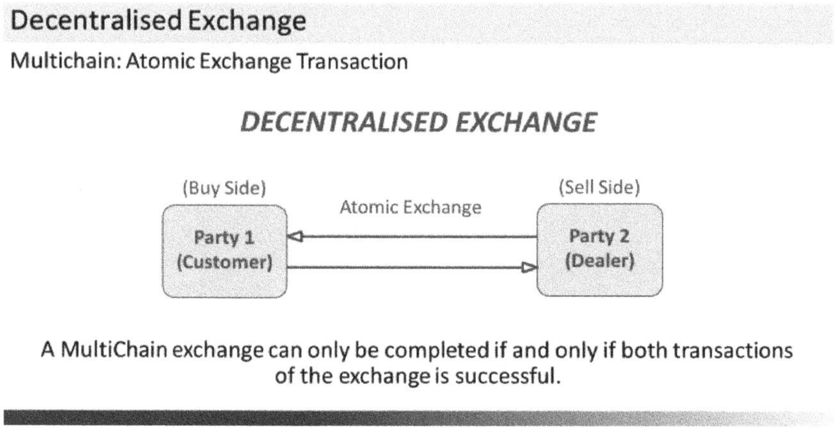

Figure 8.129: Decentralised atomic exchange.

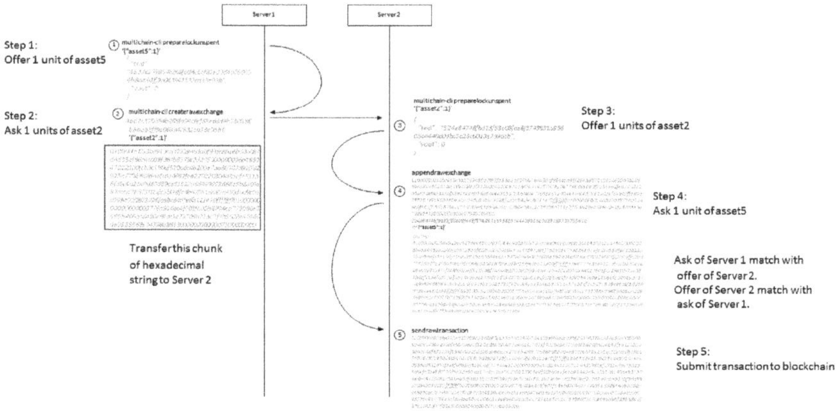

Figure 8.130: Step 1–5 summary of atomic exchange execution.

Step 4: Node 2 combines his unlocking script with the locking script from Node 2, and asks for 1 unit of asset5.

Step 5: Node 2 sends the combined script onto the blockchain.

Detailed Steps and Execution

Node 1 calls *preparelockunspent*, the command for preparing an unspent transaction output (see Figure 8.131). It imposes a lock on this unspent output amount (similar to a UTXO), and this

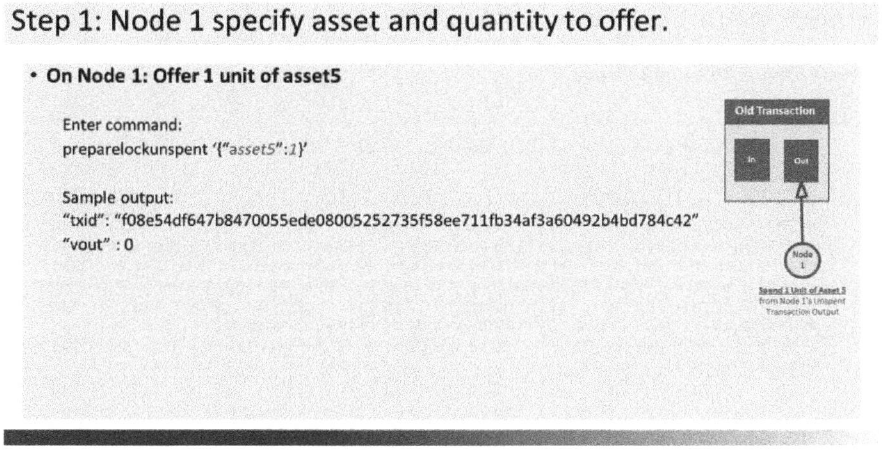

Figure 8.131: Protecting against spending with *preparelockunspent*.

transaction output will be protected against spending unless explicitly spent or unlocked.

The command returns two outputs: *txid* and *vout*. Previously, we discussed that one blockchain transaction can have multiple outputs. The "vout" here indicates that the amount of first output is zero.

Note that if some unspent transaction is locked by mistake, it can also be unlocked. The node can follow the below steps:

1. Call *listlockunspent*, which returns a list of locked unspent transaction outputs in the wallet. Find the *txid* and *vout* that need to be unlocked.
2. Call *lockunspent,* which provides the *txid* and *vout* that need to be unlocked, and sets the field "*unlock*" to "*true*". It will unlock the specified transaction. The command can also unlock all transactions if no second parameter is provided.

Node 1 then calls *createrawexchange* to create an atomic exchange transaction (see Figure 8.132). He uses the txid and vout output from Step 1, which contains the information on what he is offering, and adds in information about what he is asking: 1 unit of asset2. This forms half of the transaction (as it is only information from Node 1) and returns a string output in hexadecimal format.

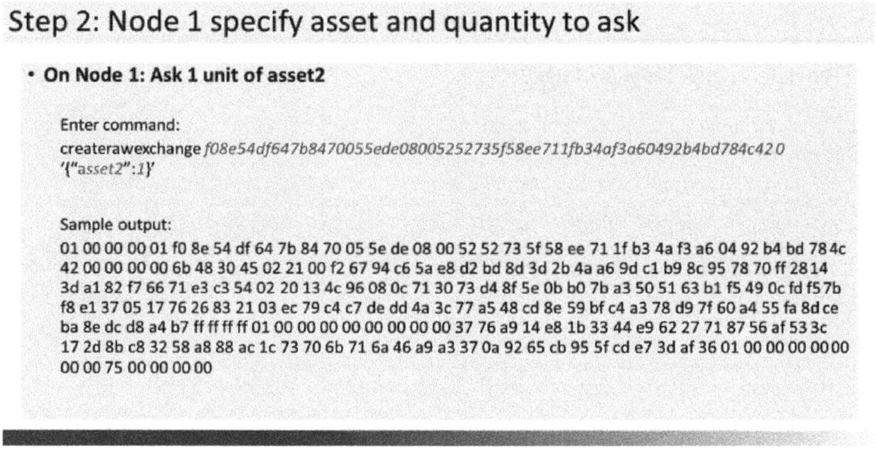

Figure 8.132: Creating atomic exchange transaction.

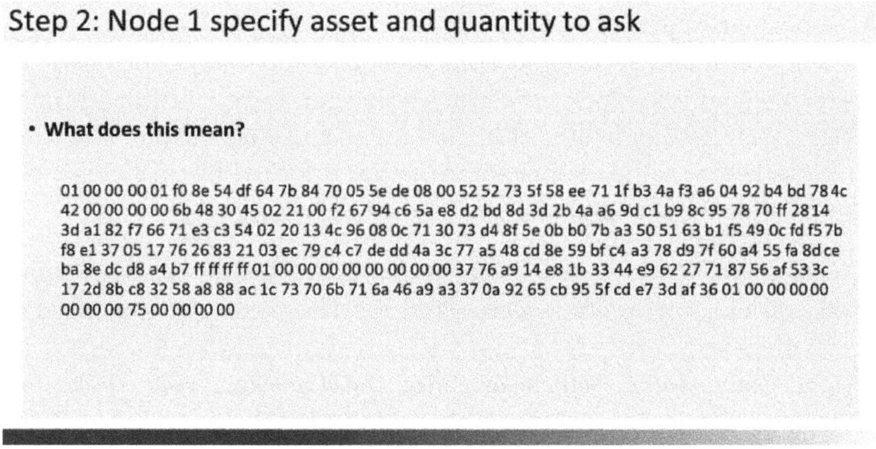

Figure 8.133: Creating atomic exchange transaction.

The output from *createrawexchange* in Figure 8.133 is the hexadecimal presentation of half of the transaction to be sent over to the other party. It can be decoded with the command *decoderawexchange*.

decoderawexchange returns details on the offer represented by the exchange and its present state (see Figure 8.134).

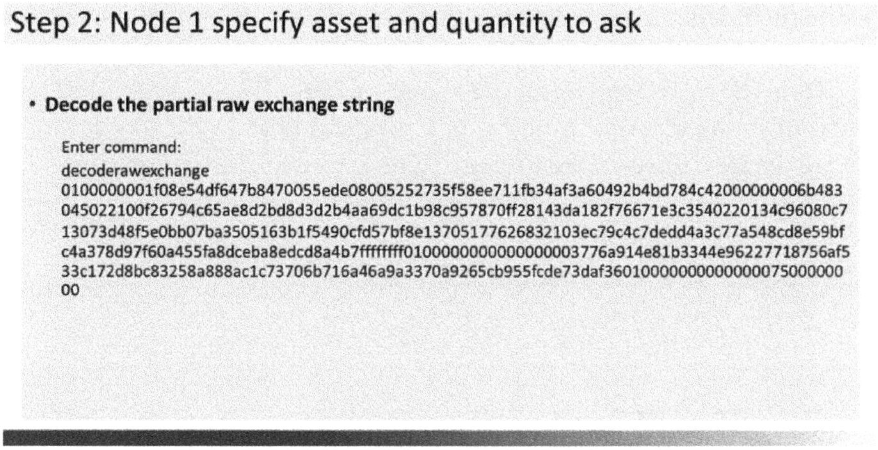

Figure 8.134: Decode the partial raw exchange string.

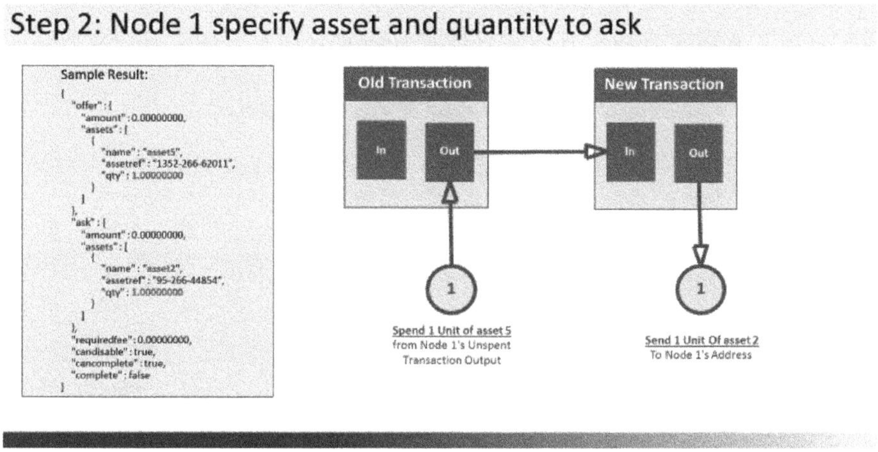

Figure 8.135: Process of transaction and result of *decoderawexchange.*

The result from the *decoderawexchange* command shows that the party who had created the raw exchange is offering 1 unit of asset5 in exchange for 1 unit of asset 2 (see Figure 8.135).

Node 1 sends the output to Node 2 via email or other channels (see Figure 8.136).

Node 2 calls *preparelockunspent* to prepare 1 unit of asset2 for transaction (see Figure 8.137).

Node 2 calls *appendrawexchange*, where he puts in the half transaction he received from Node 1, then adds on *txid* and *vout* from his *preparelockunspent* command (which is what he is offering — 1

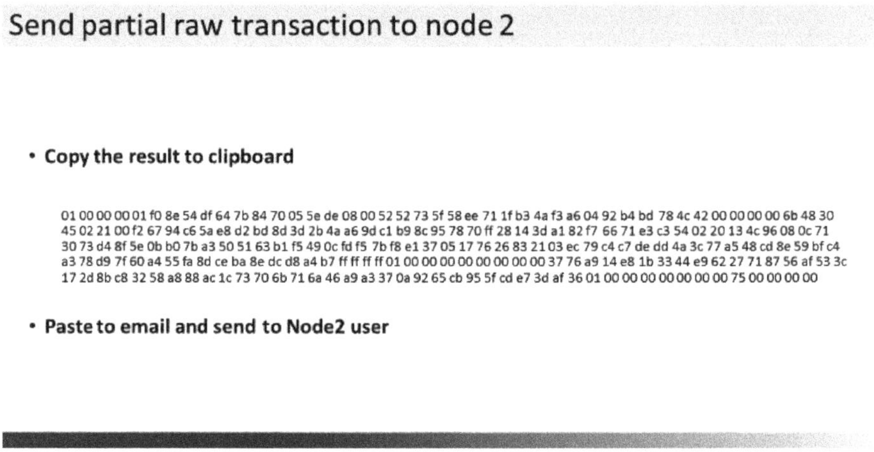

Figure 8.136: Sending output from Node 1 to Node 2.

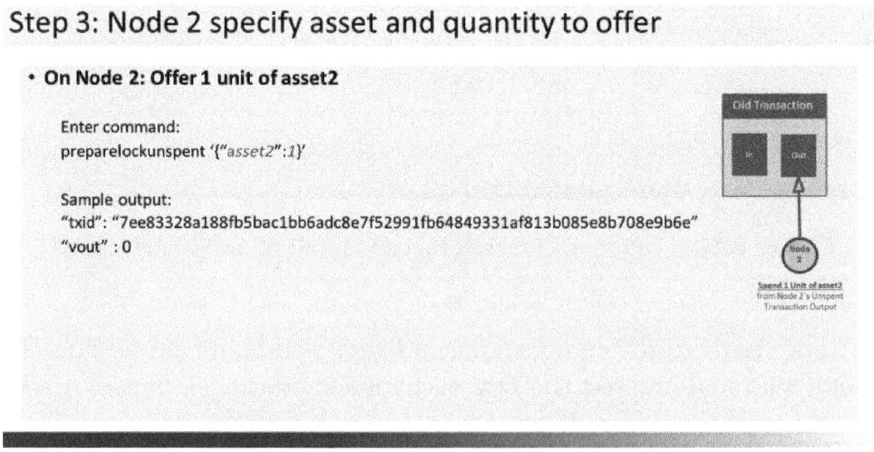

Figure 8.137: Node 2 offering 1 unit of asset 2.

unit of asset2), and adds on what he asks for: 1 unit of asset5 (see Figure 8.138).

If the transaction is constructed successfully, i.e., the asset names and quantities between the two nodes match each other, the output from *appendrawexchange* will show a *complete* field set to *true* (see Figure 8.139).

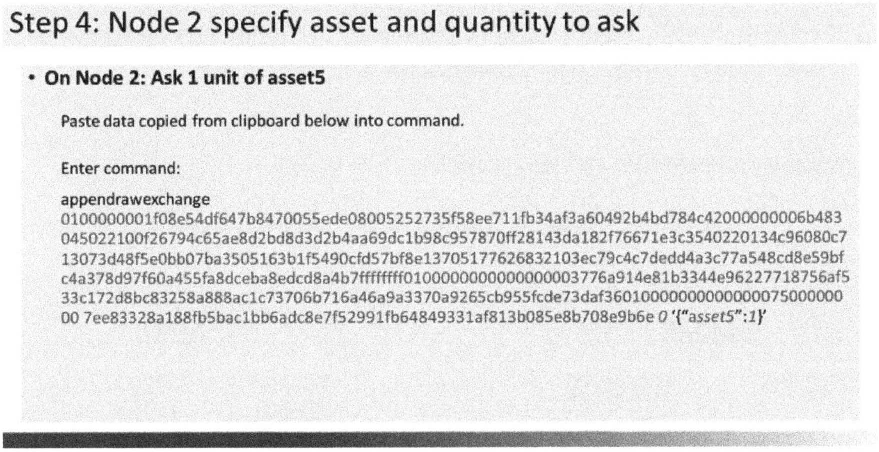

Figure 8.138: Node 1 asking for 1 unit of asset5 in return.

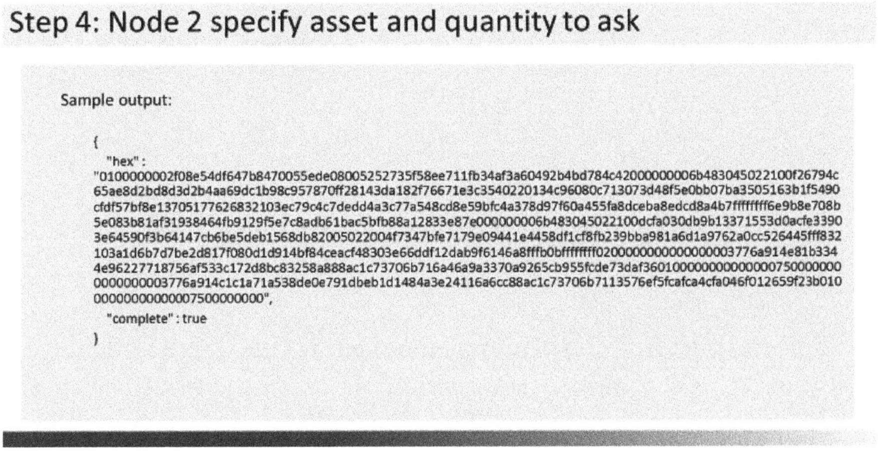

Figure 8.139: Checking for completion of trade.

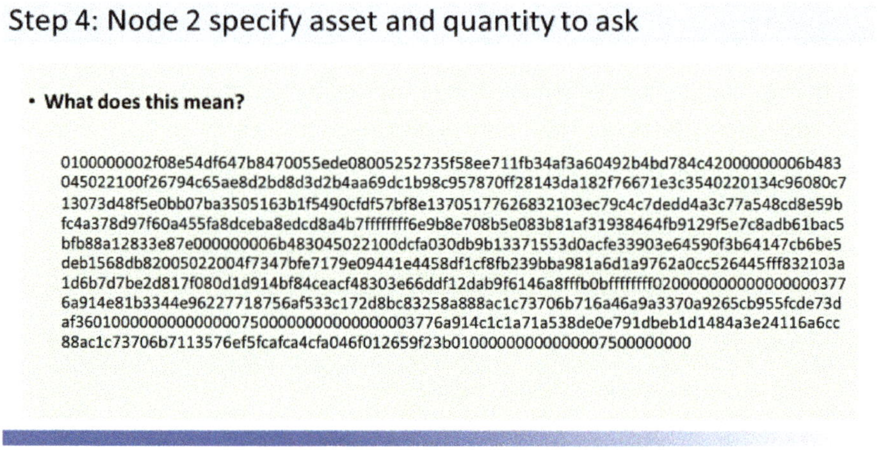

Figure 8.140: Certification of completed trade.

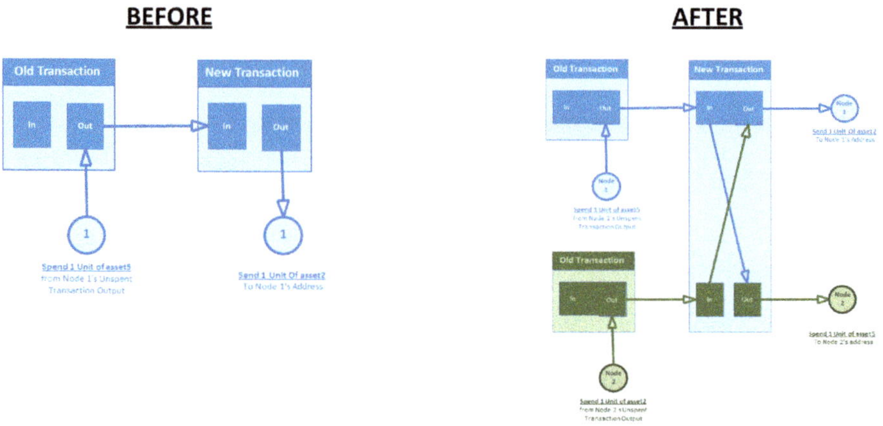

Figure 8.141: Illustration of combined transaction.

The output from *appendrawexchange* is the hexadecimal presentation of the complete transaction. It can be decoded with the command *decoderawexchange* (Figure 8.140).

Figure 8.141 illustrates the combined transaction. In this transaction, the input from Node 1 (highlighted in blue) references

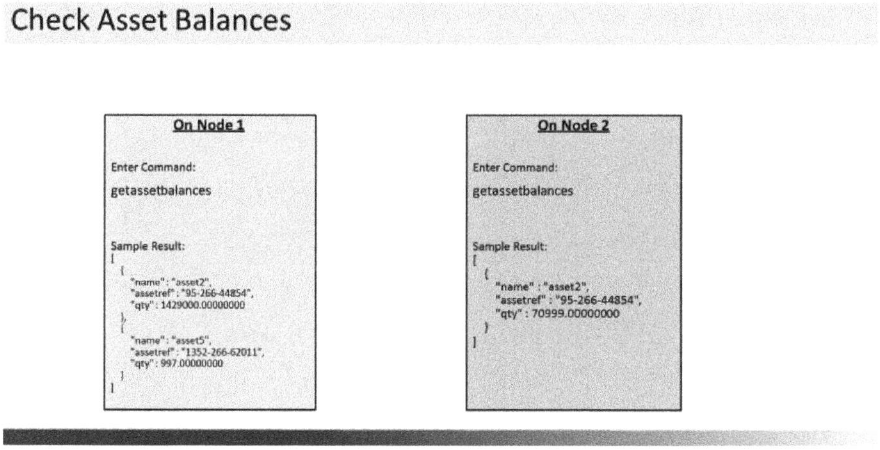

Figure 8.142: Illustration of combined transaction.

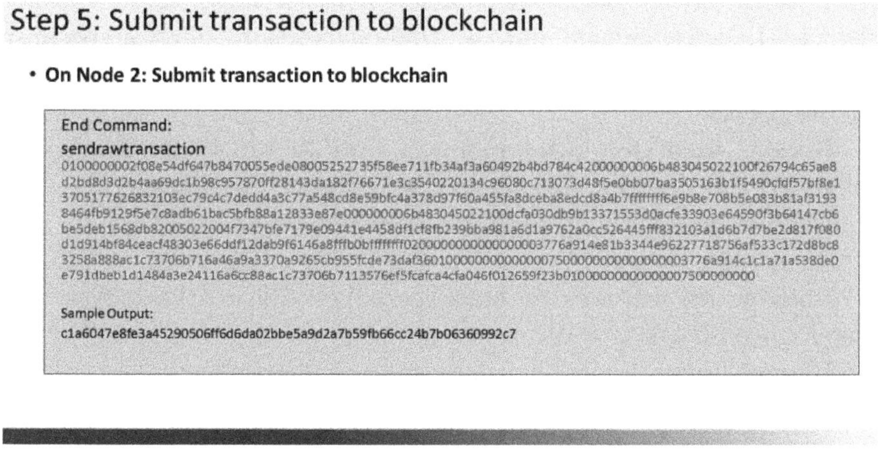

Figure 8.143: Broadcasting and execution of transaction.

unspent output of 1 unit of asset5, and the input from Node 2 (highlighted in green) references unspent output of 1 unit of asset2. The transaction is combined and completed when Node 2's unlocking script can unlock Node 1's locking script, and Node 2's input becomes output sent to Node 1, and Node 1's input becomes output sent to Node 2.

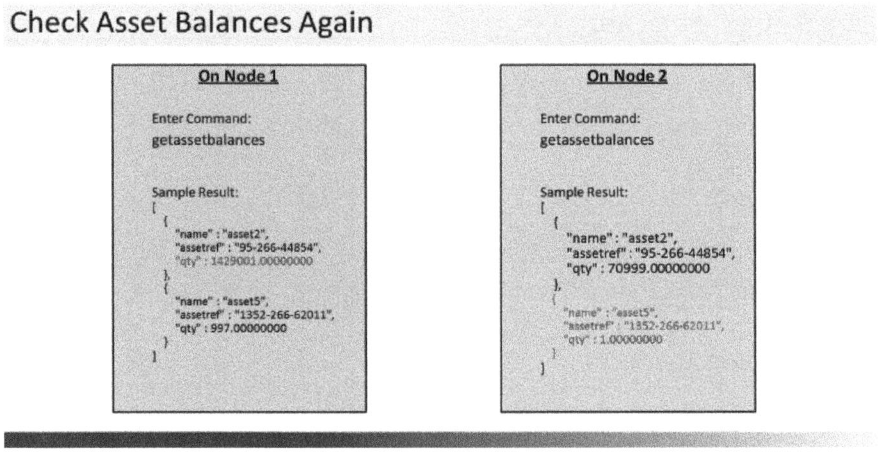

Figure 8.144: Successful transaction shown.

If both nodes check their asset balance now, they will not see the balance change due to the transaction. This is because the transaction is not confirmed yet on the blockchain (see Figure 8.142).

Node 2 then calls *sendrawtransaction* to broadcast this transaction to the network. It returns the txid for the transaction. The transaction goes through once it is confirmed by the blockchain (see Figure 8.143).

Both nodes will see the balance change due to the transaction (see Figure 8.144).

Blockchain native assets, data stream management and atomic exchange transactions are just a few instances of the extended functionality of MultiChain. The ease of deployment and customisation also make it one of the popular choices when it comes to private permissioned blockchain for industrial use.

Reference

Lamport, L., Shostak, R., and Pease, M. (1982). The Byzantine generals problem. *ACM Transactions on Programming Languages and Systems* 4(3), 382–401.

Chapter 9

Hands-On Guide to Bitcoin Layer-2 Lightning Network Node Setup

Edwan Chiam*

9.1 Introduction

The intent of this guide is to allow individuals to have a physical interaction running a bitcoin node in a more sustainable manner through affordable devices like a Raspberry Pi (Linux) according to an easy-to-follow coding instruction. The hands-on tutorial will cover running a bitcoin core, which is key to understanding Bitcoin and experiencing what it is like to be running a node, completely decentralised and not relying on any centralised cloud-hosted nodes. This tutorial will take a step further by extending beyond the underlying protocol in overcoming the scalability issue, as seen in layer-1 bitcoin, by implementing a layer-2 application known as the lightning solution, which is an almost instant confirmation in bitcoin peer-to-peer transactions with a minimal fee and increased privacy simultaneously. In preservation of Cyberpunk's work, individuals running their own node can verify and trust their own node, which is a fairly inexpensive investment that lends an extensive benefit overall.

*Founder of HelloDime.

Why do we want to run a bitcoin node? As the genesis concept of blockchain, we ought to understand how the concept of a truly decentralised blockchain network comes about. By observing and experimenting with bitcoin core nodes, you will contribute to various other factors besides understanding and visualising what it takes to run a node. As of today, May 2020, there are approximately 6700 nodes online of which a majority are running the main bitcoin core nodes. By running a bitcoin core node, you are contributing to a faster, more stable and more decentralised network. How else is it beneficial to ensure that you are following the original consensus rules of the network?

Cannot contribute to the Bitcoin hash power? *Fret* not. Node owners are more important than hashpower as they are the true validators of the network. Being curious and tinkering to be a part of this revolution deserves applause.

This guide will take you through the whole process in a testnet environment so no real money/bitcoin asset is involved. But, with just a quick flick of a line or 2, we are able to enter into the main net and explore further down the rabbit hole. If you just want to experience this up and until the testnet and not interact with the mainnet, then you do not need to download the bitcoin core application to your computer/laptop devices in the section titled "Download Bitcoin Core Application". At the end of this exercise, readers can experience all things Bitcoin core node allows (familiarise and interact with the node through CLI command lines, verify the bitcoin blockchain, perform P2P transactions by sending and receiving.), also extending to layer 2 experiencing how lightning network works (listing peers, opening new payment channels, sending and receiving) in both testnet and mainnet if they wish to extend this application. Users must understand what it entails for transacting on the mainnet as a loss of any of the keys and or sending to an unintended recipient will result in a partial or complete loss of assets. Participants need to note that layer 2 is still in constant experimentation and new versions are being developed along the way. What is stated here are good versions as of 25th May 2020, tried and tested on the bitcoin mainnet.

9.2 Setup and Tool Gathering

To begin this exercise, users do not require to have any extensive coding knowledge, but it is good to understand how command lines function, how to navigate around your own network, using tools like PUTTY, SSH, Nano text editor and to have an interest in understanding why blockchain and/or bitcoin is essential to appreciate what we are presenting here.

Tools required for this exercise include, but are not limited to, the following:

1. Having full control of your internet gateway to ensure that you can communicate with the various testnet and mainnet bitcoin ports.
2. A Raspberry Pi version 3 model B or newer.
3. USB power adapter to power up the pi (5V, 2.5A for Singapore standard).
4. A Micro SD Card for the Raspberry Pi, preferably 16 GB or higher.
5. LAN cable from your internet to the Raspberry Pi (Wi-Fi connection is fine, but may be slow).
6. External 2.5″ hard disk of at least 300 GB (Preferably SSD and >500 GB will be better for faster synchronisation of the bitcoin blockchain).
7. Existing computer/laptop running on Mac, Windows or Linux that has at least 300 GB to download the 1st instance of the Bitcoin core (taking this file from elsewhere is fine, but you cannot verify the authenticity of it).
8. Optional (External screen and HDMI cable + USB Keyboard) device for shortcut troubleshooting using a headed raspberry pi, otherwise most operations will be carried out headless.

9.2.1 *Bitcoin Core Mainnet on External Device*

This step is necessary for those who want to extend this application to the bitcoin mainnet. For those who want to just experiment the whole process in the bitcoin testnet, this step is not necessary as syncing on the testnet with the raspberry pi 3b is quite light and quick to do.

To begin, let us download the Bitcoin core on our computer/ laptop by heading to the bitcoin core official website with the respective installer file for your device. You may install the application on your local machine. You need to be the administrator of the machine as well as to be able to find the local storage for the files later on. Once you download the executable file, verify the source to ensure its integrity and then you may run it.

We will transfer the block files to the raspberry pi external hard disk once it is fully synced. It will take around 1–2 days depending on your machine's hardware and your internet connection speed. While it is synchronising, it will show the progress as seen in Figure 9.1.

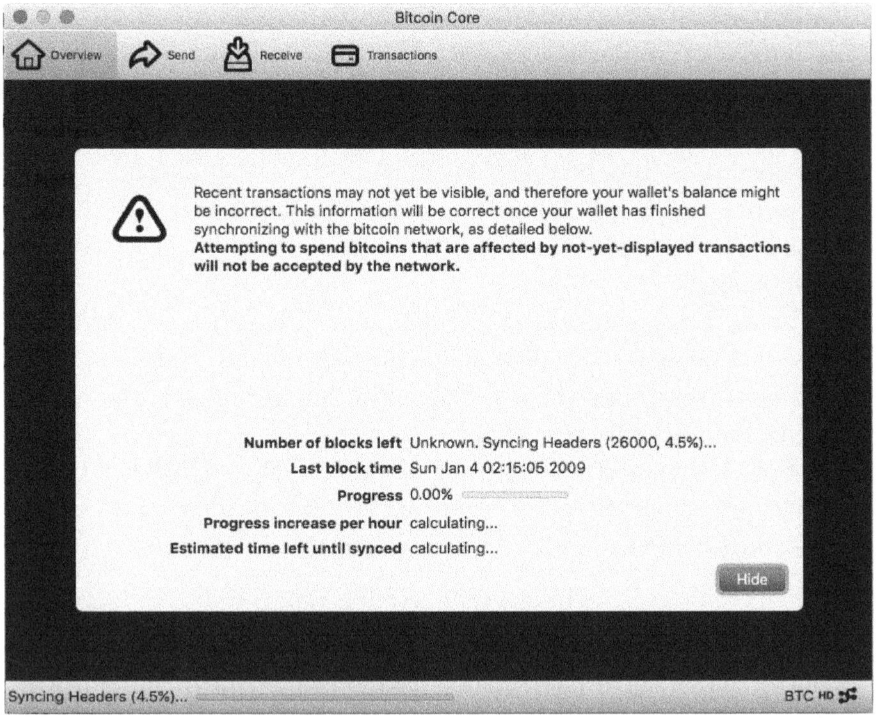

Figure 9.1: Screenshot of Bitcoin core syncing.

9.2.2 *Raspberry Pi Setup (Hardware)*

While waiting for the sync to be done, we will now set up the raspberry pi device as shown in Figure 9.2.

Ensure that the external hard disk that is to be connected to the raspberry pi is formatted or new. Ensure no important data are within the hard disk if you are using an existing hard disk for this purpose. All information will be erased and formatted for this operation. Proceed with care. Insert your Micro SD card into the raspberry pi slot. I will be using a 128 GB for this tutorial.

Connect your LAN cable from your router or your LAN socket to the LAN port of the Raspberry Pi. Ensure that you have the power adapter connected to the power socket and the back of the device.

Having an enclosure with a good heatsink for the raspberry pi as shown in Figure 9.3 will be a great alternative too, but for the coverage of this tutorial, we will not analyse at length the aesthetics of the setup.

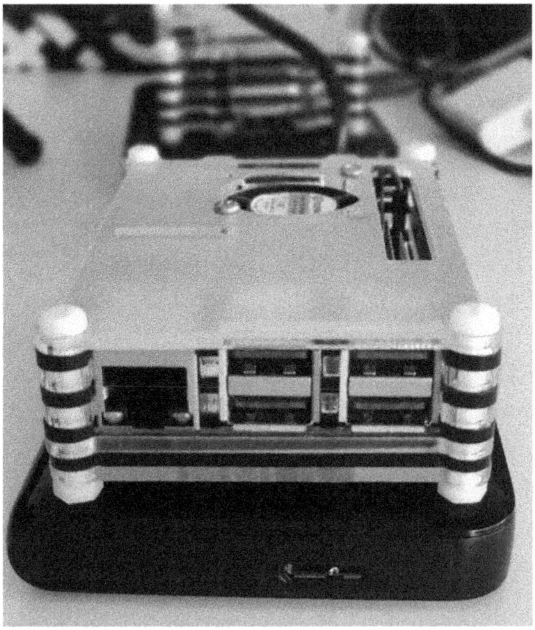

Figure 9.2: Image of raspberry pi LAN and USB ports.

Figure 9.3: Back image of the raspberry pi.

9.2.3 *Preparing the Raspberry Pi (Software)*

Once the device is connected and ready to be powered up, we will start to prepare the program for the raspberry pi device.

1. Download the raspberry pi operating system. We will be running headless operations throughout, so you may proceed to install Raspbian Buster Lite via the raspberry pi official site.
2. Once you download this ISO image file, you can write this into the micro SD memory card.
3. Enable SSH to your micro SD card via your computer when connecting to the memory card. Open the root file and add a new empty folder named SSH. Eject the card and you may disconnect it.
4. Start your raspberry pi by ensuring the memory card is installed, and the power socket is connected to the raspberry pi via the micro USB cable from the power outlet.
5. The raspberry pi has no physical power on switch besides the main adapter, but as the power is turned on, you will be able

to see the yellow blinking light and the red LED light indicating that it is turning on.

6. Here, the raspberry pi will have an IP assigned to it. We need to make this IP static.
7. Enter your router settings or your default internet gateway via an external device; key in both the admin and the password to access this. Check with the administrator if you do not have it.
8. Find the device name "Raspberry Pi" and under DHCP server, enable the Raspberry Pi to have its IP address static.
9. Configure port forwarding to allow our device to reach the Bitcoin networks. Set up in the following manner with the internal IP as above in point 8.

   a. Bitcoin Mainnet, External Port 8333, Internal Port 8333, Protocol both TCP & UDP.
   b. Bitcoin Testnet, External Port 18333, Internal Port 18333, Protocol both TCP & UDP.

10. For Windows users, please use PUTTY for the SSH connection. For Mac users, you can use the built-in native terminal for SSH. I will be using Mac and so it will be in the terminal and the codes will be the same for Windows users accessing via PUTTY. Next, we can enter into the pi IP address that we retrieve from the gateway above in point 8. By default, your raspberry pi will have a username as pi and password as raspberry. In the example here, I logged in with "pi" as my username and this results in the command starting with the username as shown in Figure 9.4.

```
pi@192.         's password:
Linux       4.19.97-v7+ #1__. SMP Thu Jan 30 13:15:58 GMT 2020 armv7l

The programs included with the Debian GNU/Linux system are free software;
the exact distribution terms for each program are described in the
individual files in /usr/share/doc/*/copyright.

Debian GNU/Linux comes with ABSOLUTELY NO WARRANTY, to the extent
permitted by applicable law.
Last login: Fri May 22 23:37:44 2020 from
pi@Edwan:~ $
```

Figure 9.4: Screenshot of login pi as default credentials.

```
pi@Pi:~ $ sudo raspi-config
Get:1 http://archive.raspberrypi.org/debian buster InRelease [25.1 kB]
Get:2 http://raspbian.raspberrypi.org/raspbian buster InRelease [15.0 kB]
Get:3 http://raspbian.raspberrypi.org/raspbian buster/main armhf Packages [13.0 MB]
Get:4 http://archive.raspberrypi.org/debian buster/main armhf Packages [328 kB]
Fetched 13.4 MB in 11s (1184 kB/s)
Reading package lists... Done
Reading package lists... Done
Building dependency tree
Reading state information... Done
raspi-config is already the newest version (20200504).
0 upgraded, 0 newly installed, 0 to remove and 4 not upgraded.
Sleeping 5 seconds before reloading raspi-config
```

Figure 9.5: Entering into the raspberry pi main configuration.

```
Raspberry Pi 3 Model B Rev 1.2

        Raspberry Pi Software Configuration Tool (raspi-config)

1 Change User Password Change password for the 'pi' user
2 Network Options      Configure network settings
3 Boot Options         Configure options for start-up
4 Localisation Options Set up language and regional settings to match your
5 Interfacing Options  Configure connections to peripherals
6 Overclock            Configure overclocking for your Pi
7 Advanced Options     Configure advanced settings
8 Update               Update this tool to the latest version
9 About raspi-config   Information about this configuration tool

              <Select>                     <Finish>
```

Figure 9.6: Menu of the raspberry pi system configuration.

SSH is enabled and the default password for the "pi" user has not been changed.

This is a security risk — please log in as the "pi" user and type "passwd" to set a new password.

Let us now set up some internal raspberry pi configurations using the code "sudo raspi-config" shown in Figure 9.5.

While in "sudo raspi-config", these are the commands to perform. The numbers are shown in Figure 9.6 in the menu order.

1. *Change password to a password of your choice [PASSWORD PI].*
2. *Boot options, choose Desktop/CLI → Console and wait for network at boot.*
3. *Localisation and choose your country for the date and time settings.*
4. *Advance option, expand file system and set memory split to 16.*
5. *Exit raspi config and you may choose not to reboot it. Either way is fine.*

Let us now get the latest updates and upgrades for the device using "sudo apt-get update" and "sudo apt-get upgrade" for this purpose.

We will now add an admin user using the code "sudo adduser admin", change password to your desired password for the admin using the command "sudo passwd root" and reboot it using command "sudo shutdown-r now". Once it is back up, you may log in to the admin user.

Then we will add another user name "bitcoin" as follows:

pi@Pi:~ $ sudo adduser bitcoin
New password:
Retype new password:
passwd: password updated successfully
Changing the user information for bitcoin

We will now mount the HDD you have attached to the pi and format it into the right format. All data will be deleted during this phase.

Getting the name and details of the hard disk attached, Figure 9.7 shows us that the raspberry pi has identified the HDD.

```
pi@Edwan:~ $ lsblk -o UUID,NAME,FSTYPE,SIZE,LABEL,MODEL
UUID                                 NAME           FSTYPE   SIZE LABEL  MODEL
af970af2-6950-4855-8b08-46703ce7355d sda            ext4   931.5G        ST1000LM01
                                     mmcblk0                29.8G
4BBD-D3E7                            |-mmcblk0p1    vfat     256M boot
45e99191-771b-4e12-a526-0779148892cb `-mmcblk0p2    ext4    29.6G rootfs
```

Figure 9.7: The HDD and the raspberry pi.

Figure 9.8: Editor screen of the fstab.

Format the hard disk by locating the name in the previous line; in my case it is "sda" as the name shows.

pi@Pi:~ $ sudo mkfs.ext4 /dev/[NAME OF HDD]

pi@Pi:~ $ sudo nano /etc/fstab [This will lead you into an editor screen shown in Figure 9.8]

Edit the "fstab" file and add the following as a new line (replace UUID=your own HDD UUID) at the end as shown in Figure 9.8 and below.

UUID=XXXXX /mnt/hdd ext4

rw,nosuid,dev,noexec,noatime,nodiratime,auto,nouser,async, nofail 0 2

As shown in Figure 9.9, make a new directory folder and add the HDD.

We then mount the HDD and check if it is mounted correctly in the following line.

Let us attach an owner to the HDD using the command "Chown-R".

If you are able to see your HDD mounted, you are doing well.

```
pi@Pi:~ $ sudo nano /et/fstab
[pi@Pi:~ $ sudo mkdir /mnt/hdd
[pi@Pi:~ $ sudo mount -a
[pi@Pi:~ $ df /mnt/hdd
[Filesystem     1K-blocks  Used Available Use% Mounted on
[/dev/sda       960381668 77852 911449304   1% /mnt/hdd
[pi@Pi:~ $ sudo chown -R bitcoin:bitcoin /mnt/hdd/
```

Figure 9.9: Screenshot to show that the HDD has been mounted.

```
bitcoin@Pi:~ $ cd /mnt/hdd
bitcoin@Pi:/mnt/hdd $ mkdir bitcoin
bitcoin@Pi:/mnt/hdd $ ls -la
total 28
[drwxr-xr-x 4 bitcoin bitcoin  4096 May 17 09:04 .
[drwxr-xr-x 3 root    root     4096 May 17 09:02 ..
[drwxr-xr-x 2 bitcoin bitcoin  4096 May 17 09:04 bitcoin
drwx------ 2 bitcoin bitcoin 16384 May 17 08:57 lost+found
bitcoin@Pi:/mnt/hdd $ touch bitcoin/test.file
bitcoin@Pi:/mnt/hdd $ rm bitcoin/test.file
bitcoin@Pi:/mnt/hdd $ exit
logout
```

Figure 9.10: Making a new directory called bitcoin within the HDD.

```
pi@Pi:~ $ sudo dphys-swapfile swapoff
pi@Pi:~ $ sudo dphys-swapfile uninstall
pi@Pi:~ $ sudo nano /etc/dphys-swapfile
[pi@Pi:~ $ sudo dd if=/dev/zero of=/mnt/hdd/swapfile count=1000 bs=1MiB
1000+0 records in
1000+0 records out
[1048576000 bytes (1.0 GB, 1000 MiB) copied, 34.1443 s, 30.7 MB/s
[pi@Pi:~ $ sudo chmod 600 /mnt/hdd/swapfile
[pi@Pi:~ $ sudo mkswap /mnt/hdd/swapfile
[Setting up swapspace version 1, size = 1000 MiB (1048571904 bytes)
no label, UUID=058ead59-1c76-4aa5-87c3-ed63d6c18e29
pi@Pi:~ $ sudo dphys-swapfile setup
computing size, want /var/swap=1970MByte, generating swapfile ... of 1970MBytes
[pi@Pi:~ $ sudo dphys-swapfile swapon
```

Figure 9.11: Creation of a new swap file.

We can change the user to bitcoin now, change directory to the HDD and make a bitcoin folder and exit it (see Figure 9.10).

We will create the swap file to shift it to the HDD instead of the Internal memory card as shown in Figure 9.11. Log in as ADMIN to do this. We will delete the old files using "swapoff" and uninstall it. We will then edit the config file and replace it with the following configuration:

"CONF_SWAPFILE=/mnt/hdd/swapfile"

You will need to remove the default CONF_SWAPSIZE line.

```
admin@Edwan:~ $ sudo su admin
[sudo] password for admin:
admin@Edwan:~ $ mkdir /home/admin/download
mkdir: cannot create directory '/home/admin/download': File exists
admin@Edwan:~ $ cd /home/admin/download
```

Figure 9.12: Logging in to admin and making a download directory.

```
admin@Edwan:~/download $ wget https://bitcoincore.org/bin/bitcoin-core-0.19.1/bitcoin-0.19.1-arm-linux-gnueabihf.tar.gz
--2020-05-21 13:51:22--  https://bitcoincore.org/bin/bitcoin-core-0.19.1/bitcoin-0.19.1-arm-linux-gnueabihf.tar.gz
Resolving bitcoincore.org (bitcoincore.org)... 107.191.99.5, 198.251.83.116
Connecting to bitcoincore.org (bitcoincore.org)|107.191.99.5|:443... connected.
HTTP request sent, awaiting response... 200 OK
Length: 27138490 (26M) [application/octet-stream]
Saving to: 'bitcoin-0.19.1-arm-linux-gnueabihf.tar.gz'

bitcoin-0.19.1-arm-linux-gnueabihf.tar.gz       100%[=====================================================================

2020-05-21 13:51:37 (1.90 MB/s) - 'bitcoin-0.19.1-arm-linux-gnueabihf.tar.gz' saved [27138490/27138490]

admin@Edwan:~/download $ tar -xvf bitcoin-0.19.1-arm-linux-gnueabihf.tar.gz
bitcoin-0.19.1/
bitcoin-0.19.1/bin/
bitcoin-0.19.1/bin/bitcoin-cli
bitcoin-0.19.1/bin/bitcoind
bitcoin-0.19.1/bin/bitcoin-qt
bitcoin-0.19.1/bin/bitcoin-tx
bitcoin-0.19.1/bin/bitcoin-wallet
bitcoin-0.19.1/bin/test_bitcoin
bitcoin-0.19.1/include/
bitcoin-0.19.1/include/bitcoinconsensus.h
bitcoin-0.19.1/lib/
```

Figure 9.13: Downloading the executable file from bitcoincore.org.

We will then create a new swap file and turn it on with swapon.

9.2.4 *Bitcoin Core Raspberry Pi Configurations*

Log in to admin "sudo su admin" (see Figure 9.12).

We create a download folder here to sit in the bitcoin core client.

We go into the download folder and download the client from the bitcoin official site command wget as shown in Figure 9.13.

Here, we will download the latest bitcoin core version and compare and verify the authentication of the downloaded bitcoin core application against the checksum of the application in the link below for this version of 0.19.1. This step is important as it ensures that the version we have downloaded is indeed an official source.

This is the link you can reach out to for the latest application version. We will be downloading and installing ARM Linux 32 bit for the raspberry pi using the "wget" function followed by its URL link of the installer. You may check against the output in Figure 9.14.

Do look out for the application version with the word OK and cross-check it with the correct signature as shown below by Wladimir J. van der Laan.

```
admin@Edwan:~/download $ wget https://bitcoincore.org/bin/bitcoin-core-0.19.1/SHA256SUMS.asc
--2020-05-21 13:26:33--  https://bitcoincore.org/bin/bitcoin-core-0.19.1/SHA256SUMS.asc
Resolving bitcoincore.org (bitcoincore.org)... 198.251.83.116, 107.191.99.5
Connecting to bitcoincore.org (bitcoincore.org)|198.251.83.116|:443... connected.
HTTP request sent, awaiting response... 200 OK
Length: 1875 (1.8K) [application/octet-stream]
Saving to: 'SHA256SUMS.asc'

SHA256SUMS.asc              100%[==================================================>]   1.83K  --.-KB/s    in 0s

2020-05-21 13:26:34 (11.7 MB/s) - 'SHA256SUMS.asc' saved [1875/1875]

admin@Edwan:~/download $ wget https://bitcoin.org/laanwj-releases.asc
--2020-05-21 13:27:29--  https://bitcoin.org/laanwj-releases.asc
Resolving bitcoin.org (bitcoin.org)... 138.68.248.245
Connecting to bitcoin.org (bitcoin.org)|138.68.248.245|:443... connected.
HTTP request sent, awaiting response... 200 OK
Length: 32242 (31K) [application/octet-stream]
Saving to: 'laanwj-releases.asc'

laanwj-releases.asc         100%[==================================================>]  31.49K  --.-KB/s    in 0.004s

2020-05-21 13:27:30 (8.42 MB/s) - 'laanwj-releases.asc' saved [32242/32242]

admin@Edwan:~/download $ sha256sum --check SHA256SUMS.asc --ignore-missing
bitcoin-0.19.1-x86_64-linux-gnu.tar.gz: OK
sha256sum: WARNING: 20 lines are improperly formatted
admin@Edwan:~/download $ gpg --import ./laanwj-releases.asc
gpg: keybox '/home/admin/.gnupg/pubring.kbx' created
gpg: key 90C8019E36C2E964: 51 signatures not checked due to missing keys
gpg: /home/admin/.gnupg/trustdb.gpg: trustdb created
gpg: key 90C8019E36C2E964: public key "Wladimir J. van der Laan (Bitcoin Core binary release signing key) <laanwj@gmail.com>" imported
gpg: Total number processed: 1
gpg:               imported: 1
gpg: no ultimately trusted keys found
admin@Edwan:~/download $ gpg --refresh-keys
gpg: refreshing 1 key from hkps://keys.openpgp.org
gpg: key 90C8019E36C2E964: "Wladimir J. van der Laan (Bitcoin Core binary release signing key) <laanwj@gmail.com>" not changed
gpg: Total number processed: 1
gpg:              unchanged: 1
admin@Edwan:~/download $ gpg --verify SHA256SUMS.asc
gpg: Signature made Mon Mar  9 18:58:04 2020 +08
gpg:                using RSA key 90C8019E36C2E964
gpg: Good signature from "Wladimir J. van der Laan (Bitcoin Core binary release signing key) <laanwj@gmail.com>" [unknown]
gpg: WARNING: This key is not certified with a trusted signature!
gpg:          There is no indication that the signature belongs to the owner.
Primary key fingerprint: 01EA 5486 DE18 A882 D4C2  6845 90C8 019E 36C2 E964
```

Figure 9.14: Download and verification process of the application.

Source: *bitcoin-0.19.1-x86_ 64-linux-gnu.tar.gz: OK*

Good signature from "Wladimir J. van der Laan (Bitcoin Core binary release signing key)⟨laanwj@gmail.com⟩" and fingerprint of 01EA 5486 DE18 A882 D4C2 6845 90C8 019E 36C2 E964

With these keys, we can do a cross-reference back to verify the application checksums that you are running from your other device — laptop/computer.

Once keys matched and are a good version, we can then extract them and install it onto our device. If the keys are incorrect, check the source of the download with the above reference once more.

Extracting and installing the file in Figure 9.15.

Once installed, please check the version again. Here, I have Bitcoin Core version V0.19.1.

Do note that you should check for the latest version. As of the end of this writing, the community just released version V0.20.0.

```
admin@Edwan:~/download $ tar -xvf bitcoin-0.19.1-arm-linux-gnueabihf.tar.gz
bitcoin-0.19.1/
bitcoin-0.19.1/bin/
bitcoin-0.19.1/bin/bitcoin-cli
bitcoin-0.19.1/bin/bitcoind
bitcoin-0.19.1/bin/bitcoin-qt
bitcoin-0.19.1/bin/bitcoin-tx
bitcoin-0.19.1/bin/bitcoin-wallet
bitcoin-0.19.1/bin/test_bitcoin
bitcoin-0.19.1/include/
bitcoin-0.19.1/include/bitcoinconsensus.h
bitcoin-0.19.1/lib/
bitcoin-0.19.1/lib/libbitcoinconsensus.so
bitcoin-0.19.1/lib/libbitcoinconsensus.so.0
bitcoin-0.19.1/lib/libbitcoinconsensus.so.0.0.0
bitcoin-0.19.1/README.md
bitcoin-0.19.1/share/
bitcoin-0.19.1/share/man/
bitcoin-0.19.1/share/man/man1/
bitcoin-0.19.1/share/man/man1/bitcoin-cli.1
bitcoin-0.19.1/share/man/man1/bitcoind.1
bitcoin-0.19.1/share/man/man1/bitcoin-qt.1
bitcoin-0.19.1/share/man/man1/bitcoin-tx.1
bitcoin-0.19.1/share/man/man1/bitcoin-wallet.1
admin@Edwan:~/download $ sudo install -m 0755 -o root -g root -t /usr/local/bin bitcoin-0.19.0.1/bin/*
install: cannot stat 'bitcoin-0.19.0.1/bin/*': No such file or directory
admin@Edwan:~/download $ sudo install -m 0755 -o root -g root -t /usr/local/bin bitcoin-0.19.0.1/bin/
install: cannot stat 'bitcoin-0.19.0.1/bin/': No such file or directory
admin@Edwan:~/download $ sudo install -m 0755 -o root -g root -t /usr/local/bin bitcoin-0.19.1/bin/*
admin@Edwan:~/download $ bitcoind --version
Bitcoin Core version v0.19.1
Copyright (C) 2009-2019 The Bitcoin Core developers
```

Figure 9.15: Installation of the verified bitcoin core application.

Next up, we want bitcoin to run automatically in the background every time our device starts. This can be achieved through what we call a bitcoin daemon also known as **bitcoind**. Bitcoind will run in the background without any user interface and stores all the data in a directory we specify.

To perform this, we require the program to point to the directory (see Figure 9.16) we have created on the HDD. Once it has been pointed to the right directory, we will be using "ln -s/mnt/hdd" directory name; we will enter "ls -la" to see if bitcoin is successfully pointed to the directory. We will then exit the program and see if it will auto restart the moment we turn it back on.

We will log in as bitcoin users, which we created previously to run bitcoin functions. Now, we will try to start up bitcoind manually by running bitcoind as the command.

You should see the script running, which indicates that bitcoin daemon is running in the background. You may stop it by exiting it with CTRL + C.

We need to configure the file for the daemon bitcoind. We will open the configuration editor with this command, "nano

```
admin@Edwan:~/download $ sudo su - bitcoin
bitcoin@Edwan:~ $ ln -s /mnt/hdd/bitcoin /home/bitcoin/.bitcoin
bitcoin@Edwan:~ $ ls -la
total 28
drwxr-xr-x 3 bitcoin bitcoin 4096 May 21 13:45 .
drwxr-xr-x 5 root    root    4096 May 17 09:03 ..
-rw------- 1 bitcoin bitcoin  217 May 21 13:50 .bash_history
-rw-r--r-- 1 bitcoin bitcoin  220 May 17 09:03 .bash_logout
-rw-r--r-- 1 bitcoin bitcoin 3523 May 17 09:03 .bashrc
lrwxrwxrwx 1 bitcoin bitcoin   16 May 21 13:44 .bitcoin -> /mnt/hdd/bitcoin
drwxr-xr-x 3 bitcoin bitcoin 4096 May 21 13:45 .local
-rw-r--r-- 1 bitcoin bitcoin  807 May 17 09:03 .profile
bitcoin@Edwan:~ $ ls
bitcoin@Edwan:~ $ exit
logout
```

Figure 9.16: Linkage pointing to the correct directory which is the bitcoin folder in the HDD.

```
  GNU nano 3.2              /home/bitcoin/.bitcoin/bitcoin.conf

# Edwan Raspberry Pi: bitcoind configuration
# /home/bitcoin/.bitcoin/bitcoin.conf

# remove the following line to enable Bitcoin mainnet
testnet=1

# Bitcoind options
server=1
daemon=1

# Connection settings
rpcuser=
rpcpassword=

onlynet=ipv4
zmqpubrawblock=tcp://127.0.0.1:28332
zmqpubrawtx=tcp://127.0.0.1:28333

# Raspberry Pi optimizations
                  [ File '/home/bitcoin/.bitcoin/bitcoin.conf' is unwritable ]
^G Get Help    ^O Write Out   ^W Where Is    ^K Cut Text    ^J Justify     ^C Cur Pos
^X Exit        ^R Read File   ^\ Replace     ^U Uncut Text  ^T To Spell    ^_ Go To Line
```

Figure 9.17: Configuration file for the bitcoin daemon.

/home/bitcoin/.bitcoin/bitcoin.conf" (see Figure 9.17), and paste the following configuration below and save it. For the rpcuser, the username is "pi" and please choose your own password 2 now. Failure to remember password 2 will result in a loss of funds.

We will save, exit and now run bitcoind. Curious to see how it is running in the background, we will now have a

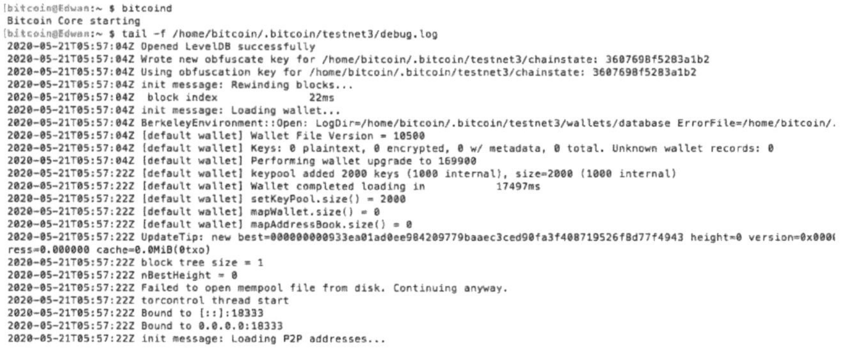

```
[bitcoin@Edwan:~ $ bitcoind
Bitcoin Core starting
[bitcoin@Edwan:~ $ tail -f /home/bitcoin/.bitcoin/testnet3/debug.log
2020-05-21T05:57:04Z Opened LevelDB successfully
2020-05-21T05:57:04Z Wrote new obfuscate key for /home/bitcoin/.bitcoin/testnet3/chainstate: 3607698f5283a1b2
2020-05-21T05:57:04Z Using obfuscation key for /home/bitcoin/.bitcoin/testnet3/chainstate: 3607698f5283a1b2
2020-05-21T05:57:04Z init message: Rewinding blocks...
2020-05-21T05:57:04Z  block index              22ms
2020-05-21T05:57:04Z init message: Loading wallet...
2020-05-21T05:57:04Z BerkeleyEnvironment::Open: LogDir=/home/bitcoin/.bitcoin/testnet3/wallets/database ErrorFile=/home/bitcoin/.
2020-05-21T05:57:04Z [default wallet] Wallet File Version = 10500
2020-05-21T05:57:04Z [default wallet] Keys: 0 plaintext, 0 encrypted, 0 w/ metadata, 0 total. Unknown wallet records: 0
2020-05-21T05:57:04Z [default wallet] Performing wallet upgrade to 169900
2020-05-21T05:57:22Z [default wallet] keypool added 2000 keys (1000 internal), size=2000 (1000 internal)
2020-05-21T05:57:22Z [default wallet] Wallet completed loading in           17497ms
2020-05-21T05:57:22Z [default wallet] setKeyPool.size() = 2000
2020-05-21T05:57:22Z [default wallet] mapWallet.size() = 0
2020-05-21T05:57:22Z [default wallet] mapAddressBook.size() = 0
2020-05-21T05:57:22Z UpdateTip: new best=000000000933ea01ad0ee984209779baaec3ced90fa3f408719526f8d77f4943 height=0 version=0x000
ress=0.000000 cache=0.0MiB(0txo)
2020-05-21T05:57:22Z block tree size = 1
2020-05-21T05:57:22Z nBestHeight = 0
2020-05-21T05:57:22Z Failed to open mempool file from disk. Continuing anyway.
2020-05-21T05:57:22Z torcontrol thread start
2020-05-21T05:57:22Z Bound to [::]:18333
2020-05-21T05:57:22Z Bound to 0.0.0.0:18333
2020-05-21T05:57:22Z init message: Loading P2P addresses...
```

Figure 9.18: Background of the bitcoin daemon running.

sneak peek at what it is running with the following command "tail -f/home/bitcoin/.bitcoin/testnet3/debug.log" as shown in Figure 9.18.

Now that it is running, let us try to get our hands on some real bitcoin core command lines called the bitcoin-cli (Figure 9.19).

What we are looking for here is the chain data. Verification progress should be near 1 to indicate full bitcoin chain synchronisation. And, the chain here is indeed testnet. We can now stop it and exit (see Figure 9.20).

Now that you have successfully got the bitcoin core to run, we will set it up to get it to autorun once your raspberry pi starts up. To do so, we will create a configuration file for it.

Entering into the editor using "sudo nano/etc/systemd/system/bitcoind.service"

Copy the whole command and paste this into the editor.

 # Your Raspberry Pi Name

[Unit]
Description=Bitcoin daemon
After=network.target

[Service]
ExecStartPre=/bin/sh -c 'sleep 30'
ExecStart=/usr/local/bin/bitcoind -daemon -conf=/home/bitcoin/.bitcoin/bitcoin.conf -pid=/home/bitcoin/.bitcoin/bitcoind.pid

```
[bitcoin@Edwan:~ $ bitcoin-cli getblockchaininfo
{
  "chain": "test",
  "blocks": 0,
  "headers": 100000,
  "bestblockhash": "000000000933ea01ad0ee984209779baaec3ced90fa3f408719526f8d77f4943",
  "difficulty": 1,
  "mediantime": 1296688602,
  "verificationprogress": 1.805138076137419e-08,
  "initialblockdownload": true,
  "chainwork": "0000000000000000000000000000000000000000000000000000000100010001",
  "size_on_disk": 293,
  "pruned": false,
  "softforks": {
    "bip34": {
      "type": "buried",
      "active": false,
      "height": 21111
    },
    "bip66": {
      "type": "buried",
      "active": false,
      "height": 330776
    },
    "bip65": {
      "type": "buried",
      "active": false,
      "height": 581885
    },
    "csv": {
      "type": "buried",
      "active": false,
      "height": 770112
    },
    "segwit": {
      "type": "buried",
      "active": false,
      "height": 834624
    }
  },
  "warnings": ""
}
```

Figure 9.19: Status of the blockchain our node is having.

```
[bitcoin@Edwan:~ $ bitcoin-cli stop
 Bitcoin Core stopping
[bitcoin@Edwan:~ $ exit
 logout
```

Figure 9.20: Stopping the bitcoin daemon.

PIDFile=/home/bitcoin/.bitcoin/bitcoind.pid
User=bitcoin
Group=bitcoin
Type=forking
KillMode=process

```
[admin@Edwan:~/download $ sudo systemctl enable bitcoind.service
 Created symlink /etc/systemd/system/multi-user.target.wants/bitcoind.service → /etc/systemd
[admin@Edwan:~/download $ mkdir /home/admin/.bitcoin
[admin@Edwan:~/download $ sudo cp /home/bitcoin/.bitcoin/bitcoin.conf /home/admin/.bitcoin/
[admin@Edwan:~/download $ sudo shutdown -r now
```

Figure 9.21: Activation of the new configuration file.

```
[admin@Edwan:~ $ systemctl status bitcoind.service
● bitcoind.service - Bitcoin daemon
   Loaded: loaded (/etc/systemd/system/bitcoind.service; enabled; vendor preset: enabled)
   Active: active (running) since Thu 2020-05-21 14:00:45 +08; 6min ago
  Process: 556 ExecStartPre=/bin/sh -c sleep 30 (code=exited, status=0/SUCCESS)
  Process: 622 ExecStart=/usr/local/bin/bitcoind -daemon -conf=/home/bitcoin/.bitcoin/bitcoin.conf -pid=/home/
 Main PID: 623 (bitcoind)
    Tasks: 17 (limit: 2319)
   Memory: 461.9M
   CGroup: /system.slice/bitcoind.service
           └─623 /usr/local/bin/bitcoind -daemon -conf=/home/bitcoin/.bitcoin/bitcoin.conf -pid=/home/bitcoin/
```

Figure 9.22: Results showing that daemon is running.

Restart=always
TimeoutSec=120
RestartSec=30

[Install]
WantedBy=multi-user.target

Save and exit. We will now activate (see Figure 9.21) and enable the configuration file above.

We will copy a copy of the following configuration to the admin user.

We will now restart the device to see if the daemon will autostart as per our configuration.

Once the red and green LED stop blinking, you may enter into the admin account and check the status of the services. Ensure that it is active and running as shown in Figure 9.22.

Now, we are done with the configuration and the setup. We will now wait for the testnet to be fully synced.

In the meantime, do check out some bitcoin command lines to call while we wait for the testnet to finish its validation progress. It is good to have a few of the common commands in hands. Once the node is synchronised, all you need to do is call certain functions to check the status of your node.

9.3 Layer-2 Application: Lightning Network

The whole idea of having this tutorial is to understand how layer-2 application solves the scalability problem that has been widely talked about for many years since the entrance of bitcoin layer 1 in comparison with that of other centralised payment solutions. This is where several companies come together to try various implementations and this topic is still under experimental research as I am writing this tutorial. We do not need to transact at the main network to experience this. We can still experience the amazing benefits and properties through alternative networks like the testnet to have a sense of what lightning network is all about.

In a nutshell, lightning network implementation is said to solve the scalability problem by aiding the trusted payment channels also termed as the side chains. Having a side chain will improve transaction speeds as a message does not require to reach the wider network and be validated across all nodes. Since it is a trusted channel, the message will be routed directly through or via other trusted channel loops, taking the shortest path to reach the intended destination. All of these are done with on-chain governance over the payment channels to dissuade cheating from either party. I will not go further into the length and breadth of the theory of lightning network for this tutorial.

As mentioned, there are a few different implementations of the network. We will be using Lightning Labs Daemon also known as LND for this guide.

9.3.1 *Download and Install Lightning Network*

Similar to what we have done for the bitcoin applications, we will go through the same process for Lightneing Networks. You should realise by now that the codes are similar in nature. We will get the application link from the source, download them, verify the application and once verified, we will extract it and install it onto the device. You can find the lightning application on the Github lightning network repository. For this tutorial, my latest release is version 0.10.1 beta.

```
admin@Edwan:~ $ cd /home/admin/download
[admin@Edwan:~/download $ rm -rf /home/admin/download/*
```

Figure 9.23: Change directory in download folder.

```
admin@Edwan:~/download $ wget https://github.com/lightningnetwork/lnd/releases/download/v0.10.1-beta.rc2/m
[--2020-05-23 00:20:48--  https://github.com/lightningnetwork/lnd/releases/download/v0.10.1-beta.rc2/manife
Resolving github.com (github.com)... 52.74.223.119
Connecting to github.com (github.com)|52.74.223.119|:443... connected.
HTTP request sent, awaiting response... 302 Found
Location: https://github-production-release-asset-2e65be.s3.amazonaws.com/49765480/1d74a100-9b90-11ea-9b66
2F20200522%2Fus-east-1%2Fs3%2Faws4_request&X-Amz-Date=20200522T162048Z&X-Amz-Expires=300&X-Amz-Signature=b
ost&actor_id=0&repo_id=49765480&response-content-disposition=attachment%3B%20filename%3Dmanifest-v0.10.1-b
--2020-05-23 00:20:49--  https://github-production-release-asset-2e65be.s3.amazonaws.com/49765480/1d74a100
NJYAX4CSVEH53A%2F20200522%2Fus-east-1%2Fs3%2Faws4_request&X-Amz-Date=20200522T162048Z&X-Amz-Expires=300&X-
SignedHeaders=host&actor_id=0&repo_id=49765480&response-content-disposition=attachment%3B%20filename%3Dman
Resolving github-production-release-asset-2e65be.s3.amazonaws.com (github-production-release-asset-2e65be.
Connecting to github-production-release-asset-2e65be.s3.amazonaws.com (github-production-release-asset-2e6
HTTP request sent, awaiting response... 200 OK
Length: 566 [application/octet-stream]
Saving to: 'manifest-v0.10.1-beta.rc2.txt.sig'

manifest-v0.10.1-beta.rc2.txt.sig            100%[==================================================

2020-05-23 00:20:50 (1.76 MB/s) - 'manifest-v0.10.1-beta.rc2.txt.sig' saved [566/566]

admin@Edwan:~/download $ wget https://github.com/lightningnetwork/lnd/releases/tag/v0.10.1-beta.rc2
[--2020-05-23 00:21:51--  https://github.com/lightningnetwork/lnd/releases/tag/v0.10.1-beta.rc2
Resolving github.com (github.com)... 13.229.188.59
Connecting to github.com (github.com)|13.229.188.59|:443... connected.
HTTP request sent, awaiting response... 200 OK
Length: unspecified [text/html]
Saving to: 'v0.10.1-beta.rc2'

v0.10.1-beta.rc2                                    [ <=>

2020-05-23 00:21:51 (5.96 MB/s) - 'v0.10.1-beta.rc2' saved [119756]

admin@Edwan:~/download $ wget https://keybase.io/roasbeef/pgp_keys.asc
[--2020-05-23 00:22:25--  https://keybase.io/roasbeef/pgp_keys.asc
Resolving keybase.io (keybase.io)... 52.20.210.27, 3.220.12.174
Connecting to keybase.io (keybase.io)|52.20.210.27|:443... connected.
HTTP request sent, awaiting response... 200 OK
Length: 6909 (6.7K) [text/plain]
Saving to: 'pgp_keys.asc'

pgp_keys.asc                                 100%[==================================================
```

Figure 9.24: Downloading of the source, verification and keys.

Let us start with admin user change directory in the download folder shown in Figure 9.23.

Here, we point to the download folder, and get the files of the application, text file, signature and keys.

We will then verify the download as what we did to the BTC core application. Screenshots of the processes are shown in Figure 9.24.

Our source application has been verified and can be trusted as shown in Figure 9.25. Again, we identify it from the fingerprint and the OK status against the right version "lnd-linux-armv7-v0.10.1-beta.rc2.tar.gz: OK ← Hooray!".

```
admin@Edwan:~/download $ sha256sum --check manifest-v0.10.1-beta.rc2.txt --ignore-missing
lnd-linux-armv7-v0.10.1-beta.rc2.tar.gz: OK
admin@Edwan:~/download $ gpg ./pgp_keys.asc
gpg: WARNING: no command supplied.  Trying to guess what you mean ...
pub   rsa4096 2019-07-10 [SC] [expires: 2020-10-02]
      9769140D255C759B1EB77B46A96387A57CAAE94D
uid           Olaoluwa Osuntokun <laolu32@gmail.com>
sub   rsa4096 2019-07-10 [A] [expires: 2020-10-02]
sub   rsa4096 2019-07-10 [S] [expires: 2020-10-02]
sub   rsa4096 2019-07-10 [E] [expires: 2020-10-02]
admin@Edwan:~/download $ gpg --import ./pgp_keys.asc
gpg: key A96387A57CAAE94D: public key "Olaoluwa Osuntokun <laolu32@gmail.com>" imported
gpg: Total number processed: 1
gpg:               imported: 1
admin@Edwan:~/download $ gpg --verify manifest-v0.10.1-beta.rc2.txt.sig
gpg: assuming signed data in 'manifest-v0.10.1-beta.rc2.txt'
gpg: Signature made Fri May 22 08:49:03 2020 +08
gpg:                using RSA key 4AB7F8DA6FAEBB3B70B1F903BC13F65E2DC84465
gpg: Good signature from "Olaoluwa Osuntokun <laolu32@gmail.com>" [unknown]
gpg: WARNING: This key is not certified with a trusted signature!
gpg:          There is no indication that the signature belongs to the owner.
Primary key fingerprint: 9769 140D 255C 759B 1EB7  7B46 A963 87A5 7CAA E94D
     Subkey fingerprint: 4AB7 F8DA 6FAE BB3B 70B1  F903 BC13 F65E 2DC8 4465
admin@Edwan:~/download $ tar -xzf lnd-linux-armv7-v0.10.1-beta.rc2.tar.gz
admin@Edwan:~/download $ sudo install -m 0755 -o root -g root -t /usr/local/bin lnd-linux-armv7-v0.10.1-beta.rc2/*
[sudo] password for admin:
admin@Edwan:~/download $ lnd --version
lnd version 0.10.1-beta.rc2 commit=v0.10.1-beta.rc2
```

Figure 9.25: Checking and verifying the downloaded application.

```
admin@Edwan:~ $ sudo ln -s /bin/ip /usr/bin/ip
[sudo] password for admin:
```

Figure 9.26: Logging into admin user.

9.3.2 *Lightning Network Configuration*

Now that the Lightning Network (LND) is installed, we need to configure it to work over our Bitcoin Core and run automatically on startup. Still as user "admin", create a symbolic link to the IP binary located in /bin/ip.

Open a "bitcoin" user session instead of an admin user (see Figure 9.26).

Create the LND working directory and the corresponding symbolic link (see Figure 9.27).

Create the LND configuration file and paste the following content (adjust to your alias). We will then save and exit the editor (see Figure 9.28).

Some explanations about this configuration

When you set nat=true, it means that your router is able to support UpnP allowing the lightning network to make your node accessible from outside by configuration port forwarding. If it is not true, then it will just be a private node without the ability to route payment for

```
admin@Edwan:~ $ sudo su - bitcoin
bitcoin@Edwan:~ $
bitcoin@Edwan:~ $ mkdir /mnt/hdd/lnd
bitcoin@Edwan:~ $ ln -s /mnt/hdd/lnd /home/bitcoin/.lnd
bitcoin@Edwan:~ $ ls -la
total 28
drwxr-xr-x 3 bitcoin bitcoin 4096 May 23 00:36 .
drwxr-xr-x 5 root    root    4096 May 17 09:03 ..
-rw------- 1 bitcoin bitcoin  396 May 21 13:58 .bash_history
-rw-r--r-- 1 bitcoin bitcoin  220 May 17 09:03 .bash_logout
-rw-r--r-- 1 bitcoin bitcoin 3523 May 17 09:03 .bashrc
lrwxrwxrwx 1 bitcoin bitcoin   16 May 21 13:44 .bitcoin -> /mnt/hdd/bitcoin
lrwxrwxrwx 1 bitcoin bitcoin   12 May 23 00:36 .lnd -> /mnt/hdd/lnd
drwxr-xr-x 3 bitcoin bitcoin 4096 May 21 13:45 .local
-rw-r--r-- 1 bitcoin bitcoin  807 May 17 09:03 .profile
bitcoin@Edwan:~ $ nano /home/bitcoin/.lnd/lnd.conf
```

Figure 9.27: Symbolic link creation.

```
  GNU nano 3.2              /home/bitcoin/.lnd/lnd.conf

        RASPBERRY PI: lnd configuration
# /home/bitcoin/.lnd/lnd.conf

[Application Options]
debuglevel=info
maxpendingchannels=5
alias=      [LND]
color=#68F442

# Your router must support and enable UPnP, otherwise delete this line
nat=true

[Bitcoin]
bitcoin.active=1

# enable either testnet or mainnet
bitcoin.testnet=1
#bitcoin.mainnet=1

bitcoin.node=bitcoind

[autopilot]
autopilot.active=1
autopilot.maxchannels=10
autopilot.allocation=0.5
```

Figure 9.28: The editor for the configuration.

others as it will not be visible from the outside. You are required to remove nat=true, your node will constantly try to connect but will be unable to and will not start till it finds a network.

```
[bitcoin@Edwan:~ $ lnd
Attempting automatic RPC configuration to bitcoind
Automatically obtained bitcoind's RPC credentials
2020-05-23 00:39:22.259 [INF] LTND: Version: 0.10.1-beta.rc2 commit=v0.10.1-beta.rc2, build=production, logging=default
2020-05-23 00:39:22.260 [INF] LTND: Active chain: Bitcoin (network=testnet)
2020-05-23 00:39:22.260 [INF] LTND: Opening the main database, this might take a few minutes...
2020-05-23 00:39:22.271 [INF] CHDB: Checking for schema update: latest_version=13, db_version=13
2020-05-23 00:39:22.271 [INF] LTND: Database now open (time_to_open=11.305646ms)!
2020-05-23 00:39:22.271 [INF] RPCS: Generating TLS certificates...
2020-05-23 00:39:22.280 [INF] RPCS: Done generating TLS certificates
2020-05-23 00:39:22.286 [INF] RPCS: password RPC server listening on 127.0.0.1:10009
2020-05-23 00:39:22.286 [INF] RPCS: password gRPC proxy started at 127.0.0.1:8080
2020-05-23 00:39:22.286 [INF] LTND: Waiting for wallet encryption password. Use `lncli create` to create a wallet, `lncli unlock` to unlock
```

Figure 9.29: Running the lnd command.

In the above configuration, I have enabled autopilot and it is set to open with a maximum of 10 channels with 50% of your funds. Do note that according to the lightning network Github repository, they recommend to have 5 channels at 0.6 of the fund.

The autopilot agent will attempt to automatically open up channels to put your node in an advantageous position within the network. This is based on preference and for a test, you can just put some numbers that make sense. If you do not wish to allow autopilot to enable channels, simply just edit the configuration to make autopilot.active=0 to disable it.

9.3.3 *Running Lightning Network*

Again, we switch to the user "bitcoin" and first start the program manually to check if everything works.

"sudo su - bitcoin"

Run lightning network using the "lnd" command (see Figure 9.29).

Just like how attaching a screen to the console works, while we let the lightning daemon run in the background, we need to load up a second console and let this console run. Open up another terminal/ PUTTY session and log back into the raspberry pi as admin without stopping this session. To better demonstrate between the first and second console, I will name it CP2 for console #2.

9.3.4 *Lightning Network Wallet Setup*

You may be aware by now that both bitcoin core and lightning have wallet functions to store your assets. Lightning wallets are different and do not share the same wallet as bitcoin core wallet.

```
admin@Edwan:~ $ sudo su - bitcoin
[sudo] password for admin:
bitcoin@Edwan:~ $ lncli --network=testnet create
Input wallet password:
password must have at least 8 characters

Input wallet password:
password must have at least 8 characters

Input wallet password:
Confirm password:


Do you have an existing cipher seed mnemonic you want to use? (Enter y/n): n
```

Figure 9.30: Creating a new wallet.

```
Your cipher seed can optionally be encrypted.
[Input your passphrase if you wish to encrypt it (or press enter to proceed without a cipher seed

Generating fresh cipher seed...

!!!YOU MUST WRITE DOWN THIS SEED TO BE ABLE TO RESTORE THE WALLET!!!

---------------BEGIN LND CIPHER SEED---------------
 1. absorb    2. public    3. icon      4. fatigue
 5.           6. friend    7.           8.
 9.          10. lake     11.          12.
13.          14. enforce  15.          16.
17.          18. desk     19.          20.
21.          22. choose   23.          24.
---------------END LND CIPHER SEED-----------------

!!!YOU MUST WRITE DOWN THIS SEED TO BE ABLE TO RESTORE THE WALLET!!!

lnd successfully initialized!
bitcoin@Edwan:~ $ exit
[logout
```

Figure 9.31: The 24-word seed phrases

By using “sudo su - bitcoin”, we now enter bitcoin users from the admin privilege of sudo pn CP2. We then create the wallet using the following command: “-network=testnet create” (see Figure 9.30).

Enter a new set of passwords for the LND wallet and you may enter N to start a new wallet by displaying the seeds of the wallet. These seeds need to be kept and held with care (a good practice to follow, even though it is on the testnet). The seed phrase (Figure 9.31) allows you to restore all your assets in the bitcoin wallet and all the LND channels.

As for the final part, it is the fun part; now that we have a wallet, we will try to get some coins into the wallet, try receiving, sending it

```
bitcoin@Edwan:~ $ exit
[logout
admin@Edwan:~ $ sudo ls -la /home/bitcoin/.lnd/
[total 28
drwxr-xr-x 4 bitcoin bitcoin 4096 May 23 00:39 .
drwxr-xr-x 5 bitcoin bitcoin 4096 May 23 00:36 ..
drwx------ 4 bitcoin bitcoin 4096 May 23 00:41 data
-rw-r--r-- 1 bitcoin bitcoin  450 May 23 00:39 lnd.conf
drwx------ 3 bitcoin bitcoin 4096 May 23 00:39 logs
-rw-r--r-- 1 bitcoin bitcoin  790 May 23 00:39 tls.cert
-rw------- 1 bitcoin bitcoin  227 May 23 00:39 tls.key
admin@Edwan:~ $ sudo ls -la /home/bitcoin/.lnd/data/chain/bitcoin/testnet/
[total 180
drwx------ 2 bitcoin bitcoin   4096 May 23 00:41 .
drwx------ 3 bitcoin bitcoin   4096 May 23 00:41 ..
-rw------- 1 bitcoin bitcoin    280 May 23 00:41 admin.macaroon
-rw-r--r-- 1 bitcoin bitcoin     83 May 23 00:41 chainnotifier.macaroon
-rw-r--r-- 1 bitcoin bitcoin     45 May 23 00:41 channel.backup
-rw-r--r-- 1 bitcoin bitcoin    132 May 23 00:41 invoice.macaroon
-rw-r--r-- 1 bitcoin bitcoin     91 May 23 00:41 invoices.macaroon
-rw------- 1 bitcoin bitcoin  20480 May 23 00:41 macaroons.db
-rw-r--r-- 1 bitcoin bitcoin    199 May 23 00:41 readonly.macaroon
-rw-r--r-- 1 bitcoin bitcoin     91 May 23 00:41 router.macaroon
-rw-r--r-- 1 bitcoin bitcoin     92 May 23 00:41 signer.macaroon
-rw------- 1 bitcoin bitcoin 114688 May 23 00:41 wallet.db
-rw-r--r-- 1 bitcoin bitcoin    114 May 23 00:41 walletkit.macaroon
```

Figure 9.32: TLS certificate and the read-only macaroon.

and opening payment channels to see the difference between layer 1. Most importantly, the whole point of this exercise is to experience the LIGHTNING effects of speed.

We want to allow admin users to have authority of the LND and call commands from the admin user instead of just solely calling commands from the bitcoin user.

We will copy the TLS certificate and the macaroon files to the admin main directory. We will check if the TLS certificates have been created, check that we have both the admin and read-only macaroon files created (see Figure 9.32).

We can see that they are indeed created; we will now copy them over. Do not move it, instead, just copy it to admin.

Let us try to see if the copy is successful and we can call LND commands from the admin user now. I will do so simply by calling commands to throw back the blockchaininfo. Do ensure that your wallet is first unlocked (network=testnet unlock) before calling the blockchaininfo (–network=testnet getinfo).

```
admin@Edwan:~ $ cd /home/bitcoin/
admin@Edwan:/home/bitcoin $ udo cp --parents .lnd/data/chain/bitcoin/testnet/admin.macaroon /home/admin/
-bash: udo: command not found
admin@Edwan:/home/bitcoin $ sudo cp --parents .lnd/data/chain/bitcoin/testnet/admin.macaroon /home/admin/
admin@Edwan:/home/bitcoin $ sudo cp /home/bitcoin/.lnd/tls.cert /home/admin/.lnd
admin@Edwan:/home/bitcoin $ sudo chown -R admin:admin /home/admin/.lnd/
admin@Edwan:/home/bitcoin $ lncli --network=testnet unlock
Input wallet password:
[lncli] Wallet is already unlocked
```

Figure 9.33: Showing CP1.

```
2020-05-23 00:41:58.127 [INF] SRVR: Initializing peer network bootstrappers!
2020-05-23 00:41:58.128 [INF] SRVR: Creating DNS peer bootstrapper with seeds: [[test.nodes.lightning.directory soa.nodes.lightning.directory]]

2020-05-23 00:41:37.849 [INF] LNWL: Opened wallet
2020-05-23 00:41:38.251 [INF] LTND: Primary chain is set to: bitcoin
2020-05-23 00:41:38.314 [INF] LTND: Initializing bitcoind backed fee estimator in CONSERVATIVE mode
2020-05-23 00:41:38.314 [INF] LNWL: Started listening for bitcoind block notifications via ZMQ on 127.0.0.1:28332
2020-05-23 00:41:38.314 [INF] LNWL: Started listening for bitcoind transaction notifications via ZMQ on 127.0.0.1:28333
2020-05-23 00:41:44.478 [INF] LNWL: The wallet has been unlocked without a time limit
2020-05-23 00:41:44.510 [INF] LTND: LightningWallet opened
2020-05-23 00:41:44.539 [INF] HSWC: Restoring in-memory circuit state from disk
2020-05-23 00:41:44.540 [INF] HSWC: Payment circuits loaded: num_pending=0, num_open=0
2020-05-23 00:41:44.540 [INF] SRVR: Scanning local network for a UPnP enabled device
2020-05-23 00:41:45.693 [INF] LNWL: Started rescan from block 00000000000006ba4dbac0968a19f847d8dfcf451d56777ddd2dbc2966750826 (height 1745799)
2020-05-23 00:41:48.828 [INF] SRVR: Automatically set up port forwarding using UPnP to advertise external IP
2020-05-23 00:41:48.863 [INF] SWPR: Migrating UTXO nursery finalized TXIDs
2020-05-23 00:41:48.867 [INF] LTND: Channel backup proxy channel notifier starting
2020-05-23 00:41:48.867 [INF] ATPL: Instantiating autopilot with active=true, max_channels=5, allocation=0.600000, min_chan_size=20000, max_chan
f_target=3
```

Figure 9.34: Information of the server line.

Here is a little cheap thrill, but notice what is happening on console 1 CP1. You are able to see the status from unlocking of the wallet to calling certain information.

Turn your attention to CP1 (see Figure 9.33) in particular these lines *[INF] SRVR (see Figure 9.34): Scanning local network for a UPnP enabled device* and *[INF] SRVR: Automatically set up port forwarding using UPnP to advertise external IP*

If there are some errors, *fret* not; it is due to the router not allowing external connection, but besides allowing for a greater audience, it still works fine privately. We will stop the LND service in CP2 (–network=testnet stop) and CP1 will reflect too with a proper end to the LND session.

We will test out to run the lnd daemon, get its information (Figure 9.35) and see that autopilot is working well, and we can then stop it (Figure 9.36).

If you are still following at this point of time, congratulations, you have gone a long way, and if you are following well and the codes work as planned, then you have now landed yourself an lnd node and you have successfully initialised it.

```
admin@Edwan:/home/bitcoin $ lncli --network=testnet getinfo
{
    "version": "0.10.1-beta.rc2 commit=v0.10.1-beta.rc2",
    "commit_hash": "ae6e84ddfd3c4d2366e151a04aca3f78b4078ed5",
    "identity_pubkey": "02e1e78b971334d76c8140270c6a4234e45a73337af01ddd3e9f3b335cd76dc9c8",
    "alias": "Edwan [LND]",
    "color": "#68f442",
    "num_pending_channels": 0,
    "num_active_channels": 0,
    "num_inactive_channels": 0,
    "num_peers": 3,
    "block_height": 1746280,
    "block_hash": "0000000000000044e98192f6f6549730316601f627e00a5a9896c6e0e88e28cfb",
    "best_header_timestamp": "1590165165",
    "synced_to_chain": true,
    "synced_to_graph": false,
    "testnet": true,
    "chains": [
        {
            "chain": "bitcoin",
            "network": "testnet"
        }
    ],
    "uris": [
    ],
    "features": {
        "0": {
            "name": "data-loss-protect",
            "is_required": true,
            "is_known": true
        },
        "5": {
            "name": "upfront-shutdown-script",
```

Figure 9.35: Lightning node information.

```
admin@Edwan:/home/bitcoin $ lncli --network=testnet stop
admin@Edwan:/home/bitcoin $ exit
logout
```

Figure 9.36: Stopping the daemon.

```
admin@Edwan:~ $ sudo nano /etc/systemd/system/lnd.service
[sudo] password for admin:
```

Figure 9.37: Admin login.

The other parts will be spring cleaning to ensure some smooth automation when booting and to test out the node by receiving, paying and listing channels and peers.

9.3.5 *Starting Lightning from Boot*

We log in as admin user (Figure 9.37) and enter into the LND configuration page (Figure 9.38).

```
GNU nano 3.2                                    /etc/systemd/system/lnd.service

#       Raspberry Pi: systemd unit for lnd
# /etc/systemd/system/lnd.service

[Unit]
Description=LND Lightning Daemon
Wants=bitcoind.service
After=bitcoind.service

[Service]
ExecStart=/usr/local/bin/lnd

User=bitcoin
Group=bitcoin
Type=simple
KillMode=process
LimitNOFILE=128000
TimeoutSec=240
Restart=always
RestartSec=60

[Install]
WantedBy=multi-user.target
```

Figure 9.38: Configuration page of the LND.

```
admin@Edwan:~ $ sudo nano /etc/systemd/system/lnd.service
[sudo] password for admin:
admin@Edwan:~ $ sudo systemctl enable lnd
Created symlink /etc/systemd/system/multi-user.target.wants/lnd.service → /etc/systemd/system/lnd.service.
admin@Edwan:~ $ sudo systemctl start lnd
admin@Edwan:~ $ systemctl status lnd
● lnd.service - LND Lightning Daemon
   Loaded: loaded (/etc/systemd/system/lnd.service; enabled; vendor preset: enabled)
   Active: active (running) since Sat 2020-05-23 00:55:04 +08; 20s ago
 Main PID: 1834 (lnd)
    Tasks: 11 (limit: 2319)
   Memory: 11.9M
   CGroup: /system.slice/lnd.service
           └─1834 /usr/local/bin/lnd
admin@Edwan:~ $ lncli --network=testnet unlock
Input wallet password:

lnd successfully unlocked!
```

Figure 9.39: Unlocking the wallet.

CP1

Now, we enable the lightning network, start it and unlock it. We shall wait for testnet to finish synchronisation with the network (see Figure 9.39).

Once you see the screen moving quickly with lots of logs (see Figure 9.40), you have successfully got it to boot automatically.

```
admin@Edwan:~ $ sudo journalctl -f -u lnd
-- Logs begin at Fri 2020-05-22 23:36:05 +08. --
May 23 00:57:14 Edwan lnd[1834]: 2020-05-23 00:57:14.956 [ERR] SRVR: Unable to connect to 027da037f45599e3c
213.39.144:9735: connect: connection timed out
May 23 00:57:14 Edwan lnd[1834]: 2020-05-23 00:57:14.956 [ERR] SRVR: Unable to connect to 02d1df64489cb934e
.24.67:9735: connect: connection timed out
May 23 00:57:15 Edwan lnd[1834]: 2020-05-23 00:57:15.426 [INF] CRTR: Pruning channel graph using block 0000
May 23 00:57:15 Edwan lnd[1834]: 2020-05-23 00:57:15.454 [INF] NTFN: New block: height=1746282, sha=0000000
May 23 00:57:15 Edwan lnd[1834]: 2020-05-23 00:57:15.455 [INF] UTXN: Attempting to graduate height=1746282:
May 23 00:57:15 Edwan lnd[1834]: 2020-05-23 00:57:15.493 [INF] CRTR: Block 00000000000002e187abef91129f80b9
May 23 00:57:17 Edwan lnd[1834]: 2020-05-23 00:57:17.719 [INF] DISC: Attempting to bootstrap with: BOLT-001
May 23 00:57:19 Edwan lnd[1834]: 2020-05-23 00:57:19.653 [INF] DISC: Obtained 2 addrs to bootstrap network
May 23 00:57:19 Edwan lnd[1834]: 2020-05-23 00:57:19.974 [ERR] SRVR: Unable to connect to 02004b8c7ce983978
May 23 00:57:19 Edwan lnd[1834]: 2020-05-23 00:57:19.974 [ERR] SRVR: Unable to connect to 02004b8c7ce983978
May 23 00:57:43 Edwan lnd[1834]: 2020-05-23 00:57:43.138 [INF] DISC: GossipSyncer(02651acf4a7096091bf42baad
May 23 00:57:52 Edwan lnd[1834]: 2020-05-23 00:57:52.076 [ERR] SRVR: Unable to connect to 0251eeb810f847a48
```

Figure 9.40: Success of auto boot once I unlock the LND wallet.

```
admin@Edwan:~ $ lncli --network=testnet newaddress np2wkh
{
    "address": "2Mw63LnBGyiaihGnRzMcvTG9iKqSvMnkrBi"
}
```

Figure 9.41: Calling the node to return me a np2wh address.

```
admin@Edwan:~ $ lncli --network=testnet walletbalance
{
    "total_balance": "40000",
    "confirmed_balance": "40000",
    "unconfirmed_balance": "0"
}
```

Figure 9.42: Balance in satoshis.

9.4 Reaping the Fruits: Testing Time

Due to the inconsistency of the testnet faucet, you may use any faucet found on the internet at the time you are trying to receive testnet coins. You can also use a bitcoin testnet explorer to verify the transactions of receiving it into your lnd node.

Generate an address and send the testnet coins to your own node (see Figure 9.41).

Check your wallet balance using the command shown in Figure 9.42.

Now, I check my peers as we have set to autopilot previously to open up channels (see Figure 9.43).

I can also check the payments that I have made (see Figure 9.44) with my network. Here, it is 0 as I have yet to make any new payments.

```
[admin@Edwan:~ $ lncli --network=testnet listpeers
{
    "peers": [
        {
            "pub_key": "02d8add8c1b7172c0615caa9f025c469625a0504fbc2c22062c522bc0c6a277bef",
            "address": "94.176.236.119:9735",
            "bytes_sent": "4475136",
            "bytes_recv": "27480522",
            "sat_sent": "0",
            "sat_recv": "0",
            "inbound": false,
            "ping_time": "180289",
            "sync_type": "ACTIVE_SYNC",
            "features": {
                "0": {
                    "name": "data-loss-protect",
                    "is_required": true,
                    "is_known": true
```

Figure 9.43: Peers connected with.

```
[admin@Edwan:~ $ lncli --network=testnet listpayments
{
    "payments": [
    ],
    "first_index_offset": "0",
    "last_index_offset": "0"
}
```

Figure 9.44: List of payments which is none at this moment.

```
[admin@Edwan:~ $ lncli --network=testnet walletbalance
{
    "total_balance": "45000",
    "confirmed_balance": "40000",
    "unconfirmed_balance": "5000"
}
```

Figure 9.45: Unconfirmed transaction.

Now that my transaction has been sent from a sender to me, this is what I got (see Figure 9.45). It still remains unconfirmed.

After 10 minutes, I check again and this is what we have. Now that it is a confirmed transaction (see Figure 9.46), UTXO, I can spend it by sending it out if I want to.

Acinq, another company experimenting with Lightning implementation, has done a cool site for testing lightning transactions over payment of coffee. Please try getting yourself a nice cold Frappe for all the effort and determination through the entire process. Wait, remember, you are on testnet. If you want to get yourself a real treat

```
[admin@Edwan:~ $ lncli --network=testnet walletbalance
{
    "total_balance": "45000",
    "confirmed_balance": "45000",
    "unconfirmed_balance": "0"
}
```

Figure 9.46: Confirmed transaction.

of coffee, you need to switch the bitcoin configuration to testnet=1 to 0. Sync all the mainnet block data into the bitcoin directory of your HDD and check the getblockinfo to ensure that you are on the mainnet as True and your verification is up-to-date. Do all these only if you are prepared to lose whatever you can afford to lose. Again, these are still in the experimental phase.

9.5 Beyond This Tutorial

Throughout this tutorial, we have experienced what it is like to be a validator of the bitcoin network by playing a part to strengthen the decentralised network and being a part of the voting rights in the chain validation. We have experienced how to download, validate and extract the bitcoin core into a palm-sized hardware connected to a hard disk, validating blocks all the way from the genesis block back in 2007. You have a copy of over a decade of chain data in your possession. Next, we experience how it is to synchronise the chain data and let it auto run from the raspberry pi. We then move on to layer-2 applications such as the lightning network to demonstrate how we can make lightning fast transactions that are useful for micro payments in a trusted environment that is low or close to negligible fees. All of these have a governance mechanism that governs the rules to prevent any party from having an incentive to cheat. All of these are done via the software together with a simple hardware like the raspberry pi.

Bitcoin or blockchain programming goes beyond just this. There are many other concepts and applications that go around the lightning network. In the case of other digital currencies such as Ethereum, the concept of layer-2 applications such as lightning works the same by having a watchtower guarding over side chains. Other useful applications include smart contracts in Ethereum which are covered in other chapters of this book.

For the tutorial in this chapter, having a node running in your office/at your home, there are readily available gadgets that aim to achieve the same objectives. At the time of writing, there are products such as Casa Node, myNode One, RaspiBlitz by Lightning in a box and Swift Cryptocurrency Bitbox Base.

The above offer a more robust setup with some having a docker file with all the dependencies and hardened with security functions to prevent various forms of network attacks. They are more hardy, aesthetically pleasing, with better user experience for troubleshooting and upgrading of versions, and offer a more sustainable operation, but all with the same fundamental concepts you have covered in the tutorial above.

This tutorial does not just end here. There are tons of other explorations available on how you can integrate your solution above to a better hardware. For example, the Raspberry Pi 4 or other services such as using it as a payment gateway for your commerce like integrating with BTC Pay server to start accepting bitcoin payments, running with TOR or running it with Electrum paired with your hardware wallets so you can send and receive bitcoins using your handy node to validate or broadcast your transactions and you can finish it off with a nice linkage to a mobile- or computer-compatible wallet application such as Zap, Zeus or Shango. All of these will not be possible without the great community out there with an open source spirit of decentralising their codes.

Chapter 10

Architecting and Designing Your Own Blockchain Solution

Ernie Teo*

10.1 Introduction

The world is gradually starting to understand blockchain and understand its benefits; more people and enterprises are discovering and experimenting on use cases. The most well-known Bitcoin use case for peer-to-peer payments has grown into an expanded world of decentralised finance: stable coins, decentralised exchanges, lending platforms, prediction markets and more. In the world of traditional finance, banks have gone beyond cryptocurrencies and have deployed solutions that are using blockchain for trade finance (letters of credit in particular); central banks such as the Monetary Authority of Singapore have experimented with interbank clearing and settlement. The use cases for blockchain are not restricted to the finance space; there are government and enterprise efforts in the areas of identity, personal records, retail, trade and manufacturing (see Figure 10.1).

An emerging technology as blockchain is, it is exciting to think about implementing blockchain in your business or use case. However, it is important to remember that not all problems can be solved

*Adjunct Senior Lecturer, National University of Singapore; Co Vice-Chairman, Blockchain Association Singapore, Singapore.

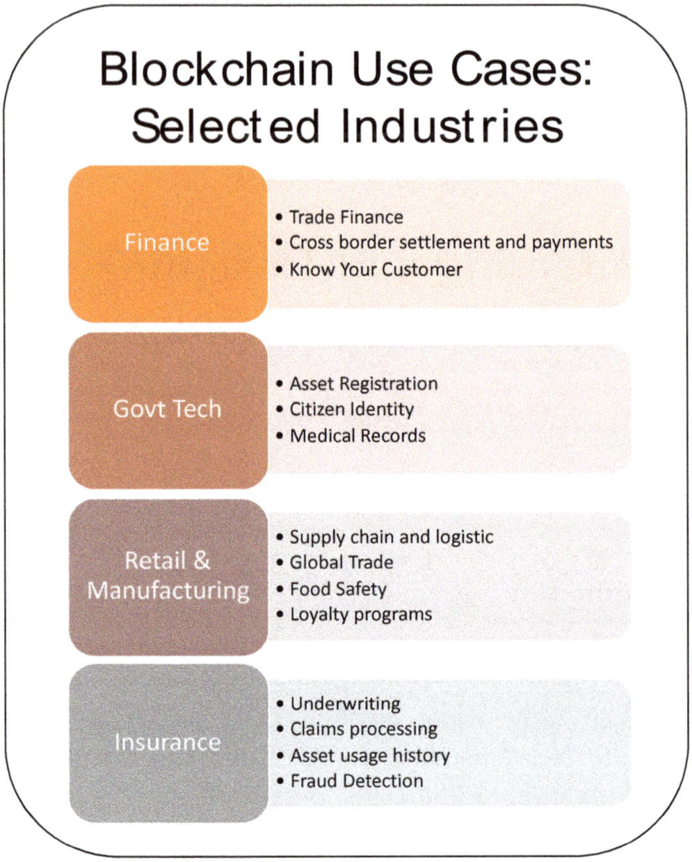

Figure 10.1: Blockchain use cases.

or improved with blockchain. A good blockchain use case should have the following attributes as shown in Figure 10.2.

The business problem (or any other problem statement) should make sense for blockchain. Sometimes, inefficiencies that exist in the industry due to a lack of digitisation or coordination can be solved with more mature technologies. There should also be a clear and identifiable network of participants, assets (that need to be held and moved within the network) and transactions (or rules which define how these assets can be moved). A good blockchain use case usually arises from a lack of trust between stakeholders. The need for the

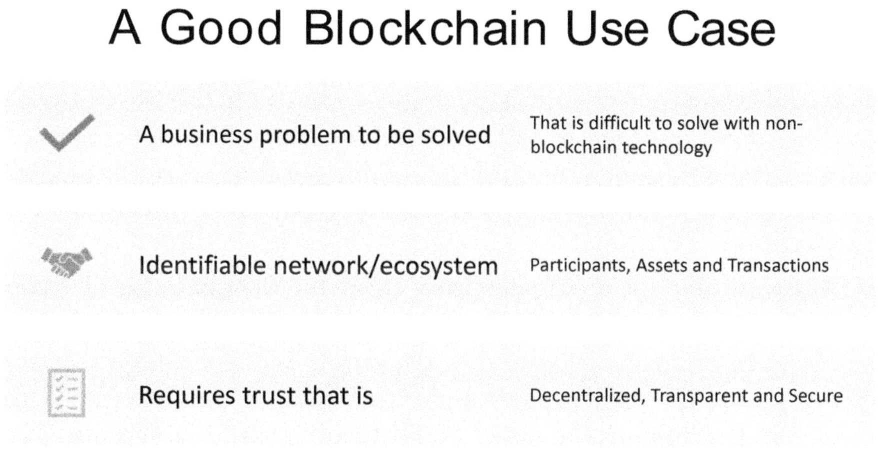

Figure 10.2: Attributes of a good blockchain use case.

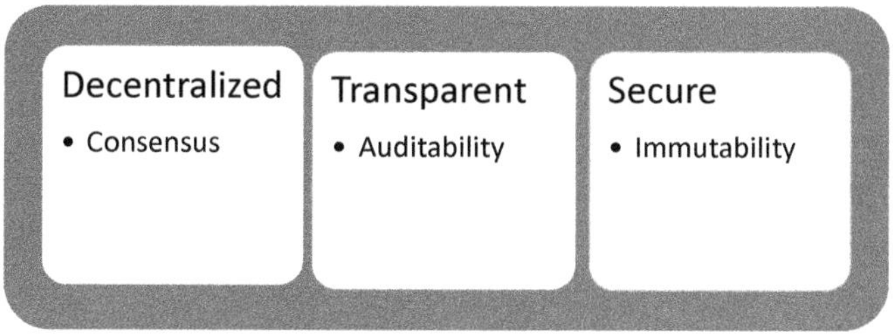

Figure 10.3: Key features of blockchain.

key features (as described in Figure 10.3) of a blockchain to solve a business problem justifies its application.

Blockchain technology can create trust within a network of participants that are not necessarily aligned in their objectives. Decentralisation ensures that there is no one point of failure and the consensus protocol ensures alignment within the network. The network agrees on the validity of the transactions that are written onto the ledger. The blockchain is also transparent to its participants (to some degree) and this makes it auditable. These features also makes the ledger secure as the data are immutable and cannot be easily changed or hacked. This creates a layer of trust for the participants on the network.

10.2 Planning Your Blockchain

Suppose you have established that you have a good blockchain use case and want to start developing the application. There are many considerations on how to put your blockchain application together. This starts with understanding the fundamental use case to deciding on the network and technology to use. The key steps are outlined in Figure 10.4.

First, outline the main purpose of using blockchain in the use case. Are there multiple parties in the process where there is a lack of trust, resulting in manual checks and bottlenecks? Is there a need to store evidence or audit trails in a decentralised way such that no centralised party can manipulate the data? Or is the use case for a decentralised economy with digital tokens or assets? Next, we take a deeper dive into understanding your use case and define the requirements, by considering its users, assets, participants and network.

10.2.1 *Define Users*

Anyone who would interact with the blockchain network is a user. This includes administrators, auditors, node operators and end users. Types of questions to ask include the following:

1. What types of actions do they need to take? Is it view only or do they need to interact with the blockchain?
2. Are they part of an organisation? What are their roles in the organisation? Is there an organisational hierarchy to consider?

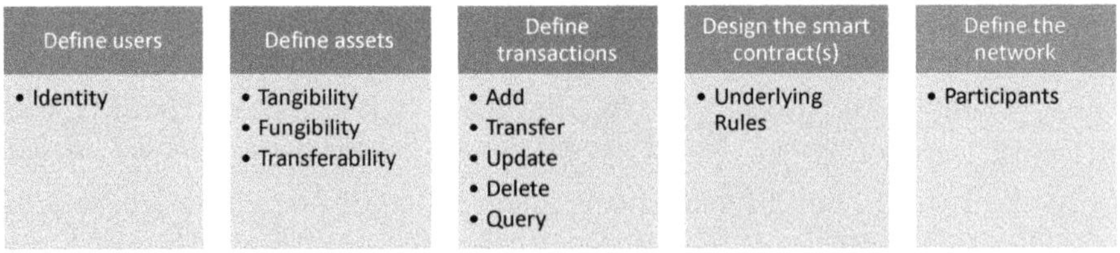

Figure 10.4: Planning your blockchain.

3. User actions include the ability to transact and hold assets. Does this ability depend on their role?
4. How would they usually interact with the system (e.g., mobile phones or laptops)?

Another important consideration is the identity (or account) of the user. There are two types of identity to consider. First, consider if a blockchain-based identity or account is needed. When users are assigned a blockchain account (or address), they can transact and hold assets. If this is needed, the other consideration is the management of user keys. Are your users technically savvy enough to manage their own private keys (i.e., manage their own blockchain wallet)? Do you need a mechanism for key recovery? Is it better to run a key management service? In this case, what are the security considerations?

The second type of identity to consider is a user's profile. This is the connection to a user's real-world identity. Should your users transact only with their blockchain accounts? Pseudo-anonymous blockchains like Bitcoin do not require user identities to be verified.

In most business use cases, some form of identity is required; there may be legal or business considerations. If there is a need for this, you also need to consider how you will verify their identity and what types of identity information is required. Does it include name, email, identity documents or more? In private or permissioned blockchains, a gateway or controller ensures that identity is verified before credentials are issued to the user. Once this information is collected, you will need to store and manage the user data in a secure manner. If you are using a public blockchain, you can also collect the users' identity on your servers and link them to blockchain accounts. Exchanges that are legally required to store KYC information are an example. Other alternatives in public blockchains are identity oracles that are linked to a trusted database. These sources can come from governments, financial institutions or utility providers. An example of this is Uport, which worked with the city of Zug to issue government-verified identities on the Ethereum blockchain.

10.2.2 *Define Assets*

Digital assets can be broadly defined as any type of information where ownership can be assigned. The most common type of asset on blockchain networks is the cryptocurrency. Cryptocurrency is an on-chain asset; they are generated through algorithms that run on the blockchain such as bitcoin mining. This type of asset only exists on the blockchain.

Other types of assets that can be digitised on the blockchain are rights over physical property such as real estate, vehicles or precious metals. In this case, a trusted party is required to act as an issuer of the digital title. There needs to be a legal process behind the issuance that ensures redeemability of the asset. The benefit of such types of digitisation is the ability to fractionalise the asset. This makes the asset more accessible to the mass market and allows the asset owners to issue tokens to the asset for financing purposes.

Intangible digital assets can also be issued on the blockchain. These can be generated digitally by entities that are part of the network. In general, these parties need to be trusted for the network to acknowledge the legitimacy of the asset. Some examples are letters of credit, bank guarantees, loyalty points, equity and intellectual property rights.

An attribute to consider is the fungibility of the digital asset/token. This also affects the technology you can use to issue the asset. Cryptocurrencies like bitcoin are non-fungible; one bitcoin is not distinguishable from another. Tokens representing properties need to be fungible as each property may have different attributes and values. However, fractionalised tokens of a particular property can be fungible as each represents a share of the property (which is no different from another share).

Digital assets/tokens generally should be transferrable to allow for changes in ownership and trading of the asset. However, there is a class of digital assets that should be non-transferrable. These are assets that are particular to an individual or entity. This includes medical records, identity registry, education credentials and employment records.

10.2.3 *Define Transactions*

Once we decide on the types of assets on the network, we should consider the rules that govern these assets. These are the transactions that will occur on the network. These rules depend on both the type of user and assets. Types of transactions include the following:

1. Add: Creating or issuing of asset
2. Transfer: Change of asset ownership
3. Update: Alteration of asset (such as updating an expiration date or status)
4. Delete: Destruction of asset
5. Query: Look up information about the asset

10.2.4 *Design the Smart Contracts*

The next step is to bundle your assets and transactions into smart contracts; the smart contracts are the rules for your assets in code. Consider what are the underlying rules or conditions for transfer of assets. This is where an understanding of the business process comes in. How are the assets created and by whom? Who is allowed to own and transfer these assets? Ensure that you have the necessary functions as smart contracts are hard to change once deployed. Consider "bad" scenarios to ensure that you have an "exit" if things go wrong, especially if your smart contracts are dealing with valuable digital assets.

10.2.5 *Determine the Network*

Once we have a clear idea of the participants, assets and transactions, we should consider the network. Who will operate and/or regulate the blockchain? Are gateways (such as exchanges or data providers) needed to connect to systems outside of the blockchain network? Do you need to integrate to external data sources?

There may be participants in your blockchain network that go beyond users. Additional questions to ask about the participants include the following: How will they access and interact with the blockchain? Are they required to be nodes on the blockchain

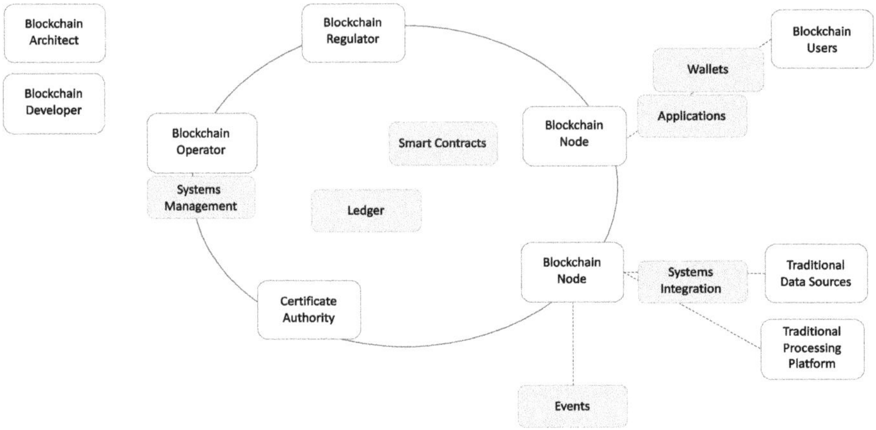

Figure 10.5: Participants in a blockchain network.

network? Figures 10.5 and 10.6 describe the types of participants that can be part of the blockchain network. Not all types are required participants of the network and it depends on the use case. Decide what are the components you need.

10.3 Choose Your Technology

The first step in deciding the technology that you will use is to determine if you need your own blockchain network. If you have a token-related use case where the token is used as a utility for running the network, you will need your own blockchain. Or if you are using a unique consensus protocol that is designed to incentivise your network participants, you will need your own blockchain. That would allow you to customise the blockchain network from the protocol level. If you intend to run a permissioned blockchain network where only your partners can join, you will also need your own permissioned blockchain network. Technologies like the Hyperledger family, Corda, Multichain and even Ethereum (Enterprise) allow you to customise and run your own blockchain network.

If you have an experienced blockchain development team that can code your blockchain from the protocol level, you can write your own consensus and rules. This might have been your only choice a few

Participants of a blockchain network	
Entities, Systems and Hardware	
Blockchain Architect	Designs the network and the software based on the system requirements.
Blockchain Developer	Develops and code the blockchain protocol and smart contracts.
Blockchain Operator	Runs and manages the blockchain daily operations.
Blockchain Regulator	Decides and enforces the rules. Manages the nodes. More likely in permissioned blockchains.
Certificate Authority	Issues authenticated certificates to users and provides proofs of identity.
Blockchain Node	A server on the blockchain network that may or may not take part in consensus and storing of the blockchain ledger.
Blockchain Users	Individuals or entities that are using the blockchain network.
Traditional Data Sources and Processing Platforms	Third party sources of data and systems which may need to be connected to the blockchain.
Software	
Wallets	For management of digital assets assigned to blockchain users.
Applications	Software that provides an interface for the user to connect to the network and interact with its functions.
Smart Contracts	Code that us deployed on the blockchain to manage assets and transactions.
Ledger	The blockchain database that records the transactions.
Events	External sources of information (or oracles) that may be used to trigger a smart contract process.
System Management	Program for managing the blockchain network such as upgrading the protocol and giving permission to nodes.
System Integration	Software written to connect the blockchain network to third party sources of information.

Figure 10.6: Participants in a blockchain network.

years ago. However, many tools for developing blockchain networks have become mature and can be utilised. It is not always practical to set up and run a network on your own. Blockchain-as-a-Service (BaaS) providers like Azure, AWS and Kaleido are offering services that can deploy a blockchain network with a few clicks. You can choose between various technology options when using BaaS.

An important consideration when deploying your own blockchain is whether to keep it permissioned or make it public. Do you want others to join your network as nodes without requiring your permission? Another factor to consider is the visibility of the blockchain data. For example, a blockchain network could be write permissioned and read public. Meaning, only the permissioned blockchain nodes can write to the blockchain, but the blockchain ledger is open for the public to access.

Both permissioned (private) and permissionless (public) blockchain networks have their pros and cons. There are varying industry opinions. One may argue that running a highly permissioned system where one control the nodes is merely opening with the same single point of failure weaknesses which blockchain was originally designed to overcome. But, others may claim that it is difficult for institutions to trust a network which anyone can join. It is difficult to answer which is better; it is subjective to the use case, company policies and mindset of stake holders. There is no rule of thumb or industry standard to decide which one is better. Some institutions will choose to trust permissioned systems, whereas a pro-decentralisation public use case may prefer the permissionless approach.

When creating your own blockchain network, you should also consider your ability to form the network. If you are intending to create an industry-wide blockchain, would you be able to get most of the industry to agree to participate as nodes? Can you get the relevant authorities like trade associations or regulators to be part of your network? If participants are potentially competitors, there may not be enough trust within the participants. If you are starting a public blockchain, will you be able to get nodes (or miners) to join your blockchain? How would you make them aware of this network? Are your incentives attractive enough to make them join? For this, you will need to consider the network economics (see the next section).

However, there are cases where you may not need to deploy your own blockchain network. If your use case is focused on just developing a decentralised application (DApp), you can deploy your smart contracts onto an existing blockchain network and can connect your DApp to the network as well. For example, many applications run on the Ethereum network. If all you need is an application, having your own blockchain network may not be necessary.

In making the decision to use an existing public blockchain, you also have to consider non-functional requirements of the solution you are developing. What is the number of users, transaction volume and speed? Is there a minimum level of service you need to provide for your users? Note that there may be a trade-off between security and speed. Larger blockchain networks (like Ethereum) may be more secure but are prone to congestion and high network transaction fees (gas). However, such networks provide a high level of data immutability and security which smaller or private networks cannot provide.

If you do decide to use an existing public blockchain network, the key considerations would be if the network is healthy (secure) and if the technical features support your use case. Ethereum is still the network of choice for deploying DApps, but many next-generation blockchain networks like QTUM, NEO, Cardano, Zilliqa, EOS, Tron and Tezos are also catching up. Ethereum 2.0 is also coming up and aims to address the scaling issues Ethereum currently faces. If there are privacy requirements, you may consider blockchain technology with built-in privacy features such as Zero Knowledge Proofs, Secure Signature Schemes or Private State Channels.

Solely permissioned or solely public blockchains are not the only options. Private permissioned blockchains may rely on public blockchains to maintain immutability and trust in a hybrid setting. This involves posting the blockchain of your permissioned network to the public blockchain of choice. This provides additional security (immutability) to the transactions on your blockchain. Such methods were first discussed in Komodo's Delayed Proof of Work using the Bitcoin network, but can also now be found in Kaleido's Ethereum tethering service.

The process of choosing the blockchain technology/network is summarised in Figure 10.7.

10.4 Designing Token Economics

The term token economics stems from mechanism design. Mechanism design is an economics approach to design incentives (or economic mechanisms) to get a strategic outcome (where players

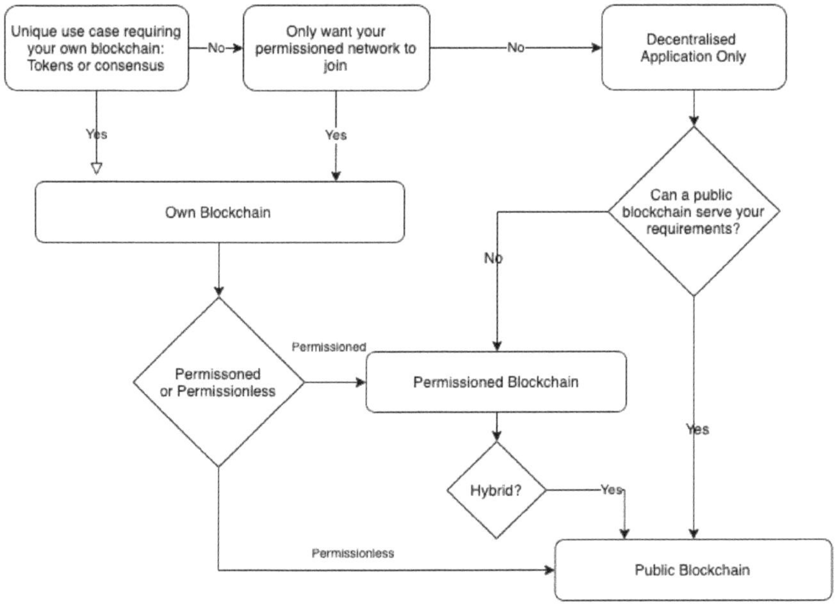

Figure 10.7: Choosing blockchain technology.

act rationally). Bitcoin's mechanism design aims to get miners to participate in validating transactions, ensures the blockchain ledger is consistent and prevents double spending of coins. The incentive used was mining rewards of bitcoins, fuelled by its limited supply. This in turn gives bitcoins economic value and drives miner incentives.

If you intend to design your own token and consensus, the key consideration is the outcome you wish to achieve. The incentives of your network participants must be aligned to drive towards that outcome, regardless of whether you are using mining or other methods as an incentive. You should also be on the lookout for undesired outcomes. When Bitcoin was designed, it was not expected that there would be consolidation of miners. When bitcoin prices in reality became extremely attractive, it led to a centralisation of mining power and the exclusion of nodes with low computational power. It was also not expected that the intense competition in mining would lead to such a large consumption of electricity for the network.

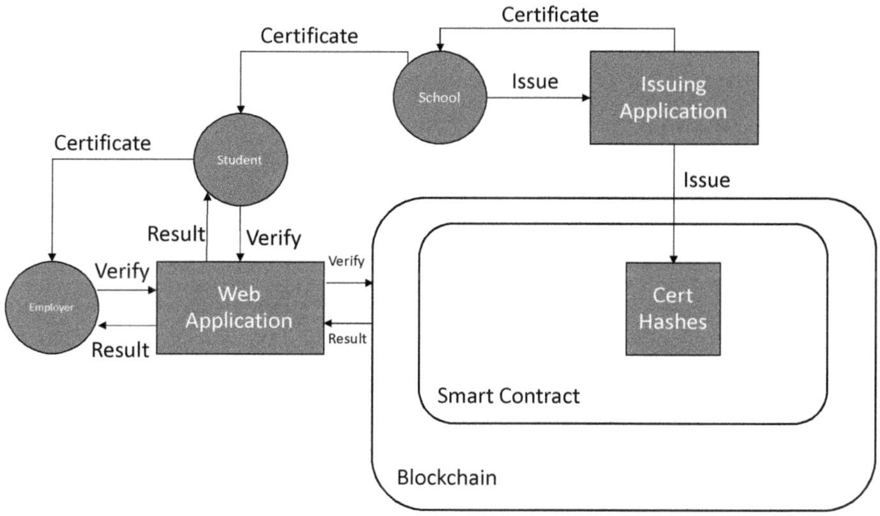

Figure 10.8: Issuing certificates on blockchain.

Points to take note when designing your tokens are attributes like how the tokens are created or generated, how the tokens are distributed to the network (is it competitive) and the utility of the token within the network. For some cases, your objectives may not be just the actions that happen within your blockchain network but also the token price. Token price is determined by factors external to your network as demand and supply is driven both internally and externally. Non-participants may trade the tokens and contribute to price volatility. The token design may affect the price and investors may attribute scarcity or high utility to potential increases in prices. If you intend for the token to power the utility within the blockchain network, you need to consider its price volatility in the external market. Bitcoin's volatile and speculative nature has prevented it from fulfilling its original intension as a payment token.

10.5 Putting it Together

Now that we have gone through the various considerations, we can put it together by describing the processes within your solution. A process flow diagram maps the user's end-to-end journey. The diagram should include the various users or participants, user interfaces or applications, the blockchain network, smart contracts and assets, and the interactions (transactions) between them. Figure 10.8 illustrates an example for the use case of education certificates on a blockchain. The school uses an Issuing Application to interact with the blockchain to store hashes of the certificates for verification. The Issuing Application returns the Certificate to the school, which then sends it to the student. The student can share this certificate with a potential employer. Both student and employer can use the Web Application to verify the authenticity of the Certificate. The Web Application queries and verifies the Certificate with the hash stored on the blockchain. If the Certificate is tampered with or fake, the Web Application will return a negative result.

To get a better idea of how to implement your use case, you can also sketch or draw the user interface. Create mock-ups of your website or mobile App; include all functions needed to interact with the smart contracts and the blockchain. Decide what the user sees from the blockchain on the UI and what happens in the background. This will help in the development of the applications and smart contracts.

Designing and architecting a blockchain solution is an art rather than a science. It takes a deep understanding of the problem statements, use cases and user requirements. It also requires an appreciation of the features of a blockchain and how to utilise and implement them in the solution that achieves your objectives. This chapter serves as a guide to get the reader started; the rest comes with experience.

Index

Singapore University of Social Sciences - World Scientific Future Economy Series

(Continued from page ii)

Forthcoming Titles

Financial Management in the Digital Economy
David Lee Kuo Chuen, Ding Ding and Guan Chong

Inclusive Disruption: Digital Capitalism, Deep Technology and Trade Disputes
David Lee Kuo Chuen and Linda Low

The Digital Transformation of Property in Greater China: Finance, 5G, AI, and Blockchain
Paul Schulte, Dean Sun and Roman Shemakov

www.ingramcontent.com/pod-product-compliance
Ingram Content Group UK Ltd.
Pitfield, Milton Keynes, MK11 3LW, UK
UKHW020351150926
8624IPUK00004B/105

9 789811 223686